A Grand Strategy for America

A volume in the series

CORNELL STUDIES IN SECURITY AFFAIRS
edited by Robert J. Art, Robert Jervis, and Stephen M. Walt
A full list of the titles in the series appears at the end of the book.

Also by Robert J. Art

The TFX Decision: McNamara and the Military. Boston: Little, Brown, 1968.

Edited with Vincent Davis and Samuel P. Huntington, *Reorganizing America's Defense.* Washington: Pergamon-Brassey's, 1985.

Edited with Seyom Brown, *U.S. Foreign Policy: The Search for a New Role.* New York: Macmillan, 1993.

Edited with Patrick Cronin, *The United States and Coercive Diplomacy.* Washington, D.C.: United States Institute of Peace Press, 2003.

A Grand Strategy for America

Robert J. Art

A CENTURY FOUNDATION BOOK

Cornell University Press ITHACA AND LONDON

Copyright © 2003 by The Century Foundation, Inc.

First published 2003 by Cornell University Press
First printing, Cornell Paperbacks, 2004

Printed in the United States of America

Library of Congress Cataloging-in-Publication Data
Art, Robert J.
  A grand strategy for America / Robert J. Art.
    p.   cm.
"A Century Foundation Book."
Includes bibliographical references (p.) and index.
    ISBN-13: 978-0-8014-4139-4 (cloth : alk. paper)
    ISBN-13: 978-0-8014-8957-0 (pbk. : alk. paper)
    1. United States—Foreign relations—2001—Philosophy.   2. United States—Foreign relations—1989-   3. United States—Military policy.   4. World politics—1995–2005.   I. Title.
    E895.A78 2003
    327.73—dc21

                                        2003000457

Cornell University Press strives to use environmentally responsible suppliers and materials to the fullest extent possible in the publishing of its books. Such materials include vegetable-based, low-VOC inks and acid-free papers that are recycled, totally chlorine-free, or partly composed of nonwood fibers. For further information, visit our website at www.cornellpress.cornell.edu.

Cloth printing   10 9 8 7 6 5 4 3 2 1
Paperback printing   10 9 8 7 6 5 4 3 2

For Suzanne, who has always been there for me

Contents

Figures and Tables

Foreword

During the 1990s, most Americans got comfortable with the fact that foreign policy and national security issues were drifting gradually to the back of the line in terms of both media and political attention. Victors in the cold war, champions of free trade, exemplars of prosperity, and marketers par excellence, America seemed to be embarked on a new era of self-absorption and even complacency after a half century of global conflict and tension. Some rough spots needed to be tidied up, but history, some said, "was over," and it was only a matter of time before everybody caught on to the advantages of emulating the American way of, well, just about everything. Then, the United States awakened to the nightmare that was September 11, 2001.

For those most involved in making or analyzing U.S. policy, the dislocation wrought by September 11 was especially acute. These "experts" had shared a common belief that this historical period would be defined by American preeminence. Their pronouncements had reinforced a belief in American invulnerability and underpinned the attitude known as American triumphalism. Their judgments were largely unchallenged, although pretty much the same group of scholars, analysts, and officials had been disquietingly off base a decade before when almost all of them failed to foresee the collapse of the Soviet Union. In the 2000 presidential election campaign, for example, foreign policy was far from a major focus of either party—and of little interest to the public. Of course, there also were scholars and policymakers at work who were aware that decisions on broader international issues and America's role as the preeminent world power were long overdue.

At The Century Foundation, as at other organizations concerned about our nation's foreign policy, we were beginning to understand and reflect on the complexity of the interests and challenges confronting the United States in the new century. As the Soviet Union began to collapse, we commenced a new series of studies aimed at enriching the quality of future debates about foreign affairs that we felt were inevitable. Robert J. Art, Christian A. Herter Professor of International Relations at Brandeis University, a former member of the secretary of defense's Long Range Planning Staff, author of *The TFX*

Decision: McNamara and the Military, and coeditor of and contributor to a number of books, including *Reorganizing America's Defense, U.S. Foreign Policy: The Search for a New Role,* and *The United States and Coercive Diplomacy,* was one of those we selected to analyze these issues and make recommendations for the future.

In this volume, Art raises what is turning out to be one of the central questions of our time: How does a power like the United States deal with both the problems and the opportunities that derive from its unique position? He reminds us that it is in our hands to decide what role we want to play in the world, and he emphasizes that it is incumbent on us to understand that that role inevitably must extend far beyond the defense of our homeland, as important as that task will be. He points out as well that great powers have never lived for "security alone."

Art writes at a time when it is clear that there is no broad national consensus about America's goals and strategies in international affairs. For five decades, we had known what our foreign policy objectives were: we understood who the enemy was, and our responses fell within an agreed-upon policy framework aimed at containing the threat posed by that enemy. Today, enemies can seem to lurk around every corner, the strength of alliances has become unclear, and the way to proceed is fraught with dangers that are almost impossible to weigh.

In this careful examination, Art looks not only at the range of foreign policy goals that America should set for itself but also at the grand strategy needed to achieve those goals. The scope of his analysis is sweeping, exploring most major questions concerning American interests and the threats to those interests. In his conclusion, Art puts forth a strategy of selective engagement as the best choice for our times. Such a strategy requires continuing to pursue our major alliances and maintaining a military presence that will enable us to influence developments in those regions he considers critical to our future interests—Europe, East Asia, and the Persian Gulf. He offers thoughtful arguments and detailed analysis of the costs and benefits of the options our nation is weighing.

This book is timely because, within the overall topic of grand strategy, Art's focus is on the military option. That is only appropriate given the preponderance of military strength the United States now enjoys and the unusual willingness of the current administration to employ that force in order to achieve its ends. But, as Art points out, "Military power is the most expensive and dangerous tool of statecraft."

Art's study joins a number of other Century Foundation books on this critical subject that have been released over the past few years, some of which also have taken on the issue of creating a broad framework for foreign policy-making, most notably Walter Russell Mead's *Special Providence* and Henry Nau's *At Home Abroad.* Some of our efforts have been aimed at specific areas that pose problems that contribute to uncertainty and conflict—Karl Meyer's *Dust of Empire* and Morton Abramowitz's two edited volumes on Turkey and Selig Harrison's *Korean Endgame*—as well as a number of examinations of ethnic conflicts that threatened to engulf whole regions, including David Callahan's *Unwinnable Wars* and Barnett Rubin's *Blood on the Doorstep*. Other Century Foundation books, such as Michael Mandelbaum's *The Dawn of Peace in Europe,* examine the future of our foreign policy alliances, while some, such as David Calleo's *Rethinking Europe's Future,* look at alliances among other nations. The new calculus of national security, not only militarily and economically but also socially and politically, has been a major focus of our work over the past year and a half.

Critics of the present administration believe that the projection of power whenever and wherever we wish has set the world's teeth on edge. Supporters see us as performing a historic mission, something well beyond mere self-defense. This gulf suggests the urgent need for a serious national dialogue on American grand strategy for the next decade and beyond. On behalf of The Century Foundation, I thank Robert Art for his contribution to the coming debate.

Richard C. Leone, President

Acknowledgments

This is a big-picture book. It concerns the fundamental direction that the United States should take in its foreign policy and grand strategy. No one person can write, unaided, a book that deals with as many subjects as this one does. Consequently, I have relied on so many people for so many things that this book is as much a product of their efforts as mine, even though many of them are not aware of this fact.

My first debt is to three role models. In writing this book, I have consciously tried to follow in the footsteps of these distinguished predecessors: Nicholas J. Spykman, Walter Lippmann, and Robert W. Tucker. Each was provoked to write by a great challenge in his particular era. Spykman's *America's Strategy in World Politics: The United States and the Balance of Power* was published in 1942, Lippmann's *U.S. Foreign Policy: Shield of the Republic* in 1943, and Tucker's *A New Isolationism: Threat or Promise* in 1972. Spykman and Lippmann were writing during World War II, before its outcome was clear, and both called for an internationalist policy on the part of the United States. Tucker wrote during the peak of public disaffection with the Vietnam War, and made an extremely powerful case for an isolationist foreign policy for the United States, even though he did not ultimately embrace it.

Although these books differ in their style, substance, and prescriptions, all three stand as models of how to do grand-strategic analysis, and for that reason they remain, in my judgment, perhaps the best books written on American grand strategy in the last half century. Each is a classic because the author delineated the big geopolitical picture: the broad contours of the international environment, America's national interests that flowed from them, the basic choices available to the United States, given that environment, and lastly the profound effects that America's choices would have not only on itself but also on that environment. In this book I have tried to follow the big geopolitical tradition set by Spykman, Lippmann, and Tucker. I am indebted to all three of them for showing the way.

My next debt is to The Century Foundation and especially to its president, Dr. Richard C. Leone. He probably thought I would never finish this book, and sometimes I wondered, too. But he never said so, and he always showed me remarkable courtesy, respect, and patient faith that I would succeed. His backing has been critical to the book's completion, and I am proud to be associated with the fine work of the Foundation.

I also owe much to my close friend and colleague, Stephen Van Evera. He told me to write this book, and then drove me crazy while I was writing it. When I asked him, "does this outline look sensible?" he said: "let's talk some more about it." When I said, "how does this chapter look?" he said: "it needs more work." When I said, "is this manuscript finished?" he said: "have you thought about this?" Stephen Van Evera set for me an intellectual standard that I could not meet. For that I will be ever grateful. If I have failed, I "failed more successfully" because of his ruthless commitment to clear thinking and concise writing.

My debt to my wife Suzanne, to whom this book is dedicated, can never be repaid. She did more than simply support and sustain me. She showed me by example how to bring a large project to completion. When I complained incessantly that I would never finish, she said: "work on it every day, even if for only ten minutes, and it will get done." I figured that because she wrote eleven books in as many years, she must know what she was talking about, and so I followed her advice. It was the wisest decision I made. Her example, support, and encouragement got me through all the hard parts of this book: the beginning, the middle, and the end.

Six people read the entire manuscript with great care and provided comments that saved me from many errors in logic and analysis. Thus, on behalf of my readers, as well as for myself, I thank Roger Haydon, Robert Ross, Glenn Snyder, Stephen Walt (who made especially detailed comments), Kenneth Waltz, and Bill Wohlforth.

In addition, others read portions of the manuscript, and their comments greatly improved specific points: Stephen Brooks, Loren Cass, Dan Drezner, Charles Glaser, Bob Keohane, David Kang, Jenny Lind, Charles Lipson, Sean Lynn-Jones, Mike Mastanduno, Rachel McCulloch, John Mearsheimer, Daryl Press, Bruce Russett, Josh Spero, Alan Stam, Jr., and Micah Zenko. On several specific matters, I have consulted at length with Tom Christensen, Gregory Gause, Paul Huth, Steven Miller, Michael O'Hanlon, Barry Posen, Ted Postol, Dick Samuels, and Cindy Williams, and they saved me much angst as a result. If there are others whom I have forgotten to mention, I apologize.

I have been blessed with able research assistants; when I asked, "can you find such and such?" they invariably did so. I thank Loren Cass, Sean Giovanello, Amy Higer, Bill Ruger, and Micah Zenko. I am especially indebted to Loren because he prepared all the tables in this book dealing with economic and war data, because he lent me his expertise in economic and environmental matters, and because he continued to provide invaluable assistance once he concluded his graduate career at Brandeis.

In addition to The Century Foundation, several other institutions supported my research. The United States Institute of Peace provided a research grant that enabled me to do extensive interviewing in Western Europe in the early 1990s. The U.S. Committee on International Relations Studies with the People's Republic of China, and its director John Watt, enabled me to teach in Beijing for two weeks in the early 1990s, where I interviewed academics and researchers at the main foreign policy and military institutes, and then to do interviews in Tokyo with Ministry of Foreign Affairs and Ministry of Defense officials, as well as many academics, politicians, and institute researchers. The Century Foundation made possible a trip to Central Europe in the mid 1990s. The Center for German and European Studies at Brandeis University made possible additional trips to Europe in the late 1990s. The Olin Institute for Strategic Studies at Harvard University and the Security Studies Program at MIT, both of which have kindly given me affiliations, provided invaluable arenas for creative thinking on national security issues that, time after time, forced me to go back and rethink what I had just written. I thank the Foreign Policy Studies Program at the Brookings Institution, the Program on International Security Policy at the University of Chicago, the Institute of War and Peace Studies at Columbia University, the John Sloan Dickey Foundation at Dartmouth, and the Olin Institute at Harvard for inviting me to give talks on portions of my manuscript.

I have learned much from my students, both undergraduates and graduates. To all of you who suffered through Politics 168b, Politics 174b, and Politics 214a over these last years, I thank you for allowing me to try out my ideas, even when they were half-baked, on you. I also thank Linda Boothroyd and Rosanne Colocouris of the Brandeis Politics Department, for their logistical help in preparation of the manuscript.

I owe special thanks to my consulting editor, Teresa Lawson, whose skills at improving a manuscript are unparalleled. She removed needless words, fixed infelicitous phrases, caught my errors in logic, fixed inconsistencies, figured out what I wanted to say when I could not, helped with the book's organization, and cheered me on in that last final month.

Finally, I thank my children, Robyn and David, for tolerating a dad who said, too often, "I have to go work on my book."

ROBERT J. ART

A Grand Strategy for America

Introduction

This book deals with America's role in world politics, and specifically with its foreign policy and military strategy. These two subjects matter because the United States is the world's preeminent actor, and because it will remain so for at least several more decades. As a consequence, the foreign policy goals that the United States sets for itself, and the ways that it employs its overwhelming military power, will greatly affect how well it fares during its moment in the sun and, to a lesser but still significant degree, how well others fare and what the world will look like after America's preeminence ends. Getting America's foreign policy and military strategy right is, therefore, a matter of the highest importance.

In this book, I use history, theory, and analysis to try to understand what the right grand strategy should be. I prescribe for the United States a set of foreign policy goals to pursue and a military posture to support them that will do the best for the United States, that will do well for others, and that will enhance the chances that, after America's preeminence passes, the next international era will be congenial to American interests. The goals that I prescribe for the United States are internationalist in nature, and the military posture that I advocate is one of forward defense. Together, the foreign policy goals and the military posture comprise a grand strategy of "selective engagement." In this chapter I sketch the outlines of the argument for selective engagement presented in this book and give an overview of its contents.

THE CHALLENGE OF GRAND STRATEGY

Grand strategy is a broad subject: a grand strategy tells a nation's leaders what goals they should aim for and how best they can use their country's military power to attain these goals. Grand strategy, like foreign policy, deals with the momentous choices that a nation makes in foreign affairs, but it differs from foreign policy in one fundamental respect. To define a nation's foreign policy is to lay out the full range of goals that a state should seek in the world and then determine how all of the instruments of statecraft—political power, military power, economic power, ideological power—should be integrated and employed with one another to achieve those goals. Grand strategy, too, deals with the full range of goals that a state should seek, but it concentrates primarily on how the military instrument should be employed to achieve them. It prescribes how a nation should wield its military instrument to realize its foreign policy goals.

Devising a grand strategy means hard thinking about basic interests and the proper role of military power in protecting them. In order to prescribe a grand strategy for the United States, I answer four fundamental questions:

- First, what are America's interests in the world and what are the threats to these interests?
- Second, what are the possible grand strategies to protect America's interests from these threats?
- Third, which of these grand strategies best protects America's national interests?
- Fourth, what specific political policies and military capabilities are required to support the grand strategy chosen?

I answer the first question in Chapters 1 and 2; the second question in Chapters 3, 4, and 5; the third question in Chapter 6; and the last question in Chapter 7. I devote most of the book to the first three questions because providing answers to them is a large and difficult undertaking. So, too, is the task of answering the last question, and it deserves its own book. However, because the fundamental strategy must be fixed before the political-military specifics to support it can be identified, I take up most of the book with getting the fundamental strategy right and only sketch in with a broad brush the specific policies required to support it.

The need for a clear grand strategy for the United States has a new urgency caused by American's current position in international politics. First, the United States possesses a margin of power over other states, especially military power, that is unparalleled in modern history; indeed, the United States is probably the most powerful global actor the world has ever seen. Consequently, what it chooses to do or not to do inevitably has profound effects not only on its own interests but also on those of most other states in the world. The choices it makes now will affect not only its future position but also the course of world politics for some time to come. Second, this margin of power will not last forever. The country has perhaps a few decades—probably three at the most—before its considerable edge over others begins to wane significantly. America's ability to shape the world is now at its peak.

Because the costs and risks of wielding its power are not likely to be as cheap or as low as they were in the 1990s, the current moment differs dramatically from the first decade after the Cold War's end. Despite the challenges of the 1990s, the United States had a fairly easy time of it then. With the collapse of the Soviet Union, America's position as the world's only superpower went largely unchallenged, and its power was mostly welcomed abroad for the stability and reassurance that an American presence provided. The United States fought wars that were quick and successful, and that involved little loss of life for its soldiers. The economic boom of the 1990s easily supported a large military force. America's brand of capitalism looked—to some, at least—as if it could do no wrong. Most importantly, Americans felt secure behind their two oceanic moats. The country faced no state of equal size and power, and experienced no attacks on its homeland by foreign non-state actors. During the 1990s, America's foreign policy was relatively successful, and the costs and risks of using its military forces, both for peacetime deployments abroad and for waging war, were not excessive.

The future is not likely to be so rosy for the United States. Other states, including America's allies, are growing restive at America's predominant position and are likely to challenge it. Thus the costs of its world role are likely to rise. The September 11, 2001, attacks by al Qaeda demonstrated that the country must now plan for the likelihood that non-state actors will engage in grand terror attacks against it—attacks that can kill thousands or millions—both with conventional means and, if they can get them, with weapons of mass destruction. Moreover, some countries that oppose the United States and that harbor aggressive designs on their neighbors' territory are likely, sooner or later, to acquire weapons of mass destruction and the capability to deliver them against the American homeland. These developments will pose tough issues for the projection of American power. The next few decades do look more ominous.

The United States is thus at a critical juncture, and the challenge for Americans now is to decide what type of international role they want the nation to play. The eradication of foreign-based terrorist organizations that want to strike the United States cannot be the only possible answer. The prime directive of any grand strategy is, of course, to protect the homeland from attack; any state would ignore that directive at its peril. Vital as homeland security is, however, it does not constitute the last word in either foreign policy or grand strategy: America's purpose in the world cannot be reduced simply to self-protection. Homeland security is the beginning of grand strategy, but it does not equal grand strategy. The United States is the world's greatest power, and great powers have never lived for security alone. It is incumbent upon Americans to decide how expansive a role they want their country to play in world affairs over the next several decades, when its power to shape that world is at its peak.

3

THE UTILITY OF MILITARY POWER

Grand strategy involves military power, and military power is the most expensive and dangerous tool of statecraft, the one that can be the most costly in both treasure and blood. Military power, however, can also promise great benefits. If used properly, it can affect the success with which the other instruments of statecraft are employed. Using military power correctly does not ensure that a state will protect all of its interests, but using it incorrectly would put a great burden on these other instruments and could make it impossible for a state to achieve its goals. Decisions about whether and how to use military power may therefore be the most fateful a state makes. As Adam Smith put it, "defense is more important than opulence."

Military power remains important in statecraft because, for the foreseeable future, there will be no world government. This is what anarchy means: the absence of government. Anarchy is not to be confused with chaos, however; in fact international politics exhibits a good deal of order, regularity, and cooperation. Unfortunately, there is also much coercion, unpredictability, and bloodshed. All politics involves coercion as well as legitimacy. In domestic politics, where consensus on norms is high and where government is effective and widely accepted, legitimacy is high, so coercion can be low. In international politics, coercion looms larger, because government is absent and legitimacy is scarcer. The politics that takes place under anarchy thus differs fundamentally from the politics that takes place under government. In international politics, states must fend for themselves because there is no one else to fend for them. In both war and peace, military power helps states fend for themselves, not simply because it provides physical protection to a state but also because its employment produces political effects.

Politics is about influence: about getting others to do what you want them to do, about who has more influence over whom in a given situation, about who alters whose behavior. Military power is one of the instruments by which a state exerts influence. Tanks may threaten or destroy other tanks, artillery may obliterate other artillery, planes may shoot down other planes, and soldiers may kill or threaten other soldiers, but, after the killing is done or a standoff is resolved, the military outcome will also significantly affect the relative bargaining power of the contestants. Even for nations that are at peace with one another, military power remains important in the background; like the force of gravity, it affects the influence that parties exert over one another. In short, military power helps shape political results. Were this not the case, states would disarm.

Military power has three political uses: deterrence, compellence (or coercion), and defense.[1] When a state employs its military power against another state or nonstate actor it wants to prevent that adversary from doing some-

4

thing (deter it), to force that adversary to change its behavior (compel it), or to protect itself against some harmful action that the adversary threatens or has taken (defend itself). *Deterrence* is the threatened use of force to dissuade an adversary from undertaking something undesirable; it involves a threat to destroy what the adversary values, with the object of dissuading it from starting an undertaking harmful to the deterrer's interests. *Compellence* is the use of military power to bring about a change in an adversary's behavior; it is designed to force an adversary to stop the objectionable actions it has already undertaken. Compellence is usually achieved by employing physical force against the adversary in order to coerce it to alter its behavior, although states can first threaten compellent actions to try to stop the objectionable behavior. If a deterrent threat is effective, the threat will not have to be executed because the adversary will not have taken (or will reverse) the objectionable steps. If a compellent action is successful, the adversary's actions will change to accord with the behavior being demanded of it. *Defense* is the deployment of military power in order either to ward off an attack or to minimize damage from an attack. Defensive preparations are directed against an adversary's military forces.[2]

Deterrence, compellence, and defense are not tactical uses of force but strategic outcomes, operating among states or among states and nonstate actors. These uses are not strictly military, but rather are political-military in nature: they are intended to change the political behavior of the state or nonstate actor against which force is being directed. This is the case whether military power is being physically wielded—to attack and destroy—or peacefully wielded—to offset, check, threaten, or hold in place.

There are other ways to think about how military power can be used. We could enumerate a whole host of reasons why a state would call upon its armed forces, such as reassurance of allies that they will be protected by putting troops on their territory (peacetime presence); a commitment to punish those who commit aggression (collective security); forceful interventions to prevent mass starvation, genocide, or savage ethnic conflict (humanitarian interventions); interposition of forces between two warring parties to keep an agreed-upon peace between them (peacekeeping); intervention in civil conflicts to impose peace among the warring parties (peacemaking or peace enforcement); occupation of a nation to provide the stability necessary to rebuild its political structure (nation-building); quick, decisive intrusion of forces to rescue foreign nationals (rescue operations); short-term actions to exact revenge for harm done by an adversary (punitive actions); and highly directed use of force to prevent supplies and war matériel from reaching a given destination (interdiction).[3]

We can categorize each of these specific uses of force by whether it produces deterrent, compellent, or defensive political effects. For example, the political goal of a reassurance action is to make allies feel secure. This is done by extending deterrence to protect them in order to dissuade their adversaries from attacking. The political goal of any collective security system is to prevent aggression; this is deterrence of attack, pure and simple. The political goal of humanitarian interventions and peacekeeping operations is to save lives; this is defense of parties from attack. The political goal of peace-making operations is to impose peace; this is done by compelling the parties to stop fighting. The political goal of nation-building is to construct a viable government; this can be viewed as compelling armed groups to obey a new central government. The political goal of a rescue operation is to snatch away persons being held by an adversary; this can be viewed as defending the parties at risk.

Thus, no matter how varied are the stated reasons for using force, each is ultimately a deterrent, a compellent, or a defensive use of force. There is a simple but important reason why this is the case. When A seeks to influence B, it is attempting to affect B's behavior. Logically, there are only three basic outcomes that A can produce in B: A stops B from doing something; A forces B to change its behavior; or A takes steps to minimize the damage it will suffer from what B has done or is planning to do. Deterrence, compellence, and defense thus represent the three fundamental outcomes of any attempt at influence, military or otherwise, among states or among states and nonstate actors.[4]

Two final notes about the political uses of military power are in order. First, although I have singled out military power in this book, I do not mean that other instruments of statecraft are irrelevant. No instrument of state-craft can, by itself, produce significant and lasting results on pivotal matters; military power is no exception. Military power must be properly integrated with the other instruments of statecraft—political, economic, diplomatic, and ideological—and they, too, must be integrated with military power for best results. Second, my emphasis on military power does not mean I embrace it enthusiastically. Even though it is necessary, force is a nasty instrument. Military power does affect political relations, but it achieves that result by coercing, maiming, or killing people or by threatening to do so. It is always better, although not always easier, to persuade people with positive induce-ments than with negative ones. When used in battle, moreover, military power all too often brings unpredictability. Its use sets off a chain of events that engages emotions, hardens positions, escalates goals, and dramatically alters the situation, often for the worse. There are also great risks in threats to use force, in guarantees of protection, or in even a simple military pres-ence in a region. Threats might not be sufficient; guarantees might have to be fulfilled; a simple presence can quickly bring political entanglement. For all of these reasons, decision makers must never treat the military instru-ment lightly.

A GRAND STRATEGY FOR CONTEMPORARY AMERICA

In the chapters that follow, I go through the essential steps of formulating a grand strategy for the United States. I define America's national interests in this era and rank them according to their importance; I identify the most likely and dangerous threats to those interests; and then, based on the first two steps, I identify the best way of deploying America's military power to counter the threats.

I postulate six overarching national interests for the United States. The first is vital; the second and the third are highly important; and the last three are important:

- First, prevent an attack on the American homeland;
- Second, prevent great-power Eurasian wars and, if possible, the intense security competitions that make them more likely;
- Third, preserve access to a reasonably priced and secure supply of oil;
- Fourth, preserve an open international economic order;
- Fifth, foster the spread of democracy and respect for human rights abroad, and prevent genocide or mass murder in civil wars;
- Sixth, protect the global environment, especially from the adverse affects of global warming and severe climate change.

The first interest—preventing an attack on the homeland—is the one truly vital interest of the United States: the physical safety and political sovereignty of its citizenry is the prime directive of any state. The second interest—preventing great-power wars in Eurasia—is highly important because these wars could drag the United States in, and because such wars would almost inevitably threaten American trade, promote the spread of weapons of mass destruction, and bring on political changes that could severely diminish American influence. The third interest—oil—is also highly important because the United States and the rest of the world are heavily dependent on oil for energy and transportation; they cannot do without it, at least in the short and medium term. The fourth interest is important because an open international economic order helps promote the growth of wealth, and that is beneficial, in turn, because it facilitates the protection and promotion of the fifth and sixth interests. Richer states, after all, are more likely to become and remain stable democracies, as I explain later in the book, and such states, in turn, are more likely to protect human rights and to have the resources to protect their environments. The fifth interest is important because of the intrinsic value that the United States puts on democracy and the protection of human rights, but also because democratic states help to promote peace. The sixth interest is important because climate change will produce adverse effects (although the United States is better placed than most other nations to deal with those effects).

7

The first goal ranks above all the others because it is vital for the other five. Taken together, the first three interests rank above the other three. If the first three interests are not protected, then the security of the United States and basic health of the American economy would be put at grave risk. In contrast, if the last three were not realized, the nation would suffer to some degree, but not as severely. Those interests can add significantly to America's security and prosperity, but only if the first three interests are realized. In their claim on American resources and leadership, the vital and highly important must take priority over the important.

These six goals encompass both realpolitik and liberal internationalist goals. The first three are classic realpolitik interests because they involve the security, safety, and basic economic health of the nation. The fourth represents a mixture of realist and liberal goals because it involves both America's prosperity and the projection of its values abroad. The fifth is a classic liberal internationalist goal because it involves the projection of American values abroad. The last is the hardest to characterize. It might fall into either category, depending on one's views about the severity of climate effects that will be induced by global warming, even though in the medium term, global warming looks to be at worst an inconvenience, rather than a disaster, for the United States. All six, however they are characterized, are consistent with the traditional American style and practice of foreign policy, which has always fused the realist and liberal strands of statecraft.

The gravest threat to the American homeland today comes from hostile states or terrorists armed with nuclear, biological, or chemical (NBC) weapons. The greatest threat to Eurasian great-power peace comes from any aggressor state that seeks to dominate either eastern or western Eurasia or both, or from intense great-power security competitions that could escalate to war. The severest threat to American and global prosperity lies in the disruption of oil supplies from the Persian Gulf. The most serious threats to international openness come from economic nationalism, fears that economic openness could be militarily disadvantageous, or from a Eurasian great-power war. The greatest threats to the spread of democracy and to human rights come from ruthless dictators, thug leaders, or civil wars where one or both parties resort to mass murder of non-combatants. The worst threat to the global environment comes from the unbridled use of fossil fuels that continue to pump carbon dioxide and other greenhouse gases into the atmosphere.

I argue that to protect America's one vital and two highly important interests from these threats, the United States should keep a peacetime military presence in the Persian Gulf, Europe, and East Asia; maintain its key alliances and forward-based forces in those regions; and preserve a healthy military capability to reinforce forces abroad when necessary. American alliances and forces deployed abroad help stabilize these three key regions by reassuring allies and deterring potential and extant adversaries. Forward-based forces also provide more effective positions from which to go after terrorist groups that threaten the United States (as demonstrated in the war against the Taliban and al Qaeda in Afghanistan) and are also valuable should the United States decide to launch preventive wars against hostile states that acquire, or are soon to acquire, NBC weapons. Thus forward-based forces, allies, and bases abroad contribute directly to protecting the three most crucial American interests.

Alliances and forward-based forces also contribute to realizing America's three important interests, but in a more diffuse fashion. Spreading democracy and protecting human rights by direct military intervention could be a bottomless pit for the United States; the demand far exceeds the supply of American forces and the willingness of the American people to commit them to such tasks. Similarly, waging war to preserve economic openness, other than protecting Persian Gulf oil, would generally be counterproductive. Global warming is not a problem against which use of military force is practical. However, the projection of American military power abroad can contribute indirectly to the realization of these three important interests. To the extent that an American military presence abroad promotes peace and political stability in Eurasia—and it does—then it contributes to global economic openness, wealth generation, the building and consolidation of democracy, respect for human rights, and the freeing up of resources for environmental protection. Eurasia is home to most of the world's people, most of its proven oil reserves, and most of its major military powers, as well as a large share of its economic growth. If Eurasia remains stable and experiences economic growth, then the rest of the world, Americans included, will ultimately benefit. If, however, Eurasia experiences great-power wars and severe, prolonged economic dislocation, then the rest of the world would suffer, as modern history has shown.

In sum, all six of its interests can best be pursued if the United States remains militarily strong, militarily engaged, forward-based, and allied with key nations. None of these interests would be well served if the United States were to sheathe its sword, cut loose from its alliances, and bring its military forces home.

I favor selective engagement as the grand strategy that would best protect America's six national interests. Selective engagement is a strategy that aims to preserve America's key alliances and its forward-based forces. It keeps the United States militarily strong. With some important changes, it continues the internationalist path that the United States chose in 1945. It establishes priorities: it assures protection of America's vital and highly important interests, while also holding out hope of furthering each of the three important interests to some degree. It steers a middle course between not doing enough and attempting too much; it takes neither an isolationist, unilater-

9

alist path at one extreme nor a world-policeman role at the other. Selective engagement requires that the United States remain militarily involved abroad for its own interests. A forward defense strategy is a prudent policy: it seeks to forestall dangers, not simply react to them, and to head off adverse events, not simply cope with their ill effects once they have occurred. Central to selective engagement are certain tasks that the United States must do well if its security, prosperity, and values are to be protected. Small in number, these tasks are large in scope and importance, and neither easy nor cheap to attain. If properly conceived and executed, however, selective engagement is politically feasible and affordable.

In this book, I evaluate seven other grand strategies that the United States might choose: dominion, global collective security, regional collective security, cooperative security, containment, isolationism, and offshore balancing. Of these seven, containment is politically feasible, but today it needs to be done only regionally, not globally, and for that reason can be easily subsumed under a more comprehensive strategy of selective engagement. The other six strategies are infeasible, politically unattainable, problematic, or undesirable, as I demonstrate; consequently, they cannot protect America's interests as well as selective engagement. Dominion—a strategy to rule the world—is infeasible because it is beyond the resources of the United States. Global collective security and cooperative security are politically unattainable; the former requires a degree of global consensus that does not exist, while the latter is a great-power condominium against the smaller powers that the latter would not accept. Regional collective security is not politically feasible in most regions of the world and remains problematic even for the region ripest for it, Europe. Isolationism and offshore balancing are politically feasible, but for reasons I spell out, they are not desirable.

To make the case for a grand strategy of selective engagement, I proceed as follows. In Chapter 1, I define the five key features of the current international environment that bear most directly on America's foreign policy interests, show how most grew out of America's prior policies, and then derive America's contemporary interests from those features. In Chapter 2, I justify the choice of these six fundamental national interests in more detail, analyze more fully the potential threats to them, and provide the rationale for the priority I assign to each. In Chapter 3, I give a brief overview of the eight grand strategies potentially available to the United States, and then show why four of them—dominion, global and regional collective security, and cooperative security—can be easily dismissed as either infeasible or politically unattainable, and why the fifth, containment, can be folded into selective engagement. In Chapters 4 and 5, I make the cases for the three strategies that remain: selective engagement and the "free hand policies" of isolationism and offshore balancing. In Chapter 6, I compare selective engagement to these two and show why it is preferable to both. Finally, in

Chapter 7, I set forth the policy guidelines necessary to implement selective engagement, speculate on how long the United States can and should persevere with it, and suggest policies that should ease the transition when its day is done.

PRESCRIPTIONS

The arguments I offer in this book lead to four major prescriptions. First, the United States should not let down its guard, but instead must keep its powder dry. In international affairs, matters can turn threatening quite swiftly, as September 11, 2001, so tragically demonstrated. There is much good sense in the old adage, "To keep the peace, prepare for war." The United States must not allow its military power to degrade significantly. Second, however, the United States must be sparing in its use of the military instrument. It cannot shrink from using military force when its interests require it, but it should not resort to force—for peaceful reassurance, for issuing threats, or for waging war—when they do not. It should be neither too quick nor too slow on the trigger. Third, the United States should not retreat into an isolationist or offshore balancing posture by abandoning its alliances, bringing its troops home, and leaving others to their fates. Some changes in America's alliances and in the disposition of its forces overseas may well be in order, but their wholesale dismantlement is not. Fourth, powerful though the United States is, it still must obtain the cooperation of its allies to realize its national interests. Unbridled unilateralism is a sort of fool's gold and would be certain to damage America's interests and reduce its global influence. The United States must proceed as multilaterally as it can in the exercise of its political-military might. In sum, if the United States allows its military instrument to degrade significantly, if it does not strike the right balance in its use of force, if it abandons its allies and pursues a unilateralist course, then the world will become a more dangerous place, and, sooner or later, that will redound to America's detriment.

If the United States is to avoid misusing its military power, it must discover the proper balance between overdoing it and underdoing it. To underuse the military instrument would weaken American statecraft and invite predatory behavior by others; to overuse it would waste a scarce resource, make the American public weary of internationalism, and accelerate the formation of counter-coalitions. To define the right balance between underdoing it and overdoing it is the basic task for grand strategy and the goal of this book.

ONE

The International Setting

To develop a grand strategy for the United States, we must begin with the international environment and America's place in it. International conditions alone do not, and should not, wholly determine a state's foreign policy, but they do impose constraints on state action, as well as offering opportunities to exploit. Our initial task, then, is to delineate those features of the contemporary environment that most directly affect America's security and prosperity and the quality of life of its citizenry.

Five features stand out: the absence of a peer state military competitor; the rise of grand terrorism; the deepening economic interdependence among Western Europe, North America, and Japan and, through the forces of globalization, the gradual incorporation of some Third World states into this interdependent arena; the growing appeal and expansion of democratic governance beyond the core zone of Western Europe, North America, and Japan; and the continuing degradation of the global environment, especially the increase in global warming and the threat of climate change associated with it. These five features capture the military, economic, political, and environmental developments of greatest significance for America's national interests. The first two features are new; they appeared only with the end of the Cold War and the collapse of the Soviet Union. The last three are not new, having become manifest during the latter half of the Cold War, but their magnitude has grown enough since then that they can be considered distinctive features of this era. Old and new, all five factors have great influence on the United States, its role in the world, and its strategic options.

In this chapter I describe each of these features in turn and show why they are the ones with the most bearing on the United States. I make the case for focusing on these five and not others that are commonly cited. Finally, I show how America's fundamental national interests in the contemporary era are shaped by these salient features. Chapter 2 then provides the full justification for these interests.

ABSENCE OF A COMPETITOR STATE

The United States currently faces no peer state competitor that can pose a compelling and immediate military threat to its homeland. No great power threatens to harness the resources of Eurasia to project military power into the Western Hemisphere or against the United States; no mighty state is targeting its military forces on America's territory with aggressive intent; no hostile coalitions are planning to move against the United States; and no great-power war looms in Eurasia to drag the United States into its maelstrom. For these reasons, the United States faces no threat of large-scale attack, wholesale destruction, military invasion, or outright conquest from state actors.

Indeed, the United States today is stronger now, relative to all other states, than at any time in its history, except for the brief period at the end of World War II when the United States enjoyed an atomic monopoly, had an army of several million, and an air force and navy second to none. Today, America's military might dwarfs that of any potential competitor, and this condition is likely to hold for a considerable time. Although no one can say for certain how long America's military dominance will last, the Pentagon made an estimate in 1998:

> The security environment between now and 2015 will . . . likely be marked by the absence of a 'global peer competitor' able to challenge the United States militarily around the world as the Soviet Union did during the Cold War. . . . The United States is the world's only superpower today, and it is expected to remain so through at least 2015.

The Pentagon reaffirmed this view in 2001:

> The United States faces no global rival today, nor is one likely to emerge for the foreseeable future.[1]

A quick look at the possible competitors demonstrates the point. Russia poses no formidable danger. Between 1992 and 1997, the Pentagon estimate of how long it would take Russia to reconstitute a major conventional threat in Eurasia was modified, from about two years to somewhere between ten and fifteen.[2] Russia's military problems are legion. In August 2001, General Anatoly Kornukov, one of Russia's military leaders, said that "air force units have practically ceased to be ready for combat" and that "the proportion of state-of-the-art planes is less than five percent."[3] The Air Force is critically short of repairs; training time for pilots is now below basic safety levels, let alone combat standards; and only 46 percent of its 2,000 aircraft are serviceable. Russia's ground forces have not trained in division-level exercises for years, and its surface and submarine crews receive inadequate training at sea. Russia's procurement budget is so low that at present levels only 10 percent of its equipment will be relatively modern by the year 2005.[4] As a consequence, "The overall state of operational readiness of all except the nuclear forces remains low due to lack of resources for training, maintenance, and new equipment."[5] In late 2000 President Putin began a serious program to reform Russia's armed forces, calling for a modern, professional, smaller, well-equipped, and well-paid military, but these reforms will take time to implement; moreover, "the fortunes of Russia's armed forces necessarily hinge on the performance of the Russian economy."[6] Although Russia's nuclear forces remain formidable, the danger to the United States is not one of deliberate attack, but rather poorly guarded nuclear weapons ("loose nukes") that could be seized by the Russia "mafia" or terrorists; rogue nuclear scientists who could sell their expertise to terrorists or states hostile to the United States; or unauthorized launch of its ballistic missiles. None of these threats is to be dismissed, but all three are qualitatively different from the one posed by the Soviet Union. Consequently, they do not demand the same urgency, resources, and attention that the Soviet threat did.

William Odom, a close analyst of Russia, sums it up: "Russia is no longer a great power and is unlikely again to become one over the next several decades."[7] This conclusion is reinforced when we take into account the relative economic power of the United States and Russia. During the height of the Cold War, the Soviet Union had a gross domestic product (GDP) approximately half that of the United States. In 2001, the GDP of Russia was about one-thirtieth the size of America's GDP ($10 trillion for the United States, $310 billion for Russia.)[8] Even if Russia's economy does well over the next several decades, it will be a long, long time before Russia could challenge the United States as a military competitor.

The other great power best positioned to challenge overall U.S. military predominance is China. Yet China remains a regional power, with a large but still poorly equipped army, a navy that, if no longer simply coastal, is clearly not yet blue-water, and an air force that still has thousands of obsolete first- and second-generation jet aircraft based on 1950s Soviet designs. China is engaged in a modernization effort whose first priority is to create "pockets of excellence," that is, to make small portions of its forces fully modernized. However, a comprehensive modernization program will take somewhere between twenty-five and forty years.[9] China deploys a small nuclear force of twenty liquid-fueled intercontinental ballistic missiles (ICBMs) and a larger number of medium-range ballistic missiles. It is in the process of modernizing these forces with submarine-launched missiles and second-generation ICBMs, but its nuclear forces are likely to remain small and useful primarily for homeland deterrence. Thus, although its military power will increase as its rapid economic growth continues, analysts concur that "China's military remains at least 20 years out of date"; that "China does not have the resources to project a major conventional force beyond its territory"; that its "power-projection capability is limited at present"; and that it "will not represent a serious strategic threat to the United States for at least twenty years."[10] Indeed, as Robert Ross concludes: "There is no false optimism in the PLA [the People's Liberation Army] that it could survive a war with the United States."[11]

The other great military powers of the world—Britain, France, Germany, and Japan—all remain allies of the United States and closely coordinate their military planning with it. None would be able singly to challenge America's military predominance. Apart from Russia, China, and these four great powers, only one other potential military competitor to the United States exists: the European Union. At present, however, the European Union, although an economic giant, remains a military pygmy. It plans to have a rapid reaction force of 60,000 troops ready in 2003, but most analysts do not believe that it will be able to meet its goals—being able to deploy such a force within sixty days and to sustain it in the field—until 2012 at the earliest.[12] Even then, the European force will represent only a fraction of America's power-projection capability. Thus, the United States today stands militarily preeminent.

Britain once deliberately maintained a "two-power" standard for her navy: the Royal Navy had to be equal in strength, and preferably superior to, the next two navies combined. In similar terms, the United States today appears to be following, by accident or by design, a six-to-nine power standard. Its defense budget in 1996—$266 billion—almost exactly equaled the combined total of the next six largest defense budgets, those of Russia, China, Japan, France, Britain, and Germany. By 1999, its defense budget of $283 billion exceeded the combined total of the next seven largest defense budgets—those six states plus Italy. By 2000, its defense budget of $295 billion exceeded the combined total of the next nine largest defense budgets—the aforementioned seven states, plus Saudi Arabia and India. The increases projected after the September 11, 2001, terrorist attacks promise to widen the gap even more.[13] Measured by the traditional standard of security—America's military power relative to other states' military power—the United States today is quite secure. However, measured by another standard—the threat of terrorist attack—the United States does not look so secure.

EMERGENCE OF GRAND TERRORISM

The terrorist threat that the United States now faces is different from anything that it has ever experienced before. In the September 11 attacks on the World Trade Center and the Pentagon, over 3000 people were killed.[14] This threat could grow even more severe, perhaps catastrophic, unless strong measures are taken to counteract it. "Grand terror"—attacks against the American homeland that could kill thousands if conventional and radiological weapons are used, or hundreds of thousands, even millions, if nuclear, biological, or chemical (NBC) weapons are used—is the prime military threat the United States confronts today.

Until the early 1990s, the terrorist acts that the United States and other countries faced were "traditional." The goals of traditional terrorists were strictly political, precisely defined, and directed toward specific goals such as ending political repression and economic injustice for a group, or attaining statehood for an ethnic minority. The groups executing such attacks usually took public credit for them in order to dramatize their causes and to produce the desired political effects. Most important, these terrorist attacks were limited in scope. Traditional terrorists fine-tuned their killing and pulled their punches, limiting the carnage they inflicted because, in the words of the terrorism expert Brian Jenkins, they wanted "a lot of people watching and a lot of people listening, and not a lot of people dead."[15] The aim of the traditional terrorists was to cause enough death to rivet attention to their political cause, but not so much death as to cause a political backlash that would hurt that cause.

Under traditional terrorism, the number of people killed worldwide was small. Using U.S. State Department data from 1968–2000, Audrey Cronin has shown that the total number of deaths worldwide from terrorist attacks ranged from a low of thirty-four in 1968, when there were 124 separate terrorist incidents, to a high of 816 in 1985, when there were 635 separate incidents. In more than half of the years, deaths from all terrorist attacks worldwide averaged fewer than four hundred.[16] Even more important, as Brian Jenkins notes, only fourteen of the more than ten thousand recorded acts of international terrorism since 1968 (and prior to September 11, 2001) had resulted in deaths of one hundred or more.[17] In the year 2000, 405 people worldwide were killed in terrorist attacks, of whom nineteen were Americans; all but two were sailors killed in the attack against the USS Cole while it was stationed in the Yemeni port of Aden.[18] Indeed, during most of the years between 1968 and the early 1990s, international terrorism was so limited in scope and killing that Thomas Schelling, accurately reflecting the times, could write in 1991: "I am . . . led to speculate on why international political terrorism is such an infinitesimal activity on the world scene when measured not in audience appeal but in damage actually accomplished or even attempted."[19] Traditional terror, although heinous, was limited and predictable.

Matters began to change in the 1990s, especially for the United States. Even though the worldwide total of terrorist incidents declined in the 1990s from what it had been in the 1980s, the attacks were increasingly directed against Americans, and the lethality of each attack increased. Throughout most of the 1970s and 1980s, about one-third of the terrorists incidents each year involved the United States. Between 1990 and 1992, however, the percentage rose to between 39 percent and 55 percent; it dipped to a low of 20 percent in 1994, but then climbed again to 40 percent in 1997, reaching 47 percent in 2000.[20] Moreover, according to State Department records, between 1968 and 2000, the three years of greatest casualties (dead and wounded) for both the United States and the world all occurred in the 1990s.[21] Because of the September 11 al Qaeda attacks in the United States, 2001 is the year in which the most Americans were killed in terrorist attacks—3,235 in the United States and 8 others abroad—and in which the largest number of people worldwide were killed, an estimated total of 3,547.[22]

Terrorists are focusing more and more on Americans because, as Paul Pillar notes, the United States is the world's "sole superpower, the leader of the West, and the only country with truly global impact and presence."[23] Terrorism is the weapon of the weak against the strong; because the United States is so strong militarily, non-state actors, or even states, cannot directly take on the United States, and so they resort to asymmetric means. It is also relatively easy for them to do so because the United States is particularly vulnerable to terrorism. Its physical presence is literally global; for example, 14,000 Americans work abroad for more than thirty U.S. government agencies that operate overseas. Its borders are porous: 520 million people were admitted to the United States in fiscal year 1999, of whom two-thirds were aliens, while in 2000, 127 million cars, 11.5 million trucks, 11.2 million shipping containers, 2.2 million railroad cars, and 211,000 ships entered the country. Its society is free and open.[24] An impregnable defense at home or abroad against determined terrorists is impossible; as Brian Jenkins puts it: "since terrorists can attack anything, anywhere, anytime, we can't protect everything, anywhere, all the time."[25] American policies generate resentment because the policies of strong states always generate resentment. America's economic interests and global military presence benefit some groups but disadvantage others. The disadvantaged see the United States as partly responsible for their disadvantaged state because it benefits from, and helps prop up, a status quo that hurts them. Many groups resent the United States as much for what it stands for as for what it does. Thus, terrorists have both motive and opportunity to strike the world's leading state.

They are also doing so with increasing effect because each individual terrorist act is producing more carnage. There are many reasons why this is so; four in particular are noted by Bruce Hoffman.[26] First, terrorists are killing more people in each attack because they believe that governments and their citizens have become inured to killing and that therefore stepping up the killing is necessary to regain political attention. Second, terrorists have become better at killing because they have gained access to better weapons. Third, terrorists have been able to kill more with each act because they have gotten help from states that have an interest in sponsoring terrorism. This has given them access to better weapons and training. Fourth, and most important for the threat to the United States, the motives of the "new" terrorists are less strictly political and more religious, political-religious, or millenarian in nature. In 1980, clearly identifiable religious groups constituted only two of the sixty-four terrorist groups operating; by 1996, thirteen of the forty-six identifiable terrorist groups were predominantly religious, and these groups committed ten of the thirteen most lethal attacks in that year.[27] Religious and millenarian groups are less constrained than traditional terrorists and use more violence because they believe their acts have divine sanction or because they are designed to overthrow a given political order, not to modify it. Hoffman put the point well:

> Whereas secular terrorists, even if they have the capacity to do so, rarely attempt indiscriminate killing on a massive scale because such tactics are not consonant with their political aims and therefore are regarded as counterproductive, if not immoral, religious terrorists often seek the elimination of broadly defined categories of enemies and accordingly regard such large-scale violence not only as morally justified but as a necessary expedient for the attainment of their goals. . . . religious terrorists see themselves not as components of a system worth preserving but as 'outsiders', seeking fundamental changes in the existing order. This sense of alienation also enables the religious terrorist to contemplate far more destructive and deadly types of terrorist operations than secular terrorists, and indeed to embrace a far more open-ended category of 'enemies' for attack.[28]

Nowhere have motive and capability come together more powerfully than in the Middle East and in al Qaeda. We do not have to accept Samuel Huntington's assertion that the West is at war with Islam to believe that the United States is at war with those Islamic fundamentalists and radicals who want to commit grand terrorism against it.[29] The causes of anti-Americanism in the Middle East and of Islamic radicals' hatred of the West are manifold: they blame the West for Islam's historical decline from power and greatness; they resent America's support of Israel against the Palestinians; they are angered by Western and American support for regimes that these groups find politically repressive, economically ineffective, and morally corrupt; and they believe that Western culture, capitalism, and democracy—and the United States as the embodiment of these things—threaten the very essence of Islam and the Islamic way of life.[30] There is no dearth of reasons for hatred of the West and the United States among extremists groups in the Middle East, but hatred provides only the motive for grand terrorism attacks; sufficient capability is also needed.

In retrospect, we can see that the Afghanistan war of the 1980s created the capability, in the form of al Qaeda. The struggle to evict the Soviets from Afghanistan brought together Islamic fighters from many different countries. It created what Pillar calls the "ultimate extremist networking opportunity," and laid the basis for a transnational terrorist organization.[31] Financed and trained in part by the United States, non-Afghan Islamic fighters learned counterinsurgency skills that were readily adaptable to terrorist activities; in this sense al Qaeda, or at least its fighting skills, is partly a creature of America's late Cold War fight against the Soviet Union. Success in evicting the Soviet Union from Afghanistan created a sense of power that such tactics could be turned to other uses. Moreover, success left the non-Afghan fighters unemployed; they constituted what Kepel terms "a kind of demobilized army of several thousand seasoned warriors, all without passports, in search of a place to fight or hide." Osama bin Laden created al Qaeda in 1986 to organize the non-Afghan fighters against the Soviet Union and to channel funds through it to the Afghan resistance. After 1990 he took this organization, created to fight against the Soviets in Afghanistan, and turned it against the United States.[32] The catalyst for bin Laden's anti-American turn was America's entry into Saudi Arabia in 1990 in order to eject Saddam Hussein's forces from Kuwait. Bin Laden argued that America troops in Arabia were infidels who were defiling the holy sites of Islam and propping up the corrupt Saudi regime.[33] In short, the Afghan war helped forge an institution—al Qaeda—with the skill required to carry out grand terror attacks against the United States at home and abroad.[34]

Al Qaeda represents the new face of terrorism—religiously motivated, organizationally decentralized but effective, technologically sophisticated, unconstrained in its use of violence, intent upon revenge and punishment, supranational in recruitment, and global in operation.[35] Al Qaeda, however, is not the only terrorist organization of this type that emerged in the 1990s, nor is it the only one with motive to target the American homeland. Hizbollah has terrorist cells on every continent save Antarctica, and the now-defunct Japanese millenarian religious cult Aum Shinrikyo apparently planned to duplicate in the United States the sarin nerve gas attacks that it executed in March 1995 in the Tokyo subway.[36] The age of multinational religious terrorism has arrived. Even if al Qaeda were to be defeated tomorrow, the United States can no longer take comfort from its two ocean moats. It must now worry about, plan against, attempt to prevent, and prepare to recover from grand terror attacks. "Terrorism has had different prime targets in different eras," writes Pillar. "It is now the turn of the United States. The turn could not be shortened unless the United States were to shrink much farther from its present stature than anyone expects and than even the most ardent isolationists hope."[37]

GROWTH OF ECONOMIC OPENNESS AND INTERDEPENDENCE

The third salient feature of the contemporary era is the economic inter-dependence among the world's rich and powerful democracies and the gradual but steady incorporation of other states into this interdependent zone. Economic interdependence among the nations of the First World is deep and well entrenched, and the forces behind it are propelling it relent-lessly outward.[38] If properly managed, this "march of the market" can be a powerful factor for peace because of the beneficial political effects that inter-dependence can foster. If not properly managed, however, interdependence might provoke political, economic, and even military conflict among nations.

I use the term "interdependence" to refer to the size and importance of the stake that a state has (or believes it has) in economic intercourse with other states—in trading with them and in seeing capital and technology flowing easily among them.[39] In this sense, interdependence can be high or low, deep or shallow.[40] The higher the perceived interdependence, the larger a state's presumed stake in the economic well-being of the countries with which it most interacts economically. At high levels of interdependence, all other things being equal, a state will want others to prosper because of the belief that this adds to its own prosperity. A high degree of interdependence can therefore foster cooperation among states because it causes them to per-ceive self-gain from others' gain. Hence, cooperation can come more easily when the possibility for mutual gains exists than when it does not.[41] Such cooperation amidst interdependence, however, is not automatic. It requires, as I argue in Chapter 2, a belief among the parties that economic entan-glements will not lead to vulnerabilities and dependencies, either economic or military, that could be turned to their disadvantage.

Several indicators demonstrate the economic interdependence that now exists both globally and among the rich First World states. They also illus-trate the marked change that occurred in the late 1970s, making the 1980s and after an era of deep interdependence.[42]

The first indicator is portrayed in Figure 1.1, and shows the ratio of world exports to gross world product (GWP) in selected years over a 170-year period. Exports are a good measure of the stake that one country has in another's economic health. The richer a nation is, the more goods it can buy from other states. The more a nation sells to other states, the greater its stake in their economic prosperity. In short, prosperous states make good customers. Rising levels of exports as a percentage of GWP therefore indi-cate greater trade and rising interdependence among states. Figure 1.1 shows that the level of interdependence has been rising. By 1970, exports as a percentage of GWP finally surpassed the level that had been reached immediately prior to World War I; by 1990, the level was three-quarters

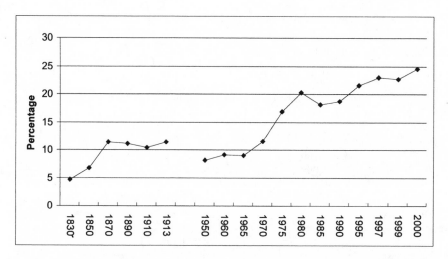

FIGURE 1.1. World Exports as a Share of Gross World Product, 1830–1913, 1950–2000.

Notes: Data for 1830–1913 include only the United States and Europe (including European and Asian Russia, but not Turkey). Data from 1913–1950 are not available, due to lack of reliable figures for the world-war and interwar years. Data from 1970 to present include the Soviet Union and the Eastern Bloc countries and their successor states. Total world exports from 1995 onward include trade among European Union member states.

Sources: For the years 1830–1965, Janice E. Thomson and Stephen D. Krasner, "Global Transactions and the Consolidation of Sovereignty," in Ernst-Otto Czempiel and James N. Rosenau, eds., *Global Changes and Theoretical Challenges* (New York: Macmillan, 1989), p. 78. 1960–1965 export data from IMF, *International Financial Statistics Yearbook.* 1960–1965 gross world product data from UN, *Yearbook of National Accounts Statistics.* 1970–2000 gross world product and export data from IMF, "World Economic Outlook Database, May 2001," <www.imf.org/external/pubs/ft/weo/2001/01/data/indexl.htm>.

greater than the 1970 level; by 2000, more than twice the 1970 level. Today, world exports as a percentage of GWP stand at their highest level in 170 years, which is one of the reasons why this era looks more deeply interdependent than the 1870–1914 era to which it is often compared.

Capital flows are also a good measure of interdependence. Investors and banks will direct funds to areas where they believe they can earn high rates of return and from which they can remit their profits. High levels of capital flow indicate confidence in the security of assets, whether direct investments or loans, and are another measure of the extent of the integration among states. The data in Tables 1.1, 1.2, and 1.3 show the explosion in capital flows that occurred beginning in the mid-1970s, when states began to relax their

TABLE 1.1. Foreign Assets of Deposit Banks as a Share of Gross World Product, 1960–1994

Year	Deposit Banks' Foreign Assets (in millions of U.S. dollars)	Gross World Product (in millions of U.S. dollars)	Foreign Assets as a Share of Gross World Product (%)
1960	3,200	1,125,800	0.3
1965	7,500	1,485,500	0.5
1970	7,700	3,411,700	0.2
1975	46,000	6,292,200	0.7
1980	1,836,100	11,811,200	15.5
1985	2,982,600	12,869,900	23.2
1990	6,790,600	22,738,300	29.9
1992	6,750,000	23,863,000	28.3
1994	7,877,100	26,234,200	30.0

Notes: Deposit banks are banks that accept transferable deposits (this excludes central banks, insurance companies, and pension funds). Foreign assets refer to all positions held by a deposit bank for non-residents. Figures for columns 2 and 3 are in millions of dollars. They include loans to business, banks, and governments, but exclude financial authority transactions. For most of 1960–1994, the Soviet Union and Russia did not report figures for foreign assets of deposit banks; for the few years that they did, the totals were insignificant.

Sources: International Monetary Fund, *International Financial Statistics* (various years). The IMF stopped publishing aggregated foreign assets of deposit banks after 1994.

controls on capital movements. Table 1.1 shows that bank activity across borders exploded in 1980. Table 1.2 shows that direct investment flows more than doubled between 1975 and 1985 and exploded in 1990, and that portfolio investment increased by a factor of more than twelve between 1975 and 1985.[43] Table 1.3 shows that direct investment flows as a percentage of GWP tripled between 1990 and 1999 and that portfolio investment flows as a percentage of GWP increased by a factor of nearly seven in the same period.[44]

A third indicator of interdependence is daily capital movements. These, rather than trade flows, dominate currency exchange rates and dwarf by a large factor the daily trade in goods, as Peter Drucker pointed out in 1986: "The London Eurodollar market, in which the world's financial institutions borrow from and lend to each other, turns over $300 billion each working day, or $75 trillion a year, a volume at least 25 times that of world trade."[45] By 1992, only six years later, the daily volume of currency trading had more than tripled to one trillion dollars, with New York accounting for $192 billion, London $303 billion, Tokyo $128 billion, and other financial centers $370 billion.[46] Table 1.4 displays daily global currency turnover from 1986–2001 as a percentage of world exports of goods and services. In these fifteen years, daily currency turnover more than doubled as a percentage of

TABLE 1.2. World Direct and Portfolio Investment Flows, 1960–1999

Year	Direct Foreign Investment (in millions of U.S. dollars)	Portfolio Investment (in millions of U.S. dollars)	Gross World Product (in millions of U.S. dollars)
1960	NA	NA	1,125,800
1965	NA	NA	1,485,500
1970	12,166	NA	3,411,700
1975	25,160	9,139	6,292,200
1980	42,497	42,697	11,811,200
1985	57,123	112,908	12,869,900
1990	238,318	183,805	22,738,300
1995	323,064	624,600	29,095,100
1999	911,192	1,632,400	30,549,700

Notes: NA means not available. Figures represent annual flows, not cumulative totals. Portfolio and direct investment figures prior to 1995 exclude the former Soviet Union, Eastern Bloc countries, and the successor states of the Soviet Union. Portfolio investment covers transactions in equity securities and debt securities (bonds, notes, money market instruments, and financial derivatives). Portfolio investments are notable for the ease with which they can be traded, and thus the speed with which money can be moved out of a country. Direct foreign investment covers the flow of equity capital, reinvested earnings, and intercompany transactions. Direct foreign investment generally involves a longer-term time frame than portfolio investment.

Source: Investment data from International Monetary Fund, *Balance of Payments Statistics* (data for 2000 was unavailable at time of publication). Gross world product data from IMF, "World Economic Outlook Database, December 2001," <www.imf.org/external/pubs/ft/weo/2001/03/data/w1.csv>.

TABLE 1.3. Investment Flows as a Share of Gross World Product, 1970–1999

Year	Gross World Product (in millions of U.S. dollars)	Direct Foreign Investment as a Share of Gross World Product (%)	Portfolio Investment as a Share of Gross World Product (%)
1970	3,411,700	0.4	0.0
1975	6,292,200	0.4	0.1
1980	11,811,200	0.4	0.4
1985	12,869,900	0.4	0.9
1990	22,738,300	1.0	0.8
1995	29,095,100	1.1	2.1
1999	30,549,700	3.0	5.3

Source: Percentages calculated from data in Table 1.2.

TABLE 1.4. Daily Currency Turnover, 1986–2001

	1986	1989	1992	1995	1998	2001
Estimated global turnover (in billions of U.S. dollars)	188	590	820	1190	1490	1210
As a share of world exports of goods and services (%)	7.4	15.8	17.4	19.1	22.3	16.2

Source: Bank for International Settlements, except 2001 world exports of goods and services from the IMF, "World Economic Outlook Database, April 2002" <www.imf.org/external/pubs/ft/weo/2002/01/data/w1.csv>.

world exports of goods and services, going from 7.4% to 16.2%. With these huge daily and annual flows of monies across their borders, national governments find it difficult to buffer their economies from the vagaries of the international capital market because all are intimately connected to it. As Raymond Vernon and Debra Spar put it: "the capacity of national monetary authorities to influence their national money supplies, to affect their national exchange rates, or even to supervise their banking systems has been reduced to new low levels."[47] This is a far cry from the pre-1914 era, when the Bank of London and the City of London had the ability to exercise a more centralized control over the flow of international funds than any single national authority can do today.[48] The era of interdependence in world financial, currency, and security markets dawned in the late 1970s and matured in the 1980s and 1990s.[49]

Taken together, these indicators—export activity, bank loans across borders, direct investment flows, daily currency trading, and the globalization of financial markets—show that the world economy changed significantly between 1975 and 1990. The 1980s represent a breakpoint in the post-1945 era: in this decade, interdependence deepened, and it deepened further in the decade of the 1990s.

The figures just reviewed present a macro picture of world trade. One more finely tuned would reveal patterns within regions or among selected groups of states. The first nations to experience a high degree of interdependence were the democratic states of Western Europe, the United States, Canada, and Japan. One rough measure of their close economic ties is trade among the G-7 nations (Germany, Italy, France, the United Kingdom, the United States, Canada, and Japan). Table 1.5 gives three pictures of G-7 exports. The first column shows that exports of the G-7 nations to one another account historically for between one-fifth and one-quarter of total world exports since the mid-1960s. The second column shows that total

TABLE 1.5. The G-7 and International Trade, 1937–2000

Year	Intra G-7 Exports as % of World Exports	Total G-7 Exports as % of World Exports	Intra G-7 Exports as % of Total G-7 Exports
1937	NA	41.1	NA
1955	17.4	48.7	35.8
1960	18.9	48.0	39.4
1965	24.0	56.8	42.2
1970	25.8	55.9	46.2
1975	20.0	50.4	39.6
1980	19.9	47.9	41.6
1985	25.9	52.4	49.5
1990	25.7	52.2	49.3
1995	22.5	49.0	45.9
1997	20.9	48.4	44.4
2000	22.0	45.7	48.0

Notes: NA means not available. The G-7 countries are the United States, Canada, Britain, France, Germany (West Germany before 1990), Italy, and Japan.

Sources: For the 1950s, United Nations, *United Nations Yearbook of International Trade Statistics*, 1955 and 1956. For subsequent years, International Monetary Fund, *Direction of Trade Statistics Yearbook* (various years).

G-7 exports account for almost half of all world exports. The third column, the most significant for measuring interdependence, shows that for about the last forty years, exports among the G-7 nations account for 40 percent to 50 percent of their total exports. The G-7 statistics understate the trade among the First World rich democracies because they do not include all the states of the European Union, which trade extensively with one another. The conclusion seems evident: the seven richest industrial democracies account for close to half the world's trade, and they also account for almost half of one another's total trade.

More specifically, trade and direct foreign investment are concentrated among the rich nations of the North. Table 1.6 shows trade among all industrial countries, which, according to International Monetary Fund convention, include the G-7, the other states of Western Europe besides the G-7, New Zealand, and Australia. As the table shows, their trade accounted for 45 percent of world exports in 2000. (Trade among the industrial nations, together with the trade between them and the developing states, accounted for 63 percent of world exports—column 1 plus column 2). Moreover, as economist Paul Krugman makes clear, the advanced economies of the world took 38 percent of one another's exports in 1953; by 1990, this figure had risen to 76 percent. (Included in advanced economies were such states as

TABLE 1.6. World Exports among and between Industrial and Developing States as a Percent of Total World Exports, 1960–2000

Year	Industrial to Industrial	Industrial to Developing	Developing to Industrial	Developing to Developing
1960	35.4	21.2	24.4	11.0
1970	49.7	23.9	21.7	4.7
1980	44.6	18.0	25.6	11.4
1990	55.2	16.6	16.9	10.8
1995	46.9	19.6	18.2	14.1
1997	45.5	20.5	19.5	15.8
2000	45.4	17.8	21.7	14.8

Source: International Monetary Fund, *Direction of Trade Statistics Yearbook* (various years).

Taiwan, South Korea, and Singapore.)[50] Direct foreign investment remains highly concentrated in the North. During the 1980s, for example, two-thirds of inward direct investment flows worldwide went into the United States and the European Union; during 1985–1989, the United States alone accounted for 46 percent of world inflows. In 1996, 40 percent of the world's direct foreign investment was located in the United States, France, the United Kingdom, and Germany. More generally, the world's wealthy states account for 97 percent of direct foreign investment outflows and 75 percent of the inflows.[51] Today's interdependence is still very much a rich-nation club.

The seeds of economic interdependence among the rich democracies were sown in the late 1950s and early 1960s, when the European Common Market was created and when the first of many multilateral talks to reduce barriers to trade in manufactured goods began under America's leadership. By the mid-1990s, the interdependence among these nations deepened to levels never before reached, at least in the modern era. The power of the market, together with its integrating force, did not stop there. Economic integration has moved far beyond the First World to include other states. The first to be incorporated were the East Asian NICs (newly industrializing countries) of South Korea, Taiwan, Hong Kong, and Singapore. By 1980, they accounted for 56.5 percent of the manufactured exports of the developing nations of the Third World; by 1990, 61.6 percent. The next states that began to move into the First World's interdependence zone were the Southeast Asian NICs (Indonesia, Malaysia, the Philippines, and Thailand), which in 1980 had accounted for only 4.3 percent of developing countries' manufactured exports, but by 1990 accounted for nearly two-and-a-half times as much, at 10.4 percent. In 1992, each of these eight states sent between 14 percent and 40 percent of its exports to the United States alone.[52] Other states from Latin America, such as Mexico, Brazil, Venezuela, and Chile, are becoming integrated into the rich nations' interdependent club. So will some countries of Eastern Europe, including Poland, the Czech Republic, Hungary, and Slovenia. If its present rates of economic growth and economic liberalization continue, China, too, will eventually join the interdependent club.

In sum, deep economic interdependence is a fact of life for the First World, based upon relatively free trade in industrialized exports, relatively unimpeded flows of capital, global access to advanced technology, and the powerful competitive forces of the market. The march of the market will continue to bring other states into the rich-nation club, if political conditions in both those states and the rich ones permit it to. Deep interdependence is not conflict-free, but to the extent that it creates interests in self-gain through mutual gain, it is a force not only for increasing material well-being but also for the peaceful resolution of disputes.[53]

PREVALENCE OF DEMOCRACY

The fourth distinguishing feature of this era is the prevalence of democracy. It is a global phenomenon, not just a Western one. It is firmly rooted within the majority of the great powers. Its spread has had multiple causes, of which economic growth has clearly been one of the most important. I touch upon each of these aspects in this section.

Today the democratic form of government is found worldwide.[54] Exactly how many nations are democratic is a judgment call; the count depends both on how the requirements of democracy are defined and on an assessment of whether a given state satisfies them. Samuel Huntington lists three ways to define democracy: according to the sources of authority for government, according to the purposes served by government, or according to the procedures for constituting government. He adopts the latter (Schumpeterian) definition, which looks to procedures and defines a twentieth-century political system as democratic "to the extent that its most powerful collective decision makers are selected through fair, honest, and periodic elections in which candidates freely compete for votes and in which virtually all the adult population is eligible to vote."[55] With this definition, Huntington found that in 1991, 45 percent of all states with populations greater than one million were democratic (fifty-eight out of 129), or about 33 percent of all the states of the world.[56] Other analysts calculate a higher percentage of the world's states as electoral democracies. Freedom House of New York, which for the last three decades has been chronicling the progress of freedom and democracy, counted 117 electoral democracies in its 1995–1996 report, or 61 percent of the 191 then-independent countries of the world. In its 2000–2001 report, it counted 120 out of 192 (63 percent of the world's states) as democracies.[57] Since the early 1980s, the number of electoral democracies has ranged between 55 percent and 63 percent of the world's states.

Electoral democracies, however, are not necessarily liberal democracies. The former term stresses the regularity and competitiveness of elections. The latter term extends beyond this to encompass, in addition, such features as a vigorous and free press, an active civic society, constitutional constraints on executive power, the rule of law, and an independent, nondiscriminatory judiciary. Electoral democracy does not necessarily guarantee that all segments of the population and their interests are taken into account in competitive elections, especially if the wealth and the political power of a governing class can determine the outcome of elections, nor does it guarantee that the rights of all citizens are observed. When an electoral democracy fails to protect the rights of its citizens fully and falls short in the other attributes of a liberal democracy, it becomes, in Fareed Zakaria's apt phrase, an "illiberal democracy."[58]

The Freedom House data show how many of today's electoral democracies are also liberal democracies. Freedom House separates states into three categories—free, partly free, and not free—according to the range of political rights that their citizens enjoy in addition to free elections. Its definition of a free state is roughly equivalent to a liberal democracy. It found, in 1990–1991, sixty-five free states, fifty that were partly free, and fifty that were not free. In 2000–2001, the number of free states had increased to eighty-six, and of partly free states to fifty-eight, while the number counted as "not free" declined slightly to forty-eight. Translating into terms of the population of these countries, Freedom House calculated that in January 1991, 39 percent of the world's population lived free, 28 percent partly free, and 33 percent not free. By January 2001, 41 percent lived free and 24 percent partly free, while 36 percent were not free.[59] Thus, the decade of the 1990s showed marked progress both in the number of countries that became free—twenty-one—and in the percentage of the world's population who lived in free states, although there was also an increase in the number of people who were neither free nor enjoyed even partial freedom.

The second aspect of democracy's advance today concerns how firmly rooted it is among the great powers. Five of the seven—the United States, Japan, Great Britain, France, and Germany—are democratic, while as yet, Russia and China are not. Russia is moving toward real democracy, while China is attempting to prevent genuine democracy while liberalizing economically, a feat at which few nations, if any, have succeeded at over the long term. In addition, the two most likely candidates for "great powerhood" in the near future—India and Brazil—are both democratic, India nearly continuously so since independence, and Brazil periodically so since 1945. In percentage terms, 71 percent of today's great powers are democratic; if India and Brazil were to join the ranks, the figure would rise to 78 percent.

These great-power percentages are not unique in the twentieth century. During two previous aftermaths of great conflicts (the decade of the 1920s and the 1945–1955 period), the number of democratic great powers equaled or exceeded this. In the 1920s, six of the era's seven great powers (86 percent) were democratic: the United States, Great Britain, France, Italy, Japan, and Germany were democratic, while Russia was not, and China was not then a great power. In the 1945–1955 period, as now, five of the seven great powers were democratic.

These statistics seem to suggest that the level of democracy among the great powers is unexceptional, but that would be the wrong conclusion. The current "aftermath era" does differ from the previous two, because democracy is more firmly rooted among the great powers than ever before. In the 1920s, democracy was a relative newcomer to Italy, Japan, and Germany. Italy's democratic experiment after World War I was very short-lived; Japan's and Germany's did not last much longer. By 1933, all three had succumbed either to military dictatorship or to authoritarian rule. In the 1945–1955 decade, it would be more appropriate to describe Japan and West Germany as in the process of being democratized than as fully functioning democracies. While they were being democratized, they were militarily occupied and were only slowly regaining their sovereignty. They were more like "great powers in waiting" than great powers. Today, democracy is neither new nor imposed in any of the democratic great powers. Both Japan and Germany have experienced over forty-five years of uninterrupted and successful democracy. For these states, democracy is now a matter of choice, not imposition. Although we should never assume that democracy is irreversible in any nation, Japan and Germany have more durable democratic systems than they had in either of the previous two aftermath eras.[60] Not quantitatively, then, but qualitatively, great-power democracy today is unique because it is more firmly rooted than at any point in modern times.

This is important because great powers are the pace-setters for international politics. What they do externally matters a great deal, for themselves and for other states. It also matters how they are politically constituted, because, historically, all great powers have sought to externalize their form of governance. None has ever been content merely to stand as a shining example of a particular form of governance; all have, instead, been vigorous political proselytizers and active missionaries. When they have chosen not to proselytize, it has only been so because they were too weak; two examples are Stalin's "socialism in one country," announced in the 1920s, and what might be called America's "republicanism in one country," enunciated in the Monroe Doctrine in 1823. Thus, the solidity of democracy within the great powers is important because that makes its advance elsewhere more likely.

The third aspect of democracy's advance is the means by which it has spread. Since 1945 it has spread either through foreign invasion and military conquest, or through non-military means. Since the end of World War II, military conquest and occupation caused the conversion of seven states to democracy: West Germany, Japan, Austria, Italy, and South Korea in the decade after World War II, during the second wave of democratization; and Panama and Grenada during the third.[61] All other conversions have involved factors other than foreign military conquest.

The non-military factors that operated during the third wave are particularly important to consider. They are the ones most likely to operate in this aftermath era. During the third wave, when twenty-nine states democratized, Huntington found five factors that explained their transitions: performance failures and consequent legitimacy problems of authoritarian systems; unprecedented global economic growth in the 1960s; a switch by the Catholic Church in the mid-1960s, away from support for authoritarian governments, toward support for political and economic reforms; economic aid and political support for democratizing efforts from external actors, including the European Community and the United States; and "snowball" or demonstration effects that were enhanced by the new technologies in global communications.[62] Some of these factors operated in every case, with varying degrees of influence. Each case was different, even when the same factors were operating. Ranking the explanatory power of each factor is therefore difficult, but fortunately not necessary for our purposes. What is significant for our analysis is that economic growth was common to nearly every one of the transitions that occurred without military conquest. At levels of economic development where per-capita income reaches $300–1,300 (in 1960 dollars), states appear to enter a transition zone that makes them ripe for democratization, although it is not inevitable.[63] As Huntington put it: "Economic development makes democracy possible; political leadership makes it real."[64] Thus, the experience of the third wave reconfirms one of the important lessons of political development: economic growth facilitates the development of democracy, even if growth by itself does not produce it.[65]

More particularly, it is the social, economic, and political changes produced by economic growth that explain why states reach the democratic transition zone. Robert Dahl captured these changes well when he described the effects of industrialization and economic growth in transforming agrarian societies into modern urban ones.[66] "Consider now what a relatively 'advanced economy' both makes possible *by* its performance and requires *for* its performance." When we do, we see that "an advanced economy automatically generates many of the conditions required for a pluralistic social order."[67] An advanced economy requires high literacy rates among the populace to function. So, too, does a modern democracy. An advanced economy requires flexible and numerous means of communication and free speech.

So, too, does a modern democracy. An advanced economy requires special-ization of function and the division of labor, which in turn creates a whole host of specialties that produce a middle class. A modern democracy, too, requires a large middle class as a stabilizing influence. An advanced economy creates a variety of private organizations, which are the basis for a civic culture and a civil society apart from the state. A modern democracy, too, requires a civic society. The list could go on. Literacy, trust, a large and stable middle class: these are the by-products of industrialization, and they are also the backbone of every successful modern democracy. Democracy is not a necessary product of economic growth and industrialization, but they do help create the building blocks of democracy. Thus, "economic development promotes democracy only by effecting changes in political culture and social structure."[68]

In sum, democracy looks highly durable among the democratic great powers. It has functioned well for fifty years in its two newest great power converts. It is spreading beyond the First World to the Third, if slowly and with challenges and some backsliding. For many if not for all of the nations that have experienced it, democracy has delivered both political freedom and economic improvement. Taken together, these aspects constitute the current demography of democracy, and they make this era look qualitatively different in this dimension from the previous ones.

GLOBAL ENVIRONMENTAL DEGRADATION

Global environmental degradation is the fifth key attribute of this era. Environmental destruction is neither a new phenomenon nor a new international political issue. The 1972 United Nations conference on the environment, held in Stockholm, first put the issue of environmental destruction on the international agenda. What is new about environmental degradation today is its accumulated magnitude, its global scale, and the sus-tained nature of the international attempts to correct it. In this era, envi-ronmental preservation has become a highly salient international political issue. Governments now regularly face highly organized, well-informed, and internationally linked environmental interest groups. Their lobbying, the backing of the citizenry, and genuine state concern for the environment have produced an explosion of international environmental conventions and treaties over the last twenty years, although states have been better at signing these agreements than implementing them.[69]

All of these efforts reached a peak in the second United Nations confer-ence on the global environment, held at Rio in 1992. The Stockholm con-ference twenty years earlier was more of a consciousness-raising exercise than a treaty-making enterprise, and the agreements concluded were hortatory,

31

not binding. Rio attempted to go one step beyond Stockholm: deliberate efforts were made to negotiate internationally binding treaties to deal with what were identified as the world's most serious environmental threats. Measured by the effectiveness of the agreements signed, Rio was not a success. Measured, however, by the fact that some binding treaties were in fact signed, it was. Rio signaled the coming of age of global environmentalism.[70]

Global environmental degradation comes in many forms: rivers, lakes, and streams polluted from industrial and agricultural runoffs; fishing stocks depleted from factory ship overfishing; rain forests destroyed or dwindling from overcutting for timber and cattle grazing; biodiversity losses from rain forest destruction and pollution; fresh water shortages, both current and looming, from population pressure and waste; loss of prime cropland due to urbanization; increase in desertification from marginal farming and tree cutting; forests stunted from acid rain; urban areas choking from automobile-induced ozone-laden ground-level smog; and on and on. The catalogue of environmental horrors is seemingly limitless.[71]

Environmentalists argue that a long list of political nightmares will flow from continuing degradation, including massive refugee movements and forced migrations, repeated severe famines, collapsing states, savage intrastate and interstate ethnic slaughters, and vicious wars among states over scarce natural resources. If all of these horrors come to pass, they will cause much misery and suffering for the populations concerned.[72]

The question for U.S. grand strategy, however, is: how will these degradations and nightmares affect the United States? The answer is that they will affect it little or not at all. Due to its favored geographical location, the United States will escape most of the degradations. Because of its richness and technological sophistication, it will be able to deal relatively easily with those that do affect it (such as, potentially, biodiversity loss due to rain forest destruction, or catastrophic failure of a large number of nuclear reactors). Nor will the country be directly damaged by any of the potential political nightmares. The reason is that, should they transpire, they will take place in regions far removed from the United States, and their effects will remain localized. Therefore, visions of hundreds of thousands or millions of people boarding boats bound for the United States after some environmental catastrophe, as an example, can be discounted as political propaganda by those who want action on the environment, rather than taken as serious portents of the future. Because environmentally induced political disasters will not reach the United States, none directly threatens the United States. Thus, in general, none of these disasters and nightmares would seriously affect America's security, economic well being, or quality of life, even though they do raise important questions about the philanthropic duties of the rich and the moral obligations of human beings to one another.

Although most environmental and ensuing political disasters will not directly affect the United States, the nation is by no means wholly immune. Two environmental threats pose a potentially severe risk to the quality of American life: the depletion of the earth's protective ozone layer and the prospect of global warming.[73] These threats are global in nature, and because they require the cooperation of other states to solve, they are rightly foreign policy issues.

Ozone depletion and global warming are both true "commons" problems.[74] A commons problem is one that affects all parties involved (even if unequally); that all parties helped bring on by their actions; that no party can solve on its own; and as to which every party wants to "free-ride" on the efforts of others to bring about a solution. Should all parties free-ride, however, no solutions to the problem will be found, and every party will continue to suffer. Commons problems are therefore those that raise collective action dilemmas and that require leadership to solve; global commons problems, in turn, require global solutions and global leaders—that is, powerful states—to produce the solutions.

Ozone depletion presents a serious threat to the United States because, if unabated, it will drastically increase human skin cancers worldwide, cause blindness due to cataracts on a massive scale, degrade immune systems, and alter the genetic makeup of plants and animals in unpredictable ways. Fortunately, the international community has taken action on ozone depletion. It has created a treaty and an ozone protection regime to stop the production of ozone-depleting industrial chemicals. If observed by all states, the regime will, in fifty years or so, return the earth's stratospheric ozone layer to an adequately protective level.[75] The regime will need continued monitoring (a black market in ozone depleting chemicals has arisen, for example), and Third World nations will require financial assistance to replace ozone-depleting chemicals with safer substitutes. Although there is no cause for complacency, the two biggest hurdles to an international solution have been surmounted: the forging of an international consensus to rectify the problem and the creation of a regime to implement the solutions devised. The same cannot be said for global warming.

Global warming, with its concomitant threat of climate change, remains the unsolved international environmental problem of greatest potential danger to the United States.[76] Global warming is an increase in the earth's average global temperature and is commonly referred to as the "enhanced greenhouse effect."[77] To explain the threat posed by global warming, we must distinguish the enhanced from the natural greenhouse effect.

For millions of years before the industrial revolution, naturally occurring greenhouse gases—primarily carbon dioxide, methane, and nitrous oxide—caused the temperature of the earth to rise higher than it would otherwise have been had these gases not been present in the atmosphere. Greenhouse gases raise the earth's temperature by allowing the visible rays of sunlight to pass through the atmosphere, thereby warming the earth's surface, while they prevent the escape back into space of longer-wavelength heat radiation reflected and emitted by the earth. Because greenhouse gases are thus partially opaque to thermal radiation (unlike oxygen and nitrogen, which constitute most of the earth's atmosphere), more heat comes to the earth's surface through sunlight than can be radiated back out into space, with the result that the temperature of the earth's surface increases. Without the natural greenhouse effect, the average surface temperature would be colder by 33 degrees C (centigrade) and unable to sustain life on earth as we know it.

The enhanced greenhouse effect refers to the increase in the earth's average global temperature beyond its natural (pre-industrial) state, and it is produced by anthropogenic (human) activities associated with the industrial era. Industrialization caused the burning of prodigious amounts of fossil fuels (coal, oil, and natural gas), which produced, as by-products, large amounts of greenhouse gases, especially carbon dioxide. Scientists estimate that the atmospheric carbon dioxide level has increased by 25–30 percent since pre-industrial days (over the last hundred years or so). Half the increase has occurred since 1958. This human-produced addition of greenhouse gases has led to an increase in the global mean surface temperature of about 0.6 degrees C over roughly the last hundred years (the twentieth century). It is this additional increase in temperature that is the enhanced greenhouse effect.[78]

The developed or First World has caused most of the enhanced greenhouse effect up to the present. Ranked according to their cumulative carbon dioxide emissions from burning fossil fuels during the 1950–1987 period, the five biggest contributors were the United States, with 38 billion metric tons of carbon; the European Community and the Soviet Union, each with 23 billion; Japan, with 6 billion; and Canada, with 3 billion. This amounts to 93 billion metric tons of carbon, or over 70 percent of total emissions, estimated at 130 billion metric tons, during the 1950–1987 period. In 1987, just eight First World nations—the United States, the Soviet Union, Japan, West Germany, France, England, Italy, and Canada, in that order—accounted for 45 percent of net greenhouse gas emissions.[79]

Given these statistics, it is not surprising that the popular view in the South is "the First World is the culprit, so let the First World fix it." However, matters are not so simple as these sets of figures imply. If we turn from cumulative stocks to present emissions, the picture changes. As far back as 1987, just four of the developing countries accounted for 23 percent of net greenhouse gas emissions: Brazil (10.5 percent), China (6.6 percent), India (3.9 percent), and Indonesia (2.4 percent). On a per-capita index for net emissions in 1987, the United States ranked ninth, England twentieth, West Germany twenty-first, the Soviet Union twenty-fifth, France thirtieth, Italy thirty-fifth, and Japan forty-second. In contrast, Qatar was second, Bahrain fourth, Brazil seventh, Côte d'Ivoire eighth, and Oman thirteenth. In 1987, total net emissions of carbon dioxide, methane, and chlorofluorocarbons (CFCs) from all global sources totaled 5.9 billion metric tons. Asia, with 1.5 billion tons, was the largest contributor; Asia, Latin America (800 million), and Africa (340,000), together accounted for 45 percent of the total. In short, as these statistics show, Third World nations now make significant contributions to greenhouse gas emissions.[80]

Moreover, their relative contribution to both annual emissions and cumulative stocks of greenhouse gases will continue to grow. Recent figures on carbon emissions illustrate this point. In 1990, the developed states emitted 10 billion tons of carbon dioxide; the developing countries, 6.8 billion tons. By 1998, the developed states emitted 10.8 billion tons and the developing countries 8.6 billion tons. The gap between the two thus had narrowed in just eight years from 3 billion to 2 billion tons.[81] At some point, the Third World will surpass the First in its emissions, because the Third World has 80 percent of the world's population (over 4 billion people) and because that is where 95 percent of the estimated population growth will take place over the next thirty years. If the Third World populates, industrializes, deforests, and desertifies itself at current projected rates, in this century it will account for the bulk of greenhouse emissions. Clearly, devising limitations to global warming is not just a First World problem; it is the entire world's problem. The First World's role should not be minimized, but neither can that of the Third World be ignored.

The case for taking corrective steps to stop global warming is strong, as I describe in the next chapter. The earth's average global temperature will continue to increase as long as human activity pumps out ever-greater amounts of greenhouse gases. Recent scientific estimates show that at present rates of production, greenhouse gas concentrations will triple by the year 2100, causing the earth's average global temperature to increase at roughly 0.3 degrees C per decade between now and the year 2100. If the emissions of greenhouse gases are not reduced, then these gases are currently projected to reach a level of concentration in the year 2100 that is higher than at any time in the last fifty million years. According to authoritative scientific estimates, this level of concentration will increase the average global temperature by 1.4–5.8 degrees C (2.5–10.4 degrees Fahrenheit) above the 1990 level. There are also credible estimates of even larger potential increases of between 2 degrees C and 9 degrees C by the year 2100.[82]

Predicting that the earth's average global temperature will rise as long as greenhouse gas concentrations increase is relatively easy, but it is difficult to predict the specific climatic results. The effects depend on the magnitude and rate of change, both of which are subject to the ranges of uncertainty described above; on extrapolations from what is currently known about how the climate operates; and on knowledge about what happened during the dramatic climate changes that occurred a long time ago. The predicted effects become particularly imprecise when climatologists try to estimate what will happen to regions of the earth smaller in scale than hemispheres and continents; this makes assessments of how specific states will fare under different scenarios especially uncertain. In the science of climate change, uncertainties abound.

In spite of the uncertainties, however, most climatologists studying global warming have reached agreement on some propositions. First, the enhanced greenhouse effect has already occurred. Second, this effect, together with its associated changes in climate, will grow larger in magnitude as long as human activities continue to pour greenhouse gases into the atmosphere. Third, greenhouse gas emissions must be reduced and then stabilized at a level significantly lower than today's if warming is to be reversed and average global temperature ultimately stabilized. (It is the concentrations of greenhouse gases in the atmosphere that must be stabilized, not their rate of emission.) Fourth, even after the stabilization level of emissions is reached, it could still take many decades, perhaps even a century, before the temperature drops back to today's level, because greenhouse gases have long lifetimes.

Finally, it is generally agreed by climate scientists that the increase in average global temperature projected for the year 2100 is of great concern. The reason is this: the high end of the estimate (5.8 degrees C) falls uncomfortably close to the estimated increase in average global temperature (5 to 10 degrees C) that occurred during the transition out of the last ice age some 18,000 to 22,000 years ago.[83] This means that the projected increase in average global temperature by 2100 could nearly match the temperature increase experienced in the world's most recent great climate change. Thus small increases in average global temperature are associated with, and may even produce, huge and unpredictable changes in the earth's climate.

Although climate change may be an inexact science, the science is good enough to convince the bulk of climatologists that the earth's climate will change, mostly for the worse, if global warming continues; that weather extremes will grow ever more frequent and severe; and that even catastrophic changes in climate could be in store if warming continues unabated long enough. How much change in climate can be expected, how quickly it will occur, how it will affect the United States, and what the nation can and should do about it—these are issues addressed in the next chapter.

WHY THESE FIVE FEATURES?

Two final questions need to be answered in this chapter. First, why it is useful to concentrate on these five international features? Second, how do they affect America's choice of a grand strategy?

These five features—absence of a peer competitor, the rise of grand terrorism, the deepening and widening of economic interdependence, the prevalence of democracy, and the increase in global warming—do not encompass all the contemporary features of world politics. A comprehensive list of what appears to be new and important would stretch many pages. To the above five features, for example, we could add the following phenomena: the collapse or breakup of states, through the outbreak of savage ethnic warfare or through the sheer incompetence of governments ("failed states"); the large and growing number of transnational and non-governmental organizations of both the malignant variety (such as international drug cartels, organized crime organizations, or terrorist organizations) and the benign variety (such as Amnesty International, the Red Cross, or the International Women's Health Coalition); the rise of religious fundamentalism, especially Islamic fundamentalism; the unprecedented rise in forced migration and international refugees; the prospect of a doubling in the world's population by the year 2015; the rapid economic development of China and its potential to become a superpower some time in the first half of the twenty-first century; the computerization of global communications; the prospect that Russia might revert to a totalitarian state or decay into a fascist one; and Europe's creation of a single currency and central bank and its continuing efforts to achieve greater political integration.

This list includes important contemporary phenomena and worrisome future developments. Some of them will cause great misery to the people caught up in them; some will harm Americans abroad; a few may even benefit Americans. But not one of these nine, nor any others that we might add to the list, could adversely affect (or significantly improve) the security, the prosperity, or the quality of life of the vast majority of Americans, unless they affect the five features on which I have chosen to focus, by increasing or decreasing the military or terror threat to the American homeland; harming or strengthening economic interdependence; reversing or furthering the spread of democracy; or making global warming more or less severe than is otherwise likely. I therefore do not deny the relevance of these nine phenomena (or any others) to the United States or to the future course of world politics, but I assert that the most efficient way to assess their importance to Americans is to ask whether and if so, how, each will affect the five international features that I claim to be of most salience to the United States.

Take, for example, the collapse of states. Most of the states likely to collapse are in Africa and will not harm the United States. State collapse per se is therefore not a calamity for America. Of concern are only those states whose collapse could affect America's security, such as the breakup of Russia or Pakistan and the consequent loss of central control over their nuclear weapons, or those whose collapse could harm America's economic interests, such as the breakup of China, or those whose collapse could provide fertile field for recruiting and training terrorists that aim to strike the United States, as was the case with Afghanistan and could perhaps be the case with Somalia. Nearly all other state collapses would be legitimate humanitarian concerns, but not a military or economic problem for the United States. Similarly, the rise of Islamic fundamentalism is worrisome, but it should result in changes to American grand strategy only if it generates more grand terror attacks against the United States and its citizens and troops abroad, or affects Western access to Persian Gulf oil. International organized crime and terrorist groups—nasty, troublesome, and dangerous as they are—should be of grave concern only if they get their hands on nuclear, biological, or chemical weapons, engage in wholesale cyber terrorism, or attack, with conventional means, high-value targets in the United States, such as nuclear power plants and chemical factories. China's emergence as a global superpower would be mostly beneficial if China were to become fully capitalist and democratic, and mostly worrisome if it were to revert to full-fledged authoritarianism and aggression. Nearly every mass refugee movement that we can envision, while a human tragedy for those caught up in it, would not threaten America because it would take place far across the oceans. Achievement of European monetary and political unification would create a more formidable political-economic competitor for the United States, but it would gravely threaten America's economic interests only if it turned inward and protectionist, and America's political interests only if it became aggressively nationalistic and non-democratic. Finally, a doubling of the world's population, much as it would stress the earth's resources, would affect America's own environment primarily through its effects on greenhouse gas emissions. A similar logic applies to any other features added to this list.

One feature of the current era, however, deserves a bit more discussion: the prevalence of civil wars and the associated ethnic warfare that has accompanied them. Some may wish to argue that civil war is a distinctive feature of the current international environment because such wars have become so much more frequent than in the previous era and so much more numerous than international war. As Table 1.7 and Figure 1.2 demonstrate, the end of the Cold War did witness a sharp surge in the number of civil wars, most of which occurred in Africa or in parts of the former Soviet Union. However, their frequency peaked in the early 1990s and declined by almost half by the end of the decade.[84] (See Appendixes A and B for a list of civil and international wars from 1991 to 2000.) It is also true that civil wars became much more numerous than international wars in the 1990s, but this is as much a late Cold War phenomenon as it is a post–Cold War phenomenon. In terms of the relative frequency of civil and international wars, the 1990s differ from the 1980s only in degree. Nor did civil wars in which mass killing took place become more frequent after the Cold War than during the Cold War. For both periods, civil wars that involved mass killing constituted

TABLE 1.7. International and Civil Wars by Region, 1991–2000

Region	Civil			International			Total		
	Started before 1991	Started 1991–2000	Total	Started before 1991	Started 1991–2000	Total	Started before 1991	Started 1991–2000	Total
Africa	8	12	20	0	3	3	8	15	23
Europe	1	10	11	0	3	3	1	13	14
Far East	5	0	5	0	0	0	5	0	5
Latin America	4	1	5	0	0	0	4	1	5
Middle East	4	1	5	0	3	3	4	4	8
South Asia	4	0	4	1	0	1	5	0	5
Total	26	24	50	1	9	10	27	33	60

Note: Because the Cold War formally ended in November 1990 at the Conference on Security and Cooperation in Europe in Paris, I use 1991 as the starting point for the post–Cold War era.

Source: Generated from data presented in Appendixes A and B.

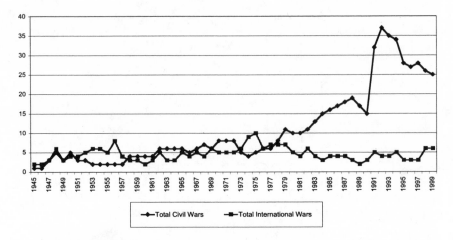

FIGURE 1.2. Annual War Occurrence, 1945–2000.

Notes: Figures show the number of wars active in any given year. International wars include wars categorized as colonial, imperial, and interstate. The large spike in the number of civil wars in 1991 is partly, but only partly, an artifact of using different data sets for the 1945–1990 and 1991–2000 periods. The COW dataset uses a consistent set of criteria, whereas the three data sets used for the 1991–2000 period vary in the criteria used to select and classify civil wars. The COW data set shows a spike in civil wars in 1991 and 1992 that is slightly less than shown by the other three sources used for 1991–2000. Nevertheless, there was an upward spike in 1991.

Sources: Data for 1945–1990 is from David J. Singer and Melvin Small, producers, *Correlates of War (COW) Project: International and Civil War Data, 1816–1992*, computer file (Ann Arbor, Mich.: Inter-university Consortium for Political and Social Research [ICPSR], 1993). Data for 1991 to 2000 is from Stockholm International Peace Research Institute, *SIPRI Yearbook: Armaments, Disarmament, and International Security* (Oxford: Oxford University Press, various years); *Defense Monitor* (1991–2000), Washington, D.C., Center for Defense Information, <www.cdi.org/dm/>, information downloaded August 17, 2001 (hard copy on file with the author); and Benjamin A. Valentino, Paul Huth, and Dylan Balch-Lindsay, *Draining the Sea: Mass Killing, Genocide, and Guerilla Warfare* (paper prepared for the Annual Meeting of the APSA, August 31, 2001). (See Appendixes A and B for full source citations and the list of wars.)

about twenty-five percent of all civil wars.[85] What appears mostly new about civil wars in the contemporary era, then, is their increased frequency.

In itself, however, the increased frequency is not important, because, with few exceptions, most of these wars have little bearing on the United States. They are of concern primarily because of the immense suffering they cause to the people entangled in them. So, although the contemporary era has experienced many more civil than international wars, the effect of most of them on the United States is negligible. Most do not threaten the United States militarily, diminish this era's economic interdependence, or have much bearing on climate change. Their most pronounced effect will be on democratic spread, but the sheer number of these wars puts severe limits on how much the United States can do to ameliorate them. Therefore, as I argue more fully in Chapter 4, only those civil wars that involve mass murder, which fortunately are relatively infrequent, or those that threaten America's strategic interests or somehow increase the likelihood of grand terror attacks against the United States (fortunately, also infrequent), can lay claim to American military intervention.

There is one feature of the international environment, however, that would critically affect America's grand strategy: a precipitous decline in the nation's power relative to other great powers. Such a decline could come about if: a global challenger or peer competitor were to emerge; America's economic power were to collapse; America were to lose its technological fighting edge; or a grand global counter-coalition or a set of regional counter-coalitions were to emerge. The second and third developments would erode America's ability to maintain a powerful military force; the first and fourth would check America's influence, even though its forces remained powerful. None of the four has as yet materialized, but should any or all occur, selective engagement would be rendered more difficult to implement.

The first contingency, the rise of a challenger, is a real possibility, but none is likely to emerge for a few decades at the earliest. The United States may be able to take some steps that would delay the emergence of a rising super-power, but ultimately it could not prevent one from arising. The prime ingre-dients for generating superpower strength—a skilled workforce, economic growth, technological advance, capital investment, large population, and abundant natural resources—are mostly indigenous to a potential super-power, not externally derived. A vigorous economic containment policy, aimed at preventing technological transfer and foreign investment, could slow down the generation of power somewhat, but only if other states coop-erated in the economic containment effort. Thus, whether China, Russia, or the European Union will eventually become superpowers lies mostly in their hands, not those of America. More to the point, however, the emergence of another superpower need not invalidate a global role for the United States nor the selective engagement strategy that I favor. If a new superpower were not unremittingly hostile, the United States could cooperate with it to some degree. If it were hostile, the United States could still remain selectively engaged abroad militarily, but would need increased cooperation from great-power allies, especially the regional neighbors of the new peer competitor. This would likely be forthcoming if the next emergent superpower were aggressive and hostile.

Thus, it is the last three developments—loss of America's economic might, loss of its military technology edge, or the rise of a counter-coalition— that would most threaten the feasibility of selective engagement. Fortunately, they are the factors over which the United States has a greater degree of control. For selective engagement to work, therefore, the United States must maintain its economic and technological prowess and must actively work to prevent either a global counter-coalition or a set of regional counter-coalitions from emerging.

As this brief analysis shows, we can achieve an economy of effort and clarity in analysis if we interpret the many contemporary international developments in light of their effects on the five international features discussed in this chapter. In this fashion, we can best separate what is insignificant for the United States from what is truly worrisome or potentially beneficial.

FROM CONDITIONS TO INTERESTS

There is another reason for dwelling on the five international features enumerated above. We can use them to identify America's national interests readily.

These conditions did not materialize by happenstance. To the contrary, in one way or another, they are the result of prior American policies. The absence of a peer competitor, the growth of economic interdependence, and the prevalence of democracy should be seen as successes of deliberate American policies, while the emergence of grand terrorism and the increase in global warming should be seen as its unintended products. The containment of the Soviet Union helped contribute to its breakup and brought about the current situation in which the United States faces no peer competitor. The organization of the free world to contain Soviet power helped to create a democratic zone of peace and deep economic interdependence among the mature democracies of Western Europe, North America, and Japan. The spread of democracy to parts of the First and Third Worlds was undertaken in part to fight communism and to bolster America's power and ideological appeal relative to the Soviet Union. In pursuit of its three successes, the United States also unintentionally helped produce its two failures. The emergence of grand terrorism directed against the United States, especially its Islamic fundamentalist manifestation, resulted in part from America's global role, its covert war against the Soviet Union in Afghanistan during the 1980s, its Middle Eastern policies, and its military presence in the Persian Gulf. Global warming and its associated threat of climate change primarily result from the profligate use of fossil fuels by the First World, especially by the United States, to sustain high living standards. Intended or not, these five features of contemporary world politics are, in one way or another, partially due to prior American actions.

If that is the case, what stance should the United States now take toward these conditions? The answer is clear: preserve those that benefit the country and change those that do not. The first, third, and fourth features are still worth protecting. Simply because the Cold War is over does not mean that the United States should ignore new military threats to its homeland, be indifferent to the spread and consolidation of democracy, or cease its efforts to deepen and extend economic interdependence. Americans today are enjoying the three fruits of their Cold War labors, and it should be the goal of American foreign policy to keep things that way. The second and fifth features are not fruits to be enjoyed but poisons to be neutralized. Grand terror could do catastrophic harm to the United States, and global warming could degrade the quality of life Americans enjoy; consequently, it makes sense to take corrective steps.

The goals of preserving the beneficial features of the contemporary era, and redressing the adverse ones, set America's national interest agenda, as shown in Table 1.8. With the absence of a peer competitor, the greatest military threats to the United States come from grand terror attacks on the American homeland, especially those executed with nuclear, biological, or chemical weapons. Consequently, preventing such weapons from falling into the wrong hands, especially terrorist hands, is the most important thing that the United States can do today to protect itself. To preserve the deep economic interdependence that obtains among Europe, North America, and Japan, as well as to extend it to other states, the United States should work to preserve a deep peace among the Eurasian great powers, to assure a stable supply of oil at reasonable prices by maintaining access to Persian Gulf reserves, and to maintain and extend international economic openness. Because intense security competitions and great-power wars would disrupt

TABLE 1.8. International Conditions and America's Interests

International Conditions	America's Interests
1. No imminent or severe state military threats	1. Defense of the homeland
2. Emergence of grand terrorist threats	
3. Deep economic interdependence	2. Deep peace among the Eurasian great powers
	3. Secure access to Persian Gulf oil at a stable, reasonable price
	4. International economic openness
4. Prevalence of democracy	5. Democracy's consolidation and spread, and the observance of human rights
5. Increase in global warming	6. No severe climate change

trade and promote economic closure, not openness, the United States should help prevent them. Until the world takes the steps necessary to wean itself from heavy dependence on fossil fuels for energy, the United States must help secure access to oil supplies (nearly two-thirds of which are in the Persian Gulf) at reasonable cost. Because international economic openness lowers the barriers to trade, capital, and technology flows, and because it facilitates the deepening and extension of economic interdependence and the generation of middle classes so central to the stability of democracy, it should be preserved. To keep the gains of democratic spread, the United States should help consolidate democracy in the recent democratic states and, in addition, seek to spread it to other states, because mature democracy is one of the most effective ways to make certain that human rights are protected, mass murders avoided, and civil and interstate wars averted. Finally, to prevent severe climate change, the United States should act to reduce carbon emissions and their equivalents in order to slow down and ultimately stop global warming.

Thus, there exists a strong connection between the five salient features of the contemporary international era, on the one hand, and the six American national interests posited in the introduction, on the other. The existence of such connections, however, does not alone constitute the case for America's pursuit of these interests. Therefore, the next steps in formulating an American grand strategy are to demonstrate conclusively why these six goals make good sense for the United States and to identify which deserve priority. These are the tasks for Chapter 2.

TWO

America's National Interests

The most fundamental task in devising a grand strategy is to determine a state's national interests. Once they are identified, they drive a nation's foreign policy and military strategy: they determine the basic direction that it takes, the types and amounts of resources that it needs, and the manner in which the state must employ them to succeed. Because of the critical role that national interests play, they must be carefully justified, not merely assumed. In this chapter, I make the case for the six interests postulated at the end of Chapter 1—those advocated by selective engagement. I begin by ranking them according to their importance; then I lay out the merits of each; and lastly, I enumerate the threats to them.

RANKING INTERESTS

We need to rank interests because they often conflict with one another, and because resources to deal with them—including the time and attention of top-level decision makers—are limited. Accordingly, I posit that the United States has one vital interest, two highly important ones, and three important ones (see Table 2.1).[1] I base this on the following criteria: the benefits if the interest is protected, and the costs if it is not; the sequence in which these interests can be achieved; and the manner in which military power can be used to support them.

According to the first criterion, a vital interest is one that is essential and that, if not achieved, will bring costs that are catastrophic or nearly so. Security is the one vital interest of a state; it means protection of the state's homeland from attack, invasion, conquest, and destruction. To protect a state's security is to ensure its physical safety and its political sovereignty. Protecting the United States from nuclear, biological, and chemical (NBC) attacks, especially by terrorists, clearly qualifies as a vital interest.

A highly important interest is one that, if achieved, brings great benefits to a state and, if denied, carries costs that are severe but not catastrophic. The United States has two such interests. First, a large-scale Eurasian great-

TABLE 2.1. Ranking America's National Interests

Interest	Ranking
1. Defense of the homeland	Vital
2. Deep peace among the Eurasian great powers	Highly Important
3. Secure access to Persian Gulf oil at a stable, reasonable price	Highly Important
4. International economic openness	Important
5. Consolidation of democracy and spread and observance of human rights	Important
6. No severe climate change	Important

power war could bring severe economic loss to the United States; under certain circumstances it could even increase the threat to the American homeland. It is therefore a highly important interest and under some scenarios could be a vital one. Second, loss of access to Persian Gulf oil, or an exorbitantly high price for oil, could bring severe economic loss to the United States; for this reason it, too, qualifies as a highly important interest.

An important interest is one that increases a nation's economic well-being and perhaps its security, and that contributes more generally to making the international environment more congenial to its interests, but whose potential value or loss is moderate, not great. There are three such interests. First, while international economic openness enhances America's prosperity, Americans would not become destitute if the international economy underwent a significant degree of closure. Nearly ninety percent of what Americans consume is produced at home, not abroad; economic closure would mean, not a total loss of imports or exports but protectionism that would increase the prices of America's imports, reduce the volume of its exports, and thereby lead to some decline in the standard of living. The severity of the decline would depend on the degree of closure. Second, the spread of democracy might well make the world more peaceful; however, failure to protect democracy and human rights in the Third World would not have an immediate effect on either America's security or its prosperity. Third, climate change will be costly to the United States, but the costs are bearable unless the change becomes severe or catastrophic.

The second way to rank interests concerns their sequence: the vital and highly important interests are the essential prerequisites to the important ones, whereas the reverse is not the case. If the United States is not secure, and if its prosperity is at risk, its ability to help maintain Eurasian peace will diminish. If Eurasia is at war or locked in intense security competitions, NBC weapons spread is more likely, and American prosperity will also likely suffer. If Persian Gulf oil is held hostage by a Gulf hegemon, then both openness and prosperity will be at risk, because affordable energy is central to each. On the other hand, openness, greenhouse gas cooperation, and democratic spread, by themselves, cannot make the United States secure and prosperous, although they can certainly enhance its security and prosperity. Thus, the causal arrow runs from the vital and highly important interests toward the important ones.

The third criterion concerns the use of force. American military power can directly advance the vital and highly important interests, but it can only indirectly advance the merely important ones. In general, military power cannot be efficiently and effectively employed to force states to lower their barriers to trade, to create democracy in states that have never experienced it, or to force others to limit their emissions of greenhouse gases. America's military power can, however, be used directly to retard the spread of nuclear, biological, and chemical weapons by providing protection to states that do not have such weapons so they will choose not to obtain them, by destroying the stocks in those states that do have them, and by rooting out terrorists who have or intend to acquire and use them. Military power can be directly used to prevent aggression against the Persian Gulf oil sheikdoms, or to reverse aggression should it occur. American power can also be used to preserve Eurasian great-power peace, by deterring would-be adversaries and reassuring America's great-power allies.

I now examine each interest in turn.

HOMELAND SECURITY

Homeland security—the prevention of attack, invasion, conquest, or destruction of a state's territory and its residents, and the maintenance of its political sovereignty—is the prime directive of any grand strategy. Conventional attacks from states and NBC threats from most states pose little risk for the foreseeable future to the American homeland. The two greatest threats to the security of America's homeland today are grand terror attacks, especially NBC ones, and the acquisition of NBC weapons by state actors who are hard to deter.

A conventional weapons attack by a state against the American homeland is a low probability event and relatively easy to handle. No other great power, and certainly no middle-rank or small power, could hope to defeat America's highly proficient and technologically sophisticated conventional forces, nor could such a power inflict much damage on American territory. The first reason is U.S. technological prowess. With its space-based intelligence assets, its long-range ground-based airpower, and its formidable naval forces, the United States could deal swiftly with any state-directed conventional threat coming from overseas. The second reason is that the United States would be

47

operating within or close to its home base, while any potential aggressor state would have to project power from far across the oceans. The only serious conventional threats would be air-launched or sea-launched cruise missiles by the thousands, or massive bomber attacks; however, there is no state today that can mount such attacks, other than the United States. Should either threat ever materialize, the United States could develop effective countermeasures. Thus, a conventional state attack that threatens wide-spread destruction or conquest of the United States is not a serious risk in the foreseeable future.[2]

The United States also need not fear deliberate nuclear, chemical, or biological attacks against its homeland from "normal" NBC-armed states. Normal states are those that have no significant expansionist designs against their neighbors, that eschew resort to terrorism for political gain, and that are governed by leaders who are good calculators. Such leaders can be dis-suaded from going to war when shown that the costs of war far exceed its benefits. They are deterrable: they will not attack another state or threaten that state's interests when faced with a credible threat of swift retaliation. Leaders of normal states are committed to the traditional rules of great-power politics, the prime one of which is the survival of the state; therefore, they would not deliberately attempt to destroy another state that they know can swiftly destroy them in return. Deterrence—the threat of unacceptable retaliation through conventional or unconventional methods—is the means by which the United States will protect itself against future NBC threats from states that calculate according to the traditional rules. This was how the United States defended itself against the Soviet nuclear threat during the Cold War and how the United States will defend itself against any other normal nuclear state that may harbor evil intentions against it.

This leaves, as the two most serious threats to the American homeland, NBC attacks by hard-to-deter state leaders—the "crazy leader" scenario—and grand terror attacks by non-deterrable terrorists using either conventional or NBC weapons. The latter threat is by far the more serious; the former is unlikely, although it cannot be wholly discounted.[3]

The crazy-leader scenario refers to leaders who run dictatorships (full-blown or partial); who oppose the territorial status quo and are committed to expanding their borders at the expense of their neighbors; who are pre-pared to use force or already have a track record of having used force; and who sponsor terrorism to expand their territory or to achieve other foreign policy objectives. Leaders of such states are cause for concern because they share three attributes that could make them harder to deter than normal actors. First, they are highly motivated to gain their aims and are therefore more prepared to use force to achieve their objectives. Second, they are more indifferent to the suffering of their citizens or supporters than are normal leaders, making them more willing to take greater losses. Third, they are poor calculators, making them more likely to misperceive a defender's threats or to ignore such threats.[4] How likely are NBC attacks against the United States by such crazy leaders?

Under most conceivable scenarios, deterrence is likely to work against even the most ruthless and motivated of such leaders simply because their goal is to wield power, not to commit suicide.[5] Attacking the United States with NBC weapons would be tantamount to committing suicide. As Kenneth Waltz argues: "Nobody but an idiot can fail to comprehend their [nuclear weapons'] destructive force. How can leaders miscalculate? For a country to strike first without certainty of success, most of those who control a nation's nuclear weapons would have to go mad at the same time."[6] Waltz's argument about nuclear weapons also holds for large-scale biological and chemical attacks. The evidence we have about NBC use supports the assessment that such NBC use against the United States is unlikely. Apart from the unrestrained use of chemical weapons on the battlefield during World War I, there have been only twelve other known episodes of NBC use by states. Only one of these was nuclear: the United States against Japan in 1945. Only one was biological: Japan against China and the Soviet Union between 1937 and 1945. The rest were chemical; only three since 1945 count as "rogue state" attacks, of which two involved Iraq. In every one of these twelve cases, the NBC attacks were made against a state or group that could not retaliate in kind.[7] With the exception of battlefield use of chemical weapons during World War I, there have been no known (and independently verified) NBC attacks by one state against another NBC-armed state, or against its forces in the field.[8]

America's experience with the one NBC-armed state that it has fought confirms this conclusion. In the 1991 Gulf War, Iraq possessed biological and chemical weapons that, while they could not be used against the American homeland, could nevertheless have been used to attack American troops in Kuwait. The United States was especially concerned that Saddam would use his chemical weapons, since he had done so in his war with Iran in the 1980s. To deter such use, President Bush sent a letter to Saddam Hussein in early January in which he stated that: "The United States will not tolerate the use of chemical or biological weapons. . . . You and your country will pay a terrible price if you order unconscionable actions of this sort." Bush's threat worked. According to information gleaned after the war from the head of Iraqi intelligence, General Wafic al-Samarrai, the United States had convinced Saddam that it would use nuclear weapons in retaliation for Iraq's use of chemical weapons; Bush's "warning was quite severe and quite effective."[9] Saddam was deterred. Thus, deterrence appears to work even against hard-to-deter state leaders under most conditions.

The one scenario where it is conceivable that such a leader might use NBC weapons against the United States would be in response to a conventional American attack whose goal is to remove the leader from power. Should the United States get into a war with such a leader, and should he possess only shorter-range NBC capabilities, then the risk of NBC attacks against American troops in the field or against America's allies in the region must be taken seriously. (This could have happened in the 1991 Gulf War. According to Kenneth Pollack, Saddam Hussein had set up a special SCUD [SS-1] ballistic missile unit armed with chemical and biological weapons, with instructions to launch the missiles against Israel if the United States used nuclear weapons or marched on Baghdad. This would have been an act of pure revenge, not deterrence, because "no one outside of Iraq knew at the time about this unit and its orders.[10]) Should such a leader possess an intercontinental NBC capability, then, while it would be an exceedingly low-probability event, a Hitler-like response—attacking the United States, and taking his country down with him when his plans do not pan out—should not be totally ruled out. Such a situation happened in the last century, when Hitler let his country go down with him; it is conceivable that such a leader could emerge again in this century. Thus, we do not want difficult-to-deter leaders to become NBC-armed if we can avoid it. If they do become NBC-armed, then the best way for the United States to avert an NBC attack on its own homeland, on its forces in the field, or on its regional allies is to avoid waging those wars whose goal is to remove such leaders from power. (In the 1991 Gulf War, President Bush decided that the best way to ensure that Saddam would not use his biological and chemical weapons, in addition to issuing the above threat, was not to go after Saddam's Ba'ath regime.)[11] Wars against such leaders may have to be fought, but they should not include as their avowed aim the toppling of the regime, unless the United States is prepared for the increased risk of NBC retaliation.

Grand terror attacks by non-state terrorists are the most worrisome threats the American homeland faces today. These attacks can involve conventional or unconventional methods. Conventional methods can produce destruction on the scale of the 2001 World Trade Center attack if terrorists succeed in crashing large planes into or otherwise destroying large structures. Conventional methods could also produce horrific destruction if suicidal terrorists were to target a large chemical complex in or near a major urban area. Probably the worst such scenario would be a conventional attack against a nuclear power reactor (American has more than 100) located near a major urban area, executed by terrorist commandos on foot or by a large airplane that is crashed into the nuclear containment shell. (Of the eighty-one commando attack tests against nuclear power plants that the Nuclear Regulatory Commission has run since 1991, the attackers succeeded thirty-seven times in getting into areas of the plant where sabotage could have produced radioactive release.)[12] Such attacks might produce a reactor meltdown that could kill tens of thousands and perhaps even hundreds of thousands of

Americans. The worst possible scenario, of course, is a nuclear, biological, or chemical attack against a major urban area, or several at once; millions might be killed.

How likely are grand terror attacks of the conventional or NBC variety? The World Trade Center attack has already happened; because other conventional attacks on the scale described above are conceivable, the United States must take all necessary precautions to prevent them. NBC attacks are also conceivable. In fact, there have been two recorded instances of a terrorist group having successfully used NBC weapons to attack large numbers of people: the June 1994 sarin nerve gas attack in the Japanese city of Matsumoto killed seven people and wounded more than 150, and the March 1995 sarin attack on the Tokyo subway killed twelve people and injured more than 5,000 others. Both attacks were carried out by the Japanese cult group Aum Shinrikyo.[13] Fortunately, only a small number of people were killed in these attacks, but it was not for want of trying on Aum Shinrikyo's part.

What makes the likelihood of NBC terrorist attacks so worrisome are two trends. First, as the Aum Shinrikyo attacks demonstrate, NBC weapons are coming increasingly within the reach of non-state terrorists groups, largely as a consequence of more education about, and greater availability of, the basic scientific and engineering knowledge to produce these weapons, as well as the greater ease of acquiring the means to produce them. Falkenrath and his co-authors chillingly describe the growing ease with which non-state actors can acquire chemical and biological weapons; their conclusions were understated because of their deliberate decision not to give greater detail on how to acquire them.[14] For example, although Aum Shinrikyo was successful in only two large-scale attacks, it attempted eighteen other chemical and biological attacks between 1990 and 1995. Five of these tries were with botulinum toxin, and four were attempts in July 1993 to disperse anthrax in the city of Tokyo. The anthrax attacks failed, not because of the delivery system, but because of the low virulence of the agent. On these eighteen occasions, only Aum's incompetence saved large numbers of people from being killed.[15] Although there is no known record of a terrorist group having yet acquired nuclear weapons, it is not for want of trying. We know that Osama bin Laden's al Qaeda terrorist organization tried to buy enriched uranium in 1993 for $1.5 million, and that in 2001 the organization consulted with scientists who worked on Pakistan's nuclear weapons program. We also know that Aum Shinrikyo tried to mine its own uranium in Australia and to buy nuclear warheads from Russia.[16] There are almost certainly other terrorist attempts to acquire fissile material and nuclear weapons that have not become publicly known.[17]

A second reason for concern is that the nature of terrorists is changing, as we saw in Chapter 1. There is a disturbing tendency among some terrorist groups toward pure revenge rather than political gain. The al Qaeda-affiliated group of terrorists that bombed New York's World Trade Center in 1993 wanted to kill 250,000 Americans by toppling one of the trade towers into the other. They were not trying to influence policy, only to inflict pain.[18] Deterring terrorists becomes nearly impossible if they are bent only on revenge, if they do not identify themselves, and if they engage in suicide attacks. If the attackers have no return address, no clear-cut political goal, and no concern for their own lives, there is no basis upon which retaliation can work; if retaliation cannot work, there can be no deterrence. Another disturbing trend is the growth of groups that are motivated by religious and millenarian imperatives.[19] Such groups aim at martyrdom and focus on the life hereafter, or they believe themselves the agents of change for a new global order. As a consequence, they do not share the same rational objectives of the traditional politically motivated terrorist; their motives are those of retribution and destruction, and they often view their adversaries as subhuman.

None of the foregoing should lead us to believe that grand terror attacks against the United States of the conventional or NBC variety are inevitable, nor that NBC attacks by crazy statesmen against the United States or its troops can be wholly discounted. Both remain distinct possibilities, although the former is more likely than the latter. What the United States now faces is a class of events whose probability of occurrence may be low, but whose consequences would be severe or even catastrophic if they happened. With such events, it is prudent to make expected-value calculations: a small number (low likelihood of occurrence) multiplied by a very large number (adverse consequences of the event) still yields an unacceptably large number. This is, after all, how the United States treated the chance of nuclear war with the Soviet Union throughout most of the Cold War—as a low-probability but high-cost event—and it therefore took steps despite great cost to try to make certain it would not happen. Although all-out nuclear war with the Soviet Union would have killed many times more Americans than a terrorist or state nuclear attack against one major American city, the loss of just one city would still be a horrific event. On the basis of these calculations, the best way to forestall NBC attacks against the American homeland or American troops abroad is to take a strong stance against NBC spread.

The logic supporting the stance against NBC spread rests on three propositions, which, although they cannot be empirically validated, cannot be discounted entirely. First, the greater the number of states that acquire NBC weapons, the greater the likelihood that rogue states and fanatical terrorists could obtain them. Wider ownership increases the chances of undesirable ownership through theft, sale, or outright transfer. Thus, for example, one of the most powerful motivations for seeking a halt to North Korea's nuclear weapons program in 1994 was the Clinton administration's concern that North Korea would sell plutonium to would-be proliferators. Similarly, since Pakistan began testing nuclear weapons in 1998, the United States has worried that some of Pakistan's nuclear weapons could fall into the hands of Islamic sympathizers should its pro-Western government fall, or that "rogue" Pakistani nuclear scientists could aid non-state terrorists such as al Qaeda in their nuclear quest. The spread of nuclear weapons to states that are undergoing rapid political transitions, or may do so soon, should be great cause for concern, as the deplorable state of the custody of nuclear weapons in Russia today testifies.[20]

A second argument for opposing NBC spread is that, although nuclear deterrence has worked up until now, we should not tempt fate by allowing these powerful weapons to spread widely. Weapons that can destroy cities or states in one fell swoop, or that can kill huge numbers of civilians easily and swiftly, should not be readily available to anyone who wants them. Deterrence may not hold forever, and the current trends in terrorist activity are unsettling.

A third reason to oppose NBC spread is that hard-to-deter leaders will markedly increase their power to do evil and to harm American interests if they acquire NBC weapons. Believing that possession of NBC weapons makes them immune to retribution by the United States, they might become more emboldened to undertake aggression with conventional weapons against their neighbors and in areas where the United States has important interests. In sum, then, the spread of NBC weapons to more states carries greater risks that terrorists will get them, that they will be used against their non-NBC armed neighbors, or that they will be used as shields behind which to engage in conventional aggression.

There are several ways to deny NBC weapons to hard-to-deter state and terrorist leaders and other undesirables. One is to maintain a vigorous global political commitment against further NBC spread. As the world's leader of this effort, the United States has little choice but to declare a clear-cut, no-exceptions policy. It cannot publicly make exceptions because that would undermine the norm against spread, and hence the cooperation of other states. Of necessity, however, if or when spread occurs, as with India and Pakistan in the late 1990s, a no-exceptions public stance would have to be modified to deal with the new reality. Another approach includes a variety of steps: strengthen institutions such as the International Atomic Energy Agency; invest more in intelligence to discover covert nuclear and biological weapons programs; develop effective covert capabilities to sabotage terrorist and rogue-state NBC programs; sign treaties that publicly commit states to forgo acquisition; offer inducements to states to forgo nuclear and biological weapons; and threaten adverse political and economic results for states that acquire NBC capabilities.

A third approach would be to use American military power to support the anti-NBC spread regime. This means, first and foremost, continued reassurance to Germany and Japan that America's nuclear umbrella will protect them. These are America's two key allies in Eurasia today. Were they to go nuclear, it would signify the end of their confidence in the American umbrella. That might risk the end of America's major alliances and the stabilizing presence that America's military presence provides at each end of Eurasia, resulting in the increased prospect of more nuclear spread to other Eurasian states, leading in turn to the further weakening of the global norm against nuclear spread, and so on. None of these are assured events, but as possibilities they cannot be ignored.

Another use of U.S. military power might be preventive attacks to disrupt or destroy a nascent NBC force if all other means, including covert sabotage attempts, have failed to prevent rogues or fanatics from acquiring these weapons. When deterrence is not viable and when interdiction is not reliable, preventive attacks may be the only recourse. Such use, even before an NBC force is operational or when it remains quite small, is by no means easy. This is partly because intelligence about capabilities and the location of facilities is difficult to come by, partly because of problems in containing the spread of biological and nuclear materials when they are attacked, partly because obtaining the needed cooperation of allies for such strikes may be difficult. During the Gulf War, for example, the United States was unable, in spite of repeated efforts and in spite of devoting huge air assets to the task, to find and destroy the mobile SCUD missiles that Iraq was able to fire from its western territory at Israel.[21] The fact that the preventive use of force to take out an emerging or just-emergent NBC capability is not easy, however, does not mean it should be ruled out in all circumstances.

There is one more anti-NBC use for American military power: to support a strong declaratory posture that any state or group that actually uses NBC weapons for aggression against unarmed NBC states will face severe military punishment. If such use were not punished, then the penalties against use would go down, and the incentives to acquire these weapons would go up. The declaratory posture here is akin to what the United States said to the Soviet Union during the Cold War: "attack us with nuclear weapons and we will devastate you in return." Whether the United States would actually have done so, or whether it would instead have pulled its punches to avoid the inevitable Soviet retaliation, was left unclear. The stance should be the same for rogue or terrorist NBC use: an unqualified United States declaratory posture of punishment, but a tacit understanding by U.S. leaders that the particular circumstances should determine the actual nature of the military response.

In the end, America's military power will probably help more in preventing the spread of nuclear weapons than of chemical and biological weapons. The latter are much easier to obtain, although they are not easy to disperse against large population centers without mastering difficult technical problems that are beyond all but the most technologically sophisticated terrorists.[22] Moreover, nuclear weapons still remain the most dangerous of the three, although the biological threat is scary enough. In preventing the spread of NBC weapons, American military power can only do so much, but what it can do should not be downplayed, because a world with fewer NBC weapons, and with fewer states possessing them, is better for the security of America as well as most other states. An American military presence at both ends of Eurasia and in the Persian Gulf is a bulwark—not the only one, but an important one—against the spread of these horrific weapons. Eurasia, after all, is where most of the regimes and groups that have the resources and the incentives to acquire them are located. Eurasia without an American military presence would probably be a more heavily armed and dangerous place; this, ultimately, would redound to America's disadvantage.

EURASIAN GREAT-POWER PEACE

America's first highly important national interest is to maintain a deep peace among the Eurasian great powers. This requires that there be neither large wars among them nor intense and sustained security competitions. It is in America's interest to prevent both.

A great-power war is one that involves at least two great powers in direct and extensive combat against each other. A non–great-power war is one that involves a great power against a smaller power, a war between smaller powers, or a war between smaller powers in which the great powers back their respective proxies with arms and economic assistance. In general, the United States has little interest in preventing these non–great-power wars in Eurasia and should stay out of them to the extent possible. There are exceptions to this rule, however. Should a non–great-power war dramatically enhance the risk of a great-power war, stimulate NBC spread, or lead to mass murder, the United States might find it necessary to intervene. If such a war were somehow to threaten America's core alliances or to involve a direct attack on an American ally, then the United States would have to intervene.

A security competition is a severe political conflict that manifests itself in the form of competitive military efforts short of war and that increases the chances of intense crises and the outbreak of war. To the extent that these competitions increase the risk of great-power wars, they are undesirable. They can be economically destructive, too, by threatening international openness, trade, and investment. Markets depend on a stable political order: they operate efficiently when their participants share expectations that the rules governing their economic interactions will be stable and fair. Stable political frameworks in turn help produce these shared expectations. If the political framework is disrupted, markets are disrupted, too.[23] If intense security competitions raise fears of war and political interference with trade and investment, they become market disrupters; they have had this effect in the past, although not invariably.[24]

The United States has a keen interest in preventing wars and intense security competitions among the great powers of Eurasia. First, any such war or competition risks harming America's policy of holding the line against NBC spread. Like most previous great-power wars, such a war would not come out of the blue; it would be preceded by a series of intense crises, a prolonged period of arms racing, and arms buildups, which would be bound to spur the acquisition and perhaps even the use of NBC weapons. All three phenomena would make the task of limiting NBC spread harder, and the use of NBC weapons in a great-power war would be a disaster of the first magnitude. It makes more sense to prevent these wars and competitions, if possible, than to deal with their adverse consequences.

Second, a great-power war, or even an intense security competition, carries great risk of dragging the United States into it. There are two possible scenarios: one in which the United States has retained its Eurasian alliances, and the other in which it has not. In the first scenario, if a war or an intense security competition involved one of America's key Eurasian allies, the United States would be sucked into the conflict, certainly diplomatically and perhaps even militarily, in order to meet its alliance commitments. In the second scenario, it seems unlikely that the United States could stand aside while several great powers engaged in war or intense competition, unless perhaps it were a strictly Russian-Chinese affair.

The record of the past in this regard is clear: every one of the large great-power Eurasian wars (although not all of the minor ones) dragged the United States in, despite its strong desires and efforts to stay out. This was true for the War of 1812 and for World Wars I and II. For one reason or another—to protect its trade, to protect the freedom of the seas, to support states with whom it had strong historical and cultural bonds, to oppose aggression, to resist the imposition of odious forms of governments on nations with which it identified, or to prevent a great power from dominating the economic and military resources of Eurasia—the United States found itself fighting in Eurasia when Eurasia was consumed with major war. Historically, great powers have not found it easy to remain outside of these major cataclysms. It is not possible to predict whether the United States could stay out, nor is it possible to predict the exact path by which it would become entangled. What is clear is that we cannot rely on the hope that the United States would be able to stay out, or merely argue that it should have enough discipline to stay out. A major great-power war is like a powerful gravitational field: it acts on bodies irrespective of their wishes. Better to prevent such a war in the first place than to have to fight in it.

A third reason that the United States has an interest in preventing great-power wars or security competitions in Eurasia is that both entail the risk that the current balance of power in Eurasia could be upset. The balance matters to the United States, not so much in terms of its security, but rather in terms of its non-security considerations. In today's world, conquest of large amounts of Eurasian territory per se no longer constitutes a security threat to the United States, because the geopolitical logic no longer affects American security the way it once did. A Eurasian great power could no longer threaten America's homeland or curtail America's political sovereignty more easily if it conquered large chunks of Eurasia; the additional resources gained thereby would not add significantly to its ability to harm the United States. America's security against hostile state actors lies primarily with its nuclear deterrent, and conquest of territory does not add significantly to a hostile state's nuclear threat, nor does it subtract significantly from America's nuclear deterrent.[25]

Instead, in today's world a major change in the Eurasian balance of power caused by war would pose different sorts of threats to the United States, arising from the conquest of states with which the United States has strong historical and cultural affinities, long-term changes in the political contours of Eurasia, and longer-term political changes in the contours of world politics. In fact, the effect of great-power wars in Eurasia has historically been to settle the fundamental political contours of world politics for long periods to come. Most of those new political contours, if wrought by a hostile, would-be Eurasian hegemon, would be highly unfavorable to the United States. They would be likely to diminish its global influence, require it to spend more to provide aid and security to those nations still under its umbrella, and pose a significant threat to its maritime forces and sea-born commerce. Again, it is better to avert such wars than to suffer their consequences.

A fourth and closely related reason is that major wars and intense security competitions that heighten tensions are not good for trade. Either would be disruptive to America's considerable economic stakes in western and eastern Eurasia, as well as in the Gulf. Peace is more stability-producing than intense security competitions and war are; it is therefore more conducive to long-term trade and investment. Other U.S. economic interests in Eurasia may not rank as high as access to Gulf oil, but they are certainly significant ones, especially for a nation whose stake in international economic activity has doubled from its historic levels in the last twenty-five years. (Exports plus imports as a percentage of U.S. gross national product, which had held at the 6–10 percent range throughout most of America's history, began a dramatic increase in the middle 1970s, reaching 18–22 percent by 1980 and since.)

Today, the Eurasian great powers are at peace, and neither intense security competitions nor great-power wars loom on the horizon. This is due to at least two factors. First, four of the great powers are solid democracies; in addition, another (Russia) has begun a rocky road to democratization, while the other (China) remains posed between the incompatible worlds of command politics and free markets. Democracies are less likely to fight one another than are non-democracies or a democratic versus a non-democratic state (as I discuss in detail below). Second, four of the great powers (Britain, France, Russia, and China) are also nuclear-armed, and the other two (Germany and Japan) are protected by the United States. It is hard to get a large war going between nuclear-armed or nuclear-protected states.

We should not, however, be wholly complacent about the pacifying effects of either democracy or nuclear weapons. The peace-among-democracies effect is a significant force, but not an iron law of history. It has not and will not invariably overpower all the other forces at work in world politics. Moreover, it is not impossible to have a war between nuclear powers: the Soviet Union and China, both nuclear-armed at the time, did fight a minor border war in 1969. Intense crises can arise among nuclear-armed states, carrying great risk of war: there were intense crises between the United States and the Soviet Union during the first half of the Cold War, as well as between India and Pakistan in 1990, 1999, and 2002.[26]

Thus, peace-inducing though these two factors are, we should retain the added insurance provided by America's military presence at either end of Eurasia. In Western Europe, it assures Germany's neighbors that Germany will not return to its ugly past; in East Asia, it reassures Japan's neighbors about Japan, and China's neighbors about China. Fears of an incipient security competition arose in Western Europe in the early 1990s, when the Europeans worried that the United States would leave Europe after the Cold War had ended. Once the United States affirmed that it would stay, these fears, and the potentially subversive effects they could have had on European stability, subsided. In East Asia, all of China's neighbors are worried about its growing military power, and many took steps to increase their arms before the 1997 Asian financial crisis. All states in the region look to the United States to balance China. At both ends of Eurasia, therefore, America's military presence makes interstate relations more stable and peace more likely.[27] While this presence is not the only factor conducive to Eurasian great power peace, and may not even be the most important one, still, it is important.

In sum, many factors contribute to peace among the Eurasian great powers today. American policy should aim to keep Eurasia peaceful.

SECURE OIL SUPPLY AT STABLE PRICES

America's second highly important national interest is to have a secure supply of oil at stable and reasonable prices. Oil remains a vital commodity for both the American economy and that of the world as a whole. Security in supply at a stable and reasonable price is important in order to avoid disruptions to both economies. Interruptions that result in severe cutbacks in supply could wreak economic havoc by lowering economic activity; so, too, could severe swings in the price of oil, because they disrupt economic calculations, subject economies to the price manipulations of oil suppliers, and make it difficult for oil-consuming states to begin weaning themselves from their heavy dependence on oil.[28]

There are many things that help keep oil supplies available at stable and reasonable prices, but one of the most important is maintaining U.S. and global access to Persian Gulf oil. This, in turn, is facilitated by preventing a regional hegemon from controlling the Persian Gulf's oil reserves, either directly by military conquest or indirectly by the threat of conquest. Hence America's third interest is served by keeping the Gulf's oil reserves divided among several of the regional states, preferably at least four. The logic for this position rests on several propositions.

First, the United States, along with most of the world's industrialized and industrializing states, will continue to rely heavily on oil and oil imports to fuel its economy for at least the next several decades. Tables 2.2 and 2.3 illustrate the dimensions of this dependence for selected countries. In Table 2.2, the first column shows the ratio of each state's total primary energy supply (TPES) to its gross domestic product (GDP) This measures the energy-efficiency of an economy, and it shows that most of the selected economies, including the United States, became more energy efficient between 1970 and 1999, with Korea being the one exception. The second column shows the ratio of oil imports to gross domestic product. This measures the dependence on oil imports; all of the states listed except Korea have decreased oil imports as a ratio of GDP between 1980 and 1999. Table 2.2 thus shows that there has been a general improvement in overall energy efficiency for both the United States and most of its important trading partners. Table 2.3 also documents the declining dependence on oil (in all except Mexico) compared to other sources of energy, such as coal, gas, nuclear, and other ("other" is mostly hydro but also includes solar). However, the decline must be put in perspective. Even though these economies consume less oil as a percentage of their total energy supply than they did several decades ago, they still rely heavily on oil, ranging from a low of 34.6 percent of its total energy supply for France, to a high of 62.5 percent for Mexico. Thus, a decline in dependence on oil does not mean that an end to oil dependence is in sight.

For the United States, the decline in oil as a percentage of total energy consumed has been accompanied by an increase in oil imports. In 1970, when domestic crude oil production peaked, the United States produced 9.6 million barrels a day (mbd) of crude oil and imported 1.3 mbd. In 1986,

TABLE 2.2. Energy Dependence and Oil Import Dependence, 1970–1999 (selected countries)

Country	1970 Ratio of TPES to GDP	1970 Ratio of Oil Imports to GDP	1980 Ratio of TPES to GDP	1980 Ratio of Oil Imports to GDP	1990 Ratio of TPES to GDP	1990 Ratio of Oil Imports to GDP	1999 Ratio of TPES to GDP	1999 Ratio of Oil Imports to GDP
European Union	0.256	0.129	0.228	0.090	0.196	0.058	0.181	0.049
France	0.228	0.119	0.211	0.097	0.199	0.059	0.194	0.053
Germany	0.306	0.097	0.277	0.082	0.220	0.054	0.182	0.050
United Kingdom	0.325	0.162	0.260	0.002	0.211	−0.011	0.189	−0.046
Japan	0.222	0.096	0.194	0.078	0.166	0.054	0.174	0.050
Korea	na	na	0.221	0.182	0.214	0.151	0.255	0.187
Mexico	na	na	0.205	−0.215	0.216	−0.264	0.196	−0.212
Canada	0.452	0.016	0.412	0.021	0.339	−0.029	0.314	−0.055
United States	0.449	0.047	0.379	0.071	0.295	0.058	0.264	0.061

Notes: Except for China, countries shown in this table and Table 2.3 constitute the majority of America's trading partners. All are heavy users of energy. "na" = not available. TPES, Total Primary Energy Supply, is expressed in tonnes of oil equivalent; GDP is expressed in billions of 1990 U.S. dollars at purchasing power parity.

Sources: Data from International Energy Agency, *Energy Balances of OECD Countries, 1998–1999* (Paris: OECD, 2001).

TABLE 2.3. Percent of Total Primary Energy Supply by Fuel Source, 1973 and 1999 (selected countries)

Country	1973					1999				
	Coal	Oil	Gas	Nuclear	Other	Coal	Oil	Gas	Nuclear	Other
European Union	25.3	59.6	10.5	1.5	3.1	14.3	41.7	22.8	15.7	5.5
France	16.5	70.3	7.7	2.2	3.3	5.9	34.6	13.2	39.5	6.8
Germany	41.4	48.1	8.5	0.9	1.1	23.5	40.1	21.4	13.1	1.9
United Kingdom	34.6	50.5	11.4	3.3	0.2	15.4	36.2	36.3	10.9	1.2
Japan	17.9	77.9	1.5	0.8	1.9	17.0	51.7	12.1	16.0	3.2
Korea	35.9	63.6	0.0	0.0	0.5	20.4	55.0	8.3	14.8	1.5
Mexico	3.3	60.1	19.0	0.0	17.6	4.3	62.5	20.8	1.8	10.6
Canada	9.4	50.0	23.0	2.5	15.1	11.4	35.4	28.8	7.8	16.6
United States	17.9	47.5	29.7	1.3	3.6	23.8	38.9	23.0	8.9	5.4

Notes: "Other" includes solar but is mostly hydropower.
Sources: Data from International Energy Agency, *Energy Balances of OECD Countries, 1998–1999* (Paris: OECD, 2001).

it produced less—8.7 mbd—and imported more—4.2 mbd. In 2000, it produced even less, at 5.9 mbd, and imported even more, at 10.4 mbd of crude oil. America's dependence on imports as a percentage of total crude oil production for domestic use increased from 12 percent in 1970 to 58 percent in 2000, and it is projected to rise to 70 percent early in this century.[29] In fact, in 1999 the United States consumed nearly as much oil as in did in the late 1970s, which was the high point of its oil consumption. At some point in the future, America's heavy dependence on oil will diminish as it continues the switch from oil to natural gas for electricity generation and as it gets serious about limiting the burning of fossil fuels in order to reduce global warming. Until that day arrives, it remains vulnerable to sustained disruptions in oil supplies and to swings in oil prices, which could wreak havoc on the American and global economies.

A second reason why it is in the U.S. interest to prevent a hegemon from dominating the Persian Gulf region is that, in spite of discoveries elsewhere, the Gulf still contains the bulk of the world's proven oil reserves and a significant percentage of its natural gas reserves. In 1949, Saudi Arabia, Iraq, the United Arab Emirates, Kuwait, Iran, Oman, and Qatar had 44 percent of the world's oil proven reserves; in 1975, they had 54 percent; and in 1993, they had 65 percent of the world's proven oil reserves and one third of the world's proven natural gas reserves. Recent oil finds, mostly in the Caspian Sea, have not changed the picture dramatically. Estimates of Caspian Sea reserves initially ranged as high as 200 billion barrels, but most authoritative sources now put them somewhere between 25 and 70 billion barrels. At the end of 2000, the Persian Gulf still contained 65 percent of the world's proven oil reserves and 36 percent of its natural gas reserves.[30] Even if Caspian oil reserves ultimately prove to be at the higher end of the estimated range, Gulf reserves will remain central to global oil usage: recent forecasts show world oil demand rising from 73.4 mbd in 1997 to 104.6 mbd in 2015, with the Gulf's share of world oil production capacity rising from its 1995 level of 28.6 percent to somewhere between 38 percent and 47 percent, depending on whether oil prices are high or low.[31] Therefore, whatever the exact figure, the Gulf's oil and natural gas reserves will continue to constitute a large percentage of the world's proven hydrocarbon reserves for the next several decades. Possession of large reserves brings market power; states with large reserves, such as Saudi Arabia, have the capacity and the interest to act as swing producers, lowering or increasing their production so as to affect supply and prices.

Third, even though the United States gets only 22 percent of its total oil imports from the Persian Gulf (2.5 mbd out of total imports of 11.5 mbd in 2000), it is still dependent on what happens there. The United States today imports about as much of its petroleum products (crude oil and refined products) from Venezuela (1.5 mbd), Canada (1.8 mbd), or Mexico (1.3

mbd) as it does from Saudi Arabia (1.6 mbd); 43 percent of its oil imports come from the Western Hemisphere. Nonetheless, these facts do not lessen the importance of Persian Gulf reserves for the United States. The world oil market is highly competitive and integrated: a major disruption in the Gulf (or in any other major producing area) would affect the world price and supply. It is therefore fallacious to argue that, because it obtains only about one-quarter of its petroleum products from the region, Gulf production and reserves are of little concern to the United States.[32]

Fourth, access to Gulf oil is made safer if proven reserves are divided among a larger number of states, preferably four or more rather than one or two. Consolidation of Gulf reserves among one or two states would facilitate collusion; division of its reserves among four or more states makes collusion more difficult.[33] To allow one or two states to control Gulf oil reserves would put one or both in a powerful position to blackmail or gouge the world. Oil is the one natural resource for which the demand is highly inelastic in the short to medium term. Oil prices, moreover, have never been determined solely by market factors, but have also been heavily influenced by political and military considerations. The Gulf's oil reserves are too important to be left to the market alone and too valuable to allow control of them to rest in the hands of just one or two regional hegemons.

Fifth, an American military presence in the Gulf helps secure access to a stable oil supply by ensuring that neither Iraq nor Iran can consolidate control over the Persian Gulf sheikdoms' considerable reserves. Since the late 1970s, the United States has followed a balance-of-power strategy in the Gulf, first favoring Iran, when Iraq looked stronger, then Iraq, when Iran looked stronger, all the while acting to protect the Kuwaiti and Saudi oil fields from dominion by either one. This has been and remains a sensible policy, and under current circumstances it requires an American military presence in the Gulf. That presence is not the answer to all the potential instabilities the Gulf faces, and American troops there do create additional difficulties. Nonetheless, this presence constitutes an important bulwark against the consolidation of the Gulf's reserves among one or two unfriendly regional hegemons.

Thus, it makes good sense to keep a division of control over oil reserves in the Gulf, because control over Gulf oil is not simply a question of oil prices but also of power, in this case raw economic power. If any single state were to dominate Gulf oil, either diplomatically or militarily, it would be in a strong position to dictate world oil prices, because it would be rich enough, might be ruthless enough, and could be fanatical enough to forgo oil income to manipulate oil prices for its own ends, whatever those ends might be. This is not a risk the United States should incur. Assuring that control over Gulf oil reserves remains divided among several states in the region is sound strategy, essential to international economic openness, and crucial to the

American economy, as long as it is so dependent on oil. To believe otherwise is to think economically, not politically, which can be a fatal mistake when power politics confronts free markets.

In sum, America's policy should be to avert a cutoff in Persian Gulf oil supplies, an exorbitant price hike, wild price swings, or near-monopoly control over Gulf reserves that could be exercised by military conquest or political-military intimidation. It must deter a Gulf war, or itself wage war there if that should prove necessary, to prevent any of these undesirable outcomes. Access to Persian Gulf oil is too vital to be left to the vagaries of the Gulf's Byzantine and internecine politics. In the case of the Gulf, "divide, but do not conquer," is the prudent American policy.

INTERNATIONAL ECONOMIC OPENNESS

The preservation of an open international economy is the fourth American national interest, and it is an important one, although somewhat lower in priority than homeland defense, great-power peace in Eurasia, or access to oil. Openness means low or non-existent barriers to the exchange of goods, services, technology, and capital flows among states. When barriers are lowered or removed, this can foster development of international markets, exchanges of goods, services, technology, and capital among states, and a high interdependence—a condition in which states have large stakes in their economic exchanges with one another. International economic openness benefits the United States in three ways, as I explain in detail below. It makes the United States richer than it would otherwise be; it makes other states richer than they would otherwise be, and therefore better customers for American goods; and under the right conditions, it strengthens the democratic nature and pacific tendencies of other states. Such contributions to prosperity and peace are the central benefits of an open international economy to the United States.

The first benefit is the increased wealth that comes from the gains of free trade. When a state engages in free trade, it becomes subject to the forces of international competition. These forces cause additional reallocations of the state's capital and labor toward its more efficient industries, whereas protectionism allows a state to shelter its inefficient industries. The results of free trade are specialization, efficiency gains, more goods to trade and, ultimately, more goods from trade.

How great are the gains from trade? These can only be estimated, and the estimate depends on calculations about two types of gains—static and dynamic.[34] Static gains refer to the gains due to the one-time increase in productivity resulting from the shift of resources to more efficient uses when a state switches from protectionism to free trade. The state will continue, however, to reap benefits from this one-time increase, in the form of the added goods that the productivity increase yields. Static gains should be understood as the amount of national income that is added by forgoing protectionism. Dynamic gains refer to the continuing increases in productivity that larger markets, fiercer competition, and economies of scale produce.

The United States has already acquired most of the static gains from trade because it is the least protected large economy in the world.[35] Dynamic gains are now the more important, because they are constantly generated anew.[36] Although they are considerable, they are difficult to estimate. They include a greater variety of products, better quality products (an example can be seen in the improved quality of American cars after competition from the Europeans and the Japanese), economies of scale in research and development, and an increased pace of innovation. Indirect evidence of the dynamic benefits that accrue from free trade can be found in a recent study of manufacturing productivity in Germany, Japan, and the United States. The study concluded that: "[manufacturing] productivity is lower in Japan and Germany than in the U.S. on average," and that "achieving and maintaining high relative productivity seems to require that companies compete directly against the best practice production [in their industry] in the global economy."[37] Overall, the American economy is both the most open to global trade and also the world's most productive. The same study argued that these two factors are linked: the first causes the second. Openness may not be the only cause of America's global lead in productivity, but it is certainly a key one. The continual need to meet the demands of global competition forces efficiency and yields on-going productivity gains.[38] Studies have shown that, compared to non-exporting firms, America's exporting firms are more productive and more innovative, experience faster employment growth, and pay their workers, both skilled and unskilled, somewhere between five to fifteen percent more in wages.[39]

The second benefit of an open international economy is to make other states richer than they would otherwise be, and this is good for the United States. Because comparative advantage is not an American monopoly, all states can gain from trade and economic openness when market forces, not political factors, determine resource allocation, although states gain unequally because their efficiencies and national circumstances differ. Empirical economic studies have found that greater openness to international trade increases a country's per-capita income. For example, the World Bank estimates that a 10 percent increase in the ratio of trade to the gross domestic product of developing states could ultimately raise per-capita incomes by 5 percent. It also found that poor countries that have been open to trade have grown slightly faster than the rich OECD countries, that they grew nearly twice as fast as poor countries closed to trade over the 1960–1995 period, and that poor people within these poor but open states also benefited.[40] A study on globalization also found that countries that integrated rapidly with the world economy experienced rates of economic growth averaging 30–50 percent higher than those that integrated more slowly.[41] It is lack of openness, not openness, that increases economic inequality among states.[42] In surveying the 1950–1998 period, one of increasing international economic openness, the *Financial Times* found that the volume of world exports multiplied eighteen times, whereas world production multiplied only six and one-half times; it concluded that "the dynamic growth in trade has been the engine of the longest and strongest period of sustained economic growth in human history."[43] When states grow richer, as they can through trade fostered by openness, they ultimately become better customers for American exports because rich customers can buy more than poor ones.

An open international economy brings a third benefit to the United States: under the proper conditions it can strengthen the forces for peace.[44] I use the word "strengthen," not "create," because by itself, neither economic openness nor interdependence guarantees peace. In 1914, for example, interdependence was high, as Figure 1.1 showed. Britain was the best customer for Germany's exports, while Germany was the second-best customer for Britain's exports. Yet these two nations, and Europe as a whole, went to war. Similarly, Japan and the United States traded a great deal with each other in the 1930s, but that did not stop them from going to war with one another in 1941. All things being equal, states would probably prefer autonomy to high interdependence: the less they depend on others, the more they control their own fates and the more secure they are. Interdependence is a second-best solution, and it is often seen as a necessary evil. As Robert Gilpin reminds us, reconciling "Keynes at home" with "Smith abroad" is not easy.[45] Participating in the international economy in order to reap its benefits— openness and free trade, or Smith abroad—while at the same time trying to insulate the domestic economy from its inevitably disruptive effects— governmental intervention, or Keynes at home—makes the management of interdependence a delicate and sometimes shaky matter. Because of these contrasting imperatives, the pacific effects of interdependence should not be taken for granted or viewed as automatic, nor should interdependence be viewed as self-sustaining. Indeed, it can work only under the proper political conditions.

Economic openness and interdependence will reduce the likelihood of war only when states believe that mutual gains, not debilitating vulnerabilities, result from interdependence. States will do so only when three conditions are met. First, states must believe that they can resort to economic rather than military means to prosper and that they will do better that way. (It was often repeated in the United States just after World War II that: "If goods can't cross borders, soldiers will."[46]) Second, states must believe that

the economic vulnerabilities and disparities that ensue from economic intercourse cannot be turned to advantage militarily, either by others against
them or by them against others.[47] Third, states must believe that if one or
both of the first two conditions were suddenly to change, either they would
have the military wherewithal to protect themselves, or else they could turn
quickly to reliable allies who would protect them. Only under these three
conditions can openness and interdependence help make states become
fat and contented, with no domestic incentives to commit aggression against
their neighbors. To the extent, therefore, that openness results in fat, contented states, it strengthens (but does not create) peace among them.[48]

Strong though the case is that the United States benefits from an open
international economy, it does not go unchallenged. There are three major
counterarguments. First is the assertion that the United States is at a disadvantage because other states engage in more protectionism than it does. This
is only partially correct. Second is the assertion that the United States cannot
compete with low-wage states and will therefore lose industries and jobs to
them. This is mostly wrong. Third is the assertion that through the transfer
of its capital and technological know-how to others, the United States is
building up its future competitors. This is a problematic assertion, at best.
The first two assertions maintain that the United States cannot do well in
an open order; the third, that it is not to America's long-run advantage to
sustain such an order.

The first assertion is misleading. Although other countries do protect
their economies more than the United States does, it does not follow from
this that the United States should therefore seek international economic
closure. The United States is the world's most competitive economy, and that
is due in part to the fact that it is also the world's most open economy. The
task for the United States, therefore, is to pressure other states to lower their
barriers, not to raise its own. This is what the United States has done since
1947, and measured by almost any indicator available, the world today has
a more open international economic order than it did when the United
States first began its sustained push for openness. The United States should
therefore continue to push for the lowering of barriers to international economic activity, not call for their resurrection.[49]

The second assertion is mostly wrong. The United States can compete well
with states that pay lower wages, and it has done so. Those who argue to the
contrary point to the decline in wages for unskilled American workers over
the last twenty years, and to the loss of American manufacturing jobs in
the 1980s, as evidence that import competition from low-wage countries has
harmed the American economy. Economic logic and fact, however, demonstrate the opposite.

As economists have shown time and again, societal increases in wealth and
workers' wages come from steady increases in productivity. These produc-

tivity increases are made possible by investments in technology, capital, education, and worker skills. Such investments can come only from sufficient savings rates. The single most important factor in the stagnation of wages in the United States is not import competition but America's low savings and investment rates.[50] Therefore, the key to steady increases in America's standard of living is not to block imports from low-wage countries but to save sufficiently in order to make productivity-improving investments.

In addition, the decline in manufacturing jobs is not exclusively a phenomenon of the 1980s, nor is it due overwhelmingly to import competition. The percentage of American workers employed in manufacturing has been declining in the United States since 1950. In that year, value added in the manufacturing sector totaled 29.6 percent of GDP and 34.2 percent of total employment. In 1970, those figures had declined to 25.0 percent and 27.3 percent, respectively. By 1990, they had dropped yet further, to 18.4 percent and 17.4 percent. What has happened to American manufacturing in the second half of the twentieth century parallels what happened to its agricultural production in the first half. Automation—the substitution of capital for labor—produced large efficiency gains, which yielded lower costs of production and lower prices for the goods produced, while fewer workers were needed to produce the goods. Two by-products of sectoral efficiency gains are lower costs and lower employment. Import competition, manifested in a trade deficit in manufactured goods (an excess of manufactured imports over manufactured exports), did contribute to the relative decline in the importance of manufacturing to the American economy (from 25.0 percent in 1970 to 18.4 percent in 1994). However, Krugman and Lawrence estimate the effect of import competition at only 23 percent of the 6.6 percent decline, or about 1.5 percent.[51]

Finally, most empirical studies by economists have shown that only about 15–20 percent of the decline in the wages of unskilled American workers in the 1980s can be attributed to imports from low-wage countries. The remaining 75–80 percent is due to technological changes in manufacturing in the United States, which decrease the demand for unskilled workers and result in lower wages for their labor; to the decline of labor unions in the United States, which, when they are present, tend to keep wages more compressed; to a change in the nature of immigration into the United States in the last twenty years, which has brought a higher level of less skilled workers; and to America's educational system, which has not provided as many skilled workers as the country needs.[52] To the extent that import competition from low-wage countries contributes to declining wages for unskilled American workers, the answer is not to stop those imports but to turn unskilled American workers into skilled ones through educational and retraining programs. The United States can make better efforts in this regard and should be doing so.

The final assertion of those opposed to openness is that it harms the long-run competitiveness of the United States. According to this logic, an open international economy builds up those who will ultimately do it in, by accelerating the diffusion of American capital and technology to America's competitors. There is some historical support for a view that states have a life cycle: they become powerful, they hold top positions for a while, and then they decline as others grow more powerful and take their places.[53] Some day that may happen to the United States, but the issues before the country now are these: must the United States inevitably suffer economic decline if others prosper? Will the United States inevitably become a second-ranked power? If so, when will that happen?

There are no definitive answers to these questions, but history offers some suggestions. Those states that "get it wrong" have a short stay at the top, while those that "get it right" can remain on top for a very long time. Historically, "getting it wrong" has meant committing two cardinal errors: paying insufficient attention to national competitiveness and engaging in overextension abroad.[54] This would produce a double whammy: competitive decline at home and dissipation of resources beyond our borders. If history is a reliable guide, "getting it right" means the continual tending of national economic competitiveness and the avoidance of overextension abroad. Therefore, whether states neglect their sources of national competitiveness or work to renew them, and whether they dissipate their resources abroad or husband them, are matters of national choice, not products of some mysterious force of historical inevitability. The best way to avert the double whammy is to be constantly on guard against it. For present purposes, this means continual economic renewal.

In sum, none of the three counterarguments offered against America's support for an open international economy bears much weight. The benefits of openness far outweigh its disadvantages, and steps can be taken to lessen its costs. Thus, not only is openness good business for the United States; under the proper conditions, it is also sound strategy.

SPREAD OF DEMOCRACY AND PROTECTION OF HUMAN RIGHTS

The fifth American national interest is to support the global spread of democracy and the protection of human rights; this, too, is an important interest. The reasons to support democracy abroad are simple but powerful: democracy is the best form of governance; it is the best guarantee for the protection of human rights and for the prevention of mass murder and genocide; it facilitates economic growth; and it aids the cause of peace. Promoting democracy is a happy but all-too-infrequent instance where power and purpose in foreign policy coincide—where what is useful is also right.

Democracy is highly valued by Americans because it is the political ideal by which we live. America's support for democracy abroad has too often been honored in the breach, especially during the Cold War, but the spread of democracy has remained a basic foreign policy goal of the nation ever since its founding, and the United States has sometimes paid dearly in pursuit of it.[55] Americans believe that the democratic form of government is the best mode of political governance; when given the chance to express themselves freely, other peoples have generally agreed, contrary to the arguments of some. Like all great powers of the past, the United States seeks to transplant its form of government abroad. No powerful nation has lived by the dictates of the balance of power alone; each has stood for some ideal (although many of these ideals have been reprehensible), and all have used their influence to spread it to other nations. "Doing something because it is right" has its place in America's foreign policy, and on these grounds alone, the support of democracy abroad is a worthy goal.

A true democracy is also the best guarantee that human rights will be observed. Implicit in democracy are respect for and protection of life, property, and freedom, which are surely three central constituents of human rights. Democracy is also the best insurance that governments will not commit mass murder and genocide against their own citizens, or those of other states. R.J. Rummel has quantified the relation between democracy and governmental killing. He finds that the more democratic the regime, the fewer internal deaths at the hands of government, and conversely, the less democratic, the more deaths.[56] The greatest internal mass murders in the twentieth century, numbering millions, occurred under the Nazis in Germany and the communists in the Soviet Union and China. Other studies have found that established democracies are less likely to experience civil wars than non-democracies.[57] Thus, democracy is the best insurance going for protecting human rights understood in the broadest sense.

The spread of democracy is also good for global economic growth. Authoritarian states and their command economies are not wholly incapable of economic growth and material improvement, but they have not proved very compatible with them over the long haul. The Soviet Union entered a long period of stagnation and economic decline; Cuba has suffered economically throughout most of Castro's rule, only partly because of America's economic embargo; China's economic record under Mao's tight rule compares badly with that under Deng's relatively looser policies. Chile under Pinochet is often cited as the exception to the rule that authoritarian states do not do well economically, but careful examination of Chile's economic experience from 1958 to 1989 shows that it fared poorly under Pinochet compared with the Alessandri, Frei, and Allende governments before it.[58] For the reasons explained in Chapter 1, industrialization and economic development unleash the forces that are most compatible with, and most supportive of, democratic regimes.[59] Recent data assembled by Freedom House support this argument. Countries that were free experienced an average rate of growth in their gross domestic product of 2.56 percent from 1990–1998; those that were partly free experienced a 1.81 percent rate during the same period; those that were not free experienced a 1.41 percent rate. Even more impressive was the performance of the poorer free states compared to the poorer non-free ones ("poorer" is defined as per-capita income of less than $5000). The free states experienced a 3.23 percent growth rate over this period, the un-free just 1.41 percent. Finally, the freer a state is, the higher its GDP per capita; the less free, the lower its GDP per capita.[60] In short, democracy is best for business and growth.

These three reasons to favor democracy's spread are relatively uncontroversial compared to the fourth—that democracy strengthens the forces for peace among states. There are two schools of thought: that democracy strengthens peace and that democracy is irrelevant to peace. I hold to the former school. I believe democratic governments are more likely to be conciliatory and pacific in their relations with one another than non-democracies are with either democracies or with each other.[61] Whereas non-democracies are more likely to shoot at each other, or at other democracies, than to argue over butter, democracies are more likely to argue over butter than to shoot at each other.[62] Through competitive elections and a critical free press, democracy gives greater influence to the voice of the people than do other forms of governance; it thereby restrains the ability of elites to wage war whenever they want. Democracies also exhibit a "liberal democratic sympathy" toward other democracies; that is, they externalize their internal norms of conciliation and compromise in resolving their disputes with each other. Because of its structure and the liberal sympathy norm, democracy's spread will enhance the global prospects for peace, and this is in America's interest. Morality aside, considerations of simple realpolitik dictate the spread of democracy, at least to those nations that critically affect American interests.[63]

A host of powerful criticisms have been leveled at the democratic peace theory.[64] First, before 1945, the absence of war among democracies is not a big puzzle because until then, there were few democracies, and, as David Spiro points out, war is a rare event for any state. If war is a rare event and if democracies were few and far between, it should not surprise us that the incidence of war among them was low.[65] For this period, therefore, we do not need the "liberal democratic sympathy" argument to explain peace among democracies. Second, as Christopher Layne has argued, in several instances before 1945 where liberal democracies experienced near misses of war, strategic considerations such as relative military capabilities, vital interests, and general geopolitical considerations explain at least as well why war was averted.[66] Third, from 1945 to the mid-1970s, bipolarity adequately explains the peace that obtained among democracies. During these three decades or so, all of the great-power democracies and most of the smaller ones were lined up in alliance with the United States against the Soviet Union, either formally or de facto.[67] Thus, in nearly two hundred years of modern international relations, one can plausibly argue that the absence of war among democracies in all but the last fifteen or twenty years is due to factors other than their liberal sympathy or democratic nature. From 1975 to 1995, however, the number of democracies doubled to about seventy, and they still did not go to war with one another. The liberal sympathy argument may well explain the democratic peace for this period, although even here alignment against the Soviet Union will account for much of the peace. In sum, evidence for the democratic peace that unequivocally explains only fifteen or twenty years out of two hundred is hardly a ringing endorsement for a theory.

All of these criticisms are valid when we consider the relation between democracy and war, and they make it clear that the pacific effects of democracy have limits, but these criticisms do not wholly invalidate the democratic peace theory. The theory's strongest support comes, not from evidence about democracies and war, but evidence about democracies and militarized disputes. A militarized interstate dispute (MID) is a serious conflict between two states that does not result in war but that involves some use of force, such as threats of force, displays of force, or the actual use of force, on a limited scale such that the total battle deaths incurred by both sides remain under 1000. (By convention, a dispute with 1,000 battle deaths or more is classified as war, and a dispute with fewer than 1,000 as a militarized dispute.) The evidence drawn from militarized disputes is important because while wars are an infrequent occurrence for a state, militarized disputes are not. Indeed, as Russett and Oneal note, militarized disputes among states are thirty times more common than war, and many if not most wars begin as militarized disputes.[68] By focusing on militarized disputes, we are looking at a phenomenon that involves the use of force (although not all-out war) that occurs far more frequently than war and that carries the greatest potential to escalate to war. The use of MIDs data therefore provides a more comprehensive and hence stronger test of the democratic peace theory than war data.

Studies using MIDs data show that the liberal democratic sympathy appears to be at work. In a survey of nearly all militarized disputes between states from 1816 to 1976, Maoz and Abdolali found that democratic dyads (pairs of democratic states) were significantly less likely to engage in militarized disputes with one another than were other types of dyads (mixed dyads—a democratic and a non-democratic state; or non-democratic dyads—two non-democratic states). Russett and Oneal found essentially the same result for the 1885–1992 period and, in addition, that democracies were less

likely to escalate a low-level dispute to a higher-level one that caused casualties. Surveying the 1820–1979 period, Raymond and Dixon found that
democratic states had a greater propensity than the other dyad types to refer
their disputes to binding arbitration by third parties. For the 1918–1988
period, Rousseau, Gelpi, Reiter, and Huth found that during an international crisis (the international event most likely to escalate to war), democracies were less likely to use violence against other democracies than against
non-democracies. Finally, in a comprehensive study of all territorial disputes
from 1919 to 1995, Huth and Allee found that democracies were less likely
than non-democracies to initiate military confrontations over territorial
claims and more likely to initiate negotiations to settle such claims with
another state (democratic or not), and, in addition, that two democracies
engaged in such confrontations were more likely to offer concessions to one
another.[69] In short, democratic dyads experience fewer militarized disputes
than other dyad types, and they do a better of job of preventing their serious
disputes from escalating into war than the other dyad types. As a consequence, they fight fewer wars with one another.

Thus, there is valid historical support for the norm-based effect of the
liberal democratic sympathy. The mechanism does not guarantee peace, nor
does it invariably override strategic and material interests. Perceptions of
which states are liberal and which illiberal can change under the impact of
adverse events, although not readily. As John Owen has documented, the
beneficent effects of the mechanism depend heavily upon perceptions: for
war to be averted or violent conflicts limited, each state must recognize the
other as adhering to the liberal norm. The liberal sympathy argument is tau-
tological: states that are committed to the peaceful resolution of disputes are
more likely to resolve them peacefully. The fact that the argument is tauto-
logical, however, does not mean that it is wrong. Because it is the mutual
perceptions of adherence to the goal of peaceful resolution of disputes that
is central to conciliatory relations among liberal democracies, the task for
the United States is clear: it should promote democracies that adhere to the
norm. Doing so will increase the forces for peace and help make the world
more peaceful.

PREVENTION OF SEVERE CLIMATE CHANGE

The sixth and last American national interest is to slow and then halt global
warming, through the reduction and then the stabilization of greenhouse
gas emissions. Why should the United States care if the world's average temperature increases? It should care because if the temperature increases are
large enough, they will induce climate change which, in turn, will produce
environmental effects that could significantly degrade the quality of life for

Americans. Depending on the amount of global warming, climate change could be moderate, severe, even catastrophic. If it is only moderate, then averting climate change is an important interest; if the risk is of severe or catastrophic change, then this can become a vital interest.

To determine whether induced climate change poses a significant threat or merely a minor inconvenience, we must make three assessments. First, how much damage could global climate change wreak on the United States? Second, is it cheaper for the United States to pay the costs of coping with the damage wrought by climate change (adaptation), or is it instead cheaper to take the measures necessary to avert climate change (abatement or mitigation)? Third, could a large increase in average global temperature trigger a change in the world's climate so swift and so adverse (by geological standards) that timely adaptation would be extremely difficult and exorbitantly costly, and would threaten a large-scale, life-threatening, worldwide calamity?

Computer-generated climate models, called "general circulation models," make predictions about what effects various increases in average global temperature will have on future weather. Most of these models predict that under moderate warming scenarios (an increase of no more than 2 to 3 degrees centigrade [C]), the United States will not be hit as hard by climate change as most other countries. This is due to two factors: America's great wealth and its large size. Its wealth provides the United States with the resources to adapt more easily than most other countries, especially the poorer ones. For example, the United States could afford to take the measures necessary to cope with the destructive effects of sea-level rise on its coastal areas more easily than Bangladesh could. Similarly, America's large size will enable it to capture some of the beneficial aspects of climate change instead of simply suffering its harmful effects. For example, under current predicted conditions, the Midwestern grain belt will get much less rainfall, but that may be offset by the greater amounts of rain and the longer growing seasons predicted for the northern part of the nation.[70]

However, neither America's ability to adapt to global warming nor its ability to capture some of its benefits should be cause for complacency. The adverse effects will be harmful enough on the country and are likely to outweigh the benefits, although the extent is highly uncertain.[71] Among the effects predicted will be sea-level rise due to thermal expansion of the oceans and polar ice cap melt, with the flooding of 9,000 square miles of American territory, directly affecting the 53 percent of Americans who live in coastal regions. Farming will be dislocated due to crop loss produced by heat stress and decreased soil moisture in some areas, partially compensated by increased rainfall and greater production in other areas. Species will be lost due to habitat changes. Other predicted effects include increases in urban pollution; increased energy demand for air conditioning and irrigation; more extreme weather, including hurricanes; stress on water supplies in

74

some areas of the country; and changes in forest productivity—a short-term gain, followed by longer-term decrease, with a potential loss of up to 40 percent of U.S. forests. Even under moderate warming scenarios, these are not trivial effects.

The second question we must address is whether it makes more sense to pay the costs of coping with the damage wrought by climate change, or to reduce the damage wrought by paying, up front, the costs of minimizing change. To make this second assessment requires a comparison of the costs of adaptation and of abatement. Adaptation is measured by the costs of repairing the damage and adapting to the changes; abatement, by the carbon taxes and other steps necessary to reduce and then stabilize greenhouse gas emissions to an amount that keeps average global temperature at a constant, satisfactory level. In fact, both adaptation and abatement will be necessary because greenhouse gases, once pumped into the atmosphere, have long lifetimes: much of the damage has already been done. A recent study of climate change impacts on the United States says that even with the reductions mandated by the Kyoto Treaty of 1997, "the planet and the nation are certain to experience more than a century of climate change, due to the long lifetimes of greenhouse gases already in the atmosphere and the momentum of the climate system. Adapting to a changed climate is consequently a necessary component of our response strategy." The study predicts that the average temperature in the United States will increase 3–5 degrees C, nearer the upper part of the predicted global increase of 1.4–5.8 degrees C.[72] The real tradeoffs between adaptation and abatement, therefore, will occur when it comes to making the decisions on how much global warming can or should be tolerated. This will involve political judgments on how much to adapt and how much to mitigate; such judgments will inevitably turn, to a considerable degree, on the costs of adaptation versus abatement. In the following discussion, therefore, the choice between abatement and adaptation should be understood as one in which the preponderant efforts are made for the former or the latter.

Adaptation cost estimates for the United States vary widely. One of the earliest but still widely respected sets of estimates is by economist William Cline. He calculates that the annual damage to the United States from global warming will run between $61.6 and $335.7 billion (in 1990 dollars), or 1.1 percent to 6 percent of GDP. (In 2002 dollars this would be $110–660 billion dollars.) The lower estimate is based on a global temperature increase of 2.5 degree C by the year 2050; the higher estimate on a 10-degree C increase by the year 2275.[73]

Abatement cost estimates also vary widely. In order to reduce the world's twenty annual gigatons of greenhouse gas emissions (predicted by 2100 if no corrective steps are taken), an 80 percent reduction in emissions would be necessary to get emissions down, by the year 2100, to the annual level of four gigatons that would be necessary to get warming to stop at somewhere close to the present (already increased) level.[74] Such a reduction would require carbon taxes between $100 and $250 per ton, costing about 2 percent of annual GWP through the end of the next century.[75] In June 1997, an intergovernmental panel set up by the Clinton administration estimated that raising the price of a ton of carbon by $100 would, in the short term, produce losses of 0.2–1.0 percent in America's GDP.[76] More recent studies conclude that the United States would lose between 0.2 and 2 percent of its GDP if it met the emissions targets set in the 1997 Kyoto Treaty.[77]

If these estimates are correct, then neither the damage nor the abatement costs for moderate temperature increases (somewhere in the mid-range of the predicted 1.4–5.8 degrees C) would be overwhelming for the United States. Still, both types of estimates do represent considerable sums and large opportunity costs when sustained over many years.

There is a catch, however. We cannot count on the fact that temperature increases will be only moderate. If nothing is done to stabilize greenhouse gas emissions, then average global temperature will continue to increase inexorably, eventually approaching ranges where annual damage costs become severe. (Cline estimates that for very long-term warming scenarios, damage costs could run as high as 13–26 percent of America's GDP.[78]) Doubling of greenhouse gas concentrations in the atmosphere may well occur by 2050; but they will go on to triple, quadruple, quintuple, and so on unless emissions are cut back.[79] Moreover, the increases in greenhouse gas concentrations persist for a long time and have long-lasting effects on the climate. The Intergovernmental Panel on Climate Change (IPCC) concludes that "several centuries after CO_2 emissions occur, about a quarter of the increase in CO_2 concentrations caused by these emissions is still present in the atmosphere."[80] Finally, it is important to emphasize that stabilizing the growth rate in emissions does not stop increases in average global temperature; it only slows down the rate at which the concentration, and hence the temperature, increase. It is therefore not sufficient merely to stabilize the growth rate of emissions. To halt and then reverse the increase so as to reach a satisfactorily stable average global temperature will require a drastic reduction in greenhouse gas emissions to a level significantly below the 1990 level.

What conclusions can be drawn from these assessments of climate change damage to the United States and of abatement versus adaptation costs? First, even at only moderate temperature increases, abatement costs may well be competitive with adaptation costs, so that steps to mitigate climate change make sense. That is, if carbon taxes nearer to $100 than $250 per ton can hold the temperature increase to under 3 degrees C, then abatement is no more expensive than adapting to climate change, and may well cost less than suffering and repairing the damage it will cause.[81] However, some of the new "integrated assessment models" (which are controversial) argue that only limited abatement steps should be taken in the short term because their costs may far outweigh their benefits, while the tougher steps should be postponed to the medium to longer term, when new, more energy-efficient technologies will be available.[82]

Several other recent models, however, strengthen the case considerably for emphasizing abatement more than adaptation.[83] These models show that the use of flexible market-based incentives—devices such as tradable permit regimes and joint implementation schemes—dramatically lower the cost of reducing greenhouse gas emissions.[84] The Clinton administration calculated that by using these market incentives, the United States could have met its Kyoto target for greenhouse gas reductions—a 7 percent cut in emissions below its 1990 level, to be reached in the 2008–2012 period—at well below the costs it had estimated in 1997. With these market incentives, the administration estimated the costs at only $14–23 per ton of carbon equivalent, for a total cost of $7–12 billion per year, roughly 0.1 percent of America's projected GDP in 2010. These figures translate into cost increases of 3–5 percent for natural gas and 3–4 percent for gasoline and electricity.[85] The estimates may be overly optimistic, but if they are even only half right, they show the dramatic impact that market-based incentives can have on lowering abatement costs.[86]

The assessments of potential damage and of costs also make it clear that, for average global temperature increases above the moderate range, the case for abatement becomes stronger. The greater the temperature increase, the more the United States will suffer damage from climate change, and the greater, consequently, will be the damage and hence the adaptation costs. Temperature increases above moderate levels (those assumed in the standard convention of doubling of emissions by 2050) tip the case decidedly for abatement, as Cline's estimates show, and the predicted temperature increase of 3–5 degrees C for the United States over the next century is at the upper limit of the "moderate" range. Overall, given moderate to large increases in average global temperatures, there is a strong case, and probably even a compelling one, for taking abatement steps.

The third assessment we must make is of the risk of non-linear climate change. It clinches the case for taking abatement steps before greenhouse gas concentrations build to dangerous levels. This means taking effective abatement steps earlier rather than later, although the meaning of "earlier" must be governed by considerations of cost-effectiveness. All of the above estimates of damage wrought, costs incurred, and damage averted depend on climate change scenarios that are gradual and linear. Mother Nature, however, may not cooperate in giving us what our models suppose. If temperature increases are large enough and rapid enough, climate change may be swift and discontinuous, not gradual and linear. Indeed, the record of past climate changes suggests that this is the more likely scenario.

An increase of a few degrees in average global temperature, predicted by most climate models, may seem small, but by climate change standards it is huge. Dramatic changes in the earth's past climate have been associated with average changes in global temperatures of only 5 to 10 degrees C. As shown in Chapter 1, the temperature increase of 1.4–5.8 degrees C predicted to occur over the next century (from 1990 to 2100) as a consequence of human-induced greenhouse gas emissions is uncomfortably close to this range. Even at the low end of the predicted temperature increase, the average rate of warming predicted for the twenty-first century is faster than anything that has occurred in the last 20,000 years.[87] Evidence now shows that ice age transitions, which involved changes in average global temperatures of up to 10 degrees C, did not occur slowly over several centuries, but took place in just decades—instantaneous by geological time. What atmospheric and climate change scientists fear greatly, and what they can be least certain about, is that warming at the current predicted rate and magnitude could trigger a rapid and highly adverse change in the earth's climate, causing it to snap into a new and decidedly non-benign state.[88] If continued global warming were to trigger such a climate change, humankind's ability to adapt would be severely tested.

The greatest fear concerns positive feedback effects, a cycle that feeds on itself and thereby magnifies change. It can potentially run out of control because it is not self-stabilizing. For example, as warming produces more evaporation, this causes more water vapor to concentrate in the atmosphere; water vapor acts like a greenhouse gas, leading to more warming, which leads to more evaporation, which leads to more water vapor, which leads to more warming, and so on.

Such a change into a new climate state could have catastrophic consequences, including disintegration of the west Antarctic ice sheet, with a consequent large rise in ocean levels; a redirection of the Gulf Stream, with large climatic impact on Europe; the spread of diseases into unresistant populations, with potentially horrendous costs in human, plant, and animal life; and most worrisome of all, a "runaway" greenhouse effect that would not stop. Scientists simply do not know whether the climate change induced by warming will be linear or discontinuous. If it is the latter, then humankind's continuing enhancement of the natural greenhouse effect is akin to playing Russian roulette with the earth's climate and humanity's life-support system.[89]

Thus, all three assessments—damage estimates, adaptation-abatement cost comparisons, and the probability of catastrophic climate change—point strongly toward a single policy. The United States should take the steps necessary to avert a large and probably severe change in the climate. These steps require unparalleled leadership by the world's great powers, asking their citizens to undergo short-term sacrifices, especially in the United States; a massive transfer of resources from the rich to the poor nations; considerable technological innovation; perhaps resort to the so-called flexible mechanisms, such as tradable permits and joint implementation; and a level of international cooperation never yet achieved in modern history.[90] The United States no longer has the luxury of averting climate change; the only questions are how much the climate will change and how severe will be its impacts. Global warming presents a potentially severe, even catastrophic threat to the United States. In order to stabilize the world's average global temperature, it is the United States that must lead. In the short term, to lead is to sacrifice, but over the long term, the United States and the world will reap benefits that will far outstrip the short-term costs.

ASSESSING THREATS

We have one final task in this chapter: to identify the threats to America's six national interests. Table 2.4 spells them out.

From the preceding discussion, the threats to America's first four interests should be evident. The greatest dangers to the physical safety and

TABLE 2.4. America's Interests and the Prime Threats to Them

Interest	Prime Threats	Status of Threats
1. Defense of the homeland	Grand terror attacks and spread of weapons of mass destruction to hard-to-deter state leaders and fanatical terrorists	Partially present
2. Deep peace among the Eurasian great powers	Aggressive great powers and hegemons	Not present
3. Secure access to Persian Gulf oil at a stable, reasonable price	A hegemonic Iran or Iraq	Not present
4. International economic openness	Great-power security competitions, great-power wars, economic nationalism	Not present
5. Consolidation of democracy and spread and observance of human rights	Ruthless leaders, civil wars, and the thwarting of economic growth	Partially present
6. No severe climate change	Unconstrained carbon emissions	Partially present

political sovereignty of the American homeland are grand terror attacks and the spread of NBC weapons to crazy leaders or fanatical terrorists. Most other imaginable dangers, except for runaway climate change, pale in comparison to these two. The greatest risks to a deep Eurasian peace come from a great power that turns aggressive and provokes a major war, or from a local war among smaller powers that draws in several great powers and then escalates to direct military confrontation among them. An aggressive Iran or Iraq engaging in outright military conquest, or in political blackmail through the threat of conquest, are scenarios that result in a quasi-monopoly control over the Gulf's oil reserves. Intense great-power security competitions, great-power wars, or public backlash against globalization, any of which could produce virulent economic nationalism, are the greatest challenges to international openness. The threats to the first four interests are clear, direct, and mostly military-oriented.

The threats to the last two interests are more varied. Thug leaders and civil wars obviously threaten democracy's spread and the protection of human rights, but probably the single most important international condition, over the long haul, for democracy's spread is uninterrupted global economic growth. Global economic growth is facilitated by a deep peace in Eurasia and secure access to energy supplies, but these are preconditions to growth, not guarantees. Third World states and post-Communist regimes may not do well even when the First World prospers, but they will surely do badly if the First World falters, either economically or politically. First World aid, markets, and stability are necessary (but not sufficient) ingredients to the economic and political success of post-Communist regimes and Third World states. Therefore, the continuing spread of democracy beyond the First World core depends in part on growth and stability at the core—the region, not just coincidentally, where America's overseas military power is currently concentrated.

Roughly the same line of argument holds true for international cooperation on global warming. The factors that threaten or facilitate democracy's spread also threaten or facilitate greenhouse cooperation. States in Eurasia and elsewhere will have fewer resources and less inclination to undertake the expensive measures to limit greenhouse gas emissions if they are waging war, spending huge resources on arms, retreating into destructive economic nationalisms, or spending their limited resources on buying exorbitantly priced energy. Achieving the cooperation necessary to bring about a reduction in greenhouse gas emissions will be difficult enough without these disturbing conditions; it will be nearly impossible with them.

What is the current state of these threats? Some, like the threat of grand terror attacks, have become manifest. Weapons of mass destruction, primarily chemical and biological, have spread to states and leaders that we would prefer not have them. We are also in the beginning stages of climate change, although it is not yet severe. Civil wars continue to erupt, and damage democracy and human rights. On the other hand, Eurasia is at peace: a deep great-power peace holds in western Europe, a stable great-power peace in Eastern Europe, a precarious peace in South Asia, and a stable if uneasy great-power peace in East Asia. Iraq has been checked; Iran, although it is building up its military power, is still relatively weak. There is no headlong rush to economic nationalism and closure. The current state of democracy's spread is healthy, and there are the beginnings of serious international cooperation to deal with global warming.

The goals of grand strategy should be to keep the latent threats latent and to remove, or if that is not possible, then to lessen, those that have become manifest. Our next step, therefore, is to determine which grand strategy can best do these things. Chapter 3 lays out eight grand strategies and shows why all but three deserve only cursory consideration.

THREE

Dominion, Collective Security, and Containment

To advance America's national interests, there are eight possible grand strategies to consider: dominion, global collective security, regional collective security, cooperative security, containment, isolationism, offshore balancing, and selective engagement. We can describe the central thrust of each strategy briefly as follows:

- *dominion* aims to rule the world;
- *global collective security*, to keep the peace everywhere;
- *regional collective security*, to keep the peace some places;
- *cooperative security*, to reduce the occurrence of war by limiting the offensive military capabilities of states;
- *containment*, to hold the line against a specific aggressor state;
- *isolationism*, to stay out of most wars and to keep a free hand for the United States;
- *offshore balancing*, to do that and, in addition, to cut down any emerging Eurasian hegemon; and
- *selective engagement*, to do a selected number of critical tasks.

All eight aim to deliver the two ultimate benefits that any nation seeks—security and prosperity—but they differ in how to pursue these ends. All but isolationism also seek to shape the international environment to suit the United States, but they differ on how much shaping is necessary and how it should be done.

This chapter disposes of five of the eight grand strategies by showing why the first four are not feasible and why the fifth—containment—is feasible, but can be easily subsumed under selective engagement. As I explain in more detail below, dominion is simply beyond the reach of America or any other country. Both global collective security and cooperative security are politically impossible to attain, while regional collective security is problematic because it is extraordinarily difficult to bring about. None of these four strategies can be adopted in their pure form, although elements from them can be incorporated into selective engagement, as I show below. The remaining three strategies—selective engagement, isolationism, and offshore balancing—as I explain in the next two chapters, are feasible, and therefore choices among them turn on issues other than their feasibility.

In this chapter and the next two, I lay out the logic and, where it is possible, the historical record of these strategies. In the current chapter, I begin with a brief comparison of all eight strategies and then show why dominion, global and regional collective security, and cooperative security are unattainable. I conclude this chapter by analyzing containment and showing why it is best incorporated under the rubric of selective engagement.

A COMPARISON OF EIGHT GRAND STRATEGIES

In this section, I differentiate the eight grand strategies along the following dimensions: their goals, their political feasibility, the degree to which they protect America's interests, their cost, the nature of their military deployment (whether forces are deployed forward), and whether they are unilateral or multilateral.[1] The strategies and their attributes on these six dimensions are laid out in Table 3.1, and the strategies are compared in each of these dimensions below.

Comparing Goals

Dominion aims to transform the world into what America thinks it should look like. This strategy would use American military power in an imperial fashion to effect the transformation. *Isolationism* aims to maintain a free hand for the United States, and its prime aim is to keep the United States out of most wars. *Offshore balancing* generally seeks the same goals as isolationism, but would go one step further and cut down an emerging hegemon in Eurasia so as to maintain a favorable balance of power there. *Containment* aims to hold the line against a specific aggressor that either threatens American interests in a given region or that strives for world hegemony, through both deterrent and defensive uses of military power. *Collective security* aims to keep the peace by preventing war by any aggressor. *Global collective security* and *cooperative security* aim to keep the peace everywhere; *regional collective security* to keep peace within specified areas. All three variants of collective security do so by tying the United States to multilateral security arrangements that guarantee military defeat for any aggressor that breaches the peace. Finally, *selective engagement* aims to do a defined number of critical things well, in order to realize America's interests as they are laid out in Chapter 2.

All eight grand strategies focus primarily on interstate relations, but each has different implications for intrastate conflicts. Dominion would require

TABLE 3.1. A Comparison of Eight Grand Strategies

Strategy	Prime Goal(s)	Feasible	Effectively Protects U.S. Interests	Cost	Is Force Forward Deployed?	Unilateral or Multilateral
Dominion	World dominance Refashion world in America's image	No	No	Prohibitive	Yes	Unilateral
Regional, collective security	Prevent war	Problematic	No	Moderate to expensive	Likely yes	Multilateral
Global collective security	Prevent war	No	No	Moderate to expensive	Likely yes	Multilateral
Cooperative security	Prevent war	No	No	Moderate to expensive	Likely yes	Multilateral
Containment	Keep any aggressor state or hegemon in check	Yes	Yes	Moderate to expensive	Yes	Multilateral
Isolationism	Keep freedom of action Stay out of most wars	Yes	No	Cheap	No	Unilateral
Offshore balancing	Stay out of most wars Cut down an emerging Eurasian hegemon	Yes	Mostly no	Moderate to expensive	Yes and no	Both
Selective engagement	Prevent spread of nuclear, biological, or chemical (NBC) weapons Maintain great-power peace Preserve energy security	Yes	Yes	Moderately expensive	Yes	Both

Note: Feasible means the strategy can be politically implemented.

American intervention whenever intrastate conflict threatened American dominance, while isolationism and offshore balancing would dictate staying out of such conflicts. Containment would mandate involvement only when necessary to thwart the growing influence and power of an aspiring hegemon. All the variants of collective security could be either interventionist or non-interventionist in intrastate wars, but on balance they would likely be interventionist for both humanitarian reasons (such wars often involve large loss of life) and political reasons (such wars risk break-out into interstate wars). Furthermore, interstate aggression is a rare event, and a system that prevents only interstate wars, while allowing intrastate ones to occur with abandon, would quickly become politically untenable. Selective engagement would not totally eschew forcible intervention in intrastate conflicts, but it would be sparing in its interventions. Only when these conflicts threatened America's strategic interests, or when the humanitarian disaster threatened to, or reached, mass-murder proportions, would selective engagement prescribe intervention. In those instances where military intervention occurs, moreover, selective engagement would mandate that it be done multilaterally, even though the United States might have to take the lead in initiating it.

Comparing Political Feasibility and Protection of American Interests

Neither dominion nor any of the three variants of collective security is politically feasible. Dominion is not, because it violates the logic of balance of power, is beyond America's resources, and is therefore inherently self-destructive. The three types of collective security are not because they presume an identity of interests among states that is unattainable. As a consequence, none can protect America's six fundamental national interests.

Containment of a would-be or actual regional or global hegemon could be feasible, but only when the affected regional or global great powers feel sufficiently threatened to act in concert. Regional containment is easier than global containment, because regional powers can see more clearly and more directly the threats from an aspiring regional hegemon than from an aspiring global hegemon. Moreover, to the extent that regional containment prescribes actions in accord with the dictates of selective engagement, it becomes a component of a selective engagement strategy and helps protect America's interests. Isolationism and offshore balancing, too, may be politically feasible, but the maintenance of a free hand that these strategies imply would cause the United States to end its alliances and bring home its troops, thereby curtailing its ability to shape regional developments to its advantage. Hence isolationism could not protect America's interests, and offshore balancing would protect only part of one interest.

Selective engagement is politically feasible, but it requires the long-term backing of the American people, the continued willingness of selected states in Eurasia and the Persian Gulf to host the peacetime deployment of American troops, and intelligent statecraft. Although these three requirements cannot be taken for granted, none is beyond the reach of the United States. If these requirements are fulfilled, selective engagement best protects America's national interests.

Comparing Cost and Deployment

The costs of the strategies turn mainly on deployment requirements. Containment and dominion require the United States to deploy forces overseas in peacetime. Global and regional collective security and cooperative security may or may not, but would be more politically effective if they did. Isolationism definitely does not. Offshore balancing deploys forces forward only when a Eurasian hegemon threatens. Selective engagement requires forward deployment of American troops in Eurasia and the Persian Gulf.

Dominion is prohibitively expensive. Isolationism is cheap but there is no fallback position should it fail. Offshore balancing is moderate in its cost if the United States has its forces only at home, but it could be expensive if those forces must be deployed to Eurasia, especially to fight a major war. Containment and the three forms of collective security are moderate to expensive strategies, depending upon the contributions of other states and upon the number and size of the states to be contained and the wars to be deterred or fought if deterrence fails. Selective engagement is not cheap, but it does not have to be exorbitant.

Going It Alone or Acting Together

Dominion and isolationism are unilateralist strategies in two senses: they rely solely on American military power, and they preserve for the United States complete freedom to decide whether and when to act. Offshore balancing is a unilateral strategy until a Eurasian hegemon threatens, whereupon it becomes a multilateral strategy. Containment and the three forms of collective security are multilateralist strategies: they require the military participation of other states, and hence they constrain the ability of the United States to act when it chooses. Selective engagement can be unilateral, because there may be rare instances in which the United States will have to act alone; in general, however, the strategy will work best when others are engaged, even if only to a degree. Selective engagement is unilateral in the sense that it requires the United States to take the initiative and lead, but multilateral in that it requires the participation of others for its success. It works best when it can rely on America's standing alliances and second best when it relies on "coalitions of the willing."

Now I turn to the five grand strategies discussed in this chapter. I begin with dominion and its close relative, primacy.

DOMINION: TRANSFORM THE WORLD

A policy of dominion, American-style, would be an imperial strategy, designed not simply to gain power and profit for the United States, although there would be plenty of that, but also to allow it to impose its dictates on the world. Dominion would create a global American imperium; it would be an aggressive, interventionist, unilateralist, and transformational strategy. It would look like Wilsonianism in action, with a vengeance: the United States would go out and make the world safe for America by forcibly making the world conform to the dictates of America's brand of democratic market capitalism. Dominion American-style would be not simply "America the global cop," but also "America in your face."

Periodic U.S. Impulses toward Dominion

The United States has never pursued a full-fledged policy of dominion, but since 1945, semblances of it have appeared four times: at the outset of the Cold War, near the end of the Cold War, immediately after the end of the Cold War, and at the turn of the twenty-first century.

In the early 1950s, from outside of government came the call for liberation, or what was commonly called "rollback" during the Cold War. This strategy originated with the hard right, those critical of the containment policy that the government was pursuing under both Democratic and Republican Administrations. Rollback rejected simply containing the Soviet Union and instead called for its forcible retreat and ultimate demise. Its goal was "freedom for the peoples and nations now enslaved by the Russian-centered Soviet state system . . . including the Russian people." Its means were: "all-sided political warfare; auxiliary military and paramilitary actions where called for; adequate preparation for whatever military action may be required in the future."[2] Rollback was to the Cold War era what dominion would be to this era, if it were adopted: an aggressive policy to spread American values abroad, by force if necessary. For rollback, that would have required the ultimate liberation of the Soviet Union and the states in the Warsaw Pact.

The United States did not publicly adopt the rollback policy and never used its own military power in a direct confrontation with Soviet or Chinese forces on the Eurasian landmass to push communist control back from a nation, with one exception. That was the attempted forcible reunification of Korea in 1950, which ultimately proved unsuccessful. Even here, except for some aerial clashes between American and Soviet pilots, the United States did not fight Soviet forces, although it did fight Chinese forces. The United States did not publicly proclaim rollback as its policy, but we now know that it did secretly adopt a version of rollback. As Gregory Mitrovich has carefully

87

documented, from 1947 until 1956 the United States covertly instituted an aggressive policy of psychological warfare against the Soviet Union and its East European satellites. The purpose of the covert policy was to destabilize the Soviet Union, or even better, to cause its collapse. The means used included disinformation, support for paramilitary resistance forces, counterinsurgency operations, and incapacitation of the administrative structures of the Communist Party.[3] Throughout the entire Cold War era, the United States also used political, economic, military, and covert instruments to thwart, block, or overthrow what it saw as communist-controlled or communist-leaning governments in the Third World, most prominently in Guatemala (1954), Cuba (1961), Vietnam, (1953–1975), Chile (1973), Angola (1974–75), Nicaragua (the early 1980s), Grenada (1983), and Afghanistan (the 1980s).

In the 1980s, rollback experienced a "second coming," but in this reincarnation, too, it was more than mere rhetoric. Under the Reagan administration, the United States adopted a highly aggressive policy toward the Soviet Union, in the hope or expectation of dealing it a mortal blow. In its first term, the administration's policy included trying to force the Soviet Union to the wall economically by causing it to spend huge sums on arms; exercising quasi-military interventionist policies to roll back Soviet-supported governments by giving covert and overt aid to guerilla groups fighting them, as in Afghanistan and Nicaragua (the so-called "Reagan Doctrine"); and dispersing funds, expertise, and propaganda to aid democratic parties abroad by creating such mechanisms as the National Endowment for Democracy.[4] The first Reagan administration undertook a vigorous renewal of the Cold War to force the Soviet Union to come to the bargaining table and accept America's terms.

In 1992, immediately after the end of the Cold War, dominion-like urges again surfaced during the Bush administration. They appeared in the Pentagon's Defense Planning Guidance (DPG), a document that sets the broad policy objectives for the United States for a five-year period, and that guides the military services and other elements of the Defense Department in planning their strategies and procurements. The 1992 DPG called for the United States to maintain its position as the world's strongest power by two means. The first was to exercise American power benevolently: the United States would "sufficiently account for the interests of the advanced industrial nations to discourage them from challenging our leadership." The second was to preserve military power of such dominance that it would deter "potential competitors from even aspiring to a larger regional or global role."[5] A key element of the latter policy was maintaining a "reconstitution" capability—the ability to rebuild American forces quickly to wage and win an all-out global conventional war.[6] The maintenance of overwhelming military power, together with its benevolent exercise, were to be the means of keeping

America supreme in the new era. Leaked to the public, the DPG incited adverse comment and was toned down, although these two basic objectives remained in effect during the administration of George H.W. Bush.[7]

In 2001–2002, a fourth appearance of dominion-like behavior became manifest under President George W. Bush. It was marked by tough rhetoric toward adversaries, a huge increase in American defense spending (only part of which could be accounted for by September 11), an unvarnished pursuit of American self-interest, a penchant for unilateralism that worried America's potential enemies and aggravated its allies, a reaffirmation of the 1992 DPG declaration of intent to maintain military power sufficient "to dissuade future military competition," and a strategic doctrine that stressed preempting threats rather than simply deterring or containing them.[8] Part of this behavior was a Republican Party correction to what it had perceived as a soft, overly multilateralist, and inconsistent Clinton foreign policy. Part was due to legitimate concerns about the spread of nuclear, chemical, or biological (NBC) weapons to states that both Republican and Democratic administrations would prefer not have them. Part, however, was due to an arrogance born of the knowledge that American power, especially its military power, bought the United States a lot of freedom of political maneuver.

As these four instances illustrate, dominion is a powerful temptation for a nation as strong as the United States. Dominion is the ideal strategy to protect America's interests: if the United States could, in fact, bend all others to its will, then by definition its interests would be protected. Dominion, however, has only one problem: it is impossible to achieve. In today's world, it is illusory, and its quest would drain America empty. The United States has neither sufficient military power nor sufficient resources to generate enough military power to subject the world to an American imperium. Two simple facts about military power today show why dominion is impossible to attain, much less sustain.

First, states with nuclear weapons cannot be militarily defeated nor easily bent to another's will. As a consequence, any military attempt to compel nuclear states would likely fail, and risk nuclear war in the process. Second, the mustering of conventional forces to intimidate or defeat all other non-nuclear adversaries, even sequentially, is beyond even the means of the United States. Subjugation of other powers with conventional forces requires the projection of American military power across the oceans to Eurasia, where the other great military powers lie. But as World War I and World War II demonstrated, and as the Persian Gulf War reaffirmed, the United States cannot project its military forces abroad unless it has allies willing to furnish bases. However, states will not be willing hosts of American military forces, if the ultimate result is their own subjugation. Without some great-power allies, an American military expedition to Eurasia would face ultimate destruction if it were ever attempted. On both counts, military dominion is impossible.

Furthermore, not only is dominion impossible, but even whiffs of it are self-defeating. Military actions that are imperious, unilateral, and of benefit to no one except the state undertaking them will provoke one of two things: the rise of countervailing coalitions to check the United States, and military buildups by those states that could compete militarily with the United States, if they chose. As a grand strategy, dominion is a self-defeating policy. It has a "backfire effect": moves toward it will provoke reactions to prevent it, and the more intensely it is pursued, the more furiously it will be resisted. As long as the United States remains the world's greatest power, however, temptations toward dominion will reappear. For the reasons described, they must be resisted.

The Value of Primacy

Although the quest for dominion is clearly foolhardy, it is fair to ask whether the goal of having military forces that are superior to those of any other state is also foolhardy and self-defeating. To answer the question, we must first distinguish dominion from superiority, or what is today called primacy.

Dominion and primacy differ in two important respects. First, dominion is a grand strategy; primacy is not. Dominion prescribes a goal—the triumph of American values—and the means to achieve it: imperial rule. Primacy is not a grand strategy, although it is often mistaken for one. Primacy does not prescribe the ends of policy but a means to help achieve them. Second, dominion and primacy differ in the margin of relative strength they call for. Dominion is absolute rule; primacy is superior influence. Dominion implies invariably prevailing; primacy means winning more often than others do. Dominion is a dictatorial position: the ability to get one's way, completely and always. Primacy is the most influential position: the ability to obtain more from others than they obtain from you, but not all that you want, and not every time. To be stronger than any other single actor is not to be in the position of dictating to each of them. To be the most important actor is not to be all-powerful, only the most powerful. Primacy, therefore, is not imperium. Dominion requires overwhelming military strength in order to prevail in every situation; primacy requires superior military strength in order to be the most influential actor. Thus, my definition of primacy requires that the United States possess the strongest national military force in the world so that it has a military edge over any other single state. For some states this edge will be large, and for others it will be small, but in comparison to any given state, the United States must have some edge.

Primacy, I argue, is both feasible and desirable for the United States, but there are those who argue that it is not, because it is too costly, not needed, or overly provocative.[9] These are important objections to consider.

Cost is always central in grand strategy. Many things simply cannot be done; others are feasible in the short term but not sustainable over the longer term. As a consequence of the collapse of the Soviet Union, the United States now has unchallenged military primacy. I assert that this primacy is both affordable and sustainable for a long time to come because the resources that the United States needs to sustain its military primacy are not inordinate. Its edge is currently so great that the United States can maintain the lead well into the future, if it so chooses. As with a company that has achieved an oligopolistic position, maintenance of the position is easier than its achievement, because the oligopolist can continually create new barriers to entry for would-be competitors. Spending to maintain military forces second to none need not be excessive, nor will it necessarily hurt America's competitive economic position. The health of the American economy, which is essential to sustain its military forces, depends primarily on what the United States does at home: fostering innovation, providing for an educated and skilled workforce, making certain that sufficient savings are available for investment, pursuing the proper macroeconomic policies, and the like. The United States is not spending more on defense now than other great powers did when they were at their peak; compared to most, it is spending substantially less. As long as America's economy remains large and growing, as long as its per-capita income is high, and as long as the United States continues to innovate, it can sustain its position as the world's strongest military power for decades to come, even though it may not always outspend several of its nearest rivals combined, as it now does, and even though this may not dissuade a potential peer competitor from challenging its military preeminence.

A second objection is whether there is a need for primacy. Need is a question of benefit and hinges on a judgment about the nature of America's interests and about whether military primacy helps protect them better than military equality or inferiority. Selective engagement, as I explain in Chapter 4, works better with military primacy than without it. For now, a brief thought experiment can help us assess the relative worth of primacy. All other things being equal, which is the best position to be in: weaker than others, equal in power to them, or stronger than others? Weakness invites predation and leads to loss of autonomy. Equality brings uncertainty as to which will get its way, and leads to fierce competition to prevail. Superiority, however, yields a margin of comfort and buys more influence. Influence is the coin of politics, whether domestic or international. To put the matter this way is to show the virtues of primacy, if it can be attained and sustained.

A third objection is that primacy is overly provocative. This is a crucial issue. If a strategy of selective engagement is to employ military primacy wisely, then it must employ it to reassure and deter more often than to provoke or compel. This is not a simple policy to implement. Primacy and especially dominion rub against the grain of balance of power. A state with a military edge will always cause wariness in other states, even among allies and even if the superior state's intentions are benign or serve the interests of its allies. The trick in wielding primacy is to convince other states that one is using it as much on their behalf as on one's own. For good reasons, states fear dominion, but they can live with primacy if it is properly wielded. If clumsily wielded, however, primacy will provoke the same types of counter-coalitions and military buildups as would the quest for dominion. The judicious use of primacy, therefore, means convincing others that it is being wielded for collective rather than unilateral purposes. This is a point that the elder Bush's Pentagon understood.

In sum, reaching for dominion is illusory, but sustaining for a lengthy period a primacy already acquired, although difficult, is by no means impossible or prohibitively expensive. For all these reasons, then, rejecting dominion makes sense; allowing America's military primacy to dissipate does not.

GLOBAL COLLECTIVE SECURITY: KEEP THE PEACE EVERYWHERE

Global collective security is a multilateralist strategy that aims to prevent interstate aggression and territorial conquest everywhere. It requires states to cooperate with one another indefinitely in order to banish war from their relations. "As an ideal, collective security is without flaws," argued Hans J. Morgenthau; "it presents indeed the ideal solution of the problem of law enforcement in a community of sovereign nations."[10] The only problem with global collective security, as Morgenthau well knew, is that it does not work, as both its logic and its history reveal.

The Flawed Logic of Collective Security

Collective security is elegantly simple. In design and intent, it is a system of deterrence. At its core is a binding political-military pledge, signed by all who enter into the arrangement, to defend militarily any of its signatories if it is attacked.[11] Collective security is a system of all-for-one, no matter who the "one" is, because an attack on one is considered an attack on all. Every state commits itself to act as if its own security is threatened whenever the security of any other state is threatened, no matter how distant the attacked state is and no matter how remote the threat may appear to its own immediate interests. Through the commitment to stop aggression wherever and whenever it occurs, a collective security system literally collectivizes security. In doing so, it makes security and peace indivisible, because no state is secure unless every state is secure, and no state can be at peace unless every state is at peace. By collectivizing security, a genuine collective security system would stop all interstate aggression, because any potential aggressor knows that its aggression would immediately provoke a crushing military counter-strike. Collective security leaves an aggressor only one answer to its calculations: it will lose any war it starts, and it will lose it big time. An eloquent expression of the all-for-one philosophy can be found in the words of Alfred Nemours, Haiti's delegate to the League of Nations, as it debated in 1935 whether and how to punish Italy for its aggression against Ethiopia: "Great or small, strong or weak, near or far, white or colored, let us never forget that one day we may be somebody's Ethiopia."[12]

Simple though it may be, collective security is difficult to achieve. For an institutional arrangement to qualify as collective security, it must pass a demanding test: unless it provides security from attack for all states, it is not truly collective. If collective security is to be for everyone, it cannot be only for some. There can be no halfway measures, no "degrees of collective security." As Inis Claude put it, collective security "permits no *ifs* or *buts*" and "is replete with absolutes, of which none is more basic than the requirement of certainty."[13] Collective security, therefore, cannot be "à la carte": there cannot be collective security for states A, B, and C, but not for M, N, O, and P, when all are members of the same collective security system. Collective security is tough to attain because if it does not exist for all states in the system at all times, then it will not exist for any state at any time.[14] Moreover, for collective security to work, the commitment to collective enforcement—attacking the aggressor and reversing its aggression—has to be totally automatic and completely binding. If one state is attacked, all others must immediately come to its aid militarily. There can be no deliberations about who is the aggressor, and there can be no stipulations that national legislatures retain the final authority to authorize war. The only issues for states to discuss can be these: how quickly can they get their troops to the theater and what is the best strategy for their use.

Because collective security must pass such demanding tests, it is not attainable in its universal form. The issue is not one of institutional design but of political will.[15] States might choose to delegate war and peace decisions to an international organization, but they do not, for several reasons. First, universal collective security demands a degree of shared outlook and consensus among states that has never been historically attained. It requires that all states evaluate the risks, costs, and benefits of each and every threatening situation in much the same way. In this regard, the prerequisite to universal collective security is a shared sense of global community. The barrier here is the same one that, as Morgenthau pointed out, prevents constructing a world state: "world community must antedate a world state."[16] The predicament is that differences in outlooks among states, and their jockeying for national advantage, work against developing the shared sense of a global community. The system of separate states works so as to perpetuate the system of separate states. Second, universal collective security demands that states value keeping the peace and punishing aggression above all their other interests. Third, all states must regard peace as indivisible: each state must consider a war far removed from it as being as detrimental to its security as a war that is close at hand. Under collective security, it is war per se, not a given war, that degrades each and every state's security. Fourth, to work, a collective security system must obtain agreement from its members on who is the aggressor in any violent conflict. In interstate wars, this can be challenging because the state that attacks first is not necessarily the aggressor; in intrastate ethnic conflicts, such agreement is nearly impossible because, more often than not, all parties to the conflict have blemished records. Finally, collective security requires the blankest of blank checks: a solemn pact to punish all aggression wherever and whenever it occurs. This demands that all states pledge to punish an aggressor without knowing who among them it will be.

If all these conditions held, then states would view peace as indivisible, and they could design genuine collective security systems. They have not, as the League of Nations and the United Nations demonstrate.

The Design of the League of Nations and the United Nations

Neither the League of Nations nor the United Nations was designed as a true collective security organization. Each moved further toward collectivizing security than had any previous attempt in world history, but neither moved far enough to convince its members that peace among them had become truly indivisible. Each organization put restrictions on its enforcement mechanism that were severe enough to make action against breaches of the peace contingent and uncertain; as a consequence, member states have not chosen to rely on these organizations to assure their security, but have instead resorted to the more traditional instruments of statecraft.

A brief look at the enforcement mechanisms illustrates the point.[17] The League's key provision for dealing with aggression is Article 16 of the Covenant: "Should any Member of the League resort to war in disregard of its covenants . . . it shall *ipso facto* be deemed to have committed an act of war against all other Members of the League."[18] On the face of it, this article appears to be collective security. In 1921, however, the Assembly of the League undermined Article 16 by passing a set of interpretive resolutions, including this key one: "It is the duty of each Member of the League to decide for itself whether a breach of the Covenant has been committed."[19] With this resolution, states took back their Covenant pledge. Aggressive acts would not be collectively and immediately resisted; instead, each state would decide for itself whether to take action, based on its views about its own stakes in the given situation. This stipulation, more than the requirement for Council unanimity, is what gutted the League's enforcement mechanism.[20] Right from the outset, states refused to issue the League a blank check to wage war, and instead reserved that judgment for national decision; they thus failed to collectivize security.

The United Nations charter did essentially the same two things, but through different means. The five great-power creators of the United Nations—the United States, the Soviet Union, Great Britain, France, and China—ensured that the Security Council would be under their control because each retained a veto on any Council actions; then they neutered its enforcement capabilities. The key enforcement provision of the United Nations charter is found in Chapter 6. Article 39 calls for the Security Council, not the individual UN members, to determine when breaches of the peace have occurred. Article 43 calls for the member states to make available to the United Nations specified armed forces for enforcement actions.[21] Ultimately, however, the five great-power members of the Security Council chose not to implement Article 43; they refused to create a standing military force to be used at the Council's discretion. Failing that, as Morgenthau points out, Article 106 of the Charter remained operative. It stipulates that the Council's five permanent members agree only to consult with one another on what actions to take if the peace is breached; it does not unequivocally commit them to take military action against aggression.[22] As with the League, the great powers that created the United Nations resisted any steps that carried even the hint of national control over the use of force, in this case by building a veto into Council actions and by failing to bring into existence a multilateral military force at the disposal of the Council, even though they had pledged to do so. The five great powers institutionally tailored the Security Council to preserve the privileged position that they had attained at the end of World War II.

Collective security enjoyed a brief resurgence in the euphoria that accompanied the end of the Cold War. In July 1991 the great powers revisited what they had done at the end of World War II. At a G-7 meeting in London, the heads of state of the world's most powerful states and richest economies proclaimed:

> We believe the conditions now exist for the United Nations to fulfill
> completely the promise and the vision of its founders. A revitalized United
> Nations will have a central role in strengthening the international order.
> We commit ourselves to making the United Nations stronger, more
> efficient, and more effective in order to protect human rights, to maintain
> peace and security for all, and to deter aggression.[23]

In January 1992, at the first ever heads-of-state meeting of the Security Council, they followed up this initiative by directing UN Secretary-General Boutros Boutros-Ghali to recommend ways "of strengthening and making more efficient . . . the capacity of the United Nations for preventive diplomacy, for peacemaking, and for peace-keeping."[24]

95

Quickly, however, both moves came to naught. In his June 1992 report entitled "Agenda for Peace," Boutros-Ghali acknowledged political realities:

> Under Article 42 of the Charter, the Security Council has the authority to take military action to maintain or restore international peace and security .... This will require bringing into being ... the special agreements foreseen in Article 43 ... whereby Member States undertake to make armed forces, assistance, and facilities available to the Security Council ... not only on an ad hoc basis but on a permanent basis .... *Such forces are not likely to be available for some time to come.*[25]

Two years later, matters had not changed. In surveying the progress made since mid-1992, Eric Schmitt, the *New York Times* UN correspondent, reported that countries had not fulfilled the terms of Article 43 and had refused "to designate forces subject to automatic call-up by the United Nations," because "no country ... has agreed to relinquish this degree of control over its troops to the United Nations."[26] By May 1994, the Clinton administration had retreated from its initial enthusiasm for the United Nations, declaring: "The President retains and will never relinquish command authority over U.S. forces."[27] The world's greatest military power made it clear that discretionary national control, not automatic collective enforcement, would continue. Thus, three years after the great powers had proclaimed the times propitious for strengthening the UN role in international security, collective enforcement had gone nowhere.[28] The great powers were no more willing in the early 1990s than they were in the mid-1940s to create the standing military force called for in Article 43 of the charter.

For both the League and the United Nations, true collective security never had a chance. Both institutions were crippled from the outset because member states refused to delegate their sovereign right to use force to an international institution. F. H. Hinsley aptly explained why the League had to fail as a collective security organization, and his words are equally applicable to the United Nations: "the lesson to be learned from the record is not that the League could have avoided these weaknesses by being given more authority. It is that it could not have avoided them because it could not have been given more authority."[29]

The Record of Collective Enforcement

The record of the League and the United Nations with collective enforcement reflects their institutional limitations. Although the League had some mediation successes in the 1920s and early 1930s, primarily with the small powers, and although the United Nations has had its own successes at peacekeeping, the track record of both with collective security is dismal.[30] They stopped few wars and they punished few aggressors.

According to a standard statistical reference on conflicts, there were seven interstate wars between 1920 and 1940, including World War II.[31] The League was unable to prevent or stop any of them. The record of the United Nations is little better. From its inception in 1948 until 2000, there were twenty-nine interstate wars, none of which the United Nations was able to prevent and nearly all of which stopped for reasons having little or nothing to do with its efforts (one party won, both sides were exhausted, or a military stalemate was achieved).[32]

Moreover, by my count, the League and the United Nations attempted collective enforcement only three times in their combined eighty-year history (1920–2000).[33] The first attempt (Ethiopia in 1935–36) was a disastrous failure, and it put the final nail into the League's coffin. The British and the French elected not to take military action against Italy after it invaded Ethiopia, and they refused to apply the only economic measure— an oil embargo—that might have stopped Mussolini.[34] Both states chose not to alienate Mussolini, hoping to keep him as an ally against Hitler, rather than upholding the principle of collective security. They put their national interests above the collective interest. The second attempt—Korea in 1950— was only an accidental success, and it solidified the Cold War East-West split within the United Nations and abetted its subsequent collective security paralysis. The United Nations did roll back North Korea's invasion of South Korea and restored its territorial integrity, but this was not a resounding blow for collective security. The military action was largely an American (and South Korean) affair, and this is what the United States expected when it undertook to defend South Korea.[35] In June 1953, at their peak strength, of the 932,000 UN forces in Korea, 96 percent were American (302,000) and South Korean (591,000). Of the 39,000 other troops, 24,000 came from the British Commonwealth (Canada sent 6,000 and Britain 14,000), while Turkey sent 5,400.[36] "Collective" security in the Korean War was not, in fact, collective, but bilateral, with a little help from some of America's friends.[37] More important, the United Nations would never have acted had the Soviet Union been present at the Security Council meeting on the day that the United States brought up the Korean matter.[38] Had it been present, it would have vetoed the Council's action, and the Korean War would have looked much more like what it was in fact: an American-led military defense against communist aggression. Thus, the international response to the North Korean attack was not so much collective security in action as the United States in action.

The final attempt—Kuwait in 1991—was a genuine success, but it was so lopsidedly an American operation and so sui generis that we should not assume it signals a glorious future for collective security. Iraq invaded Kuwait; the world community condemned the action; the United Nations Security Council imposed an economic blockade against Iraq and then sanctioned war against it. Iraq was defeated and thrown out of Kuwait.[39] The Persian Gulf case shows that an imperfectly constructed collective security institution can sometimes rise to the occasion. The emphasis has to be on "sometimes," however, because this case demonstrates that a rare confluence of events is required to produce unanimity among the great powers to do collective enforcement.

One of the unlikely conditions was that all of the great powers on the Security Council backed strong American action, although they did so for different reasons.[40] Moreover, nearly every state in the world had a stake in the outcome of Iraq's aggression because it would ultimately affect control of much of the Gulf's reserves. There was a genuine collective interest in how these reserves were divided up. Where a collective interest is at stake, collective action is feasible, although even there it is not inevitable. Finally, Saddam Hussein's drive to acquire nuclear weapons encouraged the commitment to collective enforcement. None of its neighbors wanted a nuclear-armed Iraq, and neither did the global community. These three factors—great-power unanimity, the threat to the Gulf's oil reserves, and the fear that a ruthless dictator could acquire nuclear weapons—largely explain why the potential for collective action was high in the Iraqi case. They also highlight what a rare confluence of factors it takes to produce collective enforcement.

In sum, under the League and the United Nations, collective enforcement was attempted in only 8 percent of the interstate wars of the last seventy-five years (three out of thirty-seven), and the rate of success was just 2.7 percent (one out of thirty-seven). (The thirty-seven wars include the eight that took place during the League's existence [1920–1946] and the twenty-nine that took place during the period of the United Nations [1948–2000].) This hardly constitutes a ringing endorsement for universal collective security.

Does Global Collective Security Have a Place?

In view of this dismal performance, what role should global collective security play in America's grand strategy? First, the United States should not waste its resources trying to bring about universal collective security. Today and for the foreseeable future, this is politically infeasible. States will not give blank checks to international organizations with global purviews to drag them into wars, but will instead retain the right to decide for themselves whether to fight. Even if all the permanent great-power members of the Security Council eventually become liberal democracies, national control over the use of force will persist. In the last eighty years, liberal democracies have proven fearsome and effective warriors against non-democracies, but they are no more willing than other states to delegate decisions about war and peace to an international organization. Democracies have waged war to defend their national interests, but never to defend the principle of collective security. A democratic great-power club might reduce the likelihood of war among the great powers, which is a good thing, but it will not make collective enforcement more effective in the smaller wars that have been the preoccupation of the United Nations.

Second, if universal collective security is not feasible, should the United States turn to the United Nations when it has to wage war? The answer is: "yes, whenever it can." The United States should use the institution for its own purposes in whatever way it can. In those rare circumstances where the United States can put together a wartime concert within the Security Council, it should do so. In those cases where it cannot, it may still be able to use the Council to provide political cover either for a unilateral American intervention, like Haiti in 1994, or for a military effort—like Bosnia in 1995—that the United States conducts through one of its regional alliance systems. In sum, the United States cannot count on the United Nations for waging the wars the United States wants to wage, but when it can, it should, and when it cannot, the United States should still use the organization in whatever other ways it may prove useful.

REGIONAL COLLECTIVE SECURITY

If a global collective security system is infeasible, can a regional collective security system work? An effective regional collective security system would be built on four foundations: the indivisibility-of-peace principle, an equitable sharing of burdens, widespread trust, and adequate military power. If any of these ingredients is missing, regional collective security will fail.

Requirements of Regional Collective Security

In a regional collective security system, the member states pledge themselves to fight any aggressor that attacks, even if the attacker turns out to be one of their own number. What distinguishes a regional from a global system, then, is not the indivisibility-of-peace principle but the difference in geographic scope between the two. A global system is, by definition, universal because all states are in it. A regional one is not, because it draws a clear line between insiders and outsiders and thereby does double duty: fending off attacks from without and keeping the peace within.

Moreover, all members of a regional collective security system must share the burden of keeping the peace and contributing to the war effort. They may not contribute to either task in exactly equal amounts, because states differ in their sizes and resources, but each must contribute to the best of its ability. The burden must be spread in order to prevent "free riding," the condition where some states do little or nothing but can still enjoy the

99

benefits provided by those who do contribute. The danger of free riding is that it can snowball: a little leads to more, and more leads to a lot. If free riding becomes widespread, then the burden is no longer collectively but only partially shared: a few do all the work for the many. In that event, the system collapses: either those that carry most of the burden will tire and stop, or they will act only when their direct interests are threatened. Either way, collective security no longer exists.

Free riding is a serious enough problem in a global system, but it is even more damaging in a regional system. By definition, a regional system has fewer states than a global system. With fewer states, those that shirk have more of an impact. With fewer states to share the burden, the defection of a few more quickly increases the burden of the others. With shirking more quickly noticed and more keenly felt, free riding is more likely to destroy the common effort and to do so more rapidly. A regional system is even more exacting than a global one when it comes to burden sharing.

For genuine regional collective security, each state must trust all of the others to aid it automatically and swiftly if it is attacked. If trust is not widespread, then a stab in the back, or being left in the lurch, is feared. Unless states trust one another, they cannot develop the degree of cooperation necessary to coordinate their plans and pool their efforts.

Regional collective security also requires sufficient military power to deter or defeat an aggressor. Adequacy of military power has two faces. Externally, it requires that the combined power of the regional organization be sufficient to meet all potential challengers. If the organization's power would not be sufficient, then states are not likely to pool their resources for common defense; it would be better to accommodate, appease, or bandwagon with an aggressor than to engage in futile resistance. If the organization is militarily deficient, either it will not form in the first place, or if it does, it will fall apart at the first serious challenge. Internally, a regional collective security system requires that no single member state can be so strong that it equals or surpasses all the others in military strength. If it did, then they could not make themselves secure against it if it chose to aggress. If the military power of one of the states dwarfs that of all the others combined, what exists is a sphere of influence, not a regional collective security organization. In this event, the hegemon might provide collective security to the other members, but only as long as its interests coincided with theirs.

These foundations—indivisibility of peace, equitable burden sharing, pervasive trust, and sufficient military power—constitute an extremely demanding set of conditions. There are those, however, who maintain that regional collective security can be made to work.[41] They argue that the impediments to regional collective security are not as formidable as those to global collective security, and that therefore regional collective security can succeed where global collective security cannot. These proponents are wrong, because they misjudge the severity of the impediments to regional systems, which are nearly as formidable as those for a global system. Here again, both logic and history make the case.

Impediments to Regional Collective Security

Both the League of Nations and the United Nations failed because the great powers refused to straitjacket themselves. They would not give iron-clad blanket assurances to wage war against any and all aggressors. Instead, each retained for itself the right to decide whether its interests were served by reversing any given aggression. Their refusal can be laid to one key factor: they did not have a strong enough sense of shared political community and common political fate. As Inis Claude put it: "Fundamentally, collective security requires . . . a community consciousness which overrides the divisiveness of national interests. . . . Neither peoples nor governments have undergone the transformation of viewpoints, attitudes, and values which collective security demands."[42]

This transformation is something that Morgenthau describes as "a moral revolution infinitely more fundamental than any moral change that has occurred in the history of Western civilization." It requires a change "not only in the actions of statesmen representing their countries but also in the actions of plain citizens."[43] Had the member states undergone this transformation, then they would have viewed their security as indivisible, the bedrock condition for effective collective security. It is therefore important to get the sequence correct: the strong sense of shared community and common fate produces the understanding that peace and security are indivisible, not the other way around. This means that for collective security to work, the transformation in outlook must precede the creation of the system.

It is clear why such a transformation is currently beyond reach for a global system. The large number of states, the physical remoteness of most from one another, their disparate interests, and the great diversity in their political makeup and outlook all work against the necessary transformation. Consequently, there does yet not exist a sense of world community strong enough to override the centrifugal forces of nationalism and national interests. These forces, in turn, work against the creation of such a sense because they put the parochial interests of individual states above the collective interests of them all.

At first glance, it might appear easier to create the required political transformation on a regional scale. After all, the number of states is smaller, they are in closer proximity, and they are therefore likely to have a greater sense of shared fate and regional solidarity. For these reasons it seems more likely that the sense of shared political community can flower within a region, thereby creating the political conditions that are required for regional collective security to emerge.

However, a mere reduction in scale and scope alone cannot effect the transformation in outlook. Proximity just as easily brings war as it does peace; it is, after all, neighbors, not strangers, that most often fight one another. Neighbors find many reasons to fight: their borders are in dispute; they have ideological claims that threaten each other's domestic legitimacy; or they want the same valuable natural resources. With few exceptions (Western Europe and North America), most regions of the world have on-going disputes, especially over territory, that are deep-seated, periodically violent, and almost always vicious. Moreover, regional actors are not equally affected by the conflicts among them. Some will suffer if the conflicts become violent, but others may benefit. Even if all were to suffer, still, some would suffer more than others. Regional conflicts affect their actors in different ways, and these differences will themselves become sources of conflict because they produce, in their turn, advantages and disadvantages.[44] Finally, geography amplifies or dampens the effects of these differences. States that are close neighbors are sensitive to their differences in position, advantage, and power; those that are more remote from one another can be more relaxed about their relative positions. Proximity magnifies the effect of differentials; distance dilutes it. In international relations, then, close proximity and small numbers can just as easily be curses as benefits.

In sum, the requisites for regional collective security are not so much different from global collective security that they make it easy to achieve. Indeed, none of the four necessary ingredients has yet been present in any region to the extent that would permit a genuine regional system. Consequently, in the modern world, perhaps in all of recorded history, no authentic regional collective security system has come into existence.[45]

Rio and NATO: Two Non-Exemplars of Regional Collective Security

The two regional security arrangements that have come closest to producing collective security-type results have been the Rio-OAS (Organization of American States) system and the NATO (North Atlantic Treaty Organization) alliance. Of the two, NATO has come the closest. Neither, however, meets all four tests of a genuine regional collective security organization. Moreover, although they have collective security–type attributes, each, in reality, is the security manifestation of an American sphere of influence in, respectively, Latin America and Western Europe. American power and leadership created and sustained those organizations, and without both those ingredients, neither organization would have come into existence, much less operated as effectively.

The Rio-OAS System
The Rio-OAS system has more explicit formal collective security provisions than NATO.[46] The 1947 Inter-American Treaty of Reciprocal Assistance,

known as the Rio Treaty, was the first of America's Cold War, anti-communist, multilateral alliances, and it was signed by all of the states of the Western Hemisphere except Canada. It was given firmer institutional footing with the creation of the OAS in 1948. Both the treaty and the OAS charter provide that an armed attack against any signatory state shall be considered an armed attack against all signatory states. Both explicitly define an armed attack as one emanating from either a state outside the Western Hemisphere or a state within it.[47] This system is the only modern regional arrangement that specifies that aid will be given against attacks launched by either outsiders or insiders. It is this provision that brings the Rio-OAS system the closest in its formal guarantees to the ideal of a collective security system.

However, this system still does not qualify as authentic regional collective security because two of its additional provisions significantly qualify the military guarantee. First, both the Rio Treaty and the OAS charter make important distinctions between an attack by a state outside the organization and an attack by a state that is a member of the organization. They provide stronger guarantees against the latter eventuality than they do against the former. In the event of internal attack, the signatories are required to come immediately to the assistance of the victim; for external attack, they are required only to consult on what to do. The reason for this distinction lay in the reluctance of the Latin American states to become embroiled in any Cold War conflicts that the United States might wage outside the Western Hemisphere.

Second, even the provision for defense against internal attack is weak. Article 20 of the Rio-OAS system contains an opt-out provision: "Decisions which require the application of the measures specified in Article 8 [listing the full range of punitive measures that can be taken against an aggressor] shall be binding upon all the Signatory States . . . with the sole exception that no State shall be required to use armed force without its consent." As with all would-be collective security systems, the states of the Western Hemisphere refrained from binding themselves to defend one another in the event of attack from any of their own; they chose to keep control over the use of force national, not make it international. As a consequence, in the three internal interstate wars that occurred in Latin America since 1947, the OAS did not engage in collective enforcement, although it did make mediation attempts.[48]

In addition to these formal deficiencies, the crucial element of widespread trust was usually missing among the western hemisphere states. Not only have the states of Latin America tended to be quite wary of their immediate neighbors, they have also mistrusted the United States. In fact, they have traditionally been hostile to a centralized inter-American authority precisely because of their fear that the United States might use that authority to intervene militarily in their internal affairs, as it did repeatedly in the

Caribbean. The Latin American states viewed the OAS as an instrument to "subject U.S. hegemony to an institutional discipline," more than as a mechanism to resolve their many border and other disputes through peaceful mediation.[49]

Thus, the indivisibility-of-peace principle failed internally, and it also failed its only serious external test during the Falklands (Malvinas) dispute between Britain and Argentina in 1982. Argentina claimed sovereignty over the islands and attacked the British forces there. Its fellow Latin American states supported Argentina's claim to the islands and pushed a resolution through the OAS Council to that effect. Three days later, however, the United States totally ignored the OAS resolution: it threw its backing to Britain, declared an economic boycott of Argentina, and gave limited military assistance to the British. America's loyalty to its British ally, and its belief that Argentina was the aggressor, overrode its support for the principle of hemispheric collective security.[50] Thus, in the one war since 1947 in which a Latin American state fought a non-regional power, divergence in national interests—the bane of collective security organizations—shattered OAS solidarity.

Finally, the Rio-OAS system failed in a fourth requirement of regional collective security: that there be no military hegemon. To the extent that the Rio-OAS system deterred other external attacks, it was American power that prevented them. During the Cold War, no state was in a position to challenge the United States in Latin America other than the Soviet Union, and it was deterred from doing so by American power and by the fear of nuclear war in a direct military confrontation with the United States. Just as the United States refrained from overtly intervening militarily in Eastern Europe during the Cold War, so, too, did the Soviet Union refrain in the Western Hemisphere; the one exception was the Cuban Missile Crisis, and that was resolved in America's favor. Thus, the states of the Caribbean and South America owed their security from attack by an external power to America's might, not to the Rio-OAS system per se.

In sum, the Rio-OAS system does not have the characteristics of regional collective security: indivisibility of peace, equitable sharing of burdens, or widespread trust. In addition, because America's military power dwarfs that of all others in the hemisphere, it is the United States that has largely provided whatever degree of security the other states have enjoyed. Thus, the Rio-OAS system is a great-power security sphere of influence, not a genuine regional collective security system.

The NATO Alliance
The other regional organization that comes closest to looking like collective security is the NATO alliance. NATO differs from Rio in two important respects: first, no distinction is made between internal and external attack

in NATO's treaty terms; second, NATO has been more successful than the Rio-OAS system in preventing war among its members.

The 1949 Washington Treaty that created NATO was consciously modeled on the Rio Treaty, with an important difference.[51] Article 3 of the Rio Treaty had stated that each member state would consider an armed attack against one to be "an attack against all American states," and then, together with Article 7, specified that this guarantee included both internal and external attacks against any member. NATO's Article 5 guarantee omitted Rio's explicit specification that both internal and external attack were covered. Article 5 simply reads: "an armed attack against one or more of [the signatories] in Europe or North America shall be considered an attack against them all." The omission of the additional specification was deliberate, to satisfy competing political needs.

In formulating the Washington Treaty, the Truman administration found itself subject to these conflicting pressures: French, and to an extent British, concerns about a revived and aggressive West Germany; American and Western European concerns about the increasing threat from the Soviet Union; and the need to obtain the voluntary participation of the West Germans in the brewing conflict with the Soviet Union. The French were adamant that their security concerns over a revived Germany be met before they would sign on to the NATO alliance. The United States, however, was concerned that if the alliance were formally directed against one of its own members, this would make the task of enlisting West German assistance in the economic revival and military rearmament of Western Europe difficult, and would threaten the united front against the emerging Soviet threat. It was concerned not to imply that Germany was both a potential enemy and a newfound ally. The solution was to leave Article 5 unspecific as to the location from which an attack might come. However, it was clearly understood by all that Article 5 guaranteed Western Europe against both Soviet attack and a revival of German militarism.

The other difference between the two treaty systems is that Western Europe experienced no internal war: it was more peaceful than Latin America. A number of factors were responsible: a large number of American troops were in West Germany in a semi-permanent occupation status; the Western Europeans were determined to banish war from their midst; all of the Western European members of NATO were democracies; the borders among the Western European states were fairly settled; and, most important during the Cold War, the intensity and close proximity of the Soviet threat forced a high degree of cooperation among the West Europeans. NATO was better at internal collective security than Rio, and has produced the clearest collective security–type results of any alliance in modern history.

NATO and Rio differ in some respects, but they are alike in others. Under the NATO alliance, just like the Rio-OAS system, states retained national control over the use of force, although this was stated less explicitly in the Washington treaty. Its phrases—"each . . . will assist the Party or Parties so attacked . . . with such action as it deems necessary" (Article 5), and "its provisions [shall] be carried out by the Parties in accordance with their respective constitutional processes" (Article 11)—were code words for retention of national control over the use of force. The Europeans were unhappy about these qualifications, because they rendered Article 5 something less than an automatic guarantee of military assistance. Such a guarantee had been incorporated in the Brussels Treaty (the anti-German alliance that France, Germany, and the Benelux countries had signed in 1948),[52] and the Europeans pushed hard for the same automatic guarantee in the Washington Treaty, but the Truman administration could not get it through the Congress, which refused to give up its constitutional right to declare war. The result was inclusion of those qualifying phrases, especially the reference to "respective constitutional processes." Ultimately, it was the stationing of 300,000 American troops in Europe throughout the Cold War that came to be the functional substitute for the automatic guarantee, as Secretary of State George Marshall predicted in 1948: "The French are secure against Germany as long as [the] occupation [of Germany] continues. . . . The logical conclusion is that three power occupation [by Britain, France, and the United States] may be of unforeseeable and indefinite duration."[53]

The other similarity between the two treaty systems is that both are security manifestations of an American sphere of influence. In its early years, NATO met the first test of regional collective security—indivisibility of peace—but not the next three. As it matured, it also came close to meeting, although has never fully met, the second test, that of sharing the burden, because the United States has always carried a disproportionate share of the defense burden. It came closest to meeting the third requirement, that of widespread trust, although there is still today residual concern about the power of a united Germany if it were unfettered by the European Union and NATO. NATO has not yet met the fourth test—no military hegemon—because the United States continues to dominate the alliance militarily. As a consequence, NATO remains the closest thing the modern world has seen to regional collective security, but it still falls short in one important respect, and therefore remains suspended somewhere closer to an American-run military sphere of influence than to a genuine regional collective security organization.

Is There a Future for Regional Collective Security?
There has not yet been a freestanding, authentic regional collective security system in modern times, and perhaps there never has been one. The two organizations that have come closest to it, Rio and NATO, have been, in reality, American-dominated collective defense alliances in American

spheres of influence; only NATO has produced clear collective security–type results. Moreover, collective security is unworkable for most regions of the world today because the political barriers to implementing it are simply too high. The one exception may be Europe, but collective security remains untested there. It is therefore problematic because NATO relies so heavily on American power and leadership. If peace is to be kept in regions of the world of key interest to the United States, regional collective security is not yet the mechanism to do it.

COOPERATIVE SECURITY: INCAPACITATE THE OFFENSE

No discussion of collective security is complete without a brief analysis of its newest manifestation, cooperative security. Advocates of this scheme do not aim to supplant collective security; instead, they seek to supplement it in order to make it work. To that end, cooperative security embodies a set of rigorous arms control measures designed to make military aggression difficult, and a "residual" collective security system to deal with any aggression that the arms control measures fail to prevent. For proponents of cooperative security, arms control is the more important feature because it is the one that makes the entire scheme viable.[54]

The Concept of Cooperative Security

Cooperative security seeks the same goal as collective security: to prevent aggression and war. It therefore employs the same means to deter aggression—the pledge of all states to punish any one of them that begins a war. To this deterrent pledge, however, cooperative security adds one additional ingredient: it seeks to render offensive military campaigns technically difficult to carry out. Ideally, it makes them impossible.[55]

In order to neutralize the offensive military capabilities of states, a fully implemented cooperative security regime would severely restrict conventional ground forces and tactical air assets useful for offensive thrusts, eliminate chemical and biological weapons, and relegate nuclear weapons to "background deterrent functions only." In addition, transparency in interstate military relations would be pursued: every military establishment would be fully informed about the composition, capabilities, operations, and future activities of every other military establishment. All of these arrangements would be consensually arrived at, not imposed by the threat or use of force, and would, as a consequence, have both wide acceptance and great effect. Through all these measures, cooperative security shifts the effort to prevent aggression and war "from preparing to counter threats to preventing such threats from arising—from deterring aggression to making preparation for it more difficult."[56] Finally, because there is always the possibility that one or a few states might defect from this regime, covertly develop offensive forces, and then attack others, cooperative security keeps in place a "residual" collective security system.

These elements—the arms control measures and the deterrent pledge—are synergistic, claim the proponents. The punish-the-aggressor guarantee is easier to convey and easier to underwrite than under the traditional collective security format because it is less likely to be needed when offensive military postures have been eradicated.[57] In turn, states are more willing to forgo offensive military postures because they will be protected by the punish-the-aggressor pledge if one of them defects. Cooperative security thus represents a more refined version of collective security. It grafts tough arms restrictions, consensually arrived at and institutionally monitored, onto the older notion of collective security.

The Assessment of Cooperative Security

Cooperative security is not a viable grand strategy. First, as its authors themselves admit, cooperative security is a long way from realization and probably will never be fully achieved. It therefore serves more as a beacon for the direction in which states should go than as an arrangement capable of implementation.

Second, cooperative security embodies a fundamental contradiction that its proponents do not acknowledge. The configuration of every state's military forces for defense is not compatible with the system's requirement for residual collective security. As its authors point out, "an integral part of any cooperative security regime must be the capability to organize multinational forces to defeat aggression should it occur."[58] This requires, in their words, "a reconnaissance strike complex," which means the military capability to find the aggressor's forces and destroy them. This is, however, also the ability to wage highly destructive offensive operations. If every state designed its forces only for defense, it is not clear how they would muster the capability to wage the necessary offensive operations to punish an aggressor. How can defensively designed forces be reconciled with offensively mandated punishment?

The answer offered by cooperative security proponents is that not all states will design their military forces only for defense. Some—Russia, France, Germany, Britain, and the United States—must retain offensive capabilities so as to constitute the reconnaissance strike force. The primary role in this force is reserved for the United States:

> In any multinational military force organized around a reconnaissance
> strike complex, the United States military would have a special role to play.
> It would provide most of the airlift required to quickly transport coalition
> military forces to the theater; it would provide most of the tactical
> intelligence data required to support the precision strike weapons; and it

would supply most of the stealth aircraft used to suppress enemy air
defenses. . . . In this view of cooperative security, the special military
capability of the United States would be used to give coalition forces an
advantage that insured a military victory . . . [and that] provided maximum
deterrent to any potential aggressor.[59]

In this cooperative security scheme, therefore, the United States remains
the keystone. It possesses the bulk of the offensive power and the special military capabilities required for the strike force to make punishment feasible
and the entire scheme workable. Other states must willingly accept America's
overwhelming military superiority. In return, the United States must be prepared to organize the other great powers and to use its global military reach
on behalf of the world community. In this light, cooperative security is a front
to justify the maintenance and exercise of America's global military preeminence. As such, it is neither real collective security nor is it likely to be
acceptable to other states.

Third, cooperative security would require a level of military cooperation
among states never yet achieved. The great powers would have to cooperate
in a condominium to impose peace on any aggressors, including not just
lesser powers, but potentially another great power. The lesser powers must
agree to forgo offensive military forces in return for this protection. Would
the great powers agree to punish one of their own? They never did in the
past, because collective security is a system that the great powers run to suit
their own interests. Would the lesser powers believe that the great powers
will together use their offensive forces when required to protect them?
Under the previous two attempts at collective security, the great powers never
reliably did so. Experience thus raises the legitimate fear of abandonment
among the lesser powers that is inherent in any collective security scheme.
Would the lesser states willingly join a system in which the great powers, led
by the United States, are the only ones permitted to retain "national defense
forces larger than needed for territorial [homeland] defense"? Under-
standably, the lesser powers would fear the potential for domination inherent in such an arrangement.[60] Political solutions that would provide
adequately for the punishment of a great power and salve the lesser powers'
fears of abandonment and domination are not obvious, but the cooperation
demanded by cooperative security means they are necessary. The proponents of cooperative security provide no ready-made solutions, because, to
their credit, they know they cannot.

Finally, cooperative security requires that defensive military forces be
clearly distinguishable from offensive forces. In past efforts at arms control,
this distinction has never been easy to draw; weapons per se are neither
defensive nor offensive. Tanks can be used for blitzkrieg-type strategies to
achieve rapid offensive gains, but they can also be employed to break up such

campaigns. The same goes for tactical aircraft, artillery, intelligence, and so forth. Yet cooperative security demands that the distinction be made because it seeks to neutralize the offensive forces of all states except the great powers. In practice, past attempts at arms control have forgone the distinction between offense and defense and instead have tried to constrain offensive power by limiting the number of weapons that states can have, often by equalizing them, and by limiting where they can be put.[61] If any such cooperative scheme to limit offensive power followed this route, it would only formalize by treaty, and thereby highlight, the disparity between the military forces allowed to the great powers and those allowed the lesser powers. This would inevitably raise the latter's fears of abandonment and domination.

These problems might suggest that cooperative security lacks all merit, but to conclude that would be a mistake. Cooperative security captures several features of potentially great value to a strategy of selective engagement. Properly conceived, transparency in military forces is advantageous to the United States. It is one of the important functions of NATO and the U.S.-Japanese alliance. Through these two alliances, the United States has a clear window into the military capabilities of Germany, Britain, France, and Japan. Building more transparent military relations with Russia, as the United States is trying to do with the NATO-Russia Council (NRC), and with China, for which there is not yet an institutional forum, would promote transparency among all the great powers. To the extent that tensions arise from ignorance and misperceptions about other states' military forces, transparency can help defuse them. Transparency in military relations cannot resolve all of the political conflicts between states, but it can ameliorate them and make them safer.

Two of the goals of cooperative security—abolishing chemical and biological weapons and limiting the spread of nuclear weapons—are clearly advantageous to the United States. These steps enhance the chances that such weapons will be kept out of the hands of terrorists and rogue states, for the reasons described in Chapter 2. This directly contributes to America's homeland security; by preventing other states from compensating for America's conventional superiority with these unconventional means, it also helps preserve America's global military reach. Much the same can be said for conventional arms control measures. If they succeed in limiting the size of the military forces of all states, that makes America's military edge less expensive to maintain. Finally, to the extent that other states willingly accept America's military superiority and to the extent that it can enlist the other great powers in enforcement when it decides to act, the United States clearly benefits. It will have less work to maintain its military edge, and it will be able to distribute the burdens of enforcement more widely.

In sum, although cooperative security is not attainable in its ideal form, elements of it, even if only partially attained, would clearly benefit the United States.

CONTAINMENT: HOLD THE LINE

Like collective security, containment aims to prevent territorial conquest by an aggressor state. Unlike collective security, which is directed at any potential aggressor, containment is directed at a specific potential aggressor. Containment requires collective defense, which is another name for an alliance: a pooling of efforts by states to deter, defend against, or defeat a common foe.[62]

Types of Containment

Containment can vary along two dimensions: geographic scope and degree of severity. Containment can be directed at an aspiring global hegemon or at would-be regional ones; it can aim to stalemate an aggressor state or it can attempt to weaken it so as to contain it with less effort. Whatever the scope and severity of its effort, a state that pursues containment far from its own borders must deploy its military power forward to the area where containment is to take place. Neither the state to be contained, nor those whose cooperation is necessary for the effort to be successful, will do what is expected of them if the lead state is militarily absent from the scene. This is especially the case for the United States, which is separated from areas of serious military conflict by vast oceans. If the purpose of containment is to prevent aggression and subjugation, not just to reverse them after they have taken place, then forces must be in the theater. In distant areas, America's efforts at containment will be viable only if tangible elements of its military power are visibly in place and ready to go.

Global and Regional

The United States has engaged only once in sustained global containment and just twice in what I call "preventive" global containment. The one state against which the United States applied long-term global containment was the Soviet Union. From 1947 to 1990, American policy was directed against both the growth of Soviet power and communist expansion. (The two were not necessarily the same thing, even though American decision makers usually treated them as such.) Containment of the Soviet Union largely determined America's strategy toward Europe, the Middle East, and East Asia in this period. It significantly shaped, although it did not wholly determine, U.S. policy toward Africa and Latin America. In one way or another, all major American foreign policy decisions for over forty years were affected by its worldwide rivalry with the Soviet Union. America's interventions in World Wars I and II also qualify as global containment efforts, but they are best described as preventive. They were designed to crush Germany before it could dominate Eurasia and then use that continent's resources to extend its sway overseas. Preventive containment was all-consuming but short-lived; sustained containment was intense and lengthy.[63]

Since 1947, the United States has also engaged in regional containment, but much of the time this was a by-product of its global anti-Soviet and anti-communist policy. The United States held a line against North Korea in northeast Asia; against China vis-à-vis Taiwan; against Cuba in Latin America; and against Nicaragua in Central America. It tried, unsuccessfully, to contain North Vietnam in southeast Asia. Since the early 1980s, the United States has also engaged in regional containment efforts not tied to global containment. Out of concern for access to Persian Gulf oil, the United States has sought to contain both Iraq and Iran in the Persian Gulf; out of a desire to prevent war on the Korean peninsula, it has continued to protect South Korea against North Korea; and as part of its anti-terrorist policy, it practiced containment against Libya in North Africa.

If the United States were once again to undertake worldwide containment, it would do so only against a state that had the wherewithal to challenge it globally. At present and for the next several decades, there is no state that can do this. What would a state that challenged the United States for global preeminence need? Consider the reasons for America's global preeminence: its continental size, its large and skilled population, its sophisticated industrial and technological base, its large economy, its wealth of raw materials, its abundant energy supplies, its ideological appeal, its financial markets, and its global military reach. In the next few decades, no great powers will be well positioned along these dimensions.

Germany and Japan have been touted as America's next global challengers. Each nation does have the necessary technological, industrial, and financial base to challenge the United States economically, and both could build credible nuclear forces to deter an American attack, but neither has the raw material base nor secure energy supplies to sustain itself economically in a contest that turned military. Both lack sufficient population to build a conventional force that could rival or defeat America's. Should either turn nasty and re-arm, Germany and Japan could present severe military challenges to the United States, but they would be regional, not global, in scope.

Within the next few decades, only two states have the resource base, broadly conceived, to mount a global economic-military challenge to America's preeminence: Russia and China. Both are rich enough in raw materials, population, and entrepreneurial skill to fashion considerable economic and military power if they chose. For different reasons, neither is currently well placed to do so, but each could be in a matter of a few decades. For Russia to mount such a challenge, it would have to restructure and grow its economy, and then repair and increase the size of its military. China would require continued rapid growth of its economy and the diversion of a significant chunk of it into offensive military power, which would have to be modernized. For both states, however, economic growth, military buildup, and political restructuring will be long processes.

Thus, for the next several decades, any American-led containment policies will be regional, not global, in their focus. Any regional containment
would be directed at a state that threatened important American interests in
a specific area, but that offered little or no threat beyond it. Were the United
States to engage in future regional containment efforts, the most likely
targets would be as follows: against Russian attempts to re-establish hegemony in Central Europe; German attempts to establish hegemony in Central
and Western Europe; Japan's attempts to do so in East Asia; China's, in East
and Southeast Asia; and either Iraq's or Iran's in the Persian Gulf. At present,
only China, Iraq, and Iran seek political-military hegemony in their regions,
but none has the military wherewithal to seize it. Although nearly every
region has its would-be hegemon—in addition to the above, they include
India in South Asia, Indonesia in Southeast Asia, Nigeria in Central Africa,
Brazil in South America—not all regions are of equal import to the United
States. Were the United States to apply regional containment everywhere, it
would, in effect, be engaged in a containment effort of global proportion,
even though it would not be directing its efforts against one state. For this
reason, the United States must apply regional containment discriminately.

Simple and Compound
Geographic scope is not the only dimension along which containment can
vary; also important is the severity with which it is applied. Simple containment aims to prevent an aggressor state from expanding its territorial and
political sway, and uses whatever political-military means are necessary to
hold the line against expansion. These include political suasion, waging war,
military alliances, or deployment of troops in the areas to be protected from
aggression. Thus, simple containment involves only military stalemate. In
contrast, what I call "compound containment" involves both military stalemate and economic denial to weaken the aggressor state. It seeks to prevent
an adversary from acquiring, through trade or stealth, the wherewithal that
would enable it to resist containment. For a state trying to hold the line,
compound containment is more attractive than simple containment: it
promises to achieve the same objective with fewer resources, because a weakened state is easier to contain. The practice of economic denial is especially
attractive when a state holds the line over a lengthy period, because denial
promises to save considerable resources.

Economic denial may seek to limit how strong the aggressor can grow, or
it may actually try to reduce the adversary's power. Both require measures
that interfere with the targeted state's trade; such measures can range from
highly focused embargoes on selected strategic goods to full-scale economic
warfare. The ultimate purpose of economic denial, then, is to weaken the
state militarily, either directly, by denying it access to advanced technology
and arms, or indirectly, by weakening the overall ability of its economy to

generate and sustain its military power. Following Michael Mastanduno's sensible distinction, the direct approach is termed "strategic embargo"; the indirect approach, "economic warfare."[64] The first aims to deny those items that can make a clear, immediate, and direct contribution to the adversary's military power; the second is directed at its entire economy. Because of its advantages, the modern great powers, when they have sought to hold the line, have nearly always practiced compound, not simple, containment. If the opportunity to practice economic denial against an adversary was available, it was usually seized. This has been so in both peace and war.

Examples of economic denial in war abound. During the Napoleonic wars of the early nineteenth century, Napoleon instituted the "continental system" to harm Britain's economy by denying it the trade of the continent; similarly, Britain blockaded the continent, including the areas Napoleon did not control, in order to deny him the goods he needed to wage war. In World War I, Britain instituted an economic blockade against Germany that made food scarce and German diets lean, while Germany's U-boat (submarine) warfare nearly knocked England out of the war by denying it food for its population and raw materials for its military forces. In World War II, the United States won the war in the Pacific against Japan with a naval blockade of the home islands that crippled the ability of Japan's industry to resupply its armed forces. Japan simply ran out of food, fuel, and military hardware. Similarly in Europe, the allies worked hard to deny Germany the critical raw materials it needed to sustain its war effort.[65]

Since 1945, the United States has applied the strategy of compound containment against nine nations over a sustained period: the Soviet Union, China, North Korea, North Vietnam, Iran, Iraq, Cuba, Nicaragua, and Libya.[66] Against four of these states—China, North Korea, North Vietnam, and Iraq—the United States waged war, and then followed a strategy of economic denial. Against the others, it employed some force short of all-out war, as well as economic denial. Compound containment was therefore both a peacetime and a wartime event. In every instance, the United States combined military measures with economic denial so as to weaken each of these states and to prevent, stop, or roll back its expansion.

In both peace and war, then, the modern great powers have always combined economic denial with military measures when they have sought to contain an adversary's expansion. Any future containment efforts by the United States will most likely be compound.

The Record of Containment by Economic Warfare and Strategic Embargo

How efficacious will future containment efforts be? Because they will bear some resemblance to those past, it is useful to assess how well America's previous efforts at economic warfare and strategic embargo have worked.

Economic Warfare

America's economic warfare inflicted damage on the economies of targeted states, but the extent of the damage and its ultimate effects varied considerably. The best data comes from the estimates provided by Hufbauer and his associates. For our purposes, their most useful figure is the annual cost of sanctions to the targeted state's GNP, which they calculate in terms of the annual percentage welfare loss.[67] They calculate welfare losses at: little or no loss for Iran (1984–1990); 0.1 percent of GNP for the Soviet Union for the 1950–1969 period and 0.2 percent for the 1970–1987 period; 0.5 percent for China (1949–1970); 1.2 percent for North Korea (1950–1990); 1.3 for Libya (1981–1990); 3.1 percent for North Vietnam (1955–1989); 3.2 percent for Nicaragua (1981–1990); 4.4 percent for Cuba (1960–1990); and 48 percent for Iraq (in 1990).[68]

The economies of the Soviet Union, China, North Korea, North Vietnam, Nicaragua, and Cuba suffered from America's sanctions, but these six were also command economies that proved poor at generating technological advances and productivity improvements and at achieving efficiency in their consumer sectors. The economic suffering they experienced during the Cold War, therefore, was due as much, if not more, to their own poorly structured economic systems as it was to America's economic warfare against them.

Of the nine states, the larger ones suffered less than the smaller ones, but the smaller ones (apart from Iraq) suffered less than they might otherwise have. The Soviet Union and China were minimally affected by economic warfare because, as large economies, they were less dependent on foreign trade and therefore less subject to external economic manipulation than a smaller economy. Even the smaller economies, however, suffered less than they might have, because the Soviets and the Chinese partly bailed them out. They were able to ride out America's sanctions by obtaining aid from their large communist patrons. (The disastrous decline of the Cuban and North Korean economies after Soviet-Chinese help was withdrawn illustrated the extent of their dependence.)

Two states—Iran and Libya—suffered little from America's sanctions mainly because other states did not go along with them. The Europeans, in particular, continued to buy oil and other goods from Iran and low-sulfur oil from Libya. Two of the states that suffered badly from economic warfare—Nicaragua and Iraq—did so because of the heavy use of military power that accompanied the sanctions imposed on them. By 1990, Nicaragua's economy, after nine years of sanctions, was a shambles, but Hufbauer and associates say that this was due more to the costs and disruption caused by the Contra war against the Sandinista government than to the U.S. sanctions.[69] (Of course, the United States also trained, armed, and funded the Contras.) Of the nine sanctions targets, Iraq suffered the most from economic warfare because two special conditions made it disastrously effective. Iraq is a "one-crop" export economy, and the exports of that "crop"—oil—were easy to blockade; one port and two pipelines are the prime outlets. Both before and after its war against Iraq, the United States used its navy to blockade Iraq's one port and obtained the cooperation of Turkey and Saudi Arabia to close their pipelines to Iraqi oil. Had military force not been used in both cases, America's economic warfare would have been much less effective.

The evidence on economic warfare is therefore mixed. It did not significantly weaken eight of the targeted states, although it exacted welfare losses from them. In five cases (Iran, the Soviet Union, China, North Korea, and Libya), the loss was minimal (less than 1.5 percent); in three cases (North Vietnam, Nicaragua, and Cuba), it was moderate (3–5 percent); and in only one case, that of Iraq, was the loss heavy (nearly half). The evidence demonstrates that the successful pursuit of economic warfare against entire economies is a demanding task, easily subverted by the actions of other states. Against large economies, it is especially ineffective, as Michael Mastanduno concluded after carefully analyzing the effects of American-led economic warfare on the Soviet economy for the entire Cold War period: "With the possible exception of the early 1950s, CoCom [the Coordinating Committee that organized the sanctions] was ineffective at retarding the economic growth of the Soviet Union or the amount of resources it devoted to military pursuits. As U.S. officials conceded in the early 1960s, after 1954, unilateral U.S. controls could do little to impede Soviet economic growth and development."[70] Only in the Iraqi case can the argument be made that great harm was done by economic warfare, but Iraq is the exception that proves the rule. Here economic warfare succeeded because all of the requisite conditions were satisfied: the sanctions were applied totally and all at once; they were observed by all the key states; vital exports and imports were relatively easy to cut off; sanctions were combined with, and enforced by, considerable military power; and they were applied for long enough to have their effect. Even in the Iraqi case, however, the sanctions regime began to crumble at the end of the 1990s, because some of its neighbors no longer observed the sanctions regime. Iraq began sending oil by tanker trucks to Turkey and by pipeline and rail to Syria, which enabled Syria to export its own oil. Moreover, throughout the entire period of the sanctions regime, Iraq succeeded in smuggling oil out of its borders. Although the sanctions regime against Iraq was highly effective at the beginning of the decade, by the end it leaked like a sieve.[71]

In sum, under the proper conditions economic warfare can inflict harsh results, as the Iraqi case demonstrates, but even in such instances, it is difficult to sustain for long periods, as the Iraqi case also demonstrates. More often than not, the requisite conditions for highly effective economic warfare will not be present; as a consequence, it will produce only weak to moderate effects, as in the other eight cases.

Strategic Embargo

For strategic embargoes, we have full data only on the Soviet case and some data on the Iraqi case; consequently, our assessment must be more tentative.[72]

Mastanduno best summarizes the consensus on the Soviet case. Broad economic warfare against the Soviet economy did not work because America's European allies would not accept it, but they did cooperate in a more focused and narrower embargo of advanced technology that had military applications. The narrower the list of items to be embargoed, the more successful the embargo. As a consequence, Mastanduno notes, "CoCom controls played a far more important role where the strategic embargo was concerned: they helped in maintaining U.S. lead time and in preventing the Soviet Union from attaining technological parity in military systems."[73] To the extent that the United States and its allies fielded weapons more advanced than those of the Soviets, the West could compensate for its deficiencies in quantity with an edge in quality. The burden of containing the Soviet Union was less than it might otherwise have been had the strategic embargo not enabled the West to maintain its qualitative edge over the Soviet Union. The embargo had success only with conventional weapons, however; it had no effect on the Soviets' chemical, biological, or nuclear weapons programs, which were quite extensive and sophisticated. Thus, the Soviet case is one of a reasonably successful but fairly narrow strategic embargo.

The strategic embargo against Iraq was embedded in full-scale economic warfare against that country, exercised through total economic blockade, backed up by military force and seizure of overseas assets. Denial of military equipment and technology was one of the allied coalition's central objectives in continuing with sanctions after Iraq's 1991 defeat. The coalition wanted to prevent Saddam Hussein from rebuilding his military machine. It is therefore valid to consider how well a total strategic embargo on military imports worked in this instance.

At first glance, the evidence appears contradictory. In 1993, one assessment argued that Iraq had succeeded in rebuilding many of its weapons plants, had resumed production of a wide range of conventional weaponry, and had put back into service most of the tanks, artillery, and combat aircraft damaged during the war, despite three years of a total embargo that was the most effective against any nation since 1945.[74] In 1995, however, another assessment was more positive about the effects of sanctions:

> While Iraq has rebuilt and repaired some of its prewar military machine, much of this has been due to cannibalization of existing equipment and drawing on inventories of spare parts left over from the Iran-Iraq war.

117

Sanctions have had a serious effect in degrading Iraq's military by preventing replacement of obsolescent equipment and in purchasing spare parts. Tanks frequently break down. Mobility has been hard hit since tires are one of the scarcest items in Iraq today. . . . Economic sanctions have severely hampered Iraq's industry, including its military industry, which has been repaired, but cannot function without spare parts.[75]

Both assessments are, to some extent, correct. Before the war, Iraq had stockpiled weapons and had probably stashed funds overseas in secret accounts.[76] Two months before the war, it had worked around the clock to move its manufacturing production equipment and store it underground. After the war, it kept intact its clandestine military procurement network and financed it through sales of oil (allegedly through a $5.2 billion fund set up in Jordan), and whatever other secret overseas funds it had access to.[77] Thus even in the face of sanctions, Iraq was able to rebuild its military machine to a degree. Two years of sanctions were not enough to run down the stockpiles and the funds, but, as it turned out, four years were. Ultimately, therefore, the embargo worked, but it took four years, not two, to produce its full effects on Iraq's conventional military forces. Moreover, as long the strategic embargo was effectively maintained, it limited how much Saddam could rebuild his conventional military forces.

Conventional weapons were not the only target of the strategic embargo; chemical, biological, and especially nuclear weapons were also targeted. For these weapons, the strategic embargo was much less effective, although not totally ineffective. The United Nations weapons inspectors destroyed large stocks of chemical weapons between 1991 and 1998, but were less successful with biological weapons. Once the inspectors left Iraq at the end of 1998, it was able to reconstitute its chemical and biological weapons programs; by the fall of 2002, according to both British and American intelligence sources, Iraq had a "usable chemical and biological weapons capability."[78] Sanctions may have retarded both programs, but they could not prevent Iraq from reconstituting them because of their dual-use nature: an advanced civilian chemical and biological industry can be converted to weapons production. George Tenet, director of the Central Intelligence Agency, testified in March 2002 that: "Baghdad is expanding its civilian chemical industry in ways that could be quickly diverted to CW [chemical weapons] programs."[79] Sanctions have been more successful with respect to Iraq's nuclear weapons program. By the time its inspectors left, the International Atomic Energy Agency (IAEA) concluded that it had dismantled Iraq's physical infrastructure to produce nuclear weapons and that it had removed all known fissile material from the country. (The IAEA could not verify with complete certainty that Iraq had no fissile material because there may have been some hidden and not found.) [80] Although Saddam was working hard to acquire both fissile material and the technology to produce it, the British government concluded in the fall of 2002 that: "UN sanctions on Iraq were hindering the import of crucial goods for the production of fissile material. The JIC [the British government's Joint Intelligence Committee] judged that while sanctions remain effective Iraq would not be able to produce a nuclear weapon."[81]

Based on the Soviet and Iraqi cases, we can conclude that: strategic embargoes work better against smaller powers than against big ones; that they can retard, to a degree, the technological advancement of a state's conventional military capability; that they can be expected to have little effect on retarding the development of chemical and biological weapons for advanced industrial states, no matter what their size; and that, if effective, they can prevent a non-nuclear state from acquiring the fissile material and the advanced technology necessary to produce fissile material. Strategic embargoes are not a panacea. They may work for certain types of weapons programs, but they require demanding conditions if they are to be effective.

The Uses of Compound Containment

America's experience with compound containment provides several useful guidelines for future efforts. First, containment appears better at thwarting a state's expansion than at changing the nature of its government. In only one case, that of the Soviet Union, could the United States unequivocally claim that its containment efforts contributed to altering the form of government, and that effort took forty-three years of sustained and expensive effort.[82] Although in Nicaragua it looked as if the United States were successful at changing the nature of the government, this was due more to the Sandinistas' miscalculation of their popularity at the polls than to U.S. overthrow. Had the Sandinistas predicted more accurately the results of the elections, they would never have agreed to hold them, and they might still be in power today.[83] In the remaining cases of China, North Korea, North Vietnam, Iran, Iraq, Libya, and Cuba, compound containment appears to have had little effect on the nature of the regimes, or, if it did work to some degree, it did so very, very slowly. In this regard the record of compound containment parallels the experience with economic sanctions: the less ambitious the goal, the more successful the sanctions.[84] With measures short of forcible overthrow, alteration of a regime's foreign policy is easier than changing the regime itself.

A second lesson suggests that the United States should forgo economic warfare against large states, and should only apply it to smaller states when the conditions for its success are present.[85] It will also work better when backed up by military power, as Hufbauer's data demonstrates and as Robert Pape has documented.[86] The Iraqi case is the most dramatic example of the effective use of sanctions backed up by military force.

Finally, if the United States employs strategic embargoes, it must discriminate in applying them between great powers and smaller ones, and between broad-based and highly selective embargoes. Against a great power, a full-scale strategic embargo is unlikely to work because the requisite cooperation from other states is not likely to be forthcoming. Especially if the great power is growing fast, like China, other states will not want to hurt themselves economically by imposing extensive restrictions on their exports. A broad strategic embargo has a better chance of working against a smaller power because it represents a smaller market, but even here, broad strategic embargoes cannot be maintained indefinitely. Broad embargoes, as in the Iraqi case, should be viewed as exceptions; more selective embargoes, like the Soviet case, should be seen as the norm. All other things being equal, the longer the selective embargo is to be maintained, the more narrowly it should be cast in order to maintain the required cooperation of other states.

CONCLUSION

In sum, of the five grand strategies examined in this chapter, only containment is viable, but since it must be done regionally, not globally, it can be part of a broader strategy of selective engagement. Dominion is beyond America's reach; global collective security is a chimera; cooperative security is a disguised great-power condominium that smaller powers will not accept; and regional collective security requires a set of conditions that may be applicable only in Europe, and perhaps not even there. Thus, there are only three serious contenders for an American grand strategy: selective engagement, isolationism, and offshore balancing. These are the subjects of the next two chapters.

FOUR

Selective Engagement

Selective engagement is the grand strategy I advocate, and in this chapter I explain why. Selective engagement steers a middle course between an overly restrictive and an overly expansive definition of America's interests. It allocates America's political attention and material resources first to the interests defined as vital and highly important, but it holds out hope that the important interests can also be realized at least in part. Selective engagement sets the United States on a path different from those that it pursued during both its long isolationist period and the Cold War era. In the isolationist phase, the United States did not have a policy of peacetime military engagement because it had no binding military commitments to other states. During its Cold War phase, it pursued a policy of overly extensive military engagement because it had too many commitments. Selective engagement aims to strike a balance between those two past extremes. It continues the internationalist path the United States has followed since 1945, but it does so with important modifications, as I explain in this chapter.

Six features define the strategy of selective engagement. First, it is a hybrid strategy because it combines the best features of the other grand strategies. Second, it posits a set of fundamental goals that best serve the United States in the current era. Third, it concentrates America's political-military resources on those regions of most consequence to the United States. Fourth, it maintains a forward-based defense posture that brings great peacetime benefits to the country. Fifth, it prescribes a set of judicious rules for when to wage war, and sixth, it calls for American leadership.

I discuss each of these features in turn, giving particular attention to the strategy's regional focus, its forward military posture, and its guidelines for the use of force. I then analyze the potential pitfalls of selective engagement and offer some principles for avoiding them. In Chapter 5, I discuss the other two feasible grand strategies—what I call the "free hand strategies," isolationism and offshore balancing—and then compare both to selective engagement in Chapter 6, before outlining the implications of the selective engagement strategy in Chapter 7.

HYBRID NATURE OF SELECTIVE ENGAGEMENT

Selective engagement is a hybrid strategy. By definition, a hybrid mixes different things, and the mixture is superior to the pure elements from which it is drawn. Selective engagement borrows the good features from its competitors and seeks to avoid their pitfalls and excesses.

Selective engagement borrows from the other strategies as follows. Like isolationism and offshore balancing, selective engagement understands the risks of military entanglement overseas, but unlike them, it accepts some entanglements because they lower the chances of war or because they are necessary to protect American interests even at the risk and cost of war. Like collective security, selective engagement is based on the assumption that U.S. military operations should be multilateral rather than unilateral wherever possible to spread the burdens and risks, and that standing alliances make such operations easier to organize and more likely to succeed when undertaken. Unlike collective security, however, it does not rely on an assumption that peace is indivisible. Like regional containment, selective engagement is based on the understanding that balancing against an aspiring regional hegemon requires sustained cooperation of the other powers in the area and that such cooperation cannot be sustained without a visible American military presence. Like dominion, selective engagement makes use of the power and the influence that military primacy brings, but unlike dominion, it does not seek to dictate to others. Like cooperative security, selective engagement seeks transparency in military relations, reductions in armaments, and control over the spread of nuclear, biological, and chemical (NBC) weapons, but unlike cooperative security, it does not put great faith in the reliability of collective security should these aims fail. Thus, by borrowing from the best features of its competitors, selective engagement is careful in using military power but committed to use it; multilateral in practice, but not bound to everyone or committed to do everything; visibly present militarily in regions of concern, but in ways deliberately designed to elicit rather than thwart or dampen the cooperation of other key states; prime in military power, but not so unilateralist in use to create self-defeating counter-coalitions; and cooperative with those states that reciprocate in kind, but tough with those that do not.

Because it incorporates the best features from the alternatives, selective engagement becomes more diversified than any of them. Diversification is valuable in a grand strategy: it provides a method by which to deal with uncertainty. Just as a diversified portfolio in the stock market provides a hedge against adverse changes in any one or even several of a portfolio's components, so, too, does a diversified grand strategy provide a hedge against one or several adverse external developments. Through diversification, selective engagement is more resilient, more adaptable, and more effective than the alternatives.

FUNDAMENTAL GOALS OF SELECTIVE ENGAGEMENT

Selective engagement prescribes for the United States a set of goals adapted to contemporary conditions and to America's benefit. These goals are the national interests articulated in Chapter 3, and selective engagement serves them well.

Selective engagement aims to keep the United States secure and prosperous—classic realist goals—but also goes beyond them to reach for liberal goals as well. It seeks to nudge the world toward the values (or "milieu goals") that the United States holds dear: democracy, free markets, human rights, and international openness. Selective engagement aims not only to do good for the United States, but to do some good for others, too, in the belief that if others benefit in these ways, so, too, does the United States.

REGIONAL CONCENTRATION

Selective engagement focuses America's resources, and particularly its military resources, on those portions of the globe of most significance to the United States. These are the regions with most of America's trade and investments; from which come its crucial energy imports, especially oil; and where the world's other major military powers are located. Outside of the western hemisphere, these regions are Europe, East Asia, and the Persian Gulf. The crucial states within these regions include the world's other great powers—Russia, China, Britain, France, Germany, Italy, Japan—and some middle-ranked and lesser powers, including Canada, Mexico, Brazil, Venezuela, the Netherlands, Iran, Iraq, Saudi Arabia, Kuwait, and South Korea. None of this implies that other regions and states are insignificant for the United States, but with few exceptions (among them Israel, India, Pakistan, Angola, and Nigeria), most of America's major economic interests, energy imports, alliance ties, military power considerations, and historical-cultural ties are concentrated in these three regions of the world.

Concentration of Trade

Some statistics illustrate the point, beginning with trade. Over the last thirty years, exports and imports as a percentage of America's gross domestic product (GDP) have roughly doubled. Throughout most of America's history, the ratio of exports or imports to GDP ran between 3 percent and 5 percent, or 8–10 percent combined. In the last twenty-five years, this ratio has run at 8–10 percent for exports and 10–12 percent for imports, demonstrating America's increased stake in economic openness. In 1997, Jeffrey Garten pointed out that exports supported about 11 million American jobs, and that total trade as a percentage of American GDP went from 11 percent in the early 1970s to 23 percent in the middle 1990s.[1]

TABLE 4.1. U.S. Merchandise Trade by Region, 1950–2000 (percent of U.S. total world trade)

Region/Country	1950	1960	1970	1980	1990	1995	2000
Western Hemisphere	52	41	39	33	33	36	39
Canada	21	19	24	17	20	21	20
Mexico	4	4	4	6	7	8	12
Europe	23	33	32	26	26	22	23
EU	na	18	18	20	21	18	19
Germany	3	6	7	5	5	4	4
U.K.	4	7	6	5	5	4	4
Asia	16	20	24	30	36	39	35
China	1	0	0	1	2	4	6
Japan	3	7	13	11	16	14	11
Africa	5	4	3	9	3	2	2
Other	4	2	3	2	2	1	1

Notes: Figures in Tables 4.1 and 4.2 are total of exports and imports of U.S. trade with a region. Merchandise trade means goods; it excludes services; na means not available.

Source: U.S. Department of Commerce, Bureau of the Census, *Statistical Abstract of the United States* (Washington, D.C.: U.S. Government Printing Office, various dates), Table "U.S. Exports, Imports, and Merchandise Trade Balance."

However, even though the United States trades with every region and nearly every state in the world, its trade is not uniformly distributed across them. Table 4.1 portrays America's total exports and imports by regional share, along with the most important states in each region, for the last fifty years. Table 4.2 presents the same data in dollar terms (data in these two tables are for merchandise trade—goods but not services).

Several key points emerge from these two tables. First, they show that America's merchandise trade has been historically concentrated in three regions: the western hemisphere, especially North America; Europe, especially Western Europe; and Asia, especially East Asia. Within each region, a relatively small number of states accounts for a significant percentage of the region's trade with the United States. In 2000, for example, Canada and Mexico accounted for more than four out of every five dollars of U.S. western hemisphere trade. U.S. trade with Germany and the United Kingdom constituted two-fifths of its trade with the European Union and a third of its trade with Europe. China and Japan accounted for nearly half the U.S. trade with Asia. In 2000, just two states—Canada and Mexico—accounted for almost one-third of America's total merchandise trade. Six states—Canada, Mexico, Germany, the United Kingdom, Japan, and China—accounted for nearly six in ten dollars of that total. Over the 1950–2000 period, America's trade shifted away from the western hemisphere toward Europe and Asia, then back again. By the late 1990s, the western hemisphere had once again resumed the first place it had held until 1980, largely due to Mexico's displacement of Japan as America's number-two trading partner, an effect of the North American Free Trade Agreement (NAFTA).

The concentration of American trade becomes even clearer when only exports of merchandise are considered. Table 4.3 portrays America's merchandise exports by region and by selected states from 1950 through 2000. The western hemisphere has increased in relative importance during the last ten years because of NAFTA, and now takes nearly half of America's total merchandise exports; Canada and Mexico together take more than one-third of them. Table 4.4 shows just how concentrated America's merchandise trade is. In 2000, America's top fifteen trading partners accounted for 77 percent of its total merchandise trade (exports plus imports) and 78 percent of its total merchandise exports. The importance of North America, Europe, and East Asia to American merchandise trade is thus clear.

America's trade in services is similarly concentrated, as Table 4.5 shows.[2] In 1999, for example, over one-third of America's service exports went to Europe; over one-quarter to the western hemisphere; and 16 percent to Japan, Korea, and Taiwan. Europe accounted for two-fifths of America's imports of services; the western hemisphere, over one-fourth; and Japan, Korea, and Taiwan, 14 percent. Service exports are also highly concentrated, although not quite as much. In 1999, just seven states—Japan, Britain, Canada, Germany, Mexico, France, and the Netherlands—accounted for almost half of America's total service exports. America's service trade is concentrated in the same regions as its merchandise trade and in roughly the same states in those regions.[3]

Concentration of Direct Foreign Investment

America's direct foreign investment (DFI) also displays the same concentration in North America, Europe, and East Asia as does its merchandise and service trade, although the DFI rankings by region and state differ somewhat from the trade rankings.[4] Table 4.6 displays the pattern of America's DFI from 1950–2000.[5] As is evident from the table, over this fifty-year period, America's DFI has remained relatively concentrated in three areas: Canada, Latin America, and Europe. (Until 1990, East Asia remained a distant fourth.) During the 1990s, those three areas accounted for 79–83 percent of America's DFI. Europe overtook Canada as the largest recipient of America's DFI in 1970 and has been in first place ever since; Britain is now the largest single host of America's direct foreign investment.[6] America's DFI remains highly concentrated by country, as Table 4.7 demonstrates. Three countries (the United Kingdom, Canada, and the Netherlands) account for 38 percent of America's DFI and the top fifteen countries for 77 percent. America's direct foreign investment is as concentrated as its trade, and with

TABLE 4.2. U.S. Merchandise Trade by Region, 1950–2000 (value in millions of U.S. dollars)

Region/Country	1950 Exports (X) Imports (M) Net (X − M)	1960 Exports Imports Net (X − M)	1970 Exports Imports Net (X − M)	1980 Exports Imports Net (X − M)	1990 Exports Imports Net (X − M)	2000 Exports Imports Net (X − M)
Western Hemisphere	4,813 / 5,063 / −250	7,684 / 6,864 / 820	15,612 / 16,928 / −1,316	74,114 / 78,687 / −4,573	136,713 / 155,648 / −18,935	349,573 / 440,111 / −90,538
Canada	2,000 / 1,960 / 40	3,810 / 2,901 / 909	9,079 / 11,092 / −2,013	35,395 / 41,459 / −6,064	83,674 / 91,380 / −7,706	178,941 / 230,838 / −51,897
Mexico	na / na / na	na / na / na	na / na / na	na / na / na	na / na / na	111,349 / 135,926 / −24,577
Europe	2,989 / 1,449 / 1,540	7,399 / 4,268 / 3,131	14,817 / 11,395 / 3,422	71,372 / 48,039 / 23,333	117,299 / 111,291 / 6,008	190,847 / 267,087 / −76,240
EU	na / na / na	3,974 / 2,263 / 1,711	8,423 / 6,609 / 1,814	54,601 / 36,384 / 18,217	98,130 / 91,876 / 6,254	165,064 / 220,018 / −54,954
Germany	439 / 104 / 335	1,068 / 897 / 171	2,741 / 3,127 / −386	10,960 / 11,693 / −733	18,760 / 28,162 / −9,402	29,448 / 58,513 / −29,065

U.K.	511	1,411	2,536	12,694	23,490	41,570
	335	993	2,194	9,842	20,189	43,345
	176	418	342	2,852	3,301	-1,775
Asia	1,476	4,186	10,027	60,168	120,268	226,197
	1,638	2,721	9,621	80,299	203,237	474,473
	-162	1,465	406	-20,131	-82,969	-248,276
China	37	0	0	3,756	4,806	16,185
	146	0	1	1,059	15,237	100,018
	-109	0	-1	2,697	-10,431	-83,833
Japan	417	1,447	4,652	20,790	48,580	64,924
	182	1,149	5,875	30,714	89,684	146,479
	235	298	-1,223	-9,924	-41,104	-81,555
Africa	368	793	1,580	9,060	7,663	9,545
	494	534	1,113	34,410	15,336	24,154
	-126	259	467	-25,350	-7,673	-14,608
Other	629	514	1,188	6,069	11,649	5,755
	208	267	895	3,436	9,799	12,197
	421	247	293	2,633	1,850	-6,442
World Totals	10,275	20,576	43,224	220,783	393,592	781,917
	8,852	14,654	39,952	244,871	495,311	1,218,022
	1,423	5,922	3,272	-24,088	-101,719	-436,105

Note: na means not available.

Source: U.S. Department of Commerce, Bureau of the Census, *Statistical Abstract of the United States* (Washington, D.C.: U.S. Government Printing Office (GPO), various dates), Table, "U.S. Exports, Imports, and Merchandise Trade Balance."

TABLE 4.3. U.S. Export Markets by Region, 1950–2000 (merchandise trade in millions of U.S. dollars)

Region/Country	1950 Exports	1950 % of Total	1960 Exports	1960 % of Total	1970 Exports	1970 % of Total	1980 Exports	1980 % of Total	1990 Exports	1990 % of Total	2000 Exports	2000 % of Total
Western Hemisphere	4,813	47	7,684	37	15,612	36	74,114	34	136,713	35	349,573	45
Canada	2,000	19	3,810	19	9,079	21	35,395	16	83,674	21	178,941	23
Mexico	512	5	820	4	1,704	4	15,145	7	28,279	7	111,349	14
Europe	2,989	29	7,399	36	14,817	34	71,372	32	117,299	30	190,847	24
EU	na	na	3,974	19	8,423	19	54,601	25	98,130	25	165,064	21
Germany	439	4	1,068	5	2,741	6	10,960	5	18,760	5	29,448	4
U.K.	511	5	1,411	7	2,536	6	12,694	6	23,490	6	41,570	5
Asia	1,476	14	4,186	20	10,027	23	60,168	27	120,268	31	226,197	29
China	37	0	0	0	0	0	3,756	2	4,806	1	16,185	2
Japan	417	4	1,447	7	4,652	11	20,790	9	48,580	12	64,924	8
Africa	368	4	793	4	1,580	4	9,060	4	7,663	2	9,545	1
Other	629	6	514	2	1,188	3	6,069	3	11,649	3	5,755	1
World totals	10,275		20,576		43,224		220,783		393,592		781,917	

Note: na means not available.

Source: U.S. Department of Commerce, Bureau of the Census, *Statistical Abstract of the United States* (Washington, D.C.: U.S. GPO, various dates), Table, "U.S. Exports, Imports, and Merchandise Trade Balance."

TABLE 4.4. America's Top Fifteen Trading Partners, 1980–2000 (merchandise trade)

	1980			1990			2000		
Country (by rank)	% of Total Trade	% of Exports		Country (by rank)	% of Total Trade	% of Exports	Country (by rank)	% of Total Trade	% of Exports
Canada	16.5	16.0		Canada	19.7	21.2	Canada	20.5	22.9
Japan	11.1	9.4		Japan	15.6	12.3	Mexico	12.4	14.2
Mexico	6.0	6.9		Mexico	6.6	7.2	Japan	10.6	8.3
Germany	4.9	5.0		Germany	5.3	4.8	China	5.8	2.1
United Kingdom	4.8	5.7		United Kingdom	4.9	6.0	Germany	4.4	3.8
Saudi Arabia	4.0	2.6		Taiwan	3.8	2.9	United Kingdom	4.2	5.3
France	2.7	3.4		Korea	3.7	3.7	Korea	3.4	3.6
Taiwan	2.4	2.0		France	3.0	3.5	Taiwan	3.2	3.1
Netherlands	2.3	3.9		Italy	2.3	2.0	France	2.5	2.6
Venezuela	2.1	2.1		China	2.3	1.2	Singapore	1.8	2.3
Italy	2.1	2.5		Netherlands	2.0	3.3	Malaysia	1.8	1.4
Korea	1.9	2.1		Singapore	2.0	2.0	Italy	1.8	1.4
Belgium and Luxembourg	1.8	3.0		Hong Kong	1.8	1.7	Netherlands	1.6	2.8
Brazil	1.7	2.0		Belgium and Luxembourg	1.7	2.7	Brazil	1.5	2.0
Hong Kong	1.6	1.2		Saudi Arabia	1.6	1.0	Hong Kong	1.3	1.9
Total of top 15	65.9	67.8			76.3	75.6		76.9	77.6

Source: U.S. Department of Commerce, Bureau of the Census, Statistical Abstract of the United States (Washington, D.C.: U.S. GPO, various dates), Table, "U.S. Exports, Imports, and Merchandise Trade Balance."

TABLE 4.5. U.S. Trade in Services, 1999 (in millions of U.S. dollars)

Region/country	Exports	% of Total Exports	Imports	% of Total Imports	Services Balance of Trade
Europe	96,193	38	72,079	41	24,114
France	9,821	4	8,027	5	1,794
Germany	15,326	6	10,179	6	5,147
Italy	5,300	2	4,743	3	557
Netherlands	8,396	3	3,992	2	4,404
Switzerland	4,708	2	3,670	2	1,038
U.K.	27,224	11	23,750	14	3,474
Latin America and other Western Hemisphere	70,929	28	47,568	27	23,361
Canada	21,134	8	15,222	9	5,912
Brazil	5,494	2	1,765	1	3,729
Mexico	12,544	5	9,783	6	2,761
Venezuela	3,260	1	718	0	2,542
Other countries	81,547	32	53,191	30	28,356
Australia	5,021	2	3,478	2	1,543
Japan	30,498	12	15,692	9	14,806
Korea, Rep. of	5,339	2	4,458	3	881
Taiwan	4,860	2	3,514	2	1,346
International organizations and unallocated	5,997	2	1,986	1	4,011
Total	254,665	100	174,825	100	79,840

Source: U.S. Department of Commerce, Bureau of the Census, *Statistical Abstract of the United States, 2001* (Washington, D.C.: U.S. GPO, 2001), Table No. 1283, "Private Services Transaction, by Type of Service and Country, 1990–99," <http://www.census.gov/prod/2002pubs/01statab/foreign.pdf>.

four exceptions (Bermuda, Brazil, Panama, and Australia), the bulk of its DFI is concentrated in Europe, North America, and East Asia, in that order.

America's trade and foreign investment are highly concentrated for two reasons: proximity and richness. When they are not engaged in military hostilities or protracted conflicts, states generally trade a great deal with, and invest a lot in, those states contiguous to them or close by. States also trade with, and invest in, those states that have the money to buy and the goods or resources to sell. When proximity and richness coincide, as they have since the 1960s for the countries of Western Europe, and much longer for Canada and the United States, trade and investment become even more highly con-

TABLE 4.6. U.S. Direct Foreign Investment (DFI) by Region, 1950–2000 (historical cost in millions of U.S. dollars)

Region/ Country	1950 DFI % of Total	1960 DFI % of Total	1970 DFI % of Total	1980 DFI % of Total	1990 DFI % of Total	1995 DFI % of Total	2000 DFI % of Total
Canada	3,579 30	11,198 34	22,801 29	44,640 21	69,106 16	81,387 11	126,421 10
Europe	1,733 15	6,645 20	24,471 31	95,686 45	213,368 50	363,527 51	648,731 52
Latin America	4,445 38	8,365 26	14,683 19	38,275 18	70,752 17	122,765 17	239,388 19
Africa	287 2	925 3	4,348 6	6,051 3	3,592 1	6,516 1	15,813 1
Middle East	1,001 8	2,315 7	6,631 8	2,281 1	4,007 1	7,982 1	11,851 1
Asia and Pacific	743 6	3,296 10	5,156 7	14,671 7	63,585 15	125,968 18	199,591 16
Japan	19 0	254 1	1,491 2	6,274 3	22,511 5	39,198 6	55,606 4
World	11,788	32,744	78,090	213,468	426,958	711,621	1,244,654

Notes: Data represent the value of the stock of direct foreign investment held in each region, not the flow of investment in any one year. The former Soviet Union is included in Europe. Asia and Pacific includes all of Asia except the Middle Eastern oil countries and Oceania.

Source: U.S. Department of Commerce, Bureau of Economic Analysis, *Survey of Current Business*, "U.S. Direct Investment Abroad: Detail for Historical-Cost Position and Related Capital and Income Flows" (various dates).

centrated.[7] In sum, it should not be surprising that the bulk of America's trade and investment takes place with other rich states, nor that its two neighbors loom especially large.

Some analysts argue that America's trade distribution will change in the future if the largest developing states continue to sustain their recent high growth rates. Jeffrey Garten, for example, argues that America's trade and investment patterns will shift in response to the growth of these fast-developing Third World states. He lists, as "Big Ten" emerging markets, Mexico, Brazil, Argentina, Poland, Turkey, China, South Korea, India, Indonesia, and South Africa. Garten may well be right; however, the first seven of his Big Ten are concentrated in the western hemisphere, Europe, and East Asia. Even if Garten is correct and America's trade patterns change somewhat to take account of these new emerging markets, the shift will decrease only marginally the importance of these three regions to America's trade and investment.[8]

TABLE 4.7. America's Top Fifteen DFI Recipients on a Historical Cost Basis, 1980–2000

Country (by 1980 ranking)	Total DFI Abroad (%)	Country (by 1990 ranking)	Total DFI Abroad (%)	Country (by 2000 ranking)	Total DFI Abroad (%)
Canada	20.9	Canada	17.7	United Kingdom	18.8
United Kingdom	13.2	United Kingdom	16.2	Canada	10.2
Germany	7.2	Germany	6.6	Netherlands	9.3
Switzerland	5.2	Switzerland	5.2	Japan	4.5
Bermuda	5.1	Japan	5.0	Switzerland	4.4
France	4.3	Netherlands	4.9	Bermuda	4.3
Netherlands	3.7	Bermuda	4.8	Germany	4.3
Brazil	3.6	Brazil	3.9	France	3.1
Australia	3.6	France	3.8	Brazil	2.9
Belgium	2.9	Australia	3.6	Mexico	2.8
Japan	2.9	Italy	2.8	Panama	2.8
Mexico	2.8	Belgium	2.1	Australia	2.8
Italy	2.5	Panama	2.1	Ireland	2.7
Panama	1.5	Mexico	2.0	Italy	1.9
Bahamas	1.3	Spain	1.6	Hong Kong	1.9
Total of top 15	80.7	Total of top 15	82.4	Total of top 15	76.7

Source: U.S. Department of Commerce, Bureau of Economic Analysis, *Survey of Current Business* (various dates).

Concentration of Energy Imports

Much the same pattern of concentration appears when America's energy imports of oil are examined. Table 4.8 displays oil imports by regional share over the last half-century. From 1947–2000, between 78 percent and 100 percent of America's oil imports came from three regions: the western hemisphere, the Middle East, and Africa. The western hemisphere was nearly always the single biggest regional source. The concentration of oil imports by state is even more marked, as Table 4.9 illustrates. Five states—Saudi Arabia, Canada, Mexico, Venezuela, and Nigeria—accounted for 69 percent of America's oil imports in 2000. Although the Persian Gulf as a whole does not rank first in oil exports to the United States, it does contain the largest share of the world's proven oil reserves and one-third of the world's proven natural gas reserves. Consequently, as explained in Chapter 2, because America's trading partners rely so heavily on Gulf supplies (even more than America does), the issue of who owns and controls Persian Gulf reserves must remain of central concern to the United States.

Concentration of Future Militarily Powerful States and NBC Seekers

It is not just trade or oil that dictate the regional focus of selective engagement. Data on both militarily powerful countries and potential NBC states also support the discriminating focus of selective engagement.[9] Apart from the United States, almost all of the world's strongest military powers are concentrated in Europe and East Asia. Ranked in terms of spending on defense in constant 2000 dollars, the next ten strongest military powers after the United States are Russia ($64 billion), China ($46 billion), Japan ($40 billion), Britain ($35 billion), France ($33 billion), Germany ($27 billion), Saudi Arabia ($24 billion), Italy ($21 billion), India ($14 billion), and South Korea ($11 billion). The United States, with defense spending of $332 billion in 2000, outspends all of them. The picture changes when we rank the ten largest states in terms of the size of their active armed forces. China takes first place with 2.3 million troops, followed by the United States with 1.4 million, India with 1.3 million, North Korea with 1.1 million, Russia with 1 million, South Korea with 683,000, Pakistan with 612,000, Turkey with 610,000, Iran with 513,000, and Vietnam with 443,000. Together, these are the world's fifteen most powerful military states, measured by defense spending and number of active-duty forces. (Using the combined criteria of large defense budgets and big active-duty forces omits Israel, which arguably should be added to the list. In 2001 it had a defense budget of $10 billion dollars, an active duty force of 164,000, and a highly capable reserve force of 424,000, all of which together create a formidable army. It also has nuclear weapons.)[10] Twelve of these states (all but the United States, Pakistan, and India) lie within Europe, East Asia, or the Persian Gulf. In addition, most of the states currently striving to acquire weapons of mass

TABLE 4.8. U.S. Oil Imports by Region, 1947–2000 (thousands of barrels and percent of total)

Region	1947	1950	1955	1960	1965	1970	1975	1980	1985	1990	1995	2000
Western Hemisphere	97,146	136,096	173,136	230,229	283,377	351,366	453,772	379,813	605,771	826,727	1,334,105	1,633,237
	100%	77%	61%	62%	63%	73%	30%	20%	52%	38%	51%	53%
Africa	na	na	na	1,451	24,585	44,365	488,515	731,342	213,090	451,171	476,879	502,255
				0%	5%	9%	33%	38%	18%	21%	18%	17%
Middle East	386	41,618	100,344	113,175	121,908	61,892	409,496	561,248	89,583	678,056	548,297	892,325
	0%	23%	35%	30%	27%	13%	27%	29%	8%	32%	21%	23%
Others	na	na	11,941	26,720	22,170	25,670	146,398	253,759	259,853	195,433	279,529	170,999
			4%	7%	5%	5%	10%	13%	22%	9%	11%	7%
Total	97,532	177,714	285,421	371,575	452,040	483,293	1,498,181	1,926,162	1,168,297	2,151,387	2,638,810	3,198,816
	100%	100%	100%	100%	100%	100%	100%	100%	100%	100%	100%	100%

Note: na means not available.
Source: Basic Petroleum Data Book, Vol. 21, No. 3 (August 2001), Sec. 9, Table 3 (Washington, D.C.: American Petroleum Institute).

TABLE 4.9. U.S. Oil Imports by Selected Countries, 1947–2000 (thousands of barrels and percent of total)

Country	1947	1950	1960	1970	1980	1990	2000
Algeria	na na	na na	284 0%	2,093 0%	166,980 9%	23,035 1%	211 0%
Angola	na na	na na	na na	na na	13,389 1%	86,095 4%	107,820 3%
Canada	na na	na na	41,349 11%	245,258 51%	73,002 4%	234,516 11%	493,256 15%
Columbia	10,944 11%	16,159 9%	14,799 4%	7,313 2%	na na	51,041 2%	116,311 4%
Indonesia	na na	na na	26,720 7%	25,670 5%	114,990 6%	35,912 2%	10,671 0%
Iran	na na	111 0%	13,056 4%	12,184 3%	3,086 0%	na na	na na
Iraq	na na	na na	6,363 2%	na na	10,328 1%	187,485 9%	226,804 7%
Kuwait	111 0%	26,741 15%	47,512 13%	12,123 3%	9,712 1%	28,942 1%	96,367 3%
Mexico	5,578 6%	12,307 7%	925 0%	na na	185,541 10%	251,345 12%	480,469 14%
Nigeria	na na	na na	na na	17,490 4%	307,840 16%	286,126 13%	320,137 10%
Norway	na na	na na	na na	na na	52,727 3%	34,874 2%	80,820 2%
Saudia Arabia	275 0%	14,650 8%	28,232 8%	6,140 1%	457,671 24%	436,193 20%	557,569 17%
United Kingdom	na na	na na	na na	na na	63,459 3%	56,497 3%	106,332 3%
Venezuela	75,499 77%	107,019 60%	172,887 47%	97,996 20%	56,950 3%	242,910 11%	447,736 13%
Other	5,125 5%	727 0%	19,448 5%	57,026 12%	410,487 21%	196,416 9%	275,313 8%
Total	97,532 100%	177,714 100%	371,575 100%	483,293 100%	1,926,162 100%	2,151,387 100%	3,319,816 100%

Note: na means not available.
Source: *Basic Petroleum Data Book*, Vol. 21, No. 3 (August 2001), Sec. 9, Table 4 (Washington, D.C.: American Petroleum Institute).

destruction—North Korea, Iran, Iraq, Syria, and Libya—are in or near those three regions. So, too, are those states that could quickly acquire such weapons, should they come to believe that the United States no longer could or would protect them—Germany, Japan, South Korea, and Taiwan.

These statistics show that, beyond its own hemisphere, the regions wherein lie most of America's trade, investment, and energy interests also contain the world's most powerful military states, together with those most likely and eager to acquire NBC weapons. On political, military, and economic grounds, therefore, the interests of the United States justify concentration on the western hemisphere, Europe, East Asia, and the Persian Gulf.

FORWARD DEFENSE POSTURE

Selective engagement is a forward defense strategy. As such, it retains America's core security commitments with, and keeps American combat troops deployed in, the regions where America's interests are concentrated: Europe, the Persian Gulf, and East Asia. In other regions of the world where American interests are less concentrated and of lesser importance—namely Africa, Central Asia, the Middle East outside of the Gulf, South Asia, and Southeast Asia—it refrains from standing security commitments or significant peacetime deployments.[11]

Selective engagement stresses both components of forward defense—retention of core commitments and overseas deployment of troops—because it is a preventive, precautionary strategy. The preventive bias reflects a belief that forestalling regional developments adverse to the United States is more effective and ultimately cheaper than allowing them to materialize and then having to pick up the pieces later. It favors an ounce of prevention over a pound of cure. The precautionary bias reflects a belief that should prevention fail, picking up the pieces is easier if prudent measures have been put in place in the region beforehand. A fail-safe strategy is better than one that, if it failed, had no prudent measures in place.

Security Commitments

The core security commitments that the United States should retain are those in the regions where its interests are concentrated. In the western hemisphere, these are the security treaties embodied in the Rio-OAS system. Although these treaties carry weak U.S. military guarantees to Latin American states if they attack one another they can, nevertheless, provide the institutional, legal, and moral framework for the projection of American military power within the hemisphere when circumstances require it, such as the 1994 U.S. invasion of Haiti to restore democracy. Because of America's overwhelming military dominance over the hemisphere, and its ability to deploy troops rapidly within it, it has little need to station troops south of the border and keeps only a small number there.

Essential to a forward presence are the three key alliances of the Cold War era: the North Atlantic Treaty Organization (NATO), the Japanese-American Security Alliance (JASA), and the U.S.-South Korean Alliance. The U.S. Senate has ratified all of them, but only NATO carries strong guarantees of reciprocal military aid in the event of attack; the other two are American guarantees to aid Japan and South Korea if they are attacked. (Modifications to JASA in 1996 increased the aid that Japan would render to American forces if they had to fight in the area.)[12] All three are important to retain because of their deterrent and reassurance functions, described below.

Equally important to a forward presence are the commitments to Saudi Arabia, Kuwait, Qatar, Bahrain, the United Arab Emirates, and Oman to defend them from Iraq or Iran. These are not de jure alliances, because the U.S. Senate has not ratified a formal alliance with any of these states. Rather, they are executive defense agreements that involve basing rights, porting arrangements, prepositioned equipment, joint training exercises, and the like. Nonetheless, ever since 1979, and especially after Iraq's invasion of Kuwait in 1990, the United States has acted as if it had de facto military alliances with these Gulf sheikdoms, particularly with Kuwait and Saudi Arabia, and recently with Qatar, too, and all three view their relations with the United States in roughly those terms.[13] Thus, these executive agreements should be viewed as de facto American alliances and should be retained because of their importance in preventing a regional hegemon from controlling the Gulf's oil reserves.

Besides these core security commitments, five others are worth retaining. Among them are formal bilateral alliances with Pakistan, the Philippines, and Australia. None involves the permanent peacetime deployment of American troops or great risk to the United States, but all have value: the alliance with Pakistan, to help combat terrorists and their training camps in Afghanistan and to help mediate between India and Pakistan so as to reduce the risk of war between them; those with the Philippines and Australia, to help should a major war with China break out in East Asia.

The other two security commitments, although not formal alliances, are long-standing and represent de facto alliances: one is with Israel, the other with Taiwan. Israel has little strategic value to the United States and is in many ways a strategic liability. Nonetheless, America's ties with Israel run deep, the U.S. affinity with another democracy is strong, and the moral commitment to its preservation is clear. On these grounds, the quasi-security commitment should be kept. Israel's military prowess does not require American combat forces to protect it, but it does need American economic aid and military hardware.

The security commitment to Taiwan is also worthy of retention. This is a complex and thorny issue. When the United States normalized its relations with China in January 1979, it withdrew diplomatic recognition from Taiwan and abrogated the 1954 defense treaty with it. By the 1979 Taiwan Relations Act, however, the United States made at least two quasi-security commitments to Taiwan: to see the Taiwan-China relationship resolved peacefully, which implicitly means the peaceful reunification of Taiwan with the mainland, and to retain an American capability sufficient to resist any use of force that would threaten Taiwan's security.[14] Although these understandings do not constitute a formal military alliance with Taiwan, they come very close to being the functional equivalent of one, because they commit the United States to preventing China from taking Taiwan by force. These commitments obviously complicate America's relations with China, because China does not recognize the right of the United States to interfere in what it considers its domestic affairs. Nevertheless, these commitments should be retained. To default on them would bring into question America's commitments to South Korea and Japan. Both states would rightly worry that if the United States backed out of its commitments to Taiwan, either to accommodate China or under military threat from China, then the United States might well do the same to them at some point. The commitment to Taiwan is not unqualified, however: it does not include, and should not include, backing for Taiwanese independence. Should Taiwan declare its independence, then the United States should immediately and publicly repudiate these understandings. Thus, the proper policy is this: the United States will resist with force an unprovoked Chinese attack on Taiwan, and the United States will not defend a Taiwan that declares independence.[15]

All told, these security commitments constitute American obligations to defend thirty-seven states beyond the western hemisphere. Twenty-four of these states are the European members of NATO; five states are in East Asia, six in the Persian Gulf, and two others elsewhere. America's security commitments to the states of the western hemisphere are less defined. The United States has intervened only selectively in Latin America's interstate and intra-state wars because most have been small and have not threatened American interests directly. When the United States has intervened, it was usually out of concern that such wars could enhance the influence of an external great power within the hemisphere. However, no potentially meddlesome great power is on the horizon for the foreseeable future. As a consequence, it is the thirty-seven commitments beyond the hemisphere that constitute the core of America's forward defense posture.

In-Theater Presence
To back up these commitments, the United States deployed 255,000 (or 18 percent) of its nearly 1.4 million active-duty forces outside of its borders.

(These are figures as of the end of September 2001, before the war in Afghanistan and before the Bush administration's buildup in the Persian Gulf.) Of these, 212,000 were ashore and 43,000 were afloat. This represents a decline of nearly 60 percent from the Cold War peak (609,000 troops deployed abroad in fiscal year 1990). In 2001, most of the troops were deployed in Europe (113,000 onshore and almost 5,000 afloat), East Asia (79,000 onshore and 13,000 afloat), and the Persian Gulf (11,000 onshore and 14,000 afloat nearby). About 70 percent of the troops ashore were deployed in just three states: 71,000 in Germany, 40,000 in Japan, and 38,000 in South Korea, while most of the forces afloat were in Europe, East Asia (including Southeast Asia), and the Persian Gulf.[16]

None of these deployments is unchangeable. The number of American troops in each region will vary with the region's political-military circumstances, and that number should go up or down as circumstances and American resources dictate. What remains essential, however, is that the United States should maintain forward-deployed forces powerful enough, and capable of being reinforced rapidly enough, to back up U.S. commitments. Because American troops in a region are the strongest and most tangible form of America's security commitment, an in-theater presence shapes the political contours of a region more effectively than do forces deployed from afar—that is, from the United States. In-theater balancing is politically more potent than offshore balancing.

Benefits of Forward Defense
America's forward defense posture, comprising its core security commitments and overseas deployments, bolsters selective engagement's preventive and precautionary objectives in four ways. It deters adverse military actions; it reassures key regional actors and thereby buffers regions from destabilizing influences; it enhances regional security cooperation and management; and it facilitates waging war should that become necessary.

Regional Deterrence
America's forward defense posture helps deter military actions that could harm American interests and allies in a region. If America's commitment to its key allies is clear, then attacks against them are less likely—not impossible, but less probable.[17] The 1990 Iraqi invasion of Kuwait is a case in point. This was not a failure of deterrence because the United States had no treaty to defend Kuwait, nor did it have military forces deployed there, nor did it issue any deterrent threats to Iraq. The Arab states did not expect an Iraqi attack, and the Kuwaitis did not believe that American measures were necessary. Had the United States created a viable deterrent through a military alliance and troop deployments, the Iraqi attack might very well not have

occurred.[18] Thus, America's military power adds an important ingredient to help tip a region toward peace rather than war.

Regional Reassurance and Buffering

When used properly, America's forward presence can reassure America's allies, and many other actors not allied with the United States, that highly destabilizing events are less likely to occur within their region, or that if they do occur, they are less likely to escalate out of control. Several factors enable the United States to play this reassurance role. First, America's allies and unaligned but non-hostile states know that the United States will act to manage dangerous situations that would threaten its interests and theirs. Because America's regional interests lie in trade, not territorial acquisition, these interests are best served by peace and stability, not tension and conflict. In addition, the powerful regional states know that what they do will be carefully watched and may be countered by the United States. Moreover, all know the answer to the question of which among them is the most powerful military actor: it is the United States. This reduces the need to jockey with one another for top position. A high-level German diplomat who served in the Bundeskanzleramt (the Chancellery) in the 1990s put the point well: "With the United States in Europe, there is less concern about us Germans by others. The Germans need the United States. If it leaves Europe, debate will follow on who is number one, and it is the Germans. We Germans don't want that."[19] If the United States were to leave East Asia, a similar debate would ensue over who is number one. Neither the Chinese nor the Japanese would cede that position to the other. A final factor that enables the United States to play the reassurance role well is that the United States is the most disinterested of the regional actors. It is not territorially acquisitive, and it is also less sensitive to small changes in power disparities than other regional actors because its great margin of superiority makes minor shifts in power positions immaterial. All these factors enhance America's ability to provide regional reassurance if it uses that presence intelligently.

By providing both deterrence and reassurance, the United States becomes, in essence, a regional buffer; it is able to lessen the impact of opposing forces. This is exactly what America's forward presence does for a region: it dampens military competition and crises among regional actors, thereby making a region's internal security relations more stable than they would otherwise be.

The United States plays this buffering role at both ends of Eurasia. In Europe, the small powers clearly prefer that the United States play this role, not one or several of their large continental neighbors. The European great powers would certainly not defer to one another for such a balancing and buffering role.[20] "Among Europeans, it is not acceptable that the lead nation be European. A European power broker is a hegemonic power. We can agree on U.S. leadership, but not on one of our own."[21] The United States produces the same buffering effect in East Asia, where the jockeying among the powerful regional actors—Japan, South Korea, and China—is much more pronounced. The U.S. alliances with South Korea and Japan provide both states with security, and also add significantly to regional stability. In July 2000, President Kim Dae-jung of South Korea said: "The presence of U.S. forces in northeast Asia is similar to the case of NATO. NATO was established to fight communism, but it still has the role of maintaining a balance of power for European peace even after the collapse of communism."[22] Several months later, President Kim was blunter: "We are surrounded by big powers—Russia, Japan, China—so the United States must continue to stay for stability and peace in East Asia." With these words, President Kim said, he was recounting almost the exact words that North Korea's President Kim Jong Il had used during their historic summit earlier in the year.[23]

In Southeast Asia, the same dynamic is at work. Malaysia, for example, may complain of America's economic might, and Singapore may treat some Americans who break laws there with harshness, but both, together with the other states of Southeast Asia, want an American military presence as a counter to China. Singapore, for example, has given the U.S. Navy basing rights to compensate for the loss of Subic Bay in the Philippines, building a new naval base at Changi so that American aircraft carriers can dock there.[24] Even America's former enemy Vietnam apparently views the United States as a counterweight against its large neighbor to the North: "America now is an alternative to China. To counter the Chinese threat we must lean towards the West—not because we like the West, but because the Chinese Army is 2.5 million strong."[25] Thus, the American military presence in Japan reassures China, South Korea, and the Southeast Asian nations about Japan, and the Japanese, Koreans, and Southeast Asian nations about China, just as the American military presence in Germany reassures the Europeans about Germany, and the central and western Europeans about Russia.[26]

America also plays a crucial buffering role in the Persian Gulf.[27] There, only Iraq unequivocally opposes an American presence. Iran quietly favors it as a check on Iraq as long as Saddam Hussein is in power, although over the long term, Iran would oppose the U.S. check on its own claims to regional hegemony. Kuwait welcomes the United States with open arms. Since 1990 Saudi Arabia has accepted American forces in its territory but has kept them concentrated at Prince Sultan Air Base in the middle of the desert, although its willingness to accept these forces may be ending. Should they leave, the other Gulf sheikdoms—Bahrain, Oman, Qatar, and the United Arab Emirates—will continue to welcome them because they see the United States as a power balancer that keeps at bay not only Iran and Iraq but also Saudi Arabia.

Since the end of the Cold War, Russia and China have had the most con-
flicted views about America's forward military presence. In the early 1990s,
Russia favored such a presence as insurance against a resurgent, reunited
Germany and as a stabilizing factor against uncertainties in Central Europe.[28]
At the time, Russia also hoped for a strategic partnership with the United
States, perhaps globally, or at least with regard to European affairs, particularly security affairs. However, NATO's enlargement, America's intervention
in Bosnia and especially in Kosovo, and most of all, Russia's sense of exclusion from European affairs all subsequently took their toll. By the end of the
1990s, a reunified Germany turned out to be peaceful, NATO looked like
an aggressive not a defensive alliance, and no real Russian-American strategic partnership had materialized. Russia had become marginalized in
Europe, and more than anything else, the Russian foreign policy elite abhors
exclusion from European affairs. As a consequence, Russia's attitudes
toward an American military presence in Europe became more equivocal at
the end of the 1990s than they were in the early 1990s. September 11
changed those views once again, because President Putin and President
Bush forged a close working relationship against international terrorism,
and Putin decided to throw Russia's lot in with the West. The NATO-Russia
Council (NRC), formed in 2002, began to institutionalize this turn in
Russian foreign policy.[29] The NRC represents a way to bring Russia into
NATO deliberations on relevant matters without giving Russia a veto over
NATO's negotiations, since Russia still is not a NATO member. To the extent
that the NRC diminishes Russia's sense of exclusion from the West, it will
reduce any lingering Russian opposition to an American military presence
in Europe.[30]

Two opposing dynamics affect China's view about America's military presence in East Asia.[31] On the one hand, China's public position has been that
no state should have foreign bases and troops abroad, together with a view
that the United States seeks to dominate East Asia. The logic of this position
is that the United States should withdraw its forces and bases from the
region. On the other hand, until recently, China's privately stated position
and clear preference was for the United States to remain, in order to protect
the stability of the region by preventing Japan from remilitarizing and from
acquiring nuclear weapons. China has objected to America's interposing its
Seventh Fleet between China and Taiwan, but it has also wanted the United
States to remain in the region to keep Japan under control. It put up with
the former partly because it had no choice, but also partly because it desired
the latter. Publicly, China has bewailed America's hegemony; privately, it has
supported the American military presence in the region.

Since mid-1996, however, this attitude has undergone some change, first,
because of the impact of the Taiwan Straits crisis of 1996, when the United
States sent two aircraft carriers into the Straits to signal its strong support

for the peaceful settlement of the Taiwan issue, and second, because of the 1996 revision in the guidelines of the Japanese-American alliance, which now call for more Japanese assistance to the United States in any East Asian crisis.[32] As a consequence, China is more conflicted than ever about the American military presence. Some analysts believe China now wants American forces out of the region because they are a barrier to taking Taiwan, because China believes it can now handle Japan by itself, and because American military power prevents China from assuming its proper role as East Asia's regional hegemon. Others think that China still prefers an American presence and that it favors the continuance of the Japanese-American alliance to restrain Japan, so long as the alliance is not used to support an American military position in East Asia. Still others think that China wants to drive a wedge between the United States and Japan, but not one so serious as to cause a rupture of the alliance. On balance, however, it appears that Chinese officials still favor an American military presence in East Asia: "Chinese leaders, in private conversations with American officials, have indicated that they can live with the Japanese-American Security Alliance (JASA) because they view it as a stabilizing factor."[33] Thus, even China, the one state best positioned to challenge America's dominance in any region, still favors an American military presence in its region.

In sum, Europe may be the only region where no real opposition to an American military presence exists, whereas in East Asia and the Gulf, there is some opposition. In all three regions, however, support for an American military presence remains strong enough among a sufficient number of powerful regional actors to make it politically sustainable.

Cooperative Management of Regional Security Issues
In addition to its deterrence and reassurance functions, America's forward presence also enhances the cooperative management of regional security issues. Cooperative management is produced mainly by America's military presence, but also important is the institutionalized nature of that presence. Institutionalization means a set of clearly articulated rules of interaction, stable and shared expectations about future behavior, regular meetings and consultations, coordination of actions during crises, joint exercises in peacetime, joint action in wartime, and the like. The institutionalization of regional security management under American leadership promotes greater transparency, more open dialogue, more cooperative procedures, and more beneficial outcomes among regional actors than would otherwise be the case.[34] The degree to which security management is institutionalized varies by region. It is highest in Europe, where NATO represents the most highly institutionalized multilateral security alliance ever, at least in modern times. Security management is less institutionalized in the Gulf, where no formal alliances exist and where the United States is not a member of the one mul-

tilateral security entity that does exist, the Gulf Cooperation Council. In East Asia, security management is fairly well institutionalized but it is bilateral, not multilateral as in Europe, and is based primarily on JASA and the U.S.–South Korean alliance. In all three regions, the institutionalization of security management contributes to regional stability.

Regional security management is aided, moreover, by the fact that alliances, as Paul Schroeder first pointed out, are not simply tools to aggregate resources against a common external threat. They are also mechanisms to restrain allies, dampen down conflict, and pacify regions.[35] Christopher Gelpi has built on Schroeder's original insight and undertaken empirical measurement. After analyzing 117 mediation attempts in international crises between 1918 and 1988, he concluded that:

> Great powers with equal ties to both parties are successful in mediating
> international crises only 31 percent of the time. Great powers which share
> a defense pact with one of the disputants and have no alliance with the
> other . . . are successful 81 percent of the time. Thus it appears that
> alliance ties do help powerful mediators make persuasive threats of
> abandonment against their allies and persuasive threats of intervention
> against the unallied disputant.[36]

President Clinton's active management of the Greek-Turkish dispute in early 1996 is a recent case in point. It helped avert a war between the two, arising from their perennial dispute over the Aegean islands. So, too, did Clinton's intervention in the 1999 Kargil crisis between India and Pakistan; by pressuring Prime Minister Nawaz Sharif to back down, Clinton helped prevent a limited war from turning into a large one. President George W. Bush did the same in the spring of 2002, when he pressured President Musharraf to cease his support of Pakistani terrorist operations against India.[37] Alliances are thus mechanisms of control as well as means of aggregating power.

The greater regional stability produced by America's military presence, through its deterrence, reassurance, and cooperative management effects, helps advance America's interests. Stability helps dampen, although it cannot by itself wholly eliminate, intense security competitions and arms races among states. Stability and peace can also help diminish the desire of some key regional actors to acquire NBC weapons to provide for their own defense. Potential adversaries may be stalemated in their acquisition efforts, while regional stability that fosters dialogue can improve the chances of preventing NBC spread to adversaries. Peace in the Persian Gulf helps keep Gulf oil reserves divided. Stable security relations, in turn, contribute to making a region's political environment more conducive to the growth of beneficial trade and the emergence of democratic governance than a conflict-intense and warring environment. Peace and stability do not guarantee that any of these beneficial things will happen, but they make them more likely.

Through its Eurasian alliances, then, the United States maintains direct and close political-military links with four of the world's six other great military powers—Britain, France, Germany, and Japan. To the extent that the NATO-Russia Council can be built into an institutional link with Russia that resembles a great-power concert, a fifth great power may be added to the list. China remains the one great-power "outlier," lacking institutional links with the United States, but that is not beyond the ability of both states to solve, if they have the political will to do so.

Waging Regional Wars
The final benefit of America's forward presence is that it is a "fail-safe" strategy. Should deterrence and reassurance fail, a forward presence facilitates America's ability to wage war and manage conflict. The 2001–2002 war waged against the Taliban and al Qaeda is a vivid reminder of this; together with the aircraft carriers deployed off Pakistan, America's bases in the Persian Gulf and at Diego Garcia were of central importance. Standing alliances permit more rapid and more effective action than assembling ad hoc coalitions, thereby enhancing America's military effectiveness in the regional wars it chooses to fight. The advantages of forward-deployed forces include joint exercises, overseas bases, a higher degree of interoperability, joint training, a tradition of close communication, and common, systematic contingency planning. This is a vast improvement over a situation in which allies would have to be solicited at the last minute, plans for waging war thrown together under pressure, forward bases found in haste, and joint operations improvised. Forward-based, alliance-embedded forces can react more quickly, be reinforced more effectively, and fight better than forces that have to be introduced into the region from scratch. In short, standing alliances and forward basing enable the United States to wage war more effectively if both reassurance and deterrence should fail.

For all of these reasons, America's core alliances and quasi-alliances, and their associated overseas deployments, remain valuable instruments for preserving American influence in Western Europe, East Asia, and the Persian Gulf. They enable the United States to shape the international environment in each region so as to keep it congenial to American interests and to facilitate the use of force in the region when force must be used. America's peacetime military presence makes both possible—shaping the international environment through deterrence, reassurance, and cooperative security management; the effective use of force, through the benefits provided by regional allies and in-theater bases. The ability to use force in a region serves as a hedge against the failure of reassurance and deterrence, but the premise of selective engagement is that the latter is likely to work well enough to make the use of force infrequent.

USE OF FORCE

Although forward deployment may make the need for war less frequent, it does not make war unnecessary. Severe threats to America's interests may arise in eastern and western Eurasia and the Gulf, and they might require the United States to use force to defend them. Similarly, there or elsewhere in the world, horrific events may take place, and there will be intense pressure for the United States to respond militarily. Under what conditions and for what purposes should the United States resort to force?

Selective engagement offers three general standards for judging when to use force. First, in general, the United States should wage war only for its vital and highly important interests. Second, in general, it should not wage war to defend merely important interests, and it should also, in general, stay out of the regions of lesser concern to it. Third, it should permit only three exceptions to the first two general prescriptions: it should use force when cheap, quick, and effective interventions within states to protect democracy offer themselves; it should use force to prevent deliberate mass murder in civil wars when this is feasible at reasonable cost; and it should use force when failure to defend important interests puts highly important interests at grave risk. The rationales for these standards follow.

Wage War Only for Vital and Highly Important Interests

In the event that the American homeland is attacked, either by an external state or by terrorists, the United States must respond forcefully, as it did against al Qaeda's infrastructure in Afghanistan and against the Taliban for harboring it. Waging war to defend the United States against attack is the fundamental principle of any grand strategy. In the foreseeable future, such an attack by a state is highly unlikely, for the reasons specified in Chapter 2, but additional terrorist attacks against the homeland cannot be ruled out. In either eventuality, however, the decision rule is simple: attack requires counterattack.

An equally clear-cut situation is the one where terrorists are known to be planning attacks against the United States, its forces abroad, or its allies. Here preventive actions to disrupt the planned attacks and to destroy the terrorist organizations are required. Some of those actions will require military strikes, but prevention will more often involve penetration of terrorist cells, careful intelligence, and patient police work (as I explain in Chapters 7 and 8).

Beyond North America, the regions of greatest concern to the United States are Europe, East Asia, and the Persian Gulf. These contain all of America's allies (except Israel, Australia, and Pakistan), where its highly important interests lie, and where it has placed most of its forward deployed forces. If any of America's overseas forces or its allies are attacked by a hostile state, the United States must respond with force. A credible forward presence should make the need for such responses rare (as explained above), but response is crucial when provoked; otherwise America's forward presence would lose credibility and its beneficial effects would evaporate. The defense of allies, even if infrequent, strengthens America's reassurance role; this, in turn, helps preserve the deep peace among the Eurasian great powers and access to Persian Gulf oil. Waging war in the overseas regions of greatest concern to the United States translates into defending America's allies when attacked. In this case, too, the decision rule is: attack requires counterattack.

Counterattack for attacks against it, preventive action against terrorists, and defense of allies—these are the clear-cut cases for defending vital and highly important interests. Not all cases will be as easy to decide as these, however. There will be occasions when a hostile state is believed to be contemplating an attack against one of America's allies, perhaps even making preparations for it. Here the use of force becomes more difficult because the United States cannot be certain whether the adversary will take action. It may be bluffing, probing for soft spots, strengthening its bargaining position, or planning to launch a war if it meets no opposition. In these cases, the United States must find ways to use its military power to defend its interests by shoring up deterrence, but without bringing on a war that could be avoided.

The most difficult situation of all is where a hostile state appears close to, or on the verge of, acquiring NBC weapons, especially nuclear weapons, and is believed willing to use them either directly against a U.S. ally or as shields behind which to wage conventional aggression against it. In this case, preventive attacks to destroy these nascent capabilities may become a compelling option for the United States. Such preventive wars, however, start down a dangerous road, and they should be undertaken only when the strongest case can be made that deterrence and containment will not work, as I explain more fully in Chapter 7.[38]

Avoid Wars in Regions of Lesser Concern or for Less than Highly Important Interests

Opportunity costs and efficacy considerations dictate restraint when it comes to waging war in regions of lesser concern or to advancing interests that, although they may be important, are not highly important. The opportunity costs are clear: the more of its military power the United States uses to advance its important interests, or the more it becomes bogged down in regions of lesser concern, the less military power will be available to defend its vital and highly important interests or to maintain a forward presence in the regions of greater concern to it. Efficacy considerations are equally clear: waging war is not the best way to realize America's three important interests.

Considerations regarding opportunity costs apply particularly to civil wars, the overwhelming majority of which occur in regions of lesser concern to the United States. There are two ways that the United States could intervene in a civil war: to make peace or to keep the peace. The first is commonly called peace enforcement, but as a practical matter, it means intervening in an on-going civil war and waging war to stop the war. It would most likely involve taking the side of one of the belligerents to help it win, rather than waging war against both sides. In contrast, peacekeeping means inserting forces between belligerents that have declared a ceasefire in order to help them keep the tenuous peace to which they have agreed. Peace enforcement, or intervention in on-going civil wars, is costly, especially if the forces are well armed and well supported by significant segments of the population. The bigger and more populous the state, the greater the risks and the costs of the intervention. For example, had the 1999 air war not worked, the contemplated ground intervention in Kosovo would have required somewhere between 100,000 and 175,000 western troops (depending on where the West attacked Serbian forces and what strategy was used).[39] Even in a peacekeeping intervention, the requirements can still be sizeable, although the risks are less. In Bosnia, for example, NATO initially deployed 60,000 forces to keep the peace that had been forged at Dayton in 1995. In either case, intervention is not likely to be a short-lived affair because postwar deployments for a lengthy period will be required, as both Bosnia and Kosovo demonstrated.

Both peacekeeping and peace enforcement carry significant opportunity costs. The United States has only a limited number of ground divisions (thirteen), with a significant portion committed to its strategic reserve and to a peacetime presence in Eurasia. A few "Bosnias" or "Kosovos" would severely degrade a forward presence posture, and the demand to do these types of operations far exceeds the supply of American military forces. Therefore forceful interventions of either variety should be rare and should be confined, as detailed below, to the most egregious cases and to those that directly threaten America's important interests.

Efficacy considerations dictate restraint in using military power to advance America's three important interests because in contemporary conditions, waging war is not, in general, an effective way to advance them. The United States cannot use force to coerce other states to engage in free trade or to permit the free flow of capital; that would be counterproductive. Gunboat diplomacy of the nineteenth-century variety would backfire and push states towards closure, not openness. Insecurity pushes states away from openness and interdependence toward closure and autonomy. Economic openness flourishes, instead, when the international political environment is stable and states feel secure. Similarly, waging war to coerce states to cut back their generation of greenhouse gases would also be useless. It might instead cause states to divert resources away from energy conversion and toward military defense; this is hardly an effective way to get a state to reduce its greenhouse gas emissions. Thus, the coercive use of American military power for both these important interests would be a losing proposition.

Waging war to spread democracy would also not be efficient or effective.[40] This is particularly so when the prerequisites to sustain a stable democracy are lacking, such as governmental institutions to support the rule of law, active civic institutions, a knowledgeable citizenry, the support of politically powerful elites, high per-capita income, a free and vigorous press, and a large middle class.[41] The cases of Germany and Japan are the exceptions that illustrate the rule. The United States did transform both states into viable democracies, but only after they were conquered in a total war; their constitutions were rewritten; their economies were resurrected through large amounts of American aid; their security was assured by the United States; and their adherence to democracy was monitored by several decades of American military occupation. Germany and Japan illustrate that states can be socially engineered to become democratic if enough resources are devoted to the task for a long enough period of time. In most cases today, humanitarian interventions—to protect human rights or to spread democracy—would require nation-building and national reconstruction of a similar nature.[42] Even though the scale of the effort would be less than the German and Japanese cases, doing even a few at any one time would require a military effort that far surpassed both the resources of the United States and the political will of the international community.[43] Finally, short-term military interventions to rebuild nations and to spread democracy generally bring the worst of both worlds: high risk to American soldiers but no permanent change toward democratic governance, as the cases of Haiti and Somalia in the 1990s demonstrated.[44]

Efficiency and efficacy considerations require a better way for the United States to advance democracy, protect human rights, preserve international openness, and deal with global warming. It lies in the direct application of American military power to protect its vital and highly important interests. If the line against the spread of weapons of mass destruction can be held, if the world's access to Gulf oil is assured, and if the deep peace among the Eurasian great powers can be maintained, then what results is an international system more peaceful, more prosperous, and more benign. This, in turn, advances America's important interests. If international openness facilitates economic growth, then states will have a greater stake in preserving openness. Openness helps generate the wealth that facilitates and helps sustain democratic transitions. By increasing a state's per-capita income and the size of its middle class, it improves the climate for protection of human rights.[45] The creation of wealth, facilitated by international openness and market economies, will also be necessary to deal with what is likely to prove to be humankind's biggest challenge yet: averting a global climate disaster. A more warlike world, to the contrary, is likely to be less prosperous, more contentious, and less cooperative, and none of these things benefits the United States.

Thus, the place for the United States to begin, and to stay, is in Eurasia. Here, together with North America, is where most of the world's wealth and people are concentrated and where most of the world's trade and commerce takes place. If both ends of Eurasia are at peace, aided by the commitment of American military power, then its chances of being prosperous are greater. If Eurasia is prosperous, then the global economy will be more prosperous, and wealth will spread more quickly and more abundantly to the developing states, there and elsewhere, through trade. If, however, Eurasia is at war or on the constant verge of war, these things will not happen, or will take a great deal longer. America's military presence in Eurasia can therefore make a contribution to its important interests of preserving international openness, advancing democracy, and dealing with global warming by helping to provide the stable international political framework that each of these requires.

In sum, by directing its military power to those three interests where it is most effectively and efficiently applied—the vital and highly important interests—the United States can help create the international framework most conducive to realizing its other three interests that are less susceptible to the direct application of military power—the important (but not vital and highly important) ones—and, in the process, do some good for others.

Permit Only Limited Exceptions to the First Two Rules
The last rule allows three exceptions to the injunction that the United States should keep its forces out of regions of lesser concern and should not wage war to advance its merely "important" interests. These exceptions, which are highly circumscribed, may allow interventions within a state to protect democracy, interventions in civil wars to prevent the killing of large numbers of noncombatants, and interventions in either a civil or interstate war if it threatens other more important American interests.

Interventions to Preserve Democratic Rule
There will be rare occasions when a cheap and quick military intervention by the United States can make the difference in preserving democratic rule in a state. For example, in early December 1989, the United States dispatched planes from Clark Air base in the Philippines to stop rebel planes from attacking the presidential palace and the government of President Corazon Aquino. The American planes did not fire, but the show of force in effect grounded the rebel air force; by all accounts, this averted a sixth coup attempt against Aquino by the Philippine military. As one non-Western

Manila-based diplomat put it: "Had the jets not gone up, it is likely that Cory's government would have come down."[46] Occasions like the Philippine intervention—where a democratic government requests American help, sufficient American combat forces are nearby, and a simple show of force is sufficient to face down rebel forces—will present themselves infrequently, but when they do, the United States should not pass them up.

Interventions to Stop Mass Murder in Civil Wars
Another exception for intervention within a state involves civil wars where governments, or groups trying to take control of the government, engage in deliberate mass killing of innocent civilians. Mass killing is defined here according to Benjamin Valentino's criteria: "the intentional killing of a significant number of the members of any group of noncombatants (as the group and its membership are defined by the perpetrator)" caused by direct methods (such as execution and gassing) or indirect methods (the "intentional creation of inhospitable conditions," such as starvation and malnutrition), and involving 50,000 noncombatant deaths within a five-year period.[47] The deliberate mass murder of large numbers of noncombatants is different from the unintentional killing of large numbers of them. It is the result of a calculated policy by governmental, insurgent, thug, criminal, terrorist, or paramilitary groups to achieve specific political purposes.[48] By contrast, unintentional killing would be, for example, an incidental or accidental effect of war. Civilians might be killed because they happen to be in the wrong place at the wrong time, caught in the crossfire between opposing armies, or because of conditions that arise from war but are not deliberately intended by the combatants, such as disease. Civilians are the ones who suffer most in civil wars because it is they, not the armed combatants, who generally suffer the most deaths, intentional or not. However, it is the deliberate mass killing of noncombatants, especially if it is based on ethnic, class, tribe, race, or religious reasons, that most offends humanity's moral principles and that should not be tolerated by the international community when it can prevent or stop it at a reasonable cost.

Valentino documents about sixty-three cases of mass killing in the twentieth century. Roughly half of these were outright civil wars; the others included colonial wars, wars of national liberation, strategic bombing in World War II, communist collectivization of agriculture, and political repression. Nearly every one of the outright civil wars involved at least 100,000 deaths (based on Valentino's higher estimates); sometimes many hundreds of thousands of noncombatants lost their lives. Of the approximately thirty outright civil wars of the twentieth century where deliberate mass killing occurred, five began after the Cold War ended: in Bosnia (1990–1994), 25,000–125,000 were killed; in Algeria (1992–1999), 50,000–120,000 were killed; in Burundi (1993–1998), 100,000–200,000 were killed; in Rwanda

(1994), 500,000–1,000,000 were killed; and in Russia (Chechnya, 1994–2000), 30,000–50,000 were killed.[49] Thus, roughly one in four of the twenty-four civil wars initiated since the end of the Cold War (between 1991 and 2000 [see Table 1.7 in Chapter 1]) involved deliberate mass killing, roughly the same proportion as in civil wars between 1945 and 1990.[50]

Although they are thus the minority, civil wars with mass murder have usually been the bloodiest for the noncombatants. It is such wars where the United States should contemplate intervention, because it is here that the United States can do the greatest good by saving the greatest number of innocents. The United States cannot and should not intervene in every civil war with its military forces, however; it must husband its resources and intervene only in the most egregious cases.

Even where deliberate mass murder of innocent civilians looms or takes place, the United States must follow certain guidelines.[51] It should intervene only when it can save a large number of civilian lives, only when there is high likelihood that the loss of American life can be kept low, and only when nothing short of intervention can save the civilians at risk.

Applying the criterion that intervention must hold high promise of being effective at reasonable cost means that the United States will not be able to intervene in every civil war where mass killing takes place. There will be many cases where military intervention could be effective but only at great cost to the United States, or where intervention holds little promise of being effective if the costs borne by the United States are kept low. For example, intervening in a civil war taking place within the territory of a great power would be foolhardy because it could bring on a great-power war. Intervening in a country that is large and well populated would be demanding because the size of the state and the number of people to be protected would require quite large forces (for comparison, America's interventions in three small states—Haiti, Panama, and Grenada—were undertaken with roughly 20,000 troops each). Intervening in a civil war between two well-armed, well-trained military forces (governmental and insurgent), each of which has the support of large segments of the country's population, would risk large numbers of American casualties, if one or both sides forcefully oppose intervention or wage guerilla war against American forces. In general, intervention to stop mass murder is likely to be limited to smaller states where at least one of the parties welcomes outside intervention, or where the military forces of the government, the rebels, or both are not much of a match for outside forces.

Wherever possible, the United States must avoid going into such situations alone, even when it provides the lion's share of the military forces. Multilateral interventions are best, even if they involve some sacrifice in military effectiveness (as they often do). They gain more legitimacy in the eyes of the international community than unilateral interventions and maximize the chances for gaining and sustaining public support within the United States.

Such interventions cannot be in-and-out affairs. Even when the killing has not started, an international presence may well be required for a long time to prevent its outbreak, and where killing has taken place, an international presence will be required for a long time to help prevent its reccurrence.[52] For example, five years after the Dayton Accords ended the Bosnian War, NATO still had 25,000 troops to keep the peace.[53] It is not always easy to predict when ethnic cleansing, mass murder, or genocide will occur in a civil war, but when there are strong indications that it may happen, the United States should help to avert it because preventing it is easier, cheaper, and more effective than intervening to stop it once it has started.[54] If preventive deployment is not feasible, either because the danger is hard to predict or because such deployments would tie up large numbers of American troops for long periods, intervention after the mass killing starts can still save some lives, although not as many as a preventive deployment.

Finally, no magic formula exists to determine when such interventions, either preventive or ameliorative, should be undertaken. They must be decided on a case-by-case basis because they depend on hard-to-make judgments about feasibility, likelihood of success, the effectiveness of alternatives, the availability of partners, the scale of killing likely to occur without American intervention, and the estimates of American lives that will be lost.[55] Even with all of these qualifications, however, the bias of American policy should be to consider intervention to save lives in cases where mass murder is threatened.

Rwanda in 1994 serves as an illustration. The West failed to intervene to prevent the swift mass murder of 500,000 to 800,000 Tutsis and 10,000–30,000 moderate Hutus by Hutu extremists in April 1994. By the guidelines presented above, the West should have intervened because it had some knowledge about the impending disaster, because its timely intervention could have stopped the mass murder or at least mitigated it, and because a massive intervention would not have been required.[56]

Although the West could not know for certain that Hutu extremists would systematically kill as many Tutsis and moderate Hutus as they did, there were "considerable warnings that the situation in Rwanda could explode into ethnic violence. . . . Information was available— . . . to United Nations Headquarters and to key Governments—about a strategy and threat to exterminate Tutsis."[57] Rwanda, like Burundi, had been a repeat offender at mass murder in civil wars. Moreover, as Alan Kuperman shows, a preventive deployment of 5,000 well-armed Western troops would have had a good chance of preventing the mass murder from starting in the capital, or of quickly stopping it there and keeping it from spreading to the countryside. Even if troops were not in place when the killing began, he calculates that a rapid deployment of one American division could still have saved about 125,000 of the Tutsis and moderate Hutus that were killed.[58] Finally, the evidence is clear that in the Rwanda case, like most other cases of mass murder in the twentieth century, a relatively small number of high political and military elites planned these slaughters. Although Rwanda was exceptional in that ordinary civilians also played a role in the mass killing, even here, as Valentino points out, "military and paramilitary groups were probably responsible for most of the killing. Rwandan civilians appear to have participated in killing operations primarily under the supervision of these groups and, in many instances, only after substantial coercion."[59] Thus, 5,000 well-armed Western troops might well have captured the ringleaders in the capital quickly and coerced them into ordering a halt to the violence.[60]

Rwanda may well be an "easy" case for intervention.[61] Some, including John Mueller, argue that Bosnia should have been an easy case, too, because there the mass murders were committed by thug groups, criminals, hooligans, paramilitaries, and police, not well-trained armies nor entire groups within society set against one another.[62] This may be so, but future cases will not always involve groups that are easily intimidated or swiftly curbed. Even in the Bosnian case, the Bosnian Serbs were aided by elements of the Serbian army, and it took a well-trained and well-armed Croatian military force to evict the Bosnian Serbs from Krajina in 1995. Moreover, even if a relatively small number of people devise the plans for mass murders, and even if a relatively small number of people actually do the killing, the numbers may still be large enough to make targeting the perpetrators difficult, as American attempts to kill Mohammed Farah Aideed in Somalia demonstrated.[63] Thus, although selective engagement calls for American intervention to avert or mitigate mass murder in civil wars, even here it must, regrettably, be done on a selective basis.

Interventions to Protect Alliance Credibility

The final permissible exception for military intervention involves situations in which the failure to defend an important interest could put at risk a highly important interest. This type of situation is most likely to arise when civil wars take place on the periphery of areas central to American interests, when they involve the potential for great loss of life, and when for both humanitarian and other reasons they cause great concern to America's allies nearby. In such a situation, humanitarian considerations, such as stopping the killing, will be entangled with strategic considerations, such as preserving the credibility of an American alliance.

Humanitarian and strategic factors can become conflated for several reasons. America's allies may want to intervene in the area to pacify it, but only if the United States joins them. They may have intervened in some fashion to stop the war or to ameliorate the killing, but without much success, and now want U.S. intervention to remedy matters. The United States itself, having previously intervened in the area, may now find it difficult not to act when more trouble comes. In all three situations, it is no longer simply an issue of saving innocent civilians but also one of preserving the cohesion of the alliance. After all, if the alliance does not help serve the allies' interests, they might come to question its utility for them. Humanitarian concerns might also merge with strategic concerns if the United States had taken some action to stop the killing in concert with its allies, but without real success; then the credibility not only of the alliance as an effective military instrument but also of the United States as a credible military power might come into question. A final reason might be that the United States has stopped a civil war in one area, but another war breaks out elsewhere that could adversely affect peace in the former.

By whatever route humanitarian and strategic considerations become joined, the United States faces an unpleasant choice: back down or increase the commitment. Backing down risks weakening the alliance; increasing the commitment most likely means war. The decision to escalate must be governed by calculations about how severe the costs to the alliance would be if the United States failed to follow through. If the costs are believed severe enough, then intervention is merited in order to maintain the credibility of the alliance.

America's experiences with Bosnia and Kosovo in the 1990s are cases in point. The Bush administration decided in 1991 to stay out of the Yugoslav imbroglio and leave it to the Europeans, but by mid-1995, the Clinton administration, having trained the Croatian army, seized the issue from the Europeans, pushed NATO to mount powerful air strikes against the Serbs, brokered the Dayton Peace Accords, and then sent a large contingent of American troops to Bosnia as part of a NATO peace enforcement mission.[64] What accounts for the reversal in policy?

Hubris played a minor role: the United States would show the Europeans that it could succeed where they could not, demonstrating once again the necessity of America's leadership in Europe's security affairs. Also important was American electoral politics: Clinton worried about Republican criticism of his Bosnian policy and was determined to remove it as an issue from the 1996 presidential elections. Third was the fact that Clinton, having previously promised to help with the withdrawal of the UN Protection Force in Bosnia (UNPROFOR), was facing the unpleasant prospect that the time was about to arrive to deploy 25,000 American troops for extracting UNPROFOR. Finally, the most important factor was the Clinton administration's concern about NATO's credibility. By the spring of 1995, NATO itself was in danger of becoming a casualty of the Bosnian war, largely because the alliance's airpower had inflicted only pinpricks against Serbian ethnic cleansing. These strikes had little effect on Serbian policy, and NATO was looking increasingly ineffective. Ivo Daalder put the matter well:

> It was only by resolving the Bosnia issue that NATO's continued viability could be assured. By this time [the summer of 1995] it was not only U.S. leadership of the alliance that was being called into question by [France's President] Chirac and others but also the alliance's preeminent role in managing European security. If only for that reason the United States strongly pushed its allies to accept the more forceful use of NATO air power during the London conference in late July. It also explains why the allies agreed to go along.[65]

The Kosovo War of 1999 is another case of intervention driven by concerns over alliance credibility.[66] As early as December 1992, the United States had taken a forceful position on deterring Serbian atrocities, when President Bush warned Slobodan Milosevic not to use force against the Albanians in the Serbian province of Kosovo. In October 1998, after Milosevic's brutal summer military campaign against the Kosovo Liberation Front (KLF) and the Kosovo Albanians, the United States and its NATO allies threatened to bomb Serbia unless the Serbs stopped. Faced with this threat, Milosevic ceased the campaign, but resumed it again in the spring of 1999, after the talks at Rambouillet had failed to achieve a political settlement satisfactory to him. Having once committed themselves to protecting the Albanians in Kosovo, the United States and its NATO partners now faced the tough choice of either acquiescing in Milosevic's resumed campaign or following through on its threat to stop him by force. Once again, failure to prevent massive ethnic cleansing and the threat of large loss of Albanian lives put the credibility of NATO at risk. With this credibility on the line, the United States and NATO chose to go to war.

By enforcing the peace in Bosnia and by waging war with Serbia over control of Kosovo, the United States prevented the killing of more innocent civilians, it stabilized Western Europe's eastern periphery and thereby helped pacify a region of considerable concern to its major allies, and it preserved the credibility of its major alliance.

Cases like Bosnia and Kosovo, where humanitarian and strategic interests are joined, will occur again, but they are likely to be much less frequent than America's experience with the Balkans in the 1990s might suggest. The Balkans are almost unique: its states are part of Europe, yet not fully integrated into it. They sit between two groups of American allies—the Europeans in Western Europe and the Greeks and Turks in southeastern Europe—and are therefore within easy reach of formidable American and allied military power. In addition, the Balkan wars of the 1990s generated huge waves of refugees that flooded into parts of Western Europe, putting pressure on the Western Europeans to do something to end those wars.

Finally, five new states were born in the area with the collapse of communism in Yugoslavia, and the borders of at least three of them were not settled before they became independent. These factors made the Balkans hard to ignore for America's European allies, and hence for the United States. However, the factors peculiar to the Balkans in the 1990s are not readily found in other regions of the world where America's interests are concentrated. Nevertheless, there will be occasions, either in Europe again or elsewhere, when humanitarian factors become entangled with alliance credibility or with other interests that are highly important to the United States. When these situations arise, prudence dictates military intervention if the humanitarian interests put the strategic interests at great risk.

When to Use Force

Determining when to use force to defend interests is never easy. The rules set out above cannot cover every contingency that will arise, but they do provide guidelines for most, and these guidelines flow from the fundamental goals and regional differentiation that selective engagement prescribes. Underlying all of the rules is a fundamental principle: the amount of force used should be commensurate with the intrinsic value of the interest at stake.

Applying this principle yields additional guidelines: the United States should pay large military costs only when vital and highly important interests are threatened, but it should rule out costly military action to protect secondary interests. This means that the United States should, in general, refrain from military intervention in humanitarian crises that arise from civil wars, unless its strategic interests are directly engaged or unless mass murder is likely or has begun, and it should aim to pay only small to moderate costs when it intervenes. This will satisfy neither those who want the United States to stay out of all civil wars nor those who want it to stop each and every one, but it will reserve America's military power for the civil wars that are generally the most costly to human life, to America's interests, or to both. These guidelines would preserve America's military resources for a peacetime forward presence in Eurasia and the Gulf, for waging war in those areas should that become necessary, and for military action against grand terrorists.

NECESSITY OF AMERICAN LEADERSHIP

The final feature of selective engagement is its recognition that America's global leadership is necessary to protect America's global interests. There are three reasons for this.

The first reason is that this is still the age of the state. Nationalism continues to be one of the most potent forces in world politics today, and the state remains the most important actor in international politics. Since the end of the Cold War, states have been increasing in number. Differences in national interests continue to cause the main cleavages in international politics, and are thus the main source of conflicts among states. It is states, especially the powerful ones, and not international organizations, multinational corporations, or non-governmental organizations, that are still the primary actors in world politics. Great powers may construct and run international organizations to protect their interests, but these organizations are more tools of statecraft than constraints on great-power action. States control access to their territory by multinational corporations, and regulate them within their borders; multinational corporations are still national in their nature, even though they may operate globally. Non-governmental organizations seek to influence state policy on a whole range of matters because it is states that set the rules within their territorial domains. Thus, states are more powerful than the other actors in international politics, and that is why they remain the prime actors.

In accepting the primacy of the state, selective engagement pays less heed to two other forces commonly cited as powerful factors in world politics today: economic globalization and the clash of civilizations. Some argue that state sovereignty is eroding because of economic globalization, particularly of capital markets. Markets, however, do not exist in a political vacuum; they are embedded in a political order, and international markets are embedded in an international political order created by powerful states. Markets do have powerful effects once they begin to operate, but states today are adapting to the changes wrought by markets, just as they did in the past, and they are more resilient than the proponents of globalization concede. Globalization, moreover, is primarily a phenomenon of rich and powerful states, as Chapter 1 pointed out, leaving large parts of the world beyond its reach.[67] What has been created by powerful states can be destroyed by them. (For example, at the end of World War II, the United States created the Bretton Woods system of fixed exchange rates among currencies to foster trade, but in 1971 it destroyed that system when it no longer favored American interests and replaced it with a new regime of floating exchange rates.) Trade and globalization have prospered because it is in the interest of powerful states that they do. Should those states' interests change, so, too, would the nature of trade and the scope of globalization.[68]

Selective engagement also rejects the primacy-of-civilizations argument put forward by Samuel Huntington, who argues that cultural identities at the level of civilizations are the most potent factors in world politics today.[69] Civilizational factors are significant, to a degree, but they do not capture the most important sources of violent conflict currently at work. For example, over half of the new civil wars since 1991 have occurred in Africa, but the states of Africa, according to Huntington, constitute one of the world's major civilizations. Therefore, the civil wars that have occurred there are intra-civilizational, not inter-civilizational; they derive instead from ethnic, tribal, clan, and class divisions. Similarly, the few international wars that have occurred since 1990 have also been intra-civilizational, not between civilizations. For example, the war between Ethiopia and Somalia was between two African states; the war between Peru and Ecuador was between two Latin American states; and the Great Lakes war in Africa was among seven African states. The Gulf War saw Arab states fighting with the United States, France, and England against Iraq, another Arab state, while the interventions in the former Yugoslavia saw the Judeo-Christian West intervening to protect Muslims in Bosnia and Kosovo. Civilizational differences may have important effects on world politics, but providing the focal point for civil and inter-state wars is not one of them.

A second reason that American leadership in this state-centric world is necessary is that the United States remains the world's most powerful state. Selective engagement holds that America's leadership is therefore both essential and advantaged. It is essential because no other state is as well placed on all the dimensions of national power as the United States to exert international leadership. Unless it throws its weight behind issues favored by itself and its like-minded and most weighty allies, "coalitions of the willing" will not materialize and inaction will result. As Kenneth Waltz once put it: "If the leading power does not lead, the others cannot follow. All nations may be in the same leaky world boat, but one of them wields the biggest dipper."[70]

America's leadership is also advantaged, compared to the other great powers, because none of them possesses America's political acceptability. The other great powers often resent American leadership, but nonetheless they still prefer the United States, not one of their regional competitors, to undertake the leadership role. Nearly all of these powers trust the United States more than they trust each other to assume the leadership position (but only as long as the United States acts in a multilateral, not a unilateral fashion). The United States stands in relation to the great powers of Eurasia as the most disinterested among them, the state to which nearly all are prepared to turn when they are unable to agree among themselves, in order to produce collective action. America's indispensable role, in sum, is based on both its power and its purpose, and no other state is yet able to compete with it on either ground, much less both at once.

Third, selective engagement holds that the United States must lead because of the great benefits it derives from the current world order. The United States is a status-quo power; its interests lie in making sure the public goods of international peace and prosperity are provided. "If the largest beneficiary of a public good . . . does not provide disproportionate resources towards its maintenance," as Joseph Nye argues, "the smaller beneficiaries are unlikely to."[71] If the United States is not prepared to use its resources, including its military resources, to do what is required to maintain that peace and prosperity, others will not, and therefore it will suffer disproportionately.

It is on these grounds, then, that selective engagement calls for American leadership. If the most powerful state, the one most acceptable politically to others, and the greatest beneficiary of the current international order does not lead, then no one will lead. If no one leads, then international order and stability will suffer, and so, too, will America's interests. International politics abhors a power vacuum; if the United States does not help fill those parts of the vacuum critical to its interests, others with different interests will, and not to its benefit. A great power remains great only if it uses its power judiciously to shape the international environment in ways conducive to its interests.

Our world remains one of independent states. In such a world, the interests of states will clash as much as they overlap. The centrifugal forces of national self-interest will continue to vie with the centripetal forces of democracy, economic interdependence, and the need for coordinated state action to cope with global problems such as climate change. The key to managing the tensions between national interests and collective goods is what it has always been: enlightened leadership by the great powers. In this era, the task of marshalling the great powers into regional and global concerts falls on the United States because it is the greatest power.

Summary of Selective Engagement's Key Features

These, then, are the key features of selective engagement: it seeks the fundamental goals laid out in Chapter 2; it combines beneficial features from other grand strategies; it differentiates among regions; it maintains a selective forward presence; it is judicious in the use of force for the defense of interests other than vital and highly important ones; and it maintains America's global leadership role.

The most important feature of the strategy, apart from the interests it seeks to protect, is the maintenance of a selective forward presence. In that regard, selective engagement is associated with the successes of American foreign policy in the twentieth century, and not with its failures; the last one hundred years shed a favorable light on forward defense. When the United States pursued a precautionary and preventive strategy, the nation fared well; when it did not, it ultimately paid heavily. The outstanding failure of American grand strategy occurred in the twenty years between the two world wars of the twentieth century (1919–1939), when the nation abstained from preventive action. The United States failed to join the League of Nations that it had created, and then it failed to stand firm with potential allies against Nazi aggression in Europe and Japanese aggression against China. In the interwar years, America's isolationist and offshore balancing stance simply reinforced French proclivities toward political paralysis and British proclivities toward appeasement, and thus abetted German and Japanese aggression and conquests. Having failed to deter great-power aggression in Eurasia, the United States was subsequently forced to fight a hegemonic war in order to deny these aggressors control over it. An earlier and tougher American deterrent policy in both Europe and East Asia, backed up by sufficient military power, could have forestalled German and Japanese conquests, or at least brought on war before those conquests had proceeded so far, when it would have been easier to defeat the aggressors.[72] By contrast, the outstanding success in American grand strategy in the last century was containment of the Soviet Union. Through its alliance commitments and troops deployed at both ends of Eurasia, the United States deterred potential Soviet expansion, fostered regional stability, and provided the stable political framework that enabled economic openness and interdependence to flower. Both past experience and present circumstances indicate that precautionary and preventive policies work better than stand-back or reactive ones.

PITFALLS OF SELECTIVE ENGAGEMENT

Desirable though it is, selective engagement is not risk-free. In this section I outline its pitfalls and suggest how they can be avoided.

There are six potential dangers. The first three are dissipation of America's economic might, hollowing out of America's alliances, and embroilment in war. I consider the first to be a relatively minor danger; the second, also minor, unless the United States makes major errors; and the third, a moderate danger. The other three pitfalls are the most serious: loss of selectivity, provocation of countervailing coalitions, and loss of the American public's support. They pose the greatest risks to the strategy of selective engagement because they require the most skill and discipline to avoid. I deal with the first five dangers here; I address the last—loss of the American public's support and how to prevent it—in the concluding chapter of this book.

Dissipation of Resources

Under current circumstances, we need not worry that selective engagement will drain America's economic might. The difference between a defense budget that supports isolationism or offshore balancing, on the one hand, and one that supports selective engagement, on the other, is not great.

To see why, consider American defense spending in 2000-year dollars. This is one year before the September 11, 2001, attack and the subsequent large defense budget increase for homeland defense and for the Afghanistan war. This budget serves as a convenient baseline by which to gauge the difference in magnitude between selective engagement and isolationism. Budget analyst Cindy Williams has calculated that in 2000 dollars, an isolationist defense budget would have cost $230–240 billion dollars, or roughly 2.7 percent of America's gross domestic product at the time. She calculated that a selective engagement defense budget would cost between $290 billion and $300 billion, or 3.2–3.3 percent of America's gross domestic product at the time. Williams's $300 billion figure is 9 percent below the $327 billion that the Congressional Budget Office (CBO) estimated, at the time, to be the cost of a "sustaining budget" for the Department of Defense in September 2000—defined as one "required to sustain the military forces that are in place today."[73] Based on 2000 dollars, the cost difference between isolationism and selective engagement is thus somewhere between $60 billion and $100 billion, depending on whether Williams's or CBO's estimates are used. Put another way, this means that an isolationist defense budget costs between 70 and 80 percent of a selective engagement budget, due in good part to the fact that isolationism would need a much smaller navy.[74]

The large post–September 11 defense increases of the Bush administration do not radically change this result. An isolationist budget would still have to pay for the additional costs of homeland defense, for the costs of tracking down terrorists abroad, and for the new entitlements, such as pay raises and medical benefits, that were added to the defense budget. In addition, the size of cost overruns for major weapons systems was understated in the later Clinton administration budgets, but not in the Bush budgets, and those additional costs would have to be added proportionately to the isolationist budget.[75] A defense budget for an offshore balancing strategy would likely cost more than one for an isolationist strategy, because offshore balancing would necessitate the maintenance of larger and more powerful fighting forces, especially a larger navy, in case the United States needed to return to Eurasia to battle an emerging great-power hegemon. This would narrow the gap between the cost of offshore balancing and selective engagement.

A selective engagement defense budget that cost 20 percent more than an offshore balancing budget, or 30 percent more than an isolationist defense budget, does not amount to small change, but the additional dollars involved represent less than one percent of America's gross domestic product—a sum that clearly would not break America's economic might, even when sustained over decades. In fact, defense spending today as a percentage of America's gross domestic product is lower than it was during the Cold War and throughout the first half of the 1990s. The defense budget for fiscal year 2003 represents about 3.3 percent of America's GDP. During the 1950s, the United States spent on average 10 percent of its GDP on defense; in the 1960s, the figure declined a bit to 8–9 percent; in the 1970s, it declined further to 5 percent; and in the 1980s, it was still only 5–6 percent. Defense budgets in the 1990s ranged from 4.4 percent of GDP at the beginning of the decade to 2.9 percent at the end.[76] Defense budgets did not break the bank during the Cold War, and there is no reason to believe that defense budgets in the 3.3–3.8 percent range would do so now. None of this is to argue that we should ignore the size of the defense budget, fail to control its costs, or give the Pentagon whatever it asks for. Vigilance over defense spending is always in order. The point is simply that while selective engagement is not a cheap strategy, it is also not a bank-buster.

For those concerned about America's economic health, the place to look is not the defense budget but America's savings rate. The United States still consumes more than it produces and therefore imports more than it exports. This cannot go on indefinitely, as any economist can demonstrate with national income accounting formulas. Finding ways to boost America's savings rate is the single most important thing to be done now to ensure America's long-run economic competitiveness.

Finally, a far greater danger to America's economic health than the additional dollars required to sustain a selective engagement strategy would come from defense budgets that would have to balloon to meet the demands of expanding commitments and countering powerful hostile counter-coalitions. These are the two hazards that all those who care about the effects of defense budgets on America's economic health should worry about, which is why I concentrate on them.

Hollowing Out of America's Alliances
The second danger is that America's alliances will hollow out, becoming paper commitments that neither the United States nor its allies—not to mention potential adversaries—take seriously. Formed to contain and deter the Soviet Union, these alliances have little value now that the Soviet Union is gone, so the argument goes, and they are still in existence due only to inertia. The threat gone, these alliances will soon collapse.

Alliances should never be taken for granted, but a collapse of America's core alliances in Eurasia and the Persian Gulf need not happen for a considerable time.[77] Six factors will affect the vitality and viability of these alliances. To begin with, there is the degree to which these alliances still serve the interests of all of the states that are party to them. Next is the extent to which the states in the particular region fear each other more than they fear the United States, or the extent to which they prefer American leadership to that of one of their rivals. Then there is the extent to which memories and underlying distrust remain powerful forces in eastern and western Eurasia. In addition, there is the deep fear that, if the United States were to withdraw its nuclear umbrella, regional powers would, one after another, seek nuclear weapons (what are called nuclear cascading effects). The viability of these alliances will also be affected by the strength of the socialization effects produced by America's long-standing institutionalized alliances,

NATO and JASA (the Japanese-American Security Alliance). Finally, they will also be affected by the quality of America's leadership and its willingness to work to preserve these alliances.

At present, the first five factors favor the continued viability of America's core alliances. States at the eastern and western end of Eurasia and in the Persian Gulf desire an American presence because it serves their interests. For example, the Persian Gulf sheikdoms that are allied with the United States continue to look to it for their ultimate security against Iraq and Iran. The Europeans continue to find the American military presence a stabilizing factor in their relations with one another, a residual guarantee against a Russia turned powerful and nasty, a necessary partner in dealing with threats on Europe's periphery, an important ally with a long military reach against terrorists, and a useful hedge against other potential external threats. Japan is concerned about North Korea and rising Chinese power; South Korea worries about North Korea; a united Korea would be concerned about being sandwiched between two powerful states; and both Koreas, as well as China, not an American ally, are concerned about growing Japanese military power. Therefore, although the original rationale for America's core alliances in Europe and East Asia may be gone, and although no dominant regional power has yet emerged in the Persian Gulf, none of America's allies believes that its environment is threat-free. All see transitions ahead in their regions that are unpredictable and potentially dangerous, and all believe that the American military presence helps protect them and helps keep their regions more politically stable than they would otherwise be.

Glenn Snyder may be right—that "alliances have no meaning apart from the adversary threat to which they are a response"—and that therefore when a common threat ceases to exist, so, too, does a basis for an alliance.[78] However, this has not yet happened in Europe, East Asia, or the Persian Gulf. In these three regions, America's allies view the U.S. military presence as an important insurance policy against the threats that do remain and against those that could arise. This creates the basis for shared U.S. and allied interests that are strong enough to make the alliances and forward presence politically viable.

The common interest is reinforced by the other factors at work. Memories of German and Japanese aggression in World War II are still present, much more powerfully in East Asia than in Europe; so, too, are concerns about a Germany or a Japan unfettered by alignment with the United States. Moreover, states in all three regions, both America's allies and others, fear one of their own becoming a regional hegemon more than they fear the presence of American power. All also fear a cascading spread of nuclear weapons in their regions should the United States leave. In particular, German, Japanese, Iraqi, Iranian, or North Korean acquisition of nuclear weapons would not be viewed with equanimity by their neighbors. Finally, the habits of multilateral cooperation in NATO and bilateral cooperation in JASA, nourished over four decades, have produced strong socialized and institutionalized ties.

These five factors create a sufficiently strong foundation of common interests to perpetuate America's core alliances. Nevertheless, the threats are not so potent, the interests not so strong, and the alliances not so firm, that inept or unwise American leadership could not destroy them. The quality of America's leadership is crucial if these alliances are to be preserved. They will not be as tight as they were during the Cold War, because the threats are less pronounced, but both the United States and its allies can tolerate somewhat looser ties. Looser alliances, however, do not mean hollow alliances. The alliances will only be hollowed out or destroyed if the basis of common interests were to disappear, or if the United States exercised poor leadership, especially unbridled unilateralism.

Embroilment in War

The danger of a greater likelihood of embroilment in war is not so readily dismissed. Selective engagement should be more effective than isolationism and offshore balancing in preventing wars in those regions where the United States has key interests that could be harmed by the outbreak of hostilities. The wars that are most important to prevent are those among the great powers in Eurasia, small wars that could escalate to great-power wars, and those that could threaten access to Persian Gulf oil. If properly maintained, America's alliances and military presence in Eurasia and the Persian Gulf, with their peace-inducing deterrence and reassurance effects, should make war less likely.

Selective engagement also takes the position that should the specific wars it seeks to prevent in these regions occur, then the United States should wage war because U.S. interests require it. Justification for this position depends on how America's interests and the threats to them are defined; selective engagement's definitions of interests, and threats to them, are broader than those of isolationists and offshore balancers. The difference covers not just war avoidance, but also what interests the United States should be prepared to defend with force. In the end, selective engagement holds greater promise than isolationism of preventing those wars in Europe, East Asia, and the Gulf that would be most damaging to American interests, and it is willing to fight them, if they cannot be averted, to defend American interests. Whether the result is that selective engagement carries with it a greater risk of becoming embroiled in war is not easy to say, but the answer is probably "yes." How much greater, however, is not clear.

Selective engagement's commitment to prevent, stop, or ameliorate mass killings in civil wars, where possible, will place American troops in harm's way. This is not likely to happen often, because intervention in such situations is not easy and because it must be done selectively and sparingly. However, it will happen more often under a selective engagement strategy than under an isolationist or offshore balancing one, because of their mandate to stay out of such imbroglios. On this score alone, selective engagement will mean more war than isolationism, but again, how much more is not clear.

Loss of Selectivity

The danger that selective engagement might lose its selectivity is potentially quite serious. As critics of this strategy rightly point out, commitments can become open-ended unless proper care is taken.[79] In order to understand how to limit commitments, we must first understand why they expand.

Commitments can grow in several different ways. First, success in fulfilling one task could create the ambition, and sometimes even the need, to do more. In this case initial success causes a commitment to expand. Second, the need to defend a commitment could require additional resources to be allocated to the task in order to salvage the initial commitment. This might happen because decision makers underestimated the difficulty of the initial task (bad planning), or because they legitimately miscalculated (not all things can be foreseen). Third, domestic political calculations could cause leaders to undertake additional obligations. They decide to do more, either because they believe that a foreign policy success will consolidate their grip at home, or because they believe that they face irresistible domestic forces. Fourth, alliance and prestige considerations could cause commitments to expand. This factor operates when allies demand more, when the alliance leader believes its leadership or the alliance is at stake, or when the state's leaders believe its general credibility is at issue. Each factor alone, if powerful enough, can cause a commitment to expand or lead to other commitments, but usually at least two must be present for commitments to grow. The interventions in Somalia and Bosnia—two controversial American foreign policy decisions of the 1990s—illustrate these points.

In late 1992, the United States sent a military force into Somalia on a humanitarian mission to distribute food to Somali civilians in order to avert mass starvation.[80] Having succeeded in that task by early 1993, the United States and the United Nations enlarged the mission to include the political reconstruction of Somalia. The United States was naive to believe that success in feeding civilians qualified it to rebuild a nation, but the Clinton administration was also legitimately concerned that mass starvation could recur unless the civil war was resolved. The war interfered with agricultural production, and the warring clans had used starvation as a weapon against one another. There was a case to be made for political reconstruction, which would require disarming the clans, but taking on that task caused the United States and the United Nations ultimately to move away from a position of

166

political neutrality to one of opposition to a powerful warlord, Mohammed Farah Aideed, and his organization. Moreover, while the military power the United States had deployed to feed the starving civilians was adequate to that task, after it agreed to the larger task of nation building, it cut its military forces. The result was military disaster. The United States then withdrew its forces when it decided it was not prepared to pay the price of political reconstruction. Initial success and naiveté largely explain why the United States expanded its mission from feeding Somali's civilians to trying to kill one of its warlords.

America's experience with Bosnia from 1991 to 1995 was a classic case of "mission creep," where three factors were at work: electoral politics, in Clinton's desire to neutralize Bosnia as an issue in the 1996 presidential elections; alliance considerations, as NATO's credibility was perceived to be at stake; and initial commitments, in that Clinton had promised to use U.S. forces to help extract the British and French troops of the UN peacekeeping mission, should that prove necessary.

Both cases involved a growth in commitments, and in each case the rationales were not flimsy but reasonable. Nevertheless, in retrospect each case involved a mistake in judgment that caused adverse consequences. The United States undertook a task in Somalia (nation building) that it was not prepared to see through, and the resulting loss of its soldiers there led the United States to avoid intervention in Rwanda. The United States sought at first to stay out of Bosnia, but it made two commitments that ultimately drew it in: the commitment to extract British and French forces, and the token use of air strikes in the spring of 1995. It ended up with the worst of both worlds, allowing tens of thousands of deaths, and risking the viability of NATO.

The loss of selectivity is a serious danger. Somalia teaches humility about nation building. Military intervention to reconstruct nations rent by civil war is a long-term and consuming task, one so difficult that it should be rare. Bosnia teaches that the United States should not lightly make commitments that will come back to haunt it (like the promise to extract British and French forces), and that it should not use force in a haphazard and ineffective manner (like the NATO pinprick air strikes), especially when such use risks discrediting a crucial military alliance.

One can agree or disagree with the decisions made in these cases, or with the critiques made of them, but what counts are the larger lessons regarding the expansion of commitments, or "mission creep." U.S. policy makers must always plan at least three moves beyond the initial commitment and should not initiate the use of force unless the United States is prepared to see matters through, no matter what contingencies arise. In statecraft, foresight is impossible, but strategic planning is not. None of this is to argue that commitments should never be expanded. Often they should be, but U.S.

leaders must be aware of the powerful political pressures that are nearly always present, once an initial commitment is made, to expand it. Therefore, they must be deliberate about taking the first step. When they do, they must design that step in full recognition of the pressures that will subsequently come to bear. The slope can become awfully slippery once the initial commitment is made.

Provocation of Countervailing Coalitions

An equally serious danger is that selective engagement will provoke powerful countervailing coalitions. It is not loss of selectivity that is at risk here, but rather the increased burden of implementing commitments, even those selectively made, against concerted opposition.

The argument is that, by wielding its military power, or simply by being so powerful, the United States will inevitably provoke opposition from powerful actors. They will take countermeasures to thwart American actions, such as increasing their armaments or entering into blocking coalitions. The danger is not that one or a few states will oppose the United States; there will always be opposition, if only from the state that is the target of America's deterrent or compellent actions. Rather, the danger is that several of a region's most powerful actors will ally against the United States, or that a few of the great powers, such as Russia and China, will do so. Should the former happen in several regions at once, or should great-power opposition materialize, then selective engagement would most likely impose such a heavy burden that it would become too expensive for the United States to sustain. The risk, in short, is that America's exercise of its military power would beget its own check.[81] How serious is this danger?

International relations theorists take two approaches to this matter. In one camp are the pure structuralists. They write as if they believe every state to be driven primarily by power considerations and therefore to be acutely sensitive to its relative power compared to those states about whom it cares or worries. In the other camp are the qualified structuralists. They explicitly argue that state actions are influenced not simply by power calculations, but also by a host of other factors, among which are the intentions of those states they worry about, and the purposes for which they exercise their power. In the pure structuralist view, states focus nearly single-mindedly on, and adjust nearly automatically to, perturbations in the balance of power; in the qualified structuralist view, states make a more complex set of calculations in which power is only one factor, although it is often the most important one.[82]

I hold to the latter view. Power considerations are never absent from a state's foreign policy calculations and they do count a lot, but it is absurd to argue that power explains everything. Power's function, after all, is to serve purpose: the values for which power is wielded. Besides raw power calculations, additional factors matter in state calculations: what values the state wielding its power stands for; whose interests, other than its own, its actions serve; and whether its power is wielded unilaterally or consensually, to name only three.

Whether America's actions provoke countervailing coalitions depends on how it wields its military power: for what purposes, in what fashion, under what circumstances, and with what effects. In this list the single most important element is the first—the purposes of power. Will America's exercise of power serve only its own interests, or will it also serve the interests of many or most of the significant regional actors? If the interests served are broadly shared, American power will be accepted, if not rapturously embraced. This acceptance will be reinforced by the natural rivalries and jockeying for position of the powerful actors in each region where the United States is heavily committed. If American interests are perceived by the regional actors to be exclusively and selfishly American, however, the exercise of its power will be widely resisted, sooner or later. Instead, by serving only its own interests, the United States would become the regional threat. By serving the interests of many, the United States can take advantage of the inherent competitive dynamics within each region and thereby make its exercise of power more acceptable.

Thus, the question becomes: can the United States serve the interests of others while still serving its own? In general, the answer is "yes." In East Asia, Europe, and even the Persian Gulf, enough of the key regional actors embrace the interests that the United States deems vital and highly important. America's interests overlap the most with those of influential regional actors in Europe, the least in the Persian Gulf, and somewhere in between in East Asia. The Eurasian great powers favor combating terrorists, preventing the spread of weapons of mass destruction, preserving peace among themselves, and preserving unimpeded access to Persian Gulf oil. These goals are not as widely shared in the Persian Gulf, but enough of the powerful actors there embrace them that America's goals remain acceptable, although more difficult to implement than in Eurasia. Even the American interests that, while important, are not vital or highly important—preserving an open international economic order, promoting the spread of democracy and the protection of human rights, and combating the dangers of global warming—have significant international appeal, although oftentimes more among the peoples than their governments. For all the reasons spelled out earlier in this chapter, however, it is the vital and highly important interests that are key, and it is upon those that the United States must concentrate when wielding its military power. Their broad acceptability means that the United States can also serve some of the significant interests of others while at the same time serving many of its own.[83] This proposition holds even when some of a region's influentials have clear conflicts of interests with the United States.

In each of the three regions where the United States maintains a significant military presence, the number of states that oppose its forces is astonishingly small. This fact, however, is no reason for complacency. The wrongful exercise of American power could quickly dissipate its regional acceptability. Therefore, the task for American statecraft is clear: work to persuade enough of the regional influentials that there is a significant overlap between America's interests and theirs. What makes the job of persuasion possible is the reality that there is, in fact, an underlying coincidence of many interests: what is vital and highly important for the United States tends to be highly important for the bulk of the regional influentials.

PRINCIPLES FOR IMPLEMENTING SELECTIVE ENGAGEMENT

In this chapter, I have laid out the central features and potential pitfalls of selective engagement. The strategy is demanding to implement. To be successful, America's leaders must be disciplined enough to avoid inflating commitments, deft enough to avoid provoking opposing coalitions, and successful enough to enlist the American public's continued support. Can the United States muster a sufficiently disciplined, deft, and successful statecraft? [84]

Clearly, no grand strategy is perfect, and selective engagement will never achieve perfection in discipline, deftness, or success. Mistakes are inevitable. In implementing selective engagement, the goal for the United States must be to minimize the number of mistakes and to avoid making the really big ones. To aid in this quest, I offer here three principles for implementing selective engagement; in Chapter 7, I expand upon these principles and offer specific policies to facilitate the strategy's implementation.

The first principle is to guard against commitment creep when using force by applying these tests to decisions to commit military force. The most basic test is to ask whether the commitment being considered is essential to advance or protect any of America's six national interests. The next test is to ask whether additional commitments may become necessary to salvage the original one. If the original commitment requires additional commitments, it should be reexamined to determine whether it is of sufficient importance to justify the investment of still more to protect it. Finally, when a decision has been made to add new commitments to the original one, we must ask whether the policies being implemented to support them all are mutually supportive, or are instead contradictory. If the latter, then we should either change the policy or step back from the commitment. As these tests show, maintaining a disciplined diplomacy requires hard work and continual effort; it is a never-ending task.

The second policy principle is never to rely on a coincidence of interests alone to produce concerted action. An overlap in interests between the

United States and the regional influentials only makes concerted action possible, not inevitable. Were shared interests alone sufficient to induce cooperation among states, diplomacy itself would be unnecessary. Instead, America's diplomatic task must be to convince other states that what it finds in its own interest is also in their interest, once they understand clearly where their interests lie. Deft diplomacy requires detailed elaboration of the policies that are necessary to support the shared interests, clear leadership in organizing coalitions to protect these interests, constant consultation about the best ways to attain them, concerted action to the extent feasible, and protection of the consensus on those rare occasions when unilateral American action is required. A clumsy, heavy-handed, or unilateralist diplomacy is likely to provoke strong counters to America's overseas military presence, while deft diplomacy enhances the chances that counter-coalitions can be averted. Deft diplomacy is an essential ingredient of selective engagement.

The third principle is to avoid excessive ambition. The temptation for a nation as militarily powerful as the United States is to do too much. The fatal misstep for an imperial power—and the United States is an imperial power—is overreach. The United States today has no peers and stands alone as the world's preeminent military and economic power. For that very reason, the temptation of imperial overstretch—to become the Athens of the twenty-first century and embark on self-defeating Sicilian expeditions—is ever-present and powerful. The words of Pericles ring as true today as they did in Greece in 432 B.C.: "What I fear is not the enemy's strategy, but our own mistakes."[85] American policy makers must be vigilant against succumbing to this temptation to overreach, which is born of the arrogance of power. Making certain that America's interests also serve the interests of others is the best means to avoid this well-worn path to imperial ruin.

Now that I have laid out the features of selective engagement, I turn to the free hand strategies of isolationism and offshore balancing.

FIVE

Isolationism and Offshore Balancing

As Chapter 3 showed, isolationism and offshore balancing are the only two viable alternatives to selective engagement. I call them the "free hand" strategies because they shun formal standing commitments to employ America's military power and are as sparing as possible in its use. Both are feasible in that there are no political barriers to their implementation and in that the resource demands that they make are moderate. The issue for these two strategies is not their feasibility but their desirability. Do they protect America's interests as I have postulated them, and do they do so better than selective engagement? My answer is that they do not.

To see why, in this chapter I analyze the assumptions, goals, and historical records of isolationism and offshore balancing. Then, in Chapter 6, I compare both of them to selective engagement in order to see which provides the most benefits at the lowest risk.

THE KEY FEATURES OF ISOLATIONISM

Isolationism is the grand strategy with the longest lineage in American foreign policy. With a few brief exceptions, it reigned supreme from 1789 until 1947. It first appeared in President Washington's 1796 Farewell Address, when he admonished his country to "avoid entangling alliances." Washington advocated isolationism because he had witnessed firsthand the polarizing effects that foreign entanglements could have on American domestic politics and domestic stability. Isolationism was codified in the Monroe Doctrine of 1823, when Secretary of State John Quincy Adams called for the Old World and the New to remain separate spheres. Adams sought to forestall the European great powers from reestablishing political-military footholds in Latin America, which he believed would threaten America's security and its aspirations for hegemony in Latin America.[1] During its heyday, isolationism had a powerful pull on Americans because they lived in a country whose location and size made isolationism both attractive and feasible. The United States was a continent-sized power possessing abundant natural resources, surrounded by militarily weak neighbors, and separated by two vast oceans from the bulk of the world's miseries and from easy reach by the forces of most other powers of consequence. Isolationism came to have such a grip on Americans that they imbued it with moral virtue, coming to believe that isolationism preserved their democracy's purity by removing it from the corruptions of European power politics.

Isolationism's grip on the United States was especially strong in the first half of the twentieth century, and especially in the era between the two world wars. In the immediate aftermath of World War I, Wilson's campaign to join the League of Nations foundered against isolationist opposition. In the 1930s, Roosevelt's attempts to bolster the British and the French against Hitler were undercut by an isolationist Congress and the neutrality legislation it had enacted. In 1941, on the eve of America's entry into war, while Hitler was subjugating Europe and Japan was rampaging in East Asia, the Selective Service Act (the draft) passed the House of Representatives by only a single vote. Roosevelt feared the return of isolationism so much after World War II that he devised the United Nations partly to sell internationalism to the American people. In the late 1940s, the Truman administration so feared the resurgence of isolationist sentiment that it felt compelled to exaggerate the Communist threat in order to mobilize public backing for its containment policy.[2] Even after the United States embraced containment in 1947, isolationism's hold was so powerful that a substantial segment of the American public continued to adhere to it throughout the entire Cold War era. For example, when asked "do you think it would be best for the future of the country if we take an active part in world affairs or if we stay out of world affairs," between 25 percent and 30 percent of the American public during this period regularly answered that the United States should "stay out."[3] During its long reign, isolationism's grip was so powerful that Americans saw it as the nation's natural state of affairs and valued it as an end in itself.

Isolationism is often equated with the non-use of force, an utter indifference to events in the rest of the world, or complete separation from it. This view is inaccurate.[4] Isolationism does not totally rule out the use of force; it is not morally indifferent to political events abroad; it does not seek national economic self-sufficiency (autarky). Isolationism can be compatible with sustained political engagement abroad, extensive economic intercourse with other nations, and even, on occasion, the multilateral use of force. What isolationism entails is the sparest possible use of military power to shape the international environment, based on the belief that most of what happens outside of America's borders poses no military threat to the country; the belief that America's military power, short of war, can accomplish little to shape that environment; and the belief that it is not worth the costs and risks of waging war to do so. Isolationism is a "stand back" strategy rather than a preventive strategy.

To the question of how the United States should utilize its military power, isolationism responds that the United States should undertake no binding peacetime commitments to come to the assistance of another nation with military aid, that it should use force only to protect the nation's vital interests, and that it should adhere to a very narrow definition of what interests are "vital." A pure isolationist strategy, consequently, would prescribe that the United States should discard all standing political commitments to use military power; avoid peacetime military alliances; disband all overseas bases; bring all the troops stationed abroad home; preserve complete freedom of action to determine when, where, how, in concert with whom, and against whom the United States will use its military power; reject all ambitious attempts to shape the larger international environment through the peacetime time use of military power; and go to war only for the most compelling reasons, which essentially means only to defend the nation and its citizens from attack. The heart of isolationism was well captured in 1952 by Senator Robert A. Taft, one of America's most influential isolationists, who continued to espouse isolationism well after the United States had adopted containment:

> From the days of George Washington . . . [neutrality and non-interference have] been the policy of the United States. It has . . . always avoided alliances and interference in foreign quarrels as a preventive against possible war, and it has always opposed any commitment by the United States, *in advance,* to take any military action outside of our territory. It would leave us free to interfere or not interfere according to whether we consider the case of sufficiently vital interest to the liberty of this country. It was the policy of the *free hand.*[5]

In sum, isolationism is unilateral in deciding when to use force and is very sparing in its use.[6]

Today's rationale for an isolationist posture rests on three assumptions. The first is that the United States is physically secure from attack by another state because its nuclear forces provide a robust deterrent against state-sponsored conventional, nuclear, biological, or chemical attacks against the homeland.[7] America's "strategic immunity," to use Eric Nordlinger's phrase, is likely to continue for the indefinite future. As for terrorism, an isolationist would agree that going after terrorists in the short term is militarily necessary if they attack Americans at home or abroad, but would also argue that America's overseas presence, particularly its military meddling in other people's affairs, is the root cause of such terrorist attacks against Americans abroad or at home.[8] A logical consequence would be for the United States to remove itself from the quarrels of others so that it does not become the focus of their anger. Over the longer term, according to the isolationist view, this offers the best defense against terrorism; again, it justifies bringing the troops home.

The second assumption behind the isolationist position is that America's foreign economic interests do not require the projection of its military power overseas. The United States can safely (and profitably) pursue those interests without a military escort. Yesterday's isolationists did not have to worry about protecting extensive overseas economic interests because America's stakes abroad were not that large. Those isolationists lived in an era when tariffs were high and when the bulk of America's economic energy went into developing its vast continental expanse. Today's isolationists, by contrast, note that the United States is more enmeshed in a web of global economic interdependence than ever before. The United States now has more investment abroad than ever before, and it sells to, and buys from, the rest of the world in amounts that dwarf those of earlier years.

Contemporary isolationists dismiss the salience of these new economic interests and reject the role of force in protecting them. Instead, they argue that America's economic interests have best been preserved by economic means: through the unimpeded movement of capital, technology, and goods when economic intercourse among nations is free and fair and through economic retaliation when it is not. In their view, if economic intercourse is fair, the United States will prosper; if it is not, the United States would do better to fight foreign economic discrimination by denying foreigners access to the American market when access abroad is denied, or by subsidizing its industry at home when industry abroad is subsidized. Denial of access or strategic subsidy, rather than forcible entry or exertion of political leverage through military power, are thought to be the most effective instruments to protect America's considerable economic stakes in today's interdependent world.[9]

The third assumption of isolationism is that peacetime military commitments and forward deployment of troops abroad are not only irrelevant for America's security and prosperity but are in fact downright harmful to its long-run competitive position. The worry is that the United States will dissipate its scarce resources in overseas military adventures that by their nature are expensive, needless, and fruitless. This worry is compounded by the view that in today's world it is technological innovation that holds the key to a nation's economic competitiveness, and in this competitive race the United States should steer its resources to where they will do the most good—its own economic competitiveness—rather than squandering them to protect the states that are its fiercest economic competitors. Not fear of military attack, but the prospect of causing or accelerating America's economic decline is the greatest worry of contemporary isolationists. By becoming enmeshed in military enterprises that can bring no benefits, the United States would not merely waste resources; it would also do irreparable harm to its global competitive position in the process. The logical conclusion, say the isolationists, is to avoid these enterprises.[10]

These three assumptions—confidence in America's strategic immunity, belief that economic well-being does not require the projection of military power, and fear that America would bleed itself dry in military adventures abroad—provide the underpinnings for the present-day isolationist posture. They constitute the necessary and sufficient conditions for an American military withdrawal from abroad.

THE KEY FEATURES OF OFFSHORE BALANCING

Today, there are few who adhere to the stark isolationist position. Even Robert Taft, the icon of modern isolationism, was not a pure isolationist. He understood the need, after World War II, to balance Soviet power in Europe. Taft's book, *A Foreign Policy for Americans*, is a tortured exercise in reconciling how to maintain America's free hand with the need to deter the Soviet Union through the NATO alliance and American troops in Europe.[11] Instead, most who currently declare their faith in a form of isolationism adhere, as a practical matter, to a strategy of offshore balancing.[12]

This strategy shares many of the same assumptions as isolationism, but with one key difference: a genuine isolationist is indifferent to the state of the Eurasian balance of power, while an adherent to offshore balancing is not. Isolationists believe that America's two ocean moats, its nuclear weapons, and its missile defenses can make it secure against every conceivable state threat. It can therefore remain indifferent to any war or conquest in Eurasia, even one that might lead to the emergence of a Eurasian hegemon. Offshore balancers, to the contrary, believe that should such a hegemon arise in Eurasia, through war or other means, it could pose a serious military threat to the United States by virtue of the substantial resources that it would control: either it could outspend the United States on arms and subject the country to political-military intimidation, or it could use its substantial power to attack the United States or the western hemisphere. To neutralize either threat, offshore balancers are prepared to go back to Eurasia if a potential hegemon appears on the horizon and to do whatever is necessary, including waging war, to contain it or cut it down to size. The key assumption of offshore balancing is that the United States would have sufficient time to organize the wherewithal to attack and destroy the threat before it reached the United States. If allies are required to deal with such future threats, then the United States would be able to throw together ad-hoc coalitions to deal with them. The bedrock of offshore balancing is the belief that America's margin of security is sufficiently large that military withdrawal from overseas would not endanger America's security.

Thus, a pure isolationist would do nothing to contest an emerging Eurasian hegemon; an offshore balancer would do anything, short of all-out nuclear war, to contest it.

Their differences over the Eurasian balance of power lead to other differences. Offshore balancing would spend more money on maintaining a cutting-edge, rapidly mobilizable military force that could, if necessary, be projected quickly to Eurasia. It would also devote a great deal to trying to check an emerging Eurasian hegemon through non-military means, and it would invest extensively in intelligence so as to avoid strategic surprises. Because of the potential need to intervene in Eurasia, offshore balancing would maintain a more robust military force, and especially a larger navy, than isolationism; this means that offshore balancing is a more expensive strategy to pursue than pure isolationism.

Currently, no hegemon exists in Eurasia, and no great power is well placed to become one soon. The candidate most analysts think is best positioned to achieve this status is China, but even if China were at some point to become as powerful as some now predict, it could not pose the same hegemonic threat that the Soviet Union once did. China is not as well placed geographically as the Soviet Union was to control the industrial, economic, or military power centers of Eurasia. Europe is beyond its power-projection capabilities for the foreseeable future and so, too, is Russia's industrial heartland. Between China and Japan is an ocean moat, making invasion and conquest of Japan difficult. India and Russia are each far too large and populous for China to conquer and digest. The most likely way for China to become a Eurasian hegemon through conquest would be to grab parts of Southeast Asia or part of Russia's Far East. The former scenario is a possibility, but China would confront Vietnam, a tenacious foe that would impose great costs on China to subdue, causing it to think hard before embarking on a southward advance. The latter scenario is also possible but very risky: territorial conquest of part of a nuclear-armed state's homeland is fraught with escalation scenarios that are likely to deter such an adventure. If China is to assume hegemonic status, therefore, it will most likely occur through economic growth and the conversion of some of its economic power into military power. Without substantial territorial conquest, however, China will only be a regional hegemon in East Asia, not one lording it over all of Eurasia.

Isolationism and offshore balancing can be treated as one when comparing their prescriptions to those of selective engagement. The reason is that, absent the imminent emergence of a Eurasian hegemon, the practical import of both strategies is the same: abandon America's alliances and bring the troops home. Should China become an East Asian regional threat, as some argue it will, then the prescriptions of offshore balancing will look much like those of selective engagement for East Asia.

AMERICA'S EXPERIENCE WITH THE FREE HAND

In this section, I examine how well the United States did with the two free hand strategies during its first one hundred and sixty years. In the next section, I then draw lessons from that experience for today's world.

From 1789 to 1945, the United States pursued isolationist and offshore balancing strategies at different times. It followed the dictates of isolationism from 1789–1917, then those of offshore balancing from 1917–1921; it reverted to isolationism in 1921–1941, and returned to offshore balancing in 1941–1945. During the 1945–1990 Cold War era, the United States followed the central tenet of offshore balancing: it acted to prevent the Soviet Union from dominating the Eurasian land mass by maintaining a substantial military presence in Europe and East Asia. America's Cold War balancing strategy, however, also employed extensive standing peacetime military commitments to other nations and a highly interventionist global military policy. During this period, as a consequence, offshore balancing was part of a larger global containment strategy. Thus, it is the 1789–1945 period, not the Cold War era, that provides the best evidence for assessing America's experience with the free hand approach, because the United States had no standing military alliances or peacetime military deployments in Eurasia during that time.

The Geopolitics of Isolationism and Offshore Balancing

The long reign of isolationism and the short reign of offshore balancing— the free hand era—coincided with the geopolitical era in America's foreign policy. That era began in 1789, with the nation's independence, and ended in 1945, with the advent of the nuclear age. I refer to this era as "geopolitical" because America's foreign policy turned on the interrelation of politics and geography. A geopolitical prism highlights factors such as how close or distant a state is from menacing great powers; how close or distant possible allies are from it; the extent of the industrial and raw materials those great powers control compared to what the given state controls; how resource-rich or resource-poor the state is; how much military power the state can extract from its society; and how much natural protection its frontiers provide it.[13] Before 1945, such factors weighed heavily with American leaders.

In the free hand era, the geopolitical factors that most affected America's security, and ultimately its prosperity, were the nation's great distance from Europe, which was the only area of the world with sufficient military power to harm the United States; the presence or absence of a major war among the European great powers; the possibility that one European power could emerge from such a war to dominate the industrial-military resources of western Eurasia; the benevolence or malevolence of British seapower toward the United States; and the ability of the United States to extract usable military power from its huge industrial base, and how rapidly it could do so if circumstances demanded it. The first four can be termed external factors; they were products of the nation's fortuitous geographic location, the state of European power politics, and the nature of British intentions. The fifth factor was internal to the United States, a product of American hard work and ingenuity and an abundance of natural resources. These factors were the geopolitical determinants of America's fate during the isolationist era.[14]

Each factor affected America's security and its ability to remain aloof from Europe's wars. Sitting an ocean away from Europe was of tremendous value, because it made it difficult for any European state to exert military power against the United States. So, too, was America's great productive power, because that enabled it to generate whatever military forces were necessary for defense. This factor, however, became important only when the United States became a great industrial power after the Civil War. Large great-power wars in Europe were a liability because they ultimately drew the United States in. Also a liability was the possibility that a hegemon might emerge from these large wars, because it could harness and then hurl the combined military-industrial might of Europe at the United States. Finally, Britain's maritime strength was a great asset when British intentions toward the United States were benign, but a huge liability when they were malevolent.

Historically, of course, these factors never influenced the United States in isolation from one another, and they varied in their relative importance during the nation's first one hundred and fifty years. Isolationism worked poorly from 1789 to 1815, quite well from 1815 until the mid-1880s, and then increasingly less well from the mid-1880s until the United States abandoned it after World War II.

From 1789 until 1815, isolationism failed to keep the United States out of Europe's wars. The country was too weak to defend itself or its commerce; Britain was strong and its intentions toward the United States were malign; Europe was almost constantly at war for these twenty-five years; and the wars were major because first Revolutionary France and then Napoleonic France threatened to establish a hegemony on the continent. U.S. policy made it all the more difficult to keep out of these struggles because the United States refused to give up its trade with the European belligerents and saw its commerce seized by them. As a result, the United States was treated as both prize and pawn by the European great powers and became embroiled in two wars: a quasi-naval war with France between 1798 and 1801, and the War of 1812 against Britain, which the United States lost. Even earlier, the American colonies had become embroiled in Europe's other great-power war of the eighteenth century, known as the Seven Years War in Europe and the French and Indian Wars in the new world. In these early years, America's neutrality was a wish, not a reality, and an isolationist foreign policy failed to keep it out of war.[15]

The seventy years from the end of the Napoleonic Wars to the middle of the 1880s were the heyday of America's isolationism. During this period, isolationism worked well because, although the United States remained militarily weak, Britain dominated the seas and its intentions were largely benign toward the United States, while the great-power wars that occurred in Europe were, except for the Crimean War, relatively small. Hence the United States was able to stay out of those wars. Beginning with the mid-1880s, however, isolationism worked less well for the United States because, while British intentions remained benign, its maritime supremacy waned. Two major great-power wars broke out in 1914 and 1939, in which Germany threatened to acquire hegemony unless the United States threw its weight in. Hence in the last twenty-five years of the geopolitical era, the United States once again became embroiled in Europe's wars. These last two periods most concern us: we need to understand why isolationism worked well during its heyday period, and then why it subsequently became less and less effective in the last sixty years of its reign, in order to understand the conditions under which it might again be effective.

The Heyday of Isolationism (1815–1885)

After the end of the Napoleonic Wars in 1815, the United States experienced about seventy years of security from Europe's machinations against it.[16] With its security assured, the United States proceeded to conquer a large part of the North American continent and to build an industrial powerhouse that dwarfed the British and German economies, the two largest in Europe. By 1913, for example, the United States had 32 percent of the world's manufacturing output, while Britain had just 13.6 percent and Germany 14.8 percent. The United States produced 25 percent more per worker than Britain, and twice as much per worker as Germany.[17] Moreover, except during its Civil War, America's armed forces, by comparison with Europe's, were negligible. America's army remained small, constituted mainly for killing and coercing relatively unarmed Native Americans, and its navy mostly rotted in port after the Civil War ended. In the Mexican War of 1846–1848, for example, America's armed forces totaled 39,000, while Mexico's were only 20,000. In contrast, during the 1870 Franco-Prussian war, the armed forces of Prussia and France were bigger by a factor of ten: Prussia with 452,000 and France with 319,000.[18] In America's navy during the decades after the Civil War, "there was a virulent attack of politics, graft, and corruption. . . . The Navy Department spent millions of dollars . . . with little in the end to show for it, save a collection of worthless antiquated ships, an army of enriched contractors, a host of political retainers, and partisan strength at the polls in the favored constituencies."[19] During the heyday period, in short, the United States grew both larger and richer while remaining largely disarmed—a highly unusual feat in international relations.

The United States was able to accomplish this feat because Britain's supremacy at sea made the United States safe at home. It was not America's military might but Britain's fleet that protected the United States. (That Americans benefited from Britain's maritime supremacy does not mean they were thankful for it; in fact, throughout much of the nineteenth century, hatred of Britain was a national pastime.) In this period the United States was a good example of the free-rider: its military fate depended less on what it did for itself than on what Britain did for it.

In essence, Britain's imperial strategy in the western hemisphere produced, as a by-product, a high degree of security for the United States.[20] After Nelson destroyed the French fleet at the Battle of Trafalgar in 1805, Britain became the world's dominant seapower and retained its supremacy until the century's end. No European power, consequently, could extend its political, military, or economic influence into the western hemisphere without the acquiescence of the British, who chose most of the time not to give it. Instead, they used their naval dominance to help themselves capture the lion's share of the trade of both North and South America. British capital played a large role in developing America's intercontinental railroads; it also penetrated deeply into Latin America, especially into Brazil and Argentina. Not out of altruism for the United States, but in the service of their own interests, the British threw the protective cover of their maritime supremacy across the New World. Britain's fleet became America's military deterrent and hence its first line of defense. Moreover, because the British thought their own industrial supremacy would enable them to capture Latin America's markets easily, they felt no reason to use their naval power against the United States. Commercial rivalry between the two states for these markets was intense, but it never turned violent. The absence of a major great-power war during this period (except the Crimean War), together with a stable balance of power on the European continent, enabled Britain to channel its resources into overseas commerce and seapower instead of continental entanglements and armies. Great-power peace thereby facilitated Britain's maintenance of its maritime supremacy. In sum, during the heyday period, there proved to be a free-rider relationship between America's security and Britain's imperial strategy.

The Era of Geopolitical Nightmares (1885–1945)
This fortuitous state of affairs began to change in the middle to late 1880s, when the third stage of the geopolitical era began. As this stage wore on, the international environment grew steadily less hospitable for the United States. Britain's maritime supremacy came under attack; tensions in Eurasia heightened and alliances tightened; diplomatic crises increased in frequency and

intensity and small wars broke out; ultimately two world wars erupted. Much like the period before 1815, adverse developments in Europe, this time compounded by those in East Asia, changed America's fortunes. Once again, the United States found itself hostage to developments across the oceans.

Three of these developments were crucial: the decline of Britain's maritime supremacy; the threat of Germany's victory in World War I; and the threat of a German-Japanese conquest of Eurasia. Each of these developments provoked a fear in America's political-military elite, and I call these fears "geopolitical nightmares" because if any one of them had come true, it would have imposed harsh consequences on the United States.

Britain's naval decline provoked a fear that the Caribbean could be penetrated by a hostile European power and that America's great coastal cities could be subjected to naval attack. The threat of a German victory in World War I provoked Woodrow Wilson's fear that America's democratic system would be subverted by the huge military buildup that the United States would require to protect itself from the German hegemon. The threat of a German-Japanese conquest of Eurasia provoked the fear that the United States could be subjected to a global economic blockade and ultimate military defeat by the German and Japanese hegemons. None of the three geopolitical nightmares—naval attack, militarization, or economic strangulation—materialized. This does not mean, however, that these fears were groundless. Each was rooted in real developments; each was based on reasonable assumptions about what could go wrong for the United States if preventive actions were not taken; and each was thought to pose such a serious threat to the United States that it brought forth a major American response. Indeed, one reason why none of the nightmares materialized was that America's political-military elite took them seriously and therefore took preventive steps against them. By examining each nightmare, we can understand why the international environment came to be seen as increasingly inhospitable to American interests and why, as a consequence, the United States found itself forced to become more active militarily so as to reshape the environment in ways that better suited its interests.

Naval Attack and Defensive Imperialism
The first nightmare was fear of the seizure of military bases in and around the Caribbean by a hostile European power, followed by naval attack against America's coastal cities. This nightmare arose because Britain could no longer provide the naval security that Americans had so long enjoyed, and it set in motion a chain of events that led to America supplanting Britain as the strongest naval power in the western hemisphere.

Beginning in the mid-1880s, Britain's maritime dominance and imperial position came under vigorous challenge from both European competitors and regional rivals. As a consequence, because it was overextended, Britain began to shift its naval power from abroad to home waters and to strike deals, first with its overseas regional rivals and then with its European imperial competitors.[21] The British settled first with the United States in the western hemisphere (the 1900 Hay-Pauncefote Treaty), next with Japan in East Asia (the 1902 Anglo-Japanese Treaty), then with France (the 1904 Dual Entente), and finally with Russia (the 1907 Triple Entente).

In response to what was perceived as a more competitive and threatening international environment, and to British retrenchment, the United States embarked on a twenty-year program (1885–1905) that established its political-military mastery over the Caribbean and the western hemisphere. It prevented the British from intervening in Venezuela (1894–95); it defeated Spain in a short war and acquired Cuba and Puerto Rico (1898); it annexed Hawaii (1898); it excluded the British from participation in any canal to be built across the Central American isthmus (the 1900 Hay-Pauncefote Treaty); it intervened in Santo Domingo as the bill collector for the European banks (1904); and it established the principle that the United States, not a European power, would safeguard the financial integrity of the Central American nations (the Roosevelt Corollary of 1904). Thus the United States took advantage of both British retrenchment and Spanish weakness to establish its predominance in the New World.

To back up its assertive diplomacy and territorial expansion, the United States undertook a long-term naval expansion that began in the middle 1880s and lasted through 1922. From the Civil War until the early 1880s, the United States had allowed its navy to decline technologically and materially. A modest modernization program was begun in 1883 and lasted throughout the decade, but the real turning point came in 1890, under the leadership of Secretary of the Navy Benjamin Tracy, when the United States turned from deploying a commerce-raiding and coastal-defense fleet to the construction of an ocean-going, blue-water, battleship navy.[22] From 1891 through 1919, the United States built 52 battleships. In 1890, it had a total warship tonnage of 122,000, which put it sixth in the world behind Britain (with 802,000), France, Russia, Italy, and Germany. Its naval power was no match if Britain and another European power had teamed up against it, or if Britain alone chose to act against it. By 1914, however, after twenty-five years of naval building, the United States had acquired a warship tonnage of 985,000, moving up to third behind Britain (2,714,000) and Germany (1,305,000). In 1916, during World War I, the United States passed the largest military appropriations bill in its history and vowed to build a navy "second to none." By the end of 1919, the U.S. combined fleet (the Atlantic, Pacific, and Asiatic fleets) had 29 battleships including 16 dreadnoughts, 15 cruisers, and 354 auxiliaries, for a total of 398 ships, a force larger than the combined fleets of France, Italy, and Japan. From 1919 through 1922, when a naval treaty among the big powers was concluded, the United States built

131 warships, while Britain, Japan, Italy, and France together built just 92 warships.[23]

America moved aggressively during this period to institute what became known as the "large policy," because its political-military elites reasoned they had no other choice.[24] Historian Richard Challenger writes that:

> The White House and military services were especially concerned about hypothetical dangers in the Caribbean, about the damage that might occur to the American interest if the United States did not act, well in advance, of any possible European intervention. . . . The list of possible dangers was almost inexhaustible. The United States was never viewed as in clear and present danger, but the Republic might some day be threatened if it did not move promptly in the Caribbean to forestall hypothetical dangers that might become real if there was no such preventive action.[25]

Preventive thinking was rampant among the elite, who suffered from what Greenville and Young called a sense of "vanishing security." The political-military elite believed that "isolation from complications with Europe was disappearing"; they feared that "the defenseless state of America's seaboard cities might prove a great temptation to an aggressive nation." They began to come up with all sorts of scare scenarios.[26] One of the most vivid came in a speech on the Senate floor by Senator Norton Dolph of Oregon, who conjured up a demand by the commander of five British warships for the surrender of San Francisco.

> The demand is refused. Twenty-four hours are allowed for the departure of the women and the children; then the two ships take up a position inside the bar, south of Point Lobos, within seven miles of the city hall. Suddenly a roar is heard, followed by another and another; soon the screech of the shells is followed by the crash of falling buildings; fire breaks out in a hundred different places; the fire department is helpless; the socialist and anarchist revel in the wholesale destruction, and strip and burn the buildings which the shells have spared; the whole city is on fire; men are looking out to save themselves, leaving their property to the mercy of Providence. San Francisco, the pride of the Golden State, is destroyed, and the enemy has a foothold on American soil which it will cost many lives to recover.[27]

As a consequence of these fearful contingencies, U.S. leaders took actions that they considered to be defensive, not offensive; they acted out of future rather than present concern to forestall the ability of any extra-hemispheric great power to take advantage of both Spanish weakness and the weak states in and around the Caribbean.[28] Between 1895 and 1905, Germany and Britain were (apart from Spain) the two states most vigorous in and around the Caribbean, acting primarily out of financial and economic motives (collecting debts owed them by governments and keeping the area open for their trade). Whether they would have become territorially acquisitive and established additional military bases had the United States not acted is difficult to answer. In the case of Britain, probably not, because it was in the process of imperial retrenchment. Germany, however, was seeking such footholds and might well have acquired them because it was an imperial power still "on the make." Contingent though the feared dangers were, they were enough to set the United States on a course of military rearmament and imperial expansion. The result was to transform a nation largely defenseless in 1890 into one that by 1914 was militarily secure against any potential challenger.[29]

World War I and America's Militarization

The second geopolitical nightmare arose with the prospect of a German victory in World War I. As in the first case, the danger feared was contingent, not certain, and distant, not immediate. Nonetheless, it too produced a powerful nightmare: Woodrow Wilson's fear that America's militarization, undertaken to respond to a hegemonic Germany, would ultimately undermine American democracy.

Wilson did not fear armed forays into the western hemisphere or the prospect of military conquest by a German hegemon; he believed that both could be countered. Instead, what he worried about were the corrosive effects on American democracy of a United States militarily powerful enough to hold a German hegemon at bay. For Wilson, a United States that powerful meant the militarization of America—and that was his nightmare. Wilson outlined his fears during a speech on September 5, 1919, in St. Louis, when he was in the midst of his campaign for Senate ratification of the League of Nations.

> We must be physically ready for anything to come. We must have a great standing army. We must see to it that every man in America is trained to arms. We must see to it that there are munitions and guns enough for an army. . . . You have got to think of the President of the United States, not as the chief counselor of the Nation, elected for a little while, but as the man meant constantly and everyday to be the Commander in Chief of the Army and the Navy. . . . And you know what the effect of a military government is upon social questions. You know how impossible it is to effect social reform if everybody must be under orders from the Government. *You know how impossible it is, in short, to have a free nation if it is a military nation.*[30]

Thus, not direct attack but internal subversion gripped Wilson.

How realistic was this nightmare of Wilson's? No definitive answer is possible because it requires that we imagine a history that did not happen. In this case, however, we have a good surrogate for this "unhappened history"— the Cold War. The experience of the United States during the Cold War constitutes a period long enough for the presumed effects of militarization to appear. During this era, the military forces that the United States deployed were massive, and the sums spent on them were vast, thus qualifying for Wilson's nightmare of a "great standing army." The military-industrial complex wielded great influence in American life, and military power played a large role in America's foreign policy. The adverse effects on American democracy were clear: the government too often lied, it oversold the communist threat, it got into a horrendous war in Vietnam that was not necessary, it committed outrages against some of its citizens such as testing atomic effects against unknowing soldiers, and it much too often deprived citizens of liberty, as in the McCarthy era and with the Nixon wiretaps. Ultimately, however, the quasi-militarization of American life during the Cold War, bad as its effects were, did not subvert America's democratic system. It proved resilient and bore up under the Cold War's weight. Therefore, if the Cold War is a reasonable test of the validity of Wilson's nightmare, it was clearly overstated.[31]

Fears of the effects of militarization may have motivated Wilson to oppose a would-be German hegemon, but they do not account for why the United States entered World War I. In February 1915, after Germany had declared the waters around Britain and Ireland to be a war zone and enemy merchant ships fair game, Wilson declared Germany strictly accountable for any injury to American vessels or citizens inflicted by its U-boat warfare. In May 1915, Germany sank the giant luxury liner *Lusitania*; 1,198 passengers and crew, including 128 American citizens, were lost. In response, Wilson implicitly threatened war. In April 1916, following the torpedoing of the unarmed French passenger ship *Sussex*, Wilson threatened to break diplomatic relations with Germany unless it stopped sinking unarmed ships without warning and without saving the passengers. Under threat of war with the United States, the Germans agreed to do so (the *Sussex* pledge) and their U-boats largely refrained from attacking unarmed ships until 1917. In early January, however, the German High Command decided to resume unrestricted submarine warfare against Britain. The High Command knew that this act would bring the United States into the war, but calculated that the submarine campaign would starve Britain to its knees before American military power could be brought to bear, thereby bringing a German victory. Germany's action left Wilson no choice but to declare war against it.[32]

Although Wilson's nightmare regarding the effects of militarization was not the immediate cause of America's entry into the war, it does help explain what he hoped to achieve by entering it, and it does help account for his nearly fanatical commitment to the League of Nations. In essence, Wilson waged war in order to make peace—to construct the type of peace and world order that, he reasoned, would best protect American interests.[33] It was to be a "peace without victory" because Wilson had learned from history that punitive peace settlements ultimately brought new wars in their wake. Wilson told Jusserand, the French Ambassador to the United States, on March 17, 1917, that he wanted to see a "scientific" and just peace, one with "no Alsace-Lorraine in it" that would threaten the world's future peace.[34] Such "peace without victory" would make possible the reconstruction of world order through the League of Nations. Wilson may genuinely have believed that the League of Nations would end war, but he also had a realistic appreciation of the facts: Europe could no longer manage its conflicts because Germany was too powerful to be checked by its European neighbors alone. Therefore, American power had to be brought to bear to right the balance, and the League was the device to do this. The League would bind American power to Europe and nip in the bud any new German bid for continental hegemony. With the League keeping the peace, there would be no war, and therefore, no German hegemon, thus no need for massive American forces maintained indefinitely, and no threat to America's way of life. The League would avert Wilson's nightmare by preventing the militarization of American society.[35]

World War II and Economic Strangulation

The third geopolitical nightmare—economic strangulation—arose in World War II with the prospect of a German-Japanese victory. America's entry into the war averted that outcome. Its economic aid kept Britain afloat and enhanced the Soviet Union's fighting effectiveness, and its military participation made possible the defeat of both Germany and Japan. What would have been in store for the United States had it not helped its British, Soviet, and Chinese allies to vanquish the Nazis and the Japanese?

Three outcomes were plausible. In the first, Germany could have subdued Britain, ruled western and central Europe, but failed to vanquish the Soviet Union. The Germans and the Soviets would have coexisted in an uneasy stalemate, with periodic fighting. Japan would have ruled the western Pacific and southwest Asia, but it would have continued to struggle to pacify China. Under this outcome, neither Germany nor Japan would have been a mortal threat to the United States, because neither could have diverted significant military resources from Eurasia. Germany would be guarding its eastern flank against the ever-present possibility of a Soviet attack, while Japan would be stretched thin simply trying to control China. Consequently, neither would have had spare resources to attack and defeat the United States, although Germany could have made some trouble for the United States in the Caribbean, Central America, or South America.[36]

Under the second scenario, Germany and Japan would have won a complete victory, vanquishing Britain, the Soviet Union, and China, but then they would have turned against each another and fought for the redivision of the Eurasian spoils. Neither, however, would have achieved a decisive victory, so both would constantly be consumed with fighting each other or making preparations to do so. Under the second scenario, Germany would have been even less of a bother to the United States than under the first, because it would have had no resources to spare for meddling in the western hemisphere.

It is the third scenario that would have contained the mortal danger to the United States. Germany and Japan might totally have vanquished their Eurasian great-power adversaries, pooled their resources, and then gone after the United States. With Eurasia conquered, the United States would have had no great-power allies; if the worst were to occur, the United States, too, could go down. This is the scenario that worried Americans at the time. In the summer of 1940, Roosevelt was especially worried that Hitler's conquests in Europe would enable him to acquire military bases in the western hemisphere, threaten Latin America, and then put pressure on the United States.[37] Averting a German victory was the ultimate rationale for America's entry into the war and the major outcome that the strategy of offshore balancing was designed to avert. With his usual brevity, Walter Lippmann put the matter well:

> Fundamentally, the security of the United States demands that we prevent
> the establishment of a conquering empire in any part of the great oceanic
> basin of the Atlantic and the Pacific. Eventually, it will threaten us.
> Eventually we must resist it. Sooner or later we shall be at war with it. This
> is the final reason for the Monroe Doctrine, for our championing the
> independence and territorial integrity of China, and for our intervention
> against the Kaiser's Germany and Hitler's.[38]

Had the third scenario materialized, the United States would have faced the greatest threat to its security since the War of 1812. Would it have gone down to defeat if the Germans and the Japanese had won the war? We can answer the question by turning to Nicholas Spykman's masterful book, *America's Strategy in World Politics*. It came out in 1942 during some of the darkest days of World War II, when the outcome was still in doubt, and his answer remains the most comprehensive and imaginative available.[39]

Spykman's argument was that, once Germany and Japan had conquered Eurasia, they could not swiftly defeat the United States because it was too strong. Therefore, they would first have to weaken it with a strength-sapping global blockade and embargo.[40] When the combined blockade and embargo had wrought its effects, Germany and Japan could deliver the decisive military blow. Therefore, to avert this outcome, the United States must fight while it still had powerful allies with which to defeat these two. Otherwise later, isolated and alone, it would go down in defeat. In other words, military conquest of the United States without prior strangulation was impossible, but conquest with it was inevitable.

Swift military defeat was not in the cards, reasoned Spykman, because the United States was too powerful and because it had the advantages of the defender. The feat of invading, much less conquering, a continental-sized state from across two oceans was so daunting as to be unlikely. In his view, the United States could mount a viable defense because it could occupy and hold a number of bases that were strategically situated far away from its shores. These bases would enable it to hold the enemy's long-range airpower at bay. From these bases it could then use its own long-range aircraft and naval power to destroy any invading armadas. Spykman calculated the effective combat-zone radius for bombers at 1,000 land miles and the battle fleet combat-zone radius at 2,500 land miles. In the Pacific, this put America's combat interception reach out beyond Wake Island; in the Atlantic this put its reach nearly to the Azores and sixty percent of the way to the western bulge of Africa.[41] Air and naval power would be the great equalizers for the United States. Spykman therefore concluded that, "invasion under conditions of modern warfare is very difficult if the defender is a highly industrialized nation with a modern and effective navy, air force, and army at her disposal and an adequate system of coastal defense."[42]

Sanguine as he was about a viable defense, however, Spykman did not think it could be sustained indefinitely. At some point, a global embargo imposed on the United States would cause it to experience a severe shortage in strategic raw materials, those essential to the war effort that came, in whole or in part, from outside the continental United States.[43] The shortage would hamper America's industrial production and its defense output, and could eventually cripple its military machine.

The problem for the United States was that it could do nothing to remedy the shortage or even alleviate it. The United States could not break a global embargo imposed on it; hence it could not obtain the needed raw materials from overseas. Germany and Japan would, by conquering the Soviet Union, Britain, and France, dominate not only western, central, and eastern Eurasia, but also Africa, the Middle East, and South Asia, by inheriting the overseas colonial possessions of Britain and France. As a consequence, Germany and Japan would control all of the significant landmasses on earth outside the western hemisphere and could prevent shipment of needed materials from these areas to the United States. Any attempt by the United States to break the embargo with force would be futile: without powerful allies overseas, it could not establish the footholds necessary to attack the Germans and the Japanese on their own turf. Thus, global encirclement would render a military breakout from the embargo impossible.

Stymied abroad, moreover, the United States could not rectify the raw material shortage from sources in the western hemisphere. Spykman did not believe that the United States could retain the political allegiance of the entire hemisphere, nor necessarily defend all of it; instead, he envisioned a "quarter sphere defense." This would include southern Canada, the Caribbean and its island outposts, Mexico, the Central American states, and South America down to the line that runs from the Tropic of Cancer in the west to the bulge of Brazil in the east, which meant South America down roughly through northern Brazil. (Lost to the United States through German or Japanese military action would be northern Canada, the Aleutians, Alaska, and Greenland; lost through German economic warfare would be Argentina, Chile, Bolivia, Peru, and southern Brazil.)[44] The United States could easily defend southern Canada and Mexico because both were contiguous to the heart of American military power; it could defend the Caribbean and Central America through its naval power and control of the outlying Caribbean islands; and it could defend the northern third of South America because the Amazon jungle would form a natural barrier against an upward thrust by the Germans and the Japanese.

The problem with the quarter sphere was not its military defensibility but its economic viability. It lacked the strategic raw materials for U.S. self-sufficiency, concluded Spykman, and so did not have "the power potential necessary for an adequate system of defense."[45] The United States could not defend the quarter sphere indefinitely, but indefinite defense was what the situation required. Here, in sum, was Spykman's geopolitical nightmare. The areas that could be defended by the United States did not have the raw materials required to fuel its industrial-military machine; the areas that did have them would be under German and Japanese control. Consequently, subject to a global embargo, America's military strength would ebb to the point where it would fall to a decisive military blow. In the battle of the continents, he concluded, the Eurasian hegemons would prevail.[46]

Spykman's geopolitical nightmare provided powerful reasons for the United States to join Britain and France in crushing Germany and Japan, and it probably comes close to describing President Roosevelt's ultimate fears about a German-Japanese victory. The immediate cause of America's entry into the war, however, was Japan's surprise attack on the American fleet at Pearl Harbor.

Prior to the attack, President Roosevelt had faced two big problems: how to get the United States into the war in Europe in order to prevent a Nazi victory, and how to keep it out of the war looming with Japan. Roosevelt considered Nazi Germany to be the greater threat; consequently, his preference was to defeat it first and only then to turn and deal with Japan. Isolationist sentiment was so powerful in the United States, however, that Roosevelt could not declare war on Nazi Germany. Japan's Pearl Harbor attack solved that problem: Hitler, honoring the Axis alliance, gratuitously declared war on the United States immediately after the attack. Entry into the European war, however, brought what Roosevelt had wanted to avoid: a simultaneous war with Japan and Germany.[47]

Japan's attack and Hitler's declaration of war did not, of course, come out of the blue. A deeper factor was at work: the United States opposed both aggressors, and prior to Pearl Harbor, it had taken actions short of formal war to resist them. In mid-1941, the United States had imposed an oil embargo on Japan to try to force it to halt its aggression in China and Southeast Asia. The embargo had the reverse effect, however: it drove the Japanese to seek to acquire the oil of the Dutch East Indies in order to fuel their war machine. Having decided on that course of action, the Japanese took the next two fateful steps—seizing the Philippines and attacking Pearl Harbor—to try to neutralize American military power in the Pacific.

Meanwhile, the United States had been convoying supplies to Britain to prevent Hitler from subduing it. That brought the United States into an undeclared naval war with Germany in the North Atlantic. Prior to Pearl Harbor, these clashes did not escalate into all-out war because Hitler, planning for the campaign against the Soviet Union, had imposed restraints on Germany's submarine campaign against the American navy so as to avoid such a war. Once Japan entered the war against the United States, however, Hitler unleashed his submarines in the North Atlantic. He did so because he believed that American naval power would be temporarily diverted to the Pacific, thereby making a knock-out blow against Britain possible; because he had always viewed war with the United States as inevitable and now had the formidable Japanese navy on his side; and because he wanted to honor the alliance with Japan in the hope of securing Japan's future help against the Soviet Union.[48]

Motivated by his fears of a German-Japanese victory, Roosevelt took actions short of war to prevent such a victory, and these actions, by aiding the British in their fight against Hitler and by denying the Japanese the oil they needed, did contribute to bringing the United States into the war against the would-be hegemons. The majority of Americans, however, did not share Roosevelt's fears, or else chose not to act on them; it took both a Japanese surprise attack and a German declaration of war against the United States to bring the nation into the conflict.

LESSONS FROM THE FREE HAND PERIOD

America's geopolitical years, as we have seen, divide neatly into three distinct phases. From 1789 to 1815, the United States sought to keep out of Europe's power struggles through an isolationist, neutralist posture, but the attempt failed. From 1815 to 1890, isolationism worked to America's favor, and the nation prospered economically and expanded territorially. From 1890 to 1945, isolationism was less and less effective at protecting the nation's interests, and ultimately the United States, executing the prime directive of offshore balancing, was dragged into war to protect them.

These phases were defined by the relationship between the state of America's military power and the nature of its international environment. In the earliest phase, the international environment was adverse, the United States did not have the power to alter it, and the nation subsequently became victimized by it. In the middle phase, the United States remained militarily weak, but its international environment remained benign because Britain kept it so. In the last phase, the United States confronted an international environment that had once again turned adverse, but because it could no longer count on the British to rectify matters, it was forced to help shape the international environment to protect its interests, although it did so in an episodic rather than a sustained manner.

Three lessons can be drawn from this experience with isolationism and offshore balancing. First, isolationism failed to keep the United States out of Europe's major great-power wars. Second, over the course of the isolationist era, the United States experienced a profound transformation in its geopolitical role in world politics: it went from being a consumer of security provided by others to being a provider of security for others. Third, during the critical period between 1885 and 1945, the actions taken by America's elites did not conform to the assumptions of isolationism. To the contrary, these elites acted as if they believed the assumptions invalid, and they were forced to engage in offshore balancing and even selective forms of engagement.

Involvement in Great-Power Wars

Between 1789 and 1945, the United States fought in six wars. The Mexican War (1846–1848) and Spanish-American War (1898) were imperialistic wars, initiated by the United States to take territory. The War of 1812 against Britain began initially for defense and then encompassed expansion. The remaining three—the quasi-naval war of 1798–1801 against France, World War I (1917–1918) and World War II (1941–1945)—were wars not for expansion but for defense, to protect America's maritime commerce and quality of life. Of these six wars, only the two imperialistic wars of 1846–1848 and 1898 were fought when Europe was at peace; the other four were fought because Europe was at war.

Europe's large great-power wars almost invariably dragged in the United States. Between 1792 and 1945, Europe fought five major and nine minor great-power wars. The major great-power wars almost always involved at least three European great powers; the minor ones, only two. Because of their greater number of participants, the major great-power wars had larger geographical scope, higher stakes, and usually greater loss of life. Europe's five major great-power wars were the Revolutionary Wars (1792–1799) and the Napoleonic Wars (1800–1815), each with six countries involved; the Crimean War (1854–1856), with four; World War I, with eight; and World

War II, with seven.[49] The Crimean War was the smallest of the major wars, and more limited in scope, because unlike the other four, it was fought not for supremacy over Europe but to halt Russian expansion in southeastern Europe. The United States was sucked into all the major wars except the Crimean, but into none of the minor ones.

The United States got dragged into Eurasia's major great-power wars for several reasons. The United States loomed too large economically for the Eurasian belligerents to ignore it when the issue at stake was who would rule Europe. America's trade, capital, and raw materials were weapons to be exploited to fight the enemy, or crucial resources to be denied to it. Because America's economic resources were too important to be left alone, neutrality was a luxury that the European powers refused to allow the United States to enjoy. In addition, the United States was a complicit actor in this regard because it refused to cease trading with the great-power belligerents and, in fact acted to make money off of their wars. Indeed, before its entry into World War I, the United States profited handsomely from the war, both through its trade with the European belligerents and through its ability to supplant them as the dominant exporters to Asia and South America. America did so well economically in these years that its surging trade pulled the economy out of the 1914 recession and accelerated its transition from a debtor to a creditor state.[50]

Finally, the United States was never indifferent to the outcome of these major wars; it opposed an aspiring European hegemon as much as did those European states that fought to defeat it. America's opposition to hegemony never varied, only its ability to make a significant difference militarily. In the 1798–1801 quasi-naval war and the 1812 war, the United States was a pawn in Europe's conflicts; in World Wars I and II, it was the broker. But whether pawn or broker, the United States was never a disinterested party when hegemony over Europe was at stake. Because disinterest was not possible, neither was neutrality and, as a consequence, entanglement ensued.

The relevance of this first lesson for today's world should be clear. Not every Eurasian war will affect America's interests, but the odds are high that should another major Eurasian great-power war break out, the United States would once again become involved, willingly or not. The central question then becomes: should the United States act to forestall such a war, or instead intervene once it has broken out? For the reasons explained in Chapter 2, forestalling such wars makes more sense than having to intervene once they have occurred.

From Consumer to Provider of Security
Over the course of one hundred fifty years, the United States transformed itself from a security consumer to a security provider. The transition occurred during the early part of isolationism's third phase—during the

1890–1910 period—and took place in two stages. In the first stage, the United States took on the task of ensuring its own defense. Beginning in the late 1880s, it began to extract more military power from its huge industrial machine by initiating the construction of a large navy and by expanding its geographical defense perimeter. By 1914, the United States had made the New World secure from the Old. In the second stage, the United States exported security to Eurasia by generating sufficient military power to thwart bids for hegemony by Germany in World War I and by Germany and Japan in World War II. In this stage, the New World was called in to redress the imbalances in the Old.

The great transformation from consumer to provider of security was the product both of an international environment that had become less hospitable to American interests and of the phenomenal growth of American power. As we saw earlier, throughout most of the nineteenth century, the United States rode free on the protection provided by Britain; it enjoyed security on the cheap. By the close of the nineteenth century, this became impossible because Britain had to retrench in order to bring its imperial commitments in line with its military capabilities. No longer able to count on the British for its security, the United States was forced to count on itself; by then, fortunately, the country had built an economy powerful enough to generate and sustain the military power it required for the task. The decade of the 1890s marks the turning point when the United States began to shift its reliance from fortuitous external factors to its own internal efforts for its protection. Over the course of the geopolitical era, the United States went from victim in Eurasia's power struggles to arbiter of them.

The relevance of this lesson for today's world should be clear: the United States still remains the arbiter of Eurasian power politics, because all of Europe's great powers (the rhetorical protestations of a few notwithstanding) view the United States as the only disinterested actor able to arbitrate among them. Like it or not, the United States is the "balancer of last resort" for Eurasia. The issue, therefore, is not whether the United States will play this balancing role but rather how best to play it—offshore or in Eurasia.

Assumptions versus Experience

During the last phase of the free hand era, America's elites acted in ways that did not conform to the assumptions of isolationism, and conformed only to a degree with the assumptions of offshore balancers. Most of the assumptions did not hold up well during the 1885–1945 period.

When it came to the crunch, America's political-military elites did not act as if the nation had an impregnable defense. When they perceived the external environment turning adverse, they worried that the nation's security could be at risk and therefore took steps to alter the international environment, steps best described as precautionary interventions. At the turn of the century, they expanded and strengthened America's defensive perimeter. In 1917, they went to war with Germany to prevent it from acquiring hegemony in Europe. From 1941–1945, they waged war against Germany and Japan to prevent the global encirclement of the United States. Had U.S. leaders believed, at these three critical junctures, that the United States was secure, they would not have taken these precautionary actions. The phrase "impregnable defense" was not in their vocabulary; when they acted, they followed the prescriptions of offshore balancing.

America's political-military elites also never acted as if they believed solely in the dictates of offshore balancing either, because they did not believe that the nation's economic well-being could be maintained without the projection of its military power. To the contrary, throughout the entire free hand era, they understood that the nation's economic health depended to a degree on the existence of a benign international political-military environment. In the early years of the republic, when the environment was not benign, the country experienced depredations against its shipping, impressment of its citizens into the British navy, and ultimately war with Britain—all of which negated whatever enhanced commerce the United States enjoyed from the Napoleonic wars. In the heyday of isolationism, the environment became benign because British naval power made it so; with security assured and trade thus protected, the United States prospered. At the turn of the twentieth century, the United States began to project its military power outward, not only to strengthen its defenses, but also to aid its commerce. It acquired the Philippines in order to enhance its access to the China market. Its actions thus accorded with the teachings of Alfred Thayer Mahan, who stressed the intimate connection between naval strength and a flourishing maritime commerce. Woodrow Wilson needed no reminder: the connection between Germany's drive for European hegemony and its depredations against American commerce was unmistakable.

It was during World War II, however, that Franklin Roosevelt made the broadest and most explicit acknowledgment of the connection between an adverse international environment and America's economic ill health. With German and Japanese aggression in mind, he said on April 8, 1939:

> One of the results of successful military aggression by any nation or group
> of nations is the control of commerce. . . . If military domination were to
> keep on expanding, the influence of that military aggression would be felt
> in world trade all over the world, for the very simple reason that the
> aggressor nations would extend their barter system. The nations of the
> world that pay better wages and work shorter hours are immediately faced,
> because of the barter system . . . with a loss of world trade. This is obvious
> because the aggressor nations can and do work their people much longer
> hours and for much lower pay.

Therefore, the nations that do not belong to the aggressor group are faced with three alternatives. The first is to build the old Chinese Wall around themselves and to do no world trade whatsoever. . . . The result . . . is to reduce, necessarily, the national income because they immediately are unable to export any of their surplus goods. . . . The [second] is to lower their own standard of living and try to compete in the world markets by reducing the wages they pay and increasing the hours of work. . . . The other would be to subsidize the export of American products . . . [but that] would add to the national debt or we would have to pay for it out of the taxpayer's pockets by increasing the whole of the tax system from top to bottom.[51]

Clearly, then, when the international environment turned adverse, America's leaders—from George Washington through Franklin Roosevelt—understood that America's economic well-being depended on setting the international environment to rights, and that this, in turn, required the projection of America's military might.

Finally, although history offers no clear test of the proposition that alliance entanglements would drag the nation into costly adventures abroad during this era, there was a clear test of another equally important and closely related proposition: the very failure to make peacetime alliance commitments could ultimately drag the nation into a costly war. This is exactly what happened after World War I. America's refusal to commit its military power to Europe in peacetime helped cause the nation's costliest external war, in which the United States suffered over 1 million casualties—400,000 dead and 670,000 wounded between 1941 and 1945.[52] Had the United States committed its military power to Europe after World War I, World War II might have been avoided, or at least Hitler could have been crushed more easily before he conquered continental Europe. In either case, a huge European war could have been avoided, with all its attendant costs for the United States.

Throughout the geopolitical era, isolationism never bought the nation insulation from Eurasia's great-power politics. No matter whether weak or strong, the United States could never fare well at home without regard for what happened abroad. America's well-being depended on a stable and benign international order, and that, in turn, depended on the projection of military power, first by a friendly power and then by the United States itself. When isolationism produced its greatest failure, the nation resorted to offshore balancing. That worked—the United States went to war twice, and twice prevented Germany and Japan from dominating their respective spheres of Eurasia—but at great cost. It seems obvious that it would have made more sense for the United States, especially after World War I, to commit itself to preserving a stable balance of power in Europe rather than having to fight a large war to right it once again.

This third lesson is relevant for today's world. America's security and economic well-being are inseparable from what happens abroad, and both are well served by the projection of American military power overseas, not just in wartime, but in peacetime, too. To see why this third lesson still holds, as well as the first two, we must now compare the free hand strategies with selective engagement—the subject of Chapter 6.

SIX

Selective Engagement and the Free Hand Strategies

A United States gone isolationist, or one reverting to offshore balancing, would cancel all of America's standing military alliances, starting with NATO and the U.S.-Japanese alliance. It would bring home all of its military forces stationed abroad, save for its powerful navy sailing the seas and making periodic stops in foreign ports. It would use its military forces primarily to deter or defeat an attack on the homeland, to prevent the emergence of a Eurasian hegemon, and to deal with attacks against America's commerce on the high seas or against its citizens abroad. It would then avoid nearly all other military adventures. Selective engagement, by contrast, would retain America's alliances and forward bases, keep U.S. troops deployed in Eurasia, embrace all of the national interests laid out in Chapter 2, and employ America's military power to advance them.

The choice between these two approaches—between the free hand strategies, on the one hand, and selective engagement, on the other—must rest on a comparison of the benefits, costs, and risks of each approach. In the world of foreign policy making and grand strategizing, that choice is not easy because such comparisons do not yield neat and tidy results. Instead of relying on quantitative calculations that produce clear-cut answers, we are forced instead to employ historical analogies and lessons, logical analysis, and qualitative theories, aided, of course, by as much hard data and quantitative analysis as we can muster. The best assessments that we can produce are qualitative judgments, not hard and fast answers.

Such an approach leads to the conclusion that, although in the short term the free hand strategies are less expensive and perhaps even less risky than selective engagement, in the medium to longer term, they would pose greater risks to America's interests and could, consequently, impose greater costs while bringing fewer benefits. Although it is more expensive in the short term, selective engagement does a better job of protecting America's interests in the medium to longer term; thus, overall, it entails lower risk, incurs lower costs, and promises more benefits. In this sense, it ultimately pays for itself.

In this chapter I make the case for this conclusion by comparing selective engagement with the free hand strategies along six dimensions: control of the spread of nuclear, biological, and chemical (NBC) weapons; defense against grand terror attacks; maintenance of Eurasian great-power peace and stability; protection of America's economic interests; advancement of America's democratic and humanitarian values; and hedging against future uncertainties. Having thus made the case for selective engagement, in the book's concluding chapter I outline how to implement it.

SPREAD OF NUCLEAR, BIOLOGICAL, AND CHEMICAL WEAPONS

Probably the most consequential difference between selective engagement and the free hand strategies concerns their views about the dangers of the spread of nuclear, biological, and chemical weapons. Underlying both approaches is the assumption that these weapons are more likely to spread if America abandons its military alliances; both approaches focus on Eurasia and the Persian Gulf, because those areas contain nearly all of the states with both the capability and the aspiration to acquire these weapons. Both approaches are based on the assumption that, without America's stabilizing presence and its nuclear umbrella, the states in those regions—especially Japan, South Korea, Saudi Arabia, and eventually Germany—would feel an acute need to do more for their own defense. As a consequence, regional security competitions involving these weapons, especially nuclear weapons, are likely to start, or would increase in intensity where they have already begun. Thus, both selective engagement and the free hand envision more NBC spread among states if America leaves Eurasia. Where they part company is over what this means for the United States.

Advocates of the free hand believe that NBC spread would be of little or no consequence for America's security. In their view, America's robust nuclear deterrent makes the United States so secure that it need not fear conventional or NBC attacks on its homeland by state actors, and that therefore the United States can be indifferent to NBC spread to more states. Furthermore, they argue that America's involvement in regional conflicts decreases rather than increases the nation's security. Such involvement raises the risk of drawing the United States into regional wars that could turn nuclear, biological, or chemical, and that could conceivably put the American homeland at risk. Rather than continue to extend its nuclear umbrella over its allies, then, the United States should close it, in order to stay out of any NBC cross-fires.[1] Security at home, they believe, does not require these military commitments abroad, but is in fact enhanced if the United States does not have them; consequently, the commitments should be severed.

Adherents of selective engagement believe that NBC weapons are far too dangerous for such a relaxed view. They could be used against the nation, its military forces, or its allies. Advocates of selective engagement do not discount the effectiveness of America's nuclear deterrent in dissuading attacks on its homeland; indeed, they believe in its general efficacy. What they worry about is its future effectiveness if NBC weapons spread to hard-to-deter state leaders. The latter might actually use these weapons against their neighbors, might blackmail their neighbors with them or, feeling secure in their possession, might become emboldened to aggress conventionally against them. Worse still would be terrorist acquisition of NBC weapons. Terrorists are the actors most hostile to the status quo, most likely to challenge it, most likely to threaten America's political and economic interests overseas, and most likely to resort to the first use of such weapons. If terrorists get their hands on NBC weapons, then the risk of use against American forces or the American homeland increases. Even though a precise value cannot be assigned to that enhanced risk, this does not make it any less real, and advocates of selective engagement do not want to chance it. Consequently, they take the position that the fewer states that have NBC weapons, the better off the United States will be.

The reasoning for this position was set out in Chapter 2: the more states that have such weapons, the greater the danger that rogue leaders and unbridled terrorists might get them. A smaller number of state possessors keeps the danger lower; a larger number would enhance it. Some of the states that seek these weapons, such as Iraq, Iran, and Libya, have sponsored terrorism in the past and have aspirations to alter the territorial status quo. As more states acquire nuclear and biological weapons, the technological impediments to their spread will weaken, the components necessary to construct them will become more readily available, and the chances for forcible seizure and sale, authorized or unauthorized, will grow. (Concerns about "loose nukes" in Russia and about the possibility that Islamic terrorists might acquire nuclear weapons from sympathetic elements in the Pakistani military or intelligence services should be a wakeup call.) Moreover, as the number of NBC-armed states increases, the political constraints against further spread might loosen. What now looks special and exceptional could come increasingly to look like an acceptable norm. A world of twenty-five states armed with nuclear, chemical, or biological weapons is more likely to see further spread and possible use than a world of ten such states. By keeping the number of possessors low, the hurdles can be kept higher, the controls tighter, and the political barriers stronger against acquisition by rogues and terrorists.

In sum, selective engagement gives more weight to the worry that NBC spread would enhance the risk that states and groups hostile to American interests could acquire these weapons and use them against the United States or its military forces. The increased likelihood of either eventuality constitutes a strong case for resisting NBC spread.

HOMELAND DEFENSE AGAINST GRAND TERRORISM

How selective engagement and the free hand strategies would deal with grand terror attacks is a second major difference. The issue is not which approach would do better on American territory to interdict, thwart, or recover from such attacks: both would adopt best practices to make America's borders as impermeable to terrorists as possible, find and disrupt their operations if they gain entry into the country, and respond effectively to such attacks if they could not be stopped. Rather, the differences between the two approaches center on which does a better job of prosecuting the campaign against terrorism when the United States has to go after terrorists abroad, and which approach is more likely to generate such attacks against the United States in the first place.

Most of the work against terrorists is best done before they reach the American homeland, through intelligence gathering, covert operations, and police detective action. The best defense against terrorists is to disrupt their plans and cells at the source, rather than waiting for them to attempt to enter the United States and then trying to thwart their operations once they have arrived. Disrupting terrorism requires human penetration of terrorist organizations to gather intelligence about their operations. By its nature, this phase of dealing with terrorism requires long-term patience, diligence, and quiet operations. This cannot be done alone, but requires close cooperation between the United States, its allies, and all other states from which it can enlist cooperation. War-like operations on the scale of the 2001–2002 Afghan war, in which the United States went after the al Qaeda terrorists and the Taliban government that supported them, are likely to be the exceptions rather than the rule in dealing with terrorist organizations that have the will and the capability to launch grand terror attacks against the United States.

If this is the nature of the campaign against terrorism, does selective engagement have an edge over the free hand strategies in conducting it? Clearly it does when Afghanistan-type operations are the order of the day. America's bases in the Persian Gulf aided the effort: of the 60,000 American troops at the peak of the war effort, about half were in the Persian Gulf. The United States was able to leverage its alliance with Pakistan to enlist crucial cooperation, starting with bases and with overflight rights for U.S. planes operating from aircraft carriers stationed in the Indian Ocean.[2] In this way, selective engagement is able to use America's existing bases and alliances to project its military power against terrorist training bases and concentrations. In contrast, because they would have given up allies and forward bases, neither free hand strategy would be as well placed to conduct the war; each would have to start from scratch to build alliances and gain access to bases, a difficult and problematic process. Selective engagement also has an edge when it comes to the quieter phase of fighting terrorism—the long-term intelligence and police work. Here the United States is able to take advantage of its alliances, and to use the political leverage it gains by protecting others in order to help gain the cooperation it needs from them. The free hand strategies, having forsaken these alliances, do not possess the same political leverage. Finally, as Barry Posen cogently argues:

> it will not always be possible for the United States to do the fighting. Allied military police forces are more appropriate instruments to apprehend terrorists operating within their national borders than are U.S. forces. They have the information that the United States may not have, and they know the territory and people better.[3]

Selective engagement, by virtue of its standing alliances, can enlist this type of cooperation better than the free hand strategies can. Thus, for both the "noisy" and "quiet" phases of the campaign against terrorism, selective engagement offers a better chance to defeat terrorists than the free hand approaches.

A second question is whether selective engagement generates more terrorism against the United States than the free hand strategies. Not surprisingly, free hand advocates argue that it does. They take the position that if the United States were to lower its global profile by withdrawing militarily from the world, it would be less likely to be the object of terrorist attacks, both abroad and at home.[4] As Christopher Layne put it: "If any doubt remained that U.S. hegemony would trigger a nasty geopolitical 'blowback,' it surely was erased on September 11."[5] If America gets out of other people's business and other people's conflicts, so the argument goes, then they will have little, if any reason to strike back at it. The logic of the free hand position is clear, simple, and appealing.

It is not obvious, however, that a military withdrawal of the United States from Eurasia and the Persian Gulf would lower America's profile sufficiently to remove it as a target of grand terror attacks. Paul Pillar asks: "Does the hatred stem from what the United States *does* (which presumably could be changed), or from what it *is* (which is far less alterable)?" His answer is: "Terrorist hatred involves both."[6] For example, Osama bin Laden objected to American military forces in Saudi Arabia, because, in his view, they defile the holy sites of Islam and back a corrupt regime, but as Pillar points out America's commercial and cultural presence overseas has also been an object of attack. Latin America, in particular, has historically had the largest number of attacks against Americans overseas.[7] For Islamic fanatics like bin Laden, American culture and American capitalism also threaten to eradicate their austere, backward-looking brand of Islam. What America represents stands as a threat to who they are and what they want their societies to become. On these grounds alone, as the world's preeminent power, the United States will incite the enmity and hatred of those groups that are sufficiently dissatisfied with the status quo to use terror to alter it, whether or not the United States actually exercises its military hegemony.

The effect of American policy on terrorism is more complex. The next potential generation of grand terrorists is likely to come from the Middle East, and they will be motivated to take action primarily by America's support for Israel and by its backing of the Gulf sheikdoms. Yet the United States cannot "militarily withdraw" from Israel, because it has no formal military alliance with it and no combat troops in it. An American military withdrawal from the Persian Gulf would lower the U.S. political profile in the Middle East, but the United States would probably continue to provide military assistance and arms to Saudi Arabia and the other Persian Gulf sheikdoms (and to Israel as well, along with economic aid). In fact, the United States would be likely to increase such aid if it withdrew; it would therefore continue to be viewed as a backer of the Gulf states and Israel, and thus still incite the enmity of groups opposed to them. Thus, it is not clear that a military withdrawal from the Middle East would reduce America's profile enough to avert the hatred of those groups that might plan terrorism against it.

The same line of argument holds for Pakistan's terrorist groups. They may also be part of the next generation of grand terrorists because of the political pressure that the United States put on Pakistan, both during the Afghanistan war to cut its support of the Taliban and during the 2002 Pakistani-Indian crisis over Kashmir to cease its support of terrorism against India. Neither move has been popular with the Islamic radicals in Pakistan. Yet the U.S. military profile in Pakistan is low, and once the war against al Qaeda forces in Afghanistan and Pakistan is over, it will be lower still. Moreover, the United States cannot wholly abandon the Western-oriented governments in either country. To abandon Afghanistan would risk it turning once again into a terrorist haven. To abandon Pakistan would increase the risk that groups sympathetic to the Islamic radicals would gain power and get their hands on Pakistan's nuclear weapons, which would raise the risk of terrorism to catastrophic levels.[8] Until Afghanistan is put back together again in a way that protects Western interests, a full military withdrawal from the area makes no sense, and even a full military withdrawal would not change the hatred of Pakistani radicals toward the United States. Their hatred is based on the U.S. defeat of the Islamic radicals in Afghanistan and on the crackdown by Pakistan's government against their terrorist activities in India in connection with Kashmir, brought about under American pressure to avoid a Pakistani-Indian war. Here, as in the Middle East, it is not evident that a military withdrawal from the area would lower the U.S. profile enough to avert the hatred of these groups.

None of this is to say that changes in American policies could not diminish the hatred that stokes terrorism. Military withdrawal from overseas might do little, but thoughtful changes in America's political policies could do a lot. The single most important step the United States could take would be to adopt a more even-handed approach in the Israeli-Palestinian conflict. It should insist that Israel, as well as the Palestinians, must do its part, first and foremost, by stopping its creeping annexation of the West Bank. The United States has tolerated this for far too long, and it is in neither Israel's nor America's interest that it continue. The United States must force Israel to disgorge the West Bank and Gaza and give it to the Palestinians, with all necessary assurances for Israel's security. A second important step would involve a careful look at America's military presence in Saudi Arabia. The United States does not need to be in Saudi Arabia to defend it. There are adequate places elsewhere in the region to put its troops. America's military planners are thinking along those lines already.[9] The Pakistani case is harder, but the United States might begin with its quotas and tariffs on textiles imported from Pakistan. Lifting them would benefit Pakistan economically and give its government something tangible to show for its backing of the United States. Direct financial support for secular public education in Pakistan is another measure that could have great benefits. The religious madrassas, too many of which teach hatred of the West, have taken the place of public schooling, which has virtually collapsed in Pakistan. Supplanting them with public schools that offer a modern education could help combat the anti-Western venom propagated by the madrassas. Other beneficial economic measures should be taken to show that allying with the United States pays off in real terms.

Thus, although the United States cannot change what it is, it can modify to a degree what it does without wholesale withdrawal and without looking as if it is giving in to terrorism.[10]

EURASIAN GREAT-POWER PEACE AND STABILITY

The third major difference between selective engagement and the free hand strategies concerns the importance of maintaining peace and stability among the Eurasian great powers. In this section I review the reasons why selective engagement values great-power peace and stability and why an American military presence in Europe and East Asia helps to preserve them. Then, I refute three major counterarguments to this position.

Great-Power Peace and a Forward Presence

Selective engagement seeks to preserve a deep Eurasian great-power peace because it believes that both great-power wars and intense security competitions could significantly damage America's interests; consequently, it prescribes keeping American forces in Europe and East Asia to help avert both. Isolationists are indifferent to whether the Eurasian great powers are at peace or at war, or whether they experience intense security competitions. In their view, neither affects America's one vital interest, its security. Advocates of offshore balancing do not care about Eurasian great-power peace for its own sake, only about the outcome of a Eurasian great-power war. If no hegemon emerges from it, the war is of no concern; if one threatens to emerge, then offshore balancing dictates an American return to Europe or East Asia to cut it down. Similarly, offshore balancers do not care about intense great-power security competitions, unless they would enable a state to acquire a hegemonic military position through its buildup of arms. If these competitions do not produce regional hegemons, then offshore balancers favor withdrawal of American forces from Eurasia in peacetime.[11]

Proponents of selective engagement do worry about a Eurasian hegemon, but they also worry about the destructive effects of great-power wars and intense security competitions even if no hegemon emerges from either. Such wars and competitions could disrupt America's Eurasian trade and investments, drag the United States into them, lead to the further spread of NBC weapons to those states worried about their security and able to procure them, weaken the global non-proliferation regime, and increase the chances that rogues and fanatics could acquire these weapons of mass destruction. More generally, such wars and competitions could upset the Eurasian balance of power, which is presently favorable to American interests. For all these reasons, selective engagement would seek to keep the Eurasian great-power peace and avoid the risky crises that intense security competitions can produce.

Selective engagement also favors a forward American presence in Eurasia to help keep peace and stability there. As I argued in Chapter 4, a forward presence enhances deterrence and builds reassurance, discouraging hostile states from aggressive acts and reassuring America's allies. A forward presence is also more effective and cheaper than offshore balancing. It is harder to fight back into a region than to maintain a military presence there, because beefing up a preexisting presence in an emergency is easier than re-establishing one from scratch in a crisis, while it is more expensive in the long run to go back to wage war than to stay in and prevent war. Alliances and forward deployed forces provide the United States with valuable bases, staging areas, intelligence gathering facilities, in-theater training facilities, and most important, close allies with whom it continuously trains and exercises. These are militarily significant advantages and constitute valuable assets if war must be waged. In the absence of a regional hegemon, offshore balancing would forsake an overseas peacetime presence and make the use of America's military power more difficult, should it be required. Selective engagement preserves these assets and makes waging war easier if it should prove necessary.

An additional benefit of a forward presence is that it is more likely than either isolationism or offshore balancing to maintain America's military edge. Under the free hand strategies, all American combat forces except the Navy would be brought home because of the belief that the external environment is benign for the United States. Historically, it has proven politically difficult for the United States to maintain robust military forces when it has not been forward deployed or when the international environment has not seemed threatening. It is a short political step from belief in a benign external environment to the belief that America's military forces can be cut back and their technological edge allowed to lessen. An isolationist or an offshore balancing America or an offshore balancing posture would not necessarily result in degradation of American military capabilities, but such a risk is ever-present with the free hand strategies. Selective engagement lessens that risk, because American forces would be in-theater and therefore close to, even up against, the military forces of adversaries and other great powers. The risks of allowing American forces to degrade are more readily apparent and calculable, and the costs would be more swiftly felt, when American forces are deployed forward than when they are deployed at home. Thus, selective engagement's forward deployment is politically more likely to keep America on its military toes than is pure isolationism or offshore balancing.

In essence, then, selective engagement and offshore balancing disagree about the costs, risks, and benefits of staying in Eurasia versus leaving it. Offshore balancing is prepared to risk redoing World War I and World War II: leave Eurasia, and fight to get back in only if a hegemon threatens. It calculates that the costs of going back are less than those of staying there, that the risks of leaving are low, and that the benefits of staying are less than those gained by leaving. Selective engagement believes that a withdrawal-and-then-return posture is more dangerous, more costly in the long run, and less advantageous than remaining in the region. Because the United States would have less influence over a region if it is militarily absent than if it is present, it makes more sense to remain and to shape a region's future to America's benefit than to allow the region to evolve in ways that could be harmful to America's interests. Selective engagement participates in both on-shore and in-theater balancing; it views offshore balancing not as a viable short cut but as a disastrous short circuit.

Refutation of Counterarguments

Three free hand–type arguments challenge the premium put by selective engagement on Eurasian peace and stability and a forward presence. The first argument is that a war among two or more Eurasian great powers would not significantly harm America's economic interests; the second is that the likelihood of any Eurasian great-power war is now quite low because of the stabilizing effects of nuclear weapons; and the last, that Europe is now a free-standing security community that needs no American military presence to pacify it. All three arguments have some merit, but in the end are not persuasive enough to dispense with an American military presence in Eurasia.

Eurasian Wars and America's Economic Interests

In an impressive analysis, Eugene Gholz and Daryl Press demonstrate that if a great power stands aside while other great powers wage war, it will not suffer economically, but may in fact benefit.[12] This happens, they argue, because war transfers wealth from belligerents to neutrals through the mechanism of trade. To wage war, the belligerents' demand for goods surges, but not all of the demand can be met by domestic production; consequently, the belligerents' demand for imports also surges, and it is met by increased exports from neutrals. These neutrals are also able to take over the markets once dominated by the belligerents because the latter now have to divert their economies to the war effort. Gholz and Press estimate that the United States netted more than $4 billion in exports during 1914–1916, an amount equal to 10 percent of its GDP in 1915. Overall, once adjustment costs were figured in (the costs that American business had to pay in altering their factories to produce the new goods that the war demanded), the United States at least broke even, and may have netted more than $500 million, during the years of its neutrality.[13]

Should a Eurasian great-power war occur today, Gholz and Press estimate that the United States would not do quite as well overall as it did during 1914–1916, largely because of the huge U.S. debt. Wars drive up worldwide interest rates, which would force the United States to pay more to finance its debt. The economic costs of the higher interest rates would offset the expected increase in its exports, especially if the war were short. However, although the United States would not do as well economically in a future great-power war as it did during its World War I neutrality years, the loss would still be relatively small. Gholz and Press calculate that the United States might lose $10 billion on its trade account in the first year of a major great-power war due to the initial costs of trade disruption, but might make money on trade if the war lasted a few years, while it would lose about $9 billion in higher interests costs for each year the war went on.[14]

Whatever the precise economic loss or gain in a great-power war, however, the sum is considerably less than what it costs the United States to prevent such a war from occurring in the first place, say Gholz and Press. They argue that the United States spends ten times more to keep Eurasia stable than it would lose in a major great-power war.[15] Thus they conclude that there are no compelling economic reasons for the United States to prevent a Eurasian great-power war; therefore, they ask, why should the United States bear the costs of the forces stationed in Eurasia to prevent it? Given these premises, they draw the obvious conclusion: the United States should withdraw its troops.

The analysis offered by Gholz and Press is impressive but their extrapolations are not persuasive. First, as Chapter 5 demonstrated, in the last three Eurasian great-power wars in which the United States was involved—the revolutionary and Napoleonic wars of 1792–1815, World War I, and World War II—it was America's trade with some of the belligerents that dragged it into war. Consequently, the economic gains and losses, small or large though they may be, are not the issue. If a Eurasian great-power war should once again occur, then history tells us that the United States would not only have to stand aside militarily but also cease all trade with the belligerents if it wanted to avoid being dragged into the war.[16] This has proved easier to say than to do in the past, and it will prove so in the future, if for no other reason than that the United States will not be indifferent to the outcome of any such war. Even if it does not enter the war, the United States will in one way or another aid the party that it favors, and that aid will not go unnoticed by the party's adversaries.

Second, great-power wars also affect the future shape of the region and even of the world. Great-power wars in the past have helped bring on economic closure (World War I) and economic openness (World War II). They have stalemated aspiring hegemons and prevented the spread of militaristic and totalitarian societies. In the process, these wars have shaped the international environment for decades, even centuries. We cannot look simply at the gains and losses in a given war; we must also look at how that war's outcome will affect the future international environment. A state could suffer few economic losses during a war, or even benefit somewhat, and still find the postwar environment quite costly to its own trade and investment. That is, a state could suffer little during the war, but still lose quite a lot in the subsequent peace.

Third, the lessons that Gholz and Press draw from their historical analysis of the American cases may no longer be relevant for the United States because the country now has a greater stake in international trade, investment, and economic openness than it had when these three earlier wars were fought. Throughout most of its history, that stake was roughly 3–4 percent of its gross domestic product if only exports or only imports are counted, or 6–8 percent if both are counted. These percentages began to change in the mid-1970s, and today U.S. exports and imports together account for 20–22 percent of its gross domestic product. Although these percentages are smaller than those for many other rich countries, they are larger than they used to be. If America's stake in foreign economic activity has doubled, by at least one measure, then its potential losses from disruption by war are also significantly higher.[17]

Finally, and closely related to the second point, it is wrong to advocate withdrawal from an area because one can demonstrate that the economic losses incurred in a war are much smaller than the costs paid to prevent it.

The real comparison that matters is the one between the annual costs of maintaining a military force of sufficient size to station forces in an area to help keep the peace, on the one hand, and the annual trade and investment gains that the United States receives as a result of the stable political-military framework that its presence provides, on the other. War is a brief affair; peace can be a long-term affair. It is the continuing annual economic benefits of the peace provided by America's presence, not the short-term economic losses in war, that should be compared to the annual costs of peace maintenance. By my calculation, as shown in Chapter 4, it costs the United States roughly 30 percent more to maintain the military forces of selective engagement than what a free hand force would cost. This amounts to somewhere around $100–120 billion in today's dollars.[18] America's annual trade with Eurasia alone runs over half a trillion dollars. Should the United States leave Eurasia, it would not lose all of the half-trillion dollars in annual trade, but surely its investments and its trade could suffer from the new order that would arise in its absence should a major conflict occur. We cannot put an exact price tag on those losses, but they could be substantial. When the annual economic benefits of the peace are compared to its annual economic costs, it is clear that the United States gains substantially.

Eurasian Wars and Nuclear Weapons
The second argument challenging the premium put by selective engagement on Eurasian peace and stability, and the need for American military forces to ensure them, has to do with the pacifying effects of nuclear weapons. The probability of a Eurasian great-power war is now low, if for no other reason than that four of Eurasia's six great powers—or five of seven if India is counted—have nuclear weapons (only Japan and Germany are not nuclear-armed). Since their advent, nuclear weapons have served as the ultimate instruments of defense. It is hard to conquer a nuclear-armed state; it is also dangerous to attack one. If two states are nuclear-armed, they are less likely to go to war with one another because they fear that the war between them might escalate to nuclear use. Therefore, war—both conventional and nuclear—is less likely among states that are nuclear-armed than it is among those that are only conventionally armed. Hence, so the argument goes, nuclear spread within a region may help to pacify it, if two or more of the region's powerful states have them.

The pacifying effects of nuclear weapons helped to keep the Cold War cold. The United States and the Soviet Union had as intense a rivalry as any two states since the advent of the modern state system four hundred years ago, yet they did not engage in direct war with one another. They did fight many proxy wars, they did engage in a sustained nuclear and conventional arms race that served as a surrogate for war, and they did have several intense crises that carried great risk of war, but they never fought one another directly, save for aerial dogfights during the Korean War.[19] Nuclear weapons helped keep their rivalry within bounds because both sides feared that, if they came to direct blows, the conflict could escalate to general nuclear war, thereby destroying both. If the American-Soviet experience of the Cold War is a reliable guide, then surely nuclear deterrence is a powerful pacifier, and great powers' possession of nuclear deterrents decreases the probability of great-power wars.

Despite this argument, the United States should remain in Eurasia for four reasons. First, the fact that the probability of a Eurasian great-power war is low can lead to two opposite conclusions regarding America's military presence in Eurasia. Free hand advocates conclude that the United States is no longer needed in Eurasia as a pacifier. Adherents of selective engagement conclude, by contrast, that the United States can stay in Eurasia with a significantly reduced risk because the probability of great-power war is low. Moreover, because its presence has a pacifying effect, the United States can reduce the probability of a Eurasian great-power war even lower, and that is a good thing.

Second, the probability of a Eurasian great-power war may be low, but that does not mean it is non-existent. Since the dawn of the nuclear era, we have had three clear instances of armed conflict between two nuclear-armed states. The first was the air war over the Korean peninsula between American and Soviet air forces during the Korean War. The second was the border clash over the Ussuri River boundary between the Soviet Union and China in 1969. This did not escalate to a large-scale war, but hundreds of troops were killed in the battles that ensued, and the risk of escalation to a larger war was clearly present. The third instance was the 1999 clash between India and Pakistan over Kargil in their continuing dispute over Kashmir. This was a war, although a limited one, with somewhere between 1,000 and 2,000 Indian and Pakistani troops killed.[20] (I use the convention, established by the Correlates of War Project at the University of Michigan, defining a war as a conflict in which 1,000 or more battle deaths occur.) Some analysts report that the two countries were on the verge of a full-scale war. The Kargil crisis was especially dangerous not only because there was a shooting war but also because, as American intelligence discovered, the Pakistani military was preparing its nuclear arsenal for possible use. Moreover, it appears that Pakistan's Prime Minister Nawaz Sharif did not know of this until President Clinton informed him while Sharif was in Washington in the midst of the crisis.[21] There is a possible fourth case—the Cuban missile crisis of 1962—when the U.S. Navy used depth charges against Soviet submarines in the Atlantic in attempts to force them to the surface.[22] In all of these cases, the conflict was kept limited, and while we should take comfort from that fact, we must also remember that the clashes carried great risk of escalation.

Furthermore, nuclear weapons have not proved themselves an absolute deterrent. There have been at least three instances in which non-nuclear-armed states have attacked nuclear-armed states or their military forces. In 1950, China attacked American forces that crossed into North Korea during the Korean War, and the two then fought a substantial conventional war for the next two years. In 1965, North Vietnam attacked American forces in South Vietnam during the Vietnam War, and the two fought a big and bloody conventional and guerrilla war for the next eight years. In 1973, Syria and Egypt attacked Israel, which had nuclear weapons then, and the three fought a short but furiously intense conventional war during the month of October. In all three cases, the non-nuclear state was not deterred from attacking the nuclear-armed state, because the issues at stake were too important.

It is true that nuclear weapons have worked to lower the probability of war between states that possess them and that they have strengthened the defensive power of states that have them. The record of nuclear deterrence is good, however, not perfect. They have not lowered the risk of war to zero, nor have they given their possessors a 100-percent guarantee against conventional attack.

Third, the theory of nuclear deterrence does not tell us whether nuclear weapons make war below the level of general nuclear war (all-out war) less likely or more likely. Glenn Snyder wrote many years ago about what was later called the "stability-instability paradox."[23] He argued that stability at the strategic nuclear level could produce two opposite outcomes. On the one hand, if two states possessed nuclear forces that were secure from nuclear first strikes, and both knew it, then neither leader would start a general nuclear war, and consequently both "will be less inhibited about initiating conventional war, and about the limited use of nuclear weapons, than if the strategic balance were unstable." On the other hand, "the greater likelihood of gradual escalation due to a stable strategic equilibrium tends to deter both conventional provocation and tactical nuclear strikes."[24] The stability-instability paradox says that either states start less-than-all-out wars, because they feel safe in the knowledge that escalation to all-out war will not happen, or that they do not start less-than-all-out wars, because they fear escalation to all-out war.[25] Depending on whether nuclear statesmen "run safe" or "run scared," strategic stability could bring either more war or more peace.

The U.S.-Soviet Cold War ultimately followed the second path, not the first, but it was not clear during the first fifteen years of the Cold War that this would be the case, and there were too many near-misses to take full comfort from this experience. Moreover, the U.S.-Soviet rivalry should not be viewed as the last word on what can happen between two nuclear-armed states, because this rivalry had several features that current Eurasian great-power rivalries do not share.[26] First, the Soviet and American homelands were far removed from each other, not contiguous or even close. Second, the United States and the Soviet Union contested over spheres of influence and global prestige, not territory that each claimed as an integral part of its homeland. Moreover, although their dispute was intense, it was ideological and not burdened either by religious differences or by past experiences of rapacious and barbaric invasion by one against the other. Finally, both states became nuclear powers just after having fought together as allies to defeat Nazi Germany; at that time, neither was inclined to begin another all-out war. This gave both some breathing room and time to adjust to the nuclear revolution. Even so, they still experienced a set of intense crises over a fifteen-year period, a few of which brought them close to general war.

None of these de-escalating ingredients is present in the Indian-Pakistani conflict, nor in the other potential nuclear face-offs: the Sino-Russian, Sino-Japanese, or Sino-Indian. Three of these four cases involve states contiguous to one another, not widely separated as in the U.S.-Soviet case, while the Sino-Japanese dispute involves claims over the limits of each other's territorial waters. The Indian-Pakistani case is characterized by an intense dispute over Kashmir, territory that each claims as part of its homeland, magnified by religious differences.[27] The Sino-Russian dispute is largely quiescent for now, because China and Russia have settled their Ussuri River border dispute, but a serious future rivalry between the two cannot be ruled out, especially given Russia's concerns about the immigration of large numbers of Chinese into its far eastern territories. The Sino-Japanese dispute involves animosity and a history of brutal assault by one against the other; a dispute over territory (which state owns the Diaoyutai/Senkaku islands in the East China Sea); and assertions by China that the waters through which Japan's oil passes (the South China Sea) belong to China. The fourth dispute involves a past in which India was humiliated at China's hands during the 1962 Sino-Indian war, as well as lingering disputes over territory that each claims as its own: China holds 40,000 square kilometers of Kashmir that India claims, and China claims Arunachal Pradesh, a northeastern Indian state.[28] The calming features of the U.S.-Soviet rivalry, therefore, are absent from the potential conflicts that could arise among the Eurasian great powers today. If we take the stability-instability paradox seriously, if we recognize that the U.S.-Soviet Cold War had special features that may have helped the two avert war, and if we believe that the potential conflicts of tomorrow do not share these special features, then we should have less than complete confidence that nuclear weapons will prevent another Eurasian great-power war. Should one occur, it is unlikely to go nuclear, but large-scale conventional war cannot be ruled out.

Fourth and finally, great-power wars are highly destructive, not only to the participants and their immediate neighbors, but also to world order and stability. Today, they may be low-probability events, but their costs would be extremely high. In this regard, we should treat Eurasian great-power wars the same way we do NBC terrorism, and the same way we treated the possibility of a general nuclear war between the United States and the Soviet Union during the Cold War: we should take multiple measures to prevent them and to limit them if they should break out. Great-power wars are potentially too destructive not to do everything possible to avert them; great-power peace should be over-determined, not left to chance.

America's presence in Eurasia can help over-determine peace in several ways. America's forward presence provides general reassurance and pacifying, which helps prevent or dampen down security competitions among many, if not all, of the Eurasian great powers. There is also the deterrent power—both direct and indirect—that its alliances bring. Of the four potential conflicts listed above, America's alliance system has the most influence on a potential Sino-Japanese or Indian-Pakistani conflict because of America's alliances with Japan and Pakistan. America's military presence may well have dissuasion value for the two other potential great-power conflicts too. Even though the United States does not have military alliances with any of the parties, any one of them contemplating a move against another would have to factor in an American response because it could not be certain that the United States would remain neutral. For example, during the Ussuri River clashes between the Soviet Union and China, the Soviet Union began to moot the idea of a preemptive attack against China's nuclear installations. The United States issued warnings that it would not remain indifferent to such a massive breach of the peace.[29] Moreover, even if American combat forces did not become directly engaged, the United States could threaten to provide military supplies to one of the parties in order to tip the balance of the war's outcome, as in the 1980s, during the Iran-Iraq war, when the United States provided military intelligence to the Iraqis and encouraged the French to send them advanced military equipment. The possibility of direct or indirect U.S. military intervention could well dissuade a great power from attacking in the first place. Finally, the United States could intervene with aggressive diplomacy to help keep conflicts from escalating further. In 1999, for example, President Clinton worked hard to keep the Kargil war from escalating and reportedly got Pakistan to change course, thereby helping to deflate the crisis.[30]

None of these mechanisms is foolproof for preventing or limiting Eurasian great-power conflicts, but they should not be dismissed as wholly ineffective. Moreover, none would work as well if the United States were militarily absent from Eurasia. Its presence enhances reassurance and deterrence; it makes the provision of military aid easier and swifter; it lends enhanced credibility to the threat to render military supplies and assistance; and it gives greater weight to America's diplomatic efforts to keep the peace and to contain conflicts. All of these pacifying mechanisms work better because of America's military presence in Eurasia.

Europe's Security Community and America's Presence

A final case against an American military presence in Eurasia applies only to Europe, not to East Asia or the Persian Gulf. The argument is that Europe, or at least its western half, now constitutes a pluralistic security community that no longer needs the American pacifier to keep it peaceful.[31]

Karl Deutsch and his colleagues articulated the concept of a pluralistic security community in 1957. It denotes a set of independent states that rely on the power of a norm, not on military force, to govern their relations with one another. Such a community can involve two states (bilateral) or three or more (multilateral).[32] States so constituted have attained "a sense of community and of institutions and practices strong enough and widespread enough to assure, for a long time, dependable expectations of peaceful change among its population," and therefore have real assurance that they "will not fight each other physically, but will settle their disputes in some other way."[33] Military guarantees and military force might previously have played an important role in promoting peace among the states that are now a pluralistic security community, but now the norm of peaceful dispute resolution has become so deeply rooted and so powerful that force plays no role in the community's internal life. This type of regional organization is to be understood as something more than a mere alliance of independent states, but something less than a federated state.

Of the three regions where America's overseas military power is concentrated, Western Europe is the most peaceful, and it essentially constitutes a security community, although not necessarily a free-standing one. Here is how it got that way. World War II had brought the destruction of German power, the exhaustion of Britain and France, and the entry into Central Europe of a powerful Soviet military machine. These developments thrust the United States into the role of hegemonic leader and protector of Western Europe. Canada and the United States had developed into a bilateral pluralistic security community after World War I, an evolution begun before the American Civil War when they demilitarized their long border.[34] On April 4, 1949, this bilateral security community was broadened into the North Atlantic Community (NAC), when six Western European states, together with the United States and Canada, signed the North Atlantic Treaty Organization, or NATO.

Under the umbrella of America's military protection, provided through NATO, the European component of the NAC set out on the path of economic integration and began its evolution toward a multi-state security community. America's military protection was essential to this process: it lessened the Western European states' worries about the uneven spread of economic advantages by assuring them that one another's economic advantage could not be turned to military use. This drastically mitigated the security dilemma that the European states had experienced since the advent of the modern

European state system. Josef Joffe put the matter well: "Conventional [alliance] theory holds that states coalesce in order to assure their security. In the case of NATO, however, they coalesced because their security was assured—by a powerful outsider that delivered both external protection and internal order to Western Europe. Order was the precondition of alliance and integration."[35] Thus, the North Atlantic Community and its European component grew out of the NATO alliance, and the NAC has remained largely coextensive with NATO. The expansion of NATO into Central Europe, which began in 1999, is a further demonstration of this fact.

In this sense, the European Union is an outgrowth of the sphere of influence of a powerful external hegemon. It required a sustained period of peace to emerge: the strong sense of solidarity required to make war unthinkable among the Western European states itself required a long period of peace. Certainly other factors were at work, but they, too, required sustained peace to be effective.[36] Peace, brought about by American military power, created the Western European security community, not the other way around.

If a fifty-year American military presence helped bring about the European Union, is that presence still necessary? Selective engagement answers "yes." In Europe today, the reassurance that the United States provides is more important than deterrence because most military threats to Europe (grand terrorism excepted) are greatly diminished from the previous era; some might even argue that these threats are non-existent. America's military presence in Europe does serve a low-key deterrence role against the (currently remote) possibility of a revived Russian aggressiveness, but the reassurance function is more important, because it keeps to a minimum any Western European fears that renationalization of their defense policies will somehow materialize, ending nearly fifty years of defense cooperation and military transparency. In the European context, "renationalization" refers to the fear of a return to "la géopolitique de grand'papa" (old-style geopolitics), or that these states might come once again to view their security as competitive and divisible, not quasi-harmonious and indivisible.[37] This fear was just below the surface immediately after the Cold War's end, when concerns of an American military withdrawal from Europe were high. They subsided after the United States made clear that it would remain a European military power, but today, there still remains a muted concern that if the United States were to leave Europe, the chances of renationalization would increase. Renationalization would not mean war within Europe, but it might mean competitive security and defense policies that could be destructive to further progress in strengthening and expanding the European Union. Under American leadership, therefore, NATO helps dampen renationalization fears by making it easier for the European states to maintain military transparency and to cede military dominance to an outside power.[38]

Until Europe fully develops a coherent foreign policy and its own military force to accompany it, including a truly European nuclear force, NATO helps maintain reasonably harmonious military relations among the European Union states. These relations are an essential element in enabling Europe to move further toward integration, and they are also in America's interest. It is better to have a reasonably cohesive Europe than a Europe paralyzed by squabbling among its members over competitive military policies. The former constitutes a constructive military partner for the United States; the latter does not. In sum, the European Union is still being partially underwritten by America's European military presence. It is now something between a genuine free-standing pluralistic security community and the military sphere of influence of a trans-Atlantic hegemon. America's work in Europe is not yet over. There may be a case for reducing the U.S. military footprint there, but not yet for eliminating it entirely.

Summary

Ultimately, the rationale for staying militarily engaged in Eurasia rests on whether one wants to continue to buy insurance. Contemplating the removal of American forces from Eurasia can be compared to deciding whether to maintain a fire insurance policy on one's own home. Having carried coverage for a half-century, does one now cancel the policy simply because no fire has occurred?

Selective engagement says "no." It sees the American military presence at both ends of Eurasia as good insurance because of two types of coverage it provides: to prevent and to limit damage. In terms of damage prevention, the American military presence is akin to hiring a night watchman to monitor a building continuously to make certain that nothing is done, by accident or by design, to start a fire.[39] In terms of damage limitation, the American military presence is akin to installing a sprinkler system inside a building that can quickly put out a fire once it has started. Prevention is the best value for a given expenditure because measures to prevent a fire are cheaper than those required to rebuild from one. But the American military presence can also limit damage. If a fire happens, it can be contained if steps have been taken so that it can be put out quickly. Buying insurance is a prudent strategy because it safeguards one's valuable investments. On-shore and in-theater balancing—the night watchman role—buys added insurance at reasonable cost; offshore balancing does not.

PEACETIME POWER PROJECTION AND ECONOMIC INTERESTS

The free hand approach and selective engagement also differ in the relation each presumes between power projection and economic interests. Selective engagement holds that America's military presence in Eurasia brings four economic benefits, beyond those already discussed. Advocates of the free hand approach believe that it does not or, if it does, that the gains are not worth the costs and the risks.[40]

First, an American military presence enhances a region's stability and promotes a political climate conducive to growing trade and interdependence. Economic interdependence yields clear benefits, but it also produces clear vulnerabilities. States will not allow themselves to become too economically vulnerable if those vulnerabilities could be turned to military effect against them. To the extent that America's military presence in a region lessens the concern that economic vulnerabilities can be turned to adverse military effect, it increases the willingness of states to allow interdependence to grow, thereby enhancing the region's prosperity and making it a better customer for America's trade and investment. Even more beneficial to trade are close political relations among states, especially when expressed in the form of an alliance, because an alliance fosters trade among the states party to it, as Joanne Gowa has demonstrated.[41]

Second, an American military presence in the Persian Gulf helps keep the area's oil reserves divided among the states of the region, thereby preventing any one of them from establishing hegemonic control. This division helps keep Gulf oil flowing at reasonably stable and predictable prices, which helps the world economy to grow, thereby enhancing America's trade and investment and its economic well-being.

Third, America's military alliances help keep the barriers to American goods, services, and investment lower than they might otherwise be. This occurs through the implicit linkage that exists between America's military protection, on the one hand, and the willingness of its allies to accept economic openness, on the other. In a powerful statement for isolationism, Eric Nordlinger asserts that such linkage will not work because America's alliances are weak levers with which to bargain on economic matters. He argues that attempts to link security and economics will either provoke nationalistic backlashes and prove counterproductive, or they will be ineffective because America's allies know that the United States values its military presence in their region above what happens to its trade and investment there.[42]

Nordlinger's latter point was more true of the era just past than it is now. During the Cold War, the United States put alliance solidarity ahead of its own economic interests. It perceived the Soviet threat to be so grave that its own threat to withdraw its troops from abroad was never credible, and both the United States and its allies knew that. Moreover, the need for military solidarity against the Soviet Union forced both the United States and its allies to keep their economic and other disputes within bounds.[43] In today's era, without such an overarching threat, America's implicit threat to go home is more credible because the United States faces far fewer severe military dangers than do many of its allies. In that sense, they need the United States much more than the United States needs them. The American campaign against grand terrorism does not alter this equation much, because many of America's allies are also targets, and they need the global military reach that only the United States can provide. This imbalance in need now gives the United States more inherent bargaining leverage with its allies than it ever had during the Cold War, exactly the reverse of what Nordlinger claims.

Nordlinger's first point, however, cannot be so easily dismissed. Heavy-handed linkage of security protection to the pursuit of economic openness could easily backfire. Although other states may need an American military presence in their region, they are not willing to pay an unlimited price to get it, nor are they willing to suffer unlimited humiliation to keep it. Therefore, explicit U.S. threats to go home should in general be avoided, and the United States should continue to do what it has always done: foster economic openness for all, not simply for itself. As long as the United States works for openness for all and avoids ham-handed tactics in the process, its provision of security will work gradually to reduce barriers to economic intercourse in the regions where it is involved. The reason is that all of America's allies, as well as the other regional actors that benefit from the stability it provides, understand that the United States has had a long-standing commitment to economic openness, and all know that if they engage in continuing egregious discrimination against U.S. goods, services, and investment, they will eventually erode the willingness of the American public to support an overseas military presence. The United States, therefore, will not, and should not, indefinitely protect states that fail to accept economic openness, nor should it in general provide stability to a region that closes itself off economically to the outside world. This fact alone puts a powerful weight behind America's economic diplomacy and provides a strong stimulus to America's allies, and to others that benefit from its stabilizing presence, to offer quid pro quo by lowering and by keeping low their barriers to trade and investment.

Japan is a case in point. Although it is still not as open to trade and investment as most of the other rich industrialized states, nevertheless, the Japanese economy today is more open to American trade and investment than at any previous time since 1945. The United States pushed Japan hard to open up during the 1990s, particularly in financial matters and services, but it has generally refrained from explicitly linking progress on that front to the continuance of the Japanese-American Security Treaty.[44] The United States has used its inherent security leverage to make certain that Japan does not sign on to regional arrangements that could adversely affect American trade. For example, in December 1990, when Prime Minister Mohammed Mahathir of Malaysia put forward his plan for an East Asian Economic Group that would include all of the region's big and small states except the United

States, the American government made clear its strong opposition to the idea and especially to Japan becoming a part of it. Japan decided that, "at a time when close cooperation with Washington is vital in dealing with North Korea, diplomatic wisdom dictates Japan should not do anything that could unsettle its relations with the U.S."[45]

None of this is to say that the United States will never have trade disagreements with its allies, or that it will always get its way. Disagreements will continue to occur, and the United States will not get everything it wants, in part because it also restricts trade (although less than its allies) and therefore has to accept some restrictions by them also. The main point is that the linkage between security and economics is so powerfully implicit in America's alliances that it cannot help but beneficially affect America's economic relations with its allies. Because that is the case, the linkage should in general be left implicit and allowed to produce its effects.

Fourth, on some occasions, an American military presence can produce more favored treatment for American products. The Persian Gulf is a case in point. The Europeans have traditionally taken the largest share of Gulf imports and continue to do so, while the United States lags far behind them. The disparity is due as much to Europe's colonial legacy with the area and its tilt toward the Arabs in the Arab-Israeli dispute as to America's tilt toward Israel, its emphasis on strategic over economic interests during the Cold War, and its imposition of trade sanctions against Iran and Iraq. Matters began to change in the latter part of the 1980s. Beginning in 1987, when the United States reflagged Kuwaiti ships with U.S. flags to protect them from Iranian attacks during the Iran-Iraq war, it assumed a greater role in the security of the six Persian Gulf sheikdoms. The United States solidified its position as the prime guardian of the sheikdoms with the 1991 Gulf War. A combination of close security ties and vigorous American economic diplomacy with the sheikdoms paid off. Whereas Europe's exports to the six sheikdoms were, in 1987, three times greater than America's ($15 billion to $5 billion), by 1999 they were only twice as great ($26 billion to $13 billion).[46]

I do not want to make more of the Gulf example than the facts warrant. I do not argue that America's trade with the Persian Gulf sheikdoms pays for its military presence in the Gulf; it does not. Nor do I argue that the United States should wage wars or extend military protection to a region merely to win government contracts or favored economic treatment. All I mean by the Gulf example is this: when there are other reasons for an American military presence in a region (in the Gulf, to stop the spread of NBC weapons and to keep oil reserves divided), the United States can on occasion also obtain favored economic treatment for its goods and services.

American military power produces these economic benefits because economic factors by themselves are never the only determinants of the economic relations among states. Robert Gilpin, one of the most astute observers of international economic relations, makes this clear:

> Even though economic factors will play an important role in determining the characteristics of the global economy, the most important factors are and will be political. The characteristics are and will be determined largely by the security and political relations among the major powers, including the United States, Western Europe, Japan, China, and Russia. Markets by themselves are neither morally nor politically neutral; they embody the values of society and the interests of powerful actors . . . . American political and security interests as well as economic interests are served by a united world economy. As a status quo power, the United States depends on a stable and peaceful world. To maintain that situation requires, at the least, a continuing American political and military presence in both Europe and Asia.[47]

The ultimate economic case for projecting American military power to Eurasia, then, is to shape the political-military environment in ways that advance, and do not harm, America's economic interests. Today's globalization is not an inevitable force that overwhelms all other factors; instead, it is a product of fifty years of steady progress toward economic openness, which would not have come about without the sustained exercise of American power—economic, political, and military. The United States is both the state most responsible for creating globalization and the one that has benefited the most from it. It has undertaken the responsibility because of the benefits. Consequently, if the United States leaves Eurasia, its economic interests are likely to be worse off because globalization might sputter and slow to a halt. After all, what politics (or military power) hath wrought, politics (or military power) can rend asunder. In their zeal to bring American troops home, both isolationists and offshore balancers ignore the fungibility of force and the important role that American military power has played in creating and sustaining the current international economic order. By withdrawing American military power from Eurasia, they would undercut one of the central underpinnings of the global economy.

Finally, although America's economic interests benefit from the projection of its military power, we must not exaggerate the gains, nor pretend that we can attach precise dollar figures to them. Most of the time, the economic advantages of power projection are indirect: they come primarily through their spillover and linkage effects. As a consequence, the benefits of projecting military power will be harder to pin down with precision than the costs of doing so. The fact that we cannot precisely price the benefits, however, does not make them any less real nor any less significant. We confront here what is often the case in grand strategy: in cost-benefit calculations about a given line of action, we can be quantitatively precise about the costs, but can render only qualitative judgments about the benefits. There should be no doubt, however, that on balance America's economic interests are better off with an American military presence in Eurasia than without it.

ADVANCING U.S. VALUES AND PROTECTING THE ENVIRONMENT

The fifth major difference between selective engagement and the free hand approach has to do with the goals of advancing America's values and preserving the global environment. Selective engagement will do more to advance the spread of democracy, protect human rights, avert mass murder in civil wars, and mitigate the adverse effects of global warming than would a free hand approach.

If implemented with the proper political support and policies, such as reducing America's dependence on fossil fuel use, selective engagement can make the world more stable and more prosperous. A stable and prosperous world is more conducive to democratic spread and human rights protection than an unstable, less prosperous world. No grand strategy of the United States can end all of the world's civil wars, but selective engagement can do more than the free hand strategies to save life in the worst of these wars that involve mass murder. A more stable and prosperous world is also better able to tackle the challenge of global warming than one distracted by conflict, arms racing, crisis instabilities, and economic adversities. The free hand strategies do little to advance American values and to deal with global warming. Selective engagement does not automatically produce the better world envisioned, but it works actively for it and is more likely to achieve some success than its free hand—or hands-off—competitors.

HEDGING AGAINST UNCERTAINTY

The final difference between selective engagement and the free hand approach is that the former is better able that the latter to hedge against uncertainty. To hedge is to make counterbalancing investments in order to avoid or lessen loss. Selective engagement is a hedging strategy; the free hand postures are not.

The free hand strategies are not as good at hedging against risk and uncertainty because they allow America's standing military coalitions to crumble, forsake forward deployment, and do not attempt to control the armaments of other powers. Their virtue is that they achieve complete freedom for the United States to act or not to act whenever it sees fit, but the freedom of action comes at a cost: the loss of a diversified approach. Most advocates of the free hand are prepared to trade balance and diversity for complete freedom of action because they see little worth fighting for, save direct defense of the homeland, containment or defeat of a Eurasian hegemon, or eradicating terrorists because they judge that prior military commitments are not necessary to protect these three interests and might even be injurious to them, and because they calculate that alliances will only put the United States in harm's way, largely for the benefit of others, not itself.

The free hand approach is to cope with events after they have turned adverse; in contrast, that of selective engagement is to prevent matters from turning adverse in the first place. Speaking about Asia, President Clinton put the difference between the two approaches well: "For we are not in Asia simply to respond to danger, but to be a balance wheel for stability that prevents danger from arising."[48] The free hand forgoes the opportunity to exploit fully the political utility of America's Eurasian alliances and forward deployed forces; selective engagement, by contrast, uses the political leverage yielded by those tools to shape events within Eurasia to U.S. advantage. Selective engagement makes hedging bets, primarily through alliances and overseas basing, because it believes that without America's military engagement and forward presence, the international environment will not remain benign to America's interests. The free hand strategies apparently believe that it will. Even though it does not eschew the use of force, the free hand approach is at heart a watching and reactive strategy, not, like selective engagement, a precautionary and preventive one.

CONCLUSION

In this chapter I have argued that an America dedicated to the free hand approach would let the world become more dangerous and less prosperous, while an America that follows the dictates of selective engagement will help produce a more peaceful and prosperous world. Selective engagement rejects the free hand for the selectively committed hand. It is the best strategy for the United States in the current international order.

This conclusion should not be a surprise. The most important thing that grand strategy does is to define the goals toward which the state should aim. The secondary task is to prescribe how best to use the nation's military power to attain them. The setting of goals largely shapes, although it does not wholly determine, what type of military instrument needs to be fashioned and how it should be employed. The national interests defined in Chapter 2 are internationalist in nature and call for both an activist American foreign policy and a forward defense posture. Selective engagement is the only one of the three feasible grand strategies that is internationalist, activist, and forward based, and it will be the most effective at protecting America's interests with its military power. If the interests prescribed in Chapter 2 are accepted, then selective engagement is clearly the best choice. Thus, in the concluding chapter I suggest how selective engagement should be implemented.

SEVEN

Implementing Selective Engagement

The purpose of this book has been to determine which grand strategy best suits the United States in this era. After evaluating all of the possibilities, I have argued that selective engagement is the preferred choice. It is not a strategy for all times, but it is the best for these times. It selects the goals most advantageous to the United States, and it employs America's considerable military prowess in the most effective manner to advance them. Over the medium to long term, selective engagement promises benefits to the United States that are greater, and costs and attendant risks that are smaller, than those of either isolationism or offshore balancing, its only two viable competitors.

In this chapter I give an overview of how selective engagement works, suggest the types of policies, both military and political, required to implement it, and then offer some speculation on its future and how best to negotiate a "soft landing" when its day is done.

HOW SELECTIVE ENGAGEMENT WORKS

Selective engagement is a "shaping" strategy. It emphasizes the retention of America's key alliances and forward military presence in Europe, East Asia, and the Persian Gulf, in order to help mold the political, military, and economic configurations of these regions so as to make them more congenial to America's interests. History has demonstrated that without a military presence in a region, a great power cannot hope to influence that region effectively.[1] For example, although the United States does not dominate its own hemisphere, it does significantly influence the hemisphere's political, military, and economic contours. Selective engagement aims to do the same for Europe, East Asia, and the Persian Gulf because, apart from North America, these regions contain most of the world's population, its military and economic power, and its vital natural resources. The United States cannot remain indifferent to what happens in those regions, and it must have a military presence there in order to affect the paths that they take. America's role will not be as influential in Eurasia as it is in its own hemisphere because there it has more powerful states to deal with and because influence tends to decline with distance. Nevertheless, given the preeminent position that the United States now holds in world politics, the military power that it projects overseas will have considerable effect.

It is not only in America's interest to shape the configurations of Europe, East Asia, and the Persian Gulf; it is also in the interest of those regions, as well as the rest of the world. What the United States wants for itself are not simply America's goals but also the world's goals: protection from grand terror attacks, especially by stopping the spread of nuclear, biological, and chemical weapons; preservation of peace and stability among the Eurasian great powers; secure access to stable oil supplies; international economic openness and the prosperity that comes with it; the spread of democracy and the protection of human rights; and the avoidance of severe climate change. Not every single nation, not every last citizen on earth, and certainly not every leader now in power would agree with all of these goals, but most states, most leaders, and most of humankind will.

In fact, they already have done so. To those who find suspect the argument that "what is good for America is good for the world," I would point out that these goals have been repeatedly endorsed at the United Nations and at every significant international meeting at which they are pertinent, from the Universal Declaration on Human Rights in 1948 to the Nuclear Non-Proliferation Treaty of 1968 and the 1997 Kyoto Treaty on climate change. To those who might think that democracy is only an American construct, I would point out that Africa has, over the last decade, experienced a flowering of democracy that, although imperfect, does demonstrate the desire of its people. In a recent survey of twelve African countries, 70 percent of the respondents said that democracy was "always preferable" to non-democratic governance.[2] When given the chance, once they are adequately fed, housed, and clothed, people usually want democracy.

To those who might think that globalization is simply an American ploy to open up other economies to America's rapacious economic behavior, I would point out that the developing states of the Third World have consistently argued that they need trade with the rich states at least as much as they need aid. For example, at a meeting of ten South American presidents in 2002, then President Fernando Henrique Cardoso of Brazil said that the developed states too often spoke of economic integration "as if we are the ones who don't want it, when it is we who most want a democratic integration that tears down trade barriers—but all of them, not just the ones that interest the powerful."[3] Jairam Ramesh, top economic advisor to India's Congress Party, has said: "Globalization fatigue is still very much in evidence in Europe and America, while in places like China and India, you find a great desire for participation in the economic expansion processes."[4] The developing states understand that only through trade, and especially the removal of the barriers that still keep them out of the developed states' markets, can they develop to their full potential. All these examples show that America's goals are widely shared.

That America espouses the world's goals does not, however, mean that it is universally loved as a consequence.[5] Quite the contrary: other states have objected to America's methods and specific policies to achieve these goals, sometimes with good reason. Too often the United States has been capricious, sanctimonious, hectoring, insensitive, and unilateralist.[6] Too often the United States has lagged in its own commitment to these goals—global warming being a recent and egregious example, with America's 2001 refusal to sign the Kyoto Protocol or to require of its citizens and its industry much beyond voluntary energy conservation. Too often the United States has supported governments that contravene the goals it espouses, arousing the resentment and anger of the citizens who must suffer these governments. Sometimes, the United States has faced hostility because it has called other states to account for their failure to meet the obligations that they have contracted. Finally, even when they have backed American policies, the governments and citizens of other countries more often than not have resented the United States because it is so powerful, and because it has benefited more from the current state of international affairs that they have. After all, power and success always incite some resentment and envy.

However, although America may not be universally loved, there remains strong international support for the fundamental goals espoused by selective engagement. Surely this is one of the main reasons that serious countervailing coalitions against the exercise of American power have not, so far, formed. The disputes that the United States has with its allies and its other friends are primarily over means, not ends.

Some might find selective engagement not at all selective, but instead a strategy that would lead to a grossly overextended United States. "It is not a discriminating strategy that you advocate, but a world's policeman role," they may argue. This, however, would be a fundamental misreading of the strategy of selective engagement. That it is an ambitious strategy is correct, but it is not a bottomless pit for America's power, energy, and resources. While selective engagement sets big goals for the United States, it also says that some are less weighty than others. Grand strategy must set priorities and husband scarce resources, and selective engagement does that. Defense of the American homeland comes first, followed by Eurasian peace and secure access to oil supplies. Less important are the other three interests. Spreading democracy and protecting human rights, preserving international economic openness, and avoiding severe climate change are worthy goals, but they come third, not first or second, in selective engagement's ranking. Only when measures have been taken to assure that the core goals are within reach should the United States devote some of its resources to its other worthy interests; how much gets accomplished of the lesser goals depends on what resources remain after allocation to the higher-priority goals.

It is true that the first-priority goals of selective engagement are not small tasks to accomplish, but they cannot be avoided. Should the United States instead work actively to promote the spread of weapons of mass destruction, or perhaps stand aside and allow it to happen? Should it foment Eurasian great-power conflicts in order to play these powers off against one another, or perhaps stand aside and allow such conflicts to happen? Should it encourage other states with hostile intentions to grab a stranglehold over Persian Gulf oil reserves, or perhaps withdraw and allow such grabs to run their course? These alternatives would be far worse than the goals set by selective engagement. America's core goals are big goals, but that is because they are essential if the country is to be safe, secure, and prosperous. They are within America's reach if sensibly pursued. The United States cannot be the world's policeman, but it is the world's most powerful country, and thus it can and should be the world's most important promoter of humankind's collective goods. The United States cannot move the world toward these goals by mere diktat, but the world cannot progress toward them without America's leadership, and it would certainly stand no chance of reaching them in the face of America's determined opposition.

This, in a nutshell, is the strategy of selective engagement. Now we turn to a discussion of the types of policies required to implement it.

THE REQUIREMENTS OF SELECTIVE ENGAGEMENT

What does selective engagement require? Three matters concern us here. What type of military forces does selective engagement need? What political policies are essential to complement the military measures? What is required to maintain the American public's support for this strategy?

Military Forces

There has been no dearth of recommendations about restructuring America's military forces. Numerous studies have asked how many forces the United States needs, what they should look like, where they should be placed, how they should be equipped, how they should be moved, how they should be transformed, and so on.[7] To deal adequately with all of these matters would require a book in itself, so here I only lay down some fundamental principles about the military forces that selective engagement requires. The place to begin is with the military tasks we want the strategy to perform: to defend the homeland, maintain a peacetime presence in Eurasia, preserve capabilities for peacekeeping, and be able to win wars, big or small, when war must be waged. To be able to perform all of these tasks requires a large, well equipped, well trained, technologically advanced, and diversified military force that, in its overall features, looks in many respects like what the United States has today.

Defense against Grand Terror Attacks

Defense of the American homeland requires that grand terror attacks be thwarted, and it may eventually require a missile defense against hostile states that have nuclear-armed intercontinental ballistic missiles. Neither task is easy, but the need for the former is far more pressing that the latter, and the wherewithal to deal with it more easily within America's technological reach.[8] Consequently, more resources and more urgency should be put into combating grand terror attacks than in constructing a missile defense system.

Defense against grand terror attacks involves steps both abroad and at home. Unless the United States is waging war against another regime that is willingly providing sanctuary to terrorists, the way that Afghanistan's Taliban were, or against one that has been taken over by terrorists, most of the measures taken abroad will involve intelligence, covert operations, police work, and small-scale special forces operations.[9] All of them together will not consume much of America's military resources. The same holds roughly true for the measures taken at home. Protecting the American homeland (according to the schema laid out in an excellent Brookings study) involves four steps: keeping terrorists out of the United States by defending its perimeter; preventing terrorists from operating in the United States both by tracking them should they get in and by keeping dangerous materials within the country from their grasp; protecting targets at which a large number of people may gather, or that represent critical parts of America's infrastructure; and building the capacity to respond effectively and quickly to the consequences of a grand terror attack.[10] The Brookings study estimates the likely cost of these measures at about $55 billion per year, with the government spending $45 billion each year and the private sector spending $10 billion annually more than it already does to protect its assets.[11] Most of the measures envisioned, however, do not directly involve America's armed forces. Rather, they involve such steps as better inspection of cargo containers in ships; better monitoring by the U.S. Customs service of points of entry; better FBI, police, and CIA counterintelligence work; better regulation of hazardous materials and better protection for their transport; better protection of nuclear and chemical facilities, electricity grids, and bridges; better defensive measures against cyber attack; better training of first responders; and more stockpiling of vaccines and antibiotics as well as research and development on new ones. Military involvement comes primarily with measures to enhance America's air defense system, planning against small cruise missile attacks that could deliver chemical or biological weapons, greater use of the National Guard and the reserves, and a significant enhancement and modernization of the Coast Guard (the latter, however, is not a Defense Department responsibility, but is now part of the Homeland Security Department).[12]

Homeland defense is critical, and it will be costly, but it will not involve a significant allocation of money, personnel, and material by the Department of Defense, unless war is waged against a terrorist state. Such wars should not be ruled out, but they will most likely be the exceptions in the campaign against grand terrorism. Short of such wars, Defense Department involvement in the campaign will primarily involve special operations forces abroad, air and cruise missile defenses at home, heightened security at bases abroad and at home, and more activity by the Navy looking out for terrorists traveling from one sanctuary to another.

Is Missile Defense Appropriate?

The threat to the American homeland from NBC-armed states is much less than the threat posed by NBC-armed terrorists, and the technological means at hand to combat it are not well advanced. No state that is implacably hostile to the United States now possesses intercontinental ballistic missiles, nor is such a state of affairs imminent. Moreover, missile defense technology has not advanced far enough to make it sensible to rush to deploy such a system, although it should not be totally ruled out. After all, if it could be built at reasonable cost, if it worked with a high level of confidence even against an adversary that could develop countermeasures, and if it would enhance America's ability to deter or defeat adversaries that might act against America's and its allies' regional interests—if all of these wonderful things came true, then, of course, a limited missile defense should be seriously considered.

None of these conditions is yet satisfied, however. A joint study by the Union of Concerned Scientists and the MIT Security Studies Program concluded that: "Any country capable of deploying a long-range missile would also be able to deploy countermeasures that would defeat the planned missile defense system."[13] As MIT's Ted Postol puts it, "a state that has enough technical sophistication to build a reentry vehicle with a warhead in it can also build a reentry vehicle without a warhead in it—which is, of course, another name for a decoy."[14] For this reason, interception of a ballistic missile in space (midcourse intercept) appears to be a problem that is not yet solvable, and it may never be.[15] Moreover, the best option—killing a missile when it is lifting off from Earth (boost-phase intercept)—is not yet feasible either. Boost-phase intercept envisions stationing, on ships and planes, a long-range laser capable of disabling a ballistic missile in its lift phase (kinetic-kill vehicles could also be used). Even if this system were to become operational, it would still have several disadvantages. It requires continuous patrols by planes or ships that are themselves subject to attack. Its coverage is limited. Even if it works, it would not disable the warhead but only the missile, which means that the warhead would keep on going to land somewhere, perhaps on the territory of an American ally. Most important, given the short timelines involved, boost-phase defense might require that the president pre-delegate the authority to launch—that is, give a standing authorization to the military to shoot down missiles under certain scenarios; this would be a very serious step.

Should all of these technical hurdles be surmounted at reasonable cost, we must still ask: "is a limited missile defense necessary under most scenarios that we can envision?" Missile defense for the United States is, first and foremost, about power projection; it is about America's ability to deter or to wage war abroad against an aggressor state that possesses nuclear-armed intercontinental ballistic missiles (ICBMs). For missile defense proponents, the concern is that such a state would be more emboldened to engage in aggression against its regional neighbors if the United States, itself now subject to attack, thereby became less willing and less able to deter it. As a consequence, so the argument goes, with its credibility weakened, America's regional alliances would collapse.

This concern is misplaced. If the United States is deterred from responding to an attack by, say, the state of "Ruritania" against its neighbors because Ruritania could retaliate against the American homeland, why would the same logic not apply to "Ruritania"? Would it not similarly be deterred from attacking its neighbor, which the United States has pledged to defend, by the threat of U.S. nuclear retaliation? In fact, we have been through this scenario: it was called the Cold War. The United States extended its nuclear umbrella over Western Europe to protect it from a Soviet invasion, knowing full well that its own homeland was targeted by Soviet intercontinental nuclear forces. If America's nuclear umbrella, in conjunction with its conventional forces stationed in the theater, were enough to deter a Soviet attack, why would this combination not suffice to deter the "Ruritanias" of this era? Thomas Friedman captured the fundamental illogic of limited missile defense:

> The Bush Doctrine says that rogue states are so *crazy* that they would launch a missile at us, even knowing that it would mean their certain destruction in return. But if we build a scarecrow missile shield that doesn't fully work, these rogue states are so *rational* that they would never launch one of their missiles against it, because they would realize that there was a chance it might not penetrate. In short, our perfect missiles that will destroy any rogue state with 100 percent accuracy won't deter them, but our imperfect missile shield, which may have as many holes as a Swiss cheese, will deter them.[16]

In sum, deploying a limited missile defense to protect the American homeland is currently not technologically feasible, nor is it necessary to undergird America's power projection capabilities. Moreover, should a missile defense ever become technological feasible, a much stronger analytical case for deployment than now exists would be needed. These two facts dictate a clear policy: the United States should continue to pursue a vigorous missile defense research, development, and testing program, but should not expend large resources to deploy such a system until it works and until a more compelling strategic case for it has been made.

Deter Hostile States; Preempt Terrorists

The one scenario that the United States must worry about is attacking an NBC-armed state with the express purpose of changing its regime, or destroying its NBC capability, or both. This is the contingency most likely to provoke NBC retaliation against the United States or its allies, but it is also the scenario over which the United States has the most control. Preventive wars to depose and "de-fang" such regimes are highly dangerous and should be avoided, except in the most compelling of circumstances: when an NBC attack on the United States or one of its allies appeared likely or imminent, or when the regime has been proven to have aided terrorists in acquiring NBC weapons, or when highly credible evidence suggests that it is likely to do so. A general policy of avoiding preventive wars against NBC states does not, however, preclude the United States from fighting to reverse aggression by these states should deterrence fail, but in such cases its freedom to do what it wants against them will be diminished if the state has nuclear weapons or ICBMs. The United States will have to be careful about the extent and nature of the attacks it launches against such a state, confining its military operations largely to repelling the aggressor's forces from the state it has invaded.[17] If the United States is concerned about hostile states using NBC weapons against it while it is defending its allies, it can strengthen deterrence by adopting what Steven Miller aptly calls a policy of "regime-icide," declaring that "any state that uses NBC weapons against the United States will not survive."[18]

Not only are preventive wars to depose and de-fang hostile NBC-armed regimes needlessly dangerous to the United States and its allies, they are also politically risky. As John Ikenberry points out, such wars carry a whole host of problems; three are the most serious for selective engagement.[19] By waging preventive wars, the United States risks setting a precedent that will haunt it if other states claim the same right: their preventive wars could seriously damage America's interests and perhaps even force the United States to fight wars that otherwise could have been averted. Preventive wars also risk overextension for the United States; once regimes are overthrown, they must be reconstituted. This would require extended occupation and could dangerously overstretch America's forces (as I describe below). Finally, because America's allies, as well as its enemies, generally oppose preventive war, the United States risks provoking counter-coalitions—arguably the most serious danger to selective engagement, as noted at the end of Chapter 4. A state that too easily starts wars it defines as preventive appears as an aggressor to other states; following the maxims of balance of power, these states might well ally against it. For these reasons, political considerations dictate only the most sparing resort to preventive war.

Thus, preventive and preemptive military actions should be used, whenever possible and wherever effective, against NBC-armed terrorist groups, or against groups known to be seeking such weapons, because these groups are not deterrable. However, preventive wars against hostile NBC-armed states should, in general, be avoided. Apart from the three exceptions noted above, they can be avoided because deterrence and containment are likely to work against them. Contrary to the 2002 pronouncement of the Bush Administration—that rogue states and terrorists are equally hard to deter and therefore that preventive actions should be taken against both—the rule should be: preempt terrorists (get them before they get us), but deter hostile states.[20]

Forward Deployment in Eurasia
Maintaining a peacetime military presence in Eurasia is the second major military task for selective engagement. The United States has about 250,000 troops currently stationed abroad. The most important requirement to fulfill the deterrence, reassurance, and stabilizing functions of selective engagement is to make certain that America's overseas forces are visible, respected, and capable of being reinforced quickly. This raises the question of how many troops an overseas peacetime presence requires and where they need to be. These are not simple questions to answer. The answers depend in part on careful military analysis of potential war scenarios, but such analysis will not provide all the answers because the size and placement of America's forces abroad is as much a political as a military matter.

The current peacetime placement of America's forces is not haphazard. Most are in Europe and East Asia (100,000 each), with most of the rest in and around the Persian Gulf. These are the areas where America's key interests lie; the case for keeping the troops there was laid out in Chapter 4. Drastic cuts in these deployments do not make sense barring war, severe economic conditions in the United States, or a dramatic change in the political-military environment in any of these regions. The one area for cutting may be Europe: while American troops there provide a residual deterrence function, primarily they provide reassurance, which does not require so many troops. However, bringing troops from Europe back to the United States would cost more in the short term than leaving them there, due to relocation and basing costs. Even after those initial costs are paid, moreover, relocation to the United States would not produce significant savings; the real savings would require cutting the size of America's forces. Leaving the forces in Europe has certain advantages, not the least of which is that they extend America's global military reach, especially into the Middle East. Short of decisions to cut the size of America's forces, or to reallocate a significant percentage of them from Europe to East Asia or the Persian Gulf, there is only a modest case for reducing America's military footprint in Europe.

Peacekeeping
The United States also needs capabilities for peacekeeping, but it must be sparing in undertaking these operations because there are many other demands on its forces. The United States is already engaged in a massive peacekeeping operation in the form of its peacetime presence in Eurasia and the Persian Gulf (this is too often forgotten by those who complain that the United States does not do its fair share of UN peacekeeping). The United States must also be sparing in undertaking such operations because they consume considerable resources—more than is commonly thought. James Quinlivan has shown that peacekeeping operations of just moderate size can end up making huge demands on a state's military forces, and may even significantly degrade their combat capability.[21] He calculates that such stabilizing operations can require at least four and as many as ten or more combat personnel for every thousand people in the area to be stabilized. For most places where peacekeeping has been undertaken or where it would be contemplated, stabilization would quickly require about a division of combat troops, even for small countries. For example, the United States sent 24,000 combat troops into the Dominican Republic to avert civil war there, and NATO sent 60,000 troops into Bosnia to support the 1995 Dayton Accords.

The drain on combat forces, however, is not simply the number of troops initially sent to the country to be stabilized. Peacekeeping operations, by definition, are not over quickly, but tend to last for years. Sustaining such an operation for any length of time requires rotation of the forces in the field. This necessitates three sets of forces: the current forces in the field, forces in training to replace those in the field, and the retraining of the forces that have returned from the field for their regular combat missions. Due to the rotation demands of sustained missions, the size of any initial force required for stabilization must be multiplied by a factor of two to three. (For example, the European Union's decision to create a rapid reaction force of 60,000 troops that can be sent quickly to the field and sustained there for a year actually requires a force of 180,000–200,000.) The peacekeeping drain on combat forces can be ameliorated somewhat by the use of National Guard units, but these units cannot wholly substitute for combat forces, especially when the environment is dangerous. Thus, even peace-keeping operations that look modest can make very large demands on a nation's military forces.

The United States does not have a great many ground forces to spare. It has ten active Army divisions and three active Marine divisions. Of these thirteen divisions, four are on garrison duty overseas: a Marine division in Okinawa, an Army division in Korea, and two Army divisions in Germany. Substantial participation in just two moderate-size peacekeeping operations that lasted any length of time could easily tie up several combat divisions. The United States must conserve its resources for other demands that would claim higher priority. This does not mean it should avoid UN peacekeeping operations altogether, but the United States must carefully choose which ones to undertake: it cannot afford to do more than one or perhaps two at any one time. Peacekeeping is an activity in which the more mobile and sustainable of the European forces could complement America's military efforts; thus, the United States should continue to encourage the Europeans to develop their rapid reaction forces for service both inside and outside of Europe.

Maintaining the U.S. Competitive Advantage

The fourth demand on military forces made by a strategy of selective engage-ment is that the United States must maintain forces to win the wars that it will have to wage. These wars may range from low-intensity conflicts such as special forces operations against terrorist cells, to peace enforcement oper-ations in Rwanda-like scenarios, to Kosovo and Afghanistan-type operations, up to a full-scale war with North Korea or its equivalent. A global war on the order of World War II is a highly unlikely event, but even here, the United States must maintain some mobilization capability. The most difficult task for the United States in waging war will be to maintain its competitive advantages, including its use of space, its command, control, computers, and communications technologies, its precision guided munitions, and its easy access to overseas bases.[22] Future adversaries will not all be as primitive as Afghanistan's Taliban, who were poorly equipped, nor will they all choose tactics as easy to defeat as the Taliban did: concentrating their forces in the countryside where they were easy targets for American airpower, rather than hiding in cities where the prospect of civilian deaths would have severely complicated America's war effort. Not all opponents will wait until the United States builds up its forces in an area. America's adversaries will learn from America's successes, and they will engage in asymmetric warfare: they will not go head-to-head where the United States is strong, but will instead attack where it is vulnerable. Changes in the present composition, tactics, weaponry, and skills of America's armed forces will surely be necessary, and many of these are not now foreseeable. To thwart such future adversaries will require that America's armed forces continue to innovate in both weaponry and tactics.

In sum, to perform the military tasks that selective engagement demands, the United States needs a strong and diversified military force, with about 15–20 percent of it deployed abroad. Selective engagement requires a military force second to none in its fighting capability, although it need not necessarily equal the spending of the next nine to fifteen military powers combined as the United States now appears to do.

Political Policies

Many of the political policies required to implement selective engagement have already been spelled out in Chapter 4, but two are especially important to revisit. The United States should avoid the twin evils of excessive ambition and excessive unilateralism: that is, it should avoid trying to do too much, and it should avoid doing too much on its own. Most of the ills that could befall selective engagement can be avoided if these two mistakes are avoided. A United States that tries to do too much would destroy selective engagement's selectivity, dissipate America's resources, embroil the country in too many conflicts, and provoke opposition that would make selective engagement impossibly expensive. A United States that does whatever it wants, whenever it wants, to whomever it wants will eventually hollow out or shatter its alliances and bring about deadly counter-coalitions.

Avoid Excessive Ambition and Excessive Unilateralism
America's impulses toward excessive ambition and excessive unilateralism are fueled by the fact that the United States is so powerful today. It is all too tempting for the United States, like every powerful state of the past, to believe that it can impose its will on others; succeed where others before have failed; make rules for others but violate the rules itself; ignore the counsel of others because it is so easy to go its own way; and ride roughshod over others' interests to serve its own.

These temptations must be resisted because they would lead to certain ruin. America's alliances are the keystone of selective engagement, and they must be preserved if the strategy is to succeed. Without them, there would be no forward presence and no ability to shape the international environment through the projection of military power. America's allies need not go so far as to form coalitions against the United States in order to thwart it. They could simply refuse, en bloc or singly, to cooperate with the United States. The ability even of allies and friends to undermine American actions should not be underestimated. Richard Haass, head of policy planning in the George W. Bush administration's State Department, put the point well: "There's very little we can do in the world unilaterally. There's almost

nothing we can do better unilaterally."[23] America's alliances are too important to be destroyed by the unilateralist temptation. To be preserved, the
United States must follow the three "Cs" of alliance management: it must
consult, it must compromise, and it must coordinate.

The reasons for avoiding excessive unilateralism are especially clear when
we understand why America's Cold War alliances have persisted beyond the
Cold War. These alliances remain viable, not only because the United States
has provided valuable goods to its allies, but also because it has managed its
alliances in ways that have been more multilateral than unilateral. The form
of alliance management has been as important as the nature of the alliance
benefits.

Political scientist John Ikenberry argues that the international institutions
set up by the United States after World War II, and that have persisted to
this day, comprise a semi-constitutional order.[24] Institutions and alliances
such as NATO operate in predictable, semi-legal ways and serve to bind not
only lesser members but also the United States itself. Moreover, the nature
of the American political system allows America's allies to participate in its
foreign policy decisions. The competition among the executive branch's
foreign policy bureaucracies and the institutionalized struggle between Congress and the presidency make the American political system an especially
open one with many points of access. Not just domestic actors, but foreign
actors as well, particularly American's allies, can find access points to influence decisions. I am not persuaded by all of the conclusions Ikenberry draws,
but there is merit to his argument. For example, the United States is the
weightiest member of NATO, but NATO still requires unanimity to take
action. The United States can cajole and threaten, and on rare occasions it
can dictate, but even when it is strong-arming its allies, it must take account
of their concerns.

I warn against excessive unilateralism, but not against unilateralism per
se. There will be occasions when the United States will have to act unilaterally, either because others oppose it but the need for action is urgent, or
because only the United States has the power to act. In addition, as Joseph
Nye has astutely observed, there will be occasions when the United States
should act unilaterally: when multilateral action would lead to inaction;
when unilateral action would advance multilateral interests; or when unilateral action would facilitate multilateral compromises that could lead to multilateral action later.[25] Even in these cases, he enjoins, the United States
should still try to obtain as much international support as possible.

Implement Other Policies
Avoidance of excessive ambition and rejection of excessive unilateralism are
the two most fundamental political prescriptions for selective engagement,
but there are other, more specific policies that will facilitate its implemen-

tation. The list is potentially long, and a few have already been touched on in the preceding chapters. Here I emphasize five political prescriptions that are especially salient to the goals of selective engagement.

First, the United States and its allies must do more to lock down the unsecured fissile material and the chemical and biological weapons of the former Soviet Union, and to find constructive employment for its scientists skilled in these areas. The program instituted by the United States since 1991, called the Cooperative Threat Reduction (CTR) program (or Nunn-Lugar), has had its successes, but it has been run too much as a foreign aid program and not enough as a national security program.[26] After a decade of insufficient funding, the United States and its allies allocated more funds to these tasks, but still not enough. Given the real risks of NBC grand terror attacks on the United States and its allies, this matter requires the sustained high-level attention of American governmental officials. Concomitant with the effort in Russia must be a global program to secure the plutonium and highly enriched uranium that currently sit, poorly guarded, in hundreds of sites around the world, including civilian research reactors.[27] The main thing that keeps states and non-state organizations from acquiring nuclear weapons is the scarcity of weapons-grade material; all of the potential supplies must be put out of reach.

Second, the United States needs to do much more than it has to conserve energy and especially to lessen its reliance on fossil fuels. These steps would reduce the carbon dioxide that the United States pours into the atmosphere (roughly 20 percent of the world's total annual emissions), and would also lessen the world's demand for oil and thus ease the severity of any disruption of Persian Gulf oil supplies that might occur. When oil prices rose dramatically in the 1970s, it proved possible at relatively modest cost to increase U.S. GDP without necessarily increasing energy consumption. That is, a 1 percent increase in GDP was possible with an increase in energy consumption that was less than 1 percent.[28] Many studies have shown that modest investments in energy efficiency and conservation can produce large results. For example, a recent study demonstrated that increases in the federally mandated corporate average fuel economy (CAFE) standards for automobiles could reduce oil imports by 11 percent in 2010 and by 27 percent in 2020.[29] Increases in U.S. energy efficiency and conservation are necessary to help avert severe climate change. The public may well be ahead of America's leaders on this issue. The Program on International Policy Attitudes at the University of Maryland found that "to mitigate the effects of global warming the American public is ready to take steps with real consequence—more than is generally realized."[30] America's political leaders should show as much common sense and courage about this issue as the public does. To be so gluttonous with energy, when matters could be dramatically changed with reasonable investments and when such benefits to

U.S. foreign policy and to the environment could result, is nothing short of outrageous and extremely short-sighted and dangerous.

Third, the United States should continue to encourage Europe's efforts to forge a common foreign and security policy and to enhance its defense capabilities, especially its ability to project military power outside of Europe. Some hard-bitten realists might argue that the United States should prefer European disunity rather than unity, because this would enable the United States to play divide-and-conquer and thereby maximize its power vis-à-vis Europe. It is true that a more powerful and cohesive Europe would dimin-ish America's freedom of international maneuver to a degree. However, the United States and Europe share many values, and there is much work to be done internationally; the more Europe can do, the less the United States has to do. Although power clearly counts in international relations, so, too, do values. A more cohesive group of generally like-minded democracies in Europe is a better bet for the United States over the long haul than a bunch of squabbling states that are too preoccupied with their competitive jockey-ing to help with the international work that needs to be done.[31] Along with Canada, Europe is, or should be, America's most reliable partner.

Fourth, in order to keep the current backlash against globalization from destroying international economic openness, the United States must act to deal with inequality at home and capitalistic rapaciousness abroad. Those workers in the United States that lose from openness must be given a finan-cial safety cushion and retraining. Robert Rubin, the architect of Clinton's economic policy, pointed out that, "change is key to growth . . . [but] change inevitably creates winners, losers, and dislocations." As a consequence, "con-tinued trade liberalization and movement toward market based economics" must be combined with "programs to help those dislocated by change."[32] Those states that open themselves up to capital flows must be protected from the vicious downside of international capital movements: the sudden with-drawal of capital when trouble threatens. (Investors are motivated by two of the most powerful human emotions—greed and fear—and to make matters worse, they travel in packs, like wolves. They all rush into a state together, lusting for profit, and when trouble looms, they all run away at the same time, bringing on the catastrophe they fear.) Together with the other rich nations of the world, the United States must do a much better job of regu-lating capital flows to avoid repeats of financial crises like the one that hit Asia in 1997.[33]

Finally, the United States cannot allow the campaign against terrorism to hijack its foreign policy. Protecting the American homeland from grand terror attacks is the prime directive of grand strategy, but this cannot constitute its sole purpose. The United States must not adopt a policy that ignores the political causes of terrorism to wage primarily a military campaign against it. Military means clearly have their role in defeating terrorism, along with intelligence, financial controls, covert operations, and the like, but these military and other measures must be complemented with political policies designed to deal with the political causes of terrorism, some of which were discussed in Chapter 6. This does not require the United States to solve all of the world's problems in order to defeat terrorism, but the United States must devise policies that target the political irritants in the key regions where terrorist organizations with global reach are being generated. In the long term, the most effective way to deal with terrorists is to delegitimate them within the societies from which they arise. The most effective way to do this, in turn, is to deal with the political grievances that give rise to these organizations; such grievances are usually widely shared by the populace from which the terrorist organizations arise. In the Middle East, for example, this will require that the United States produce genuine progress in the Israeli-Palestinian dispute and that it support political liberalization in those regimes over which it has some influence.

The United States must also not lose its political and moral compass in the campaign against terrorism. It must not make the mistake of containment, when the United States backed any regime that lined up against the Soviet Union, no matter what its political complexion. Although the United States will have to make some compromises with regimes that are unsavory in order to secure their cooperation against terrorists, this cannot become a U.S. license for such leaders to do whatever they wish in the name of fighting terrorism. If this were allowed to happen, then the United States would forfeit its political standing and become identified with the repressive policies of the leaders it backs, a sure-fire way to generate even more terrorism against itself.

It will not be easy to find the right balance between military measures to combat terrorists and political policies to undercut their appeal, and between enlisting the needed support of undesirable regimes and leaders and yet distancing the United States from their unsavory aspects, but it must be done. If these balances are not struck, and a clumsy and short-sighted campaign against terrorism is waged, it would end up isolating the United States from its real friends and generating more enemies against it.

These five substantive policies are not all of the political prescriptions that would facilitate selective engagement, but they are the ones most pertinent to its goals and most likely to make its implementation successful.

Domestic Support

No matter how acceptable selective engagement might be to other countries, if it does not have the support of the American public, it will fail. The most fundamental point to understand is that the public continues to support an active American role in world affairs. This was true before September 11, 2001, and it remained true afterwards. In February 2001, the Gallup organization asked Americans what role they thought the United States should play in solving international problems. Sixteen percent favored a "leading" role; 57 percent, a "major" role; and only 25 percent a "minor" or no role. One year later, after the September 11 attacks, support for an active U.S. role had increased: 26 percent favored a leading role; 52 percent, a major role; and only 20 percent a minor or no role.[34] In other words, 73 percent to 78 percent of Americans believe that the United States should take a major or leading role in world affairs. These recent figures accord well with historical data, which has found that for the last twenty-five years, nearly two-thirds of the American public has believed that it would be "best for the future of the country if we take an active part in world affairs rather than stay out of world affairs."[35] The American public's support for an active world role has not diminished from its Cold War levels, and the September 11 attacks appear to have enhanced that support.

A second, equally important finding is that U.S. citizens want their country to avoid the hegemonic role of a world policeman; they prefer instead a cooperative role with other nations. In a June 1996 poll, only 13 percent wanted the United States to play the role of dominant world leader, and 74 percent wanted the United States to play its fair share in multilateral efforts, while just 12 percent wanted to withdraw from the world.[36] As a 2001 Council on Foreign Relations study put it: "the general public wants the nation to be no more or less active than others."[37] The public is prepared to be active in world affairs, but only in cooperation with others. A June 1995 poll found that, when there was a problem in the world that required the use of force, 89 percent of Americans favored using force multilaterally through the United Nations; only 8 percent favored using it alone. The same poll found that 66 percent of Americans favored working through the United Nations and only 29 percent favored going it alone because the United States could act more quickly and effectively.[38] A July 2002 poll found that the majority of Americans (77 percent) wanted defense spending to be "based on the assumption that Washington will fulfill its obligations to protect other countries as part of multilateral efforts, not on its own."[39] In short, Americans do not reject an active world role, but they do reject a hegemonic world role, and they strongly prefer a multilateral approach because they want to share the burden, not bear it alone.

Third, the public puts a high value on several of the specific goals of selective engagement. In 1999, when asked to identify critical threats to the United States, 84 percent listed international terrorism; 76 percent, chemical and biological weapons; 75 percent, unfriendly countries acquiring nuclear weapons; and 43 percent, global warming. A poll just before September 11, 2001, found that three of the top five foreign policy priorities of the public included protecting the United States from terrorist attack, preventing the spread of weapons of mass destruction, and ensuring adequate energy supplies (the other two priorities were protecting the jobs of American workers and reducing the spread of AIDS).[40]

Fourth, the public is more supportive of the use of force than is commonly thought, although that support is qualified. The 1993 firefight in Mogadishu, Somalia, in which eighteen American soldiers were killed was thought by many to indicate that the American public is casualty-averse. (This had a major significance: largely because of Somalia, the Clinton administration avoided forceful intervention in the Rwandan genocide, even after it found out the terrible scale of the killing.) This view of public attitudes is incorrect. In fact, after the firefight in Mogadishu, 55 percent, 56 percent, or 61 percent of Americans—depending on whether one read the CNN/USA Today, ABC, or NBC polls—favored sending in more American troops, at least in the short run. Seventy-five percent favored retaliating militarily against the Somali warlord Aideed if he did not release American prisoners.[41] Other researchers have found that the critical determinant of the public's support for the use of force is not whether vital American interests are involved, but whether the military operation appears likely to succeed.[42] Success breeds support; fatalities in a successful operation do not cause the American public to withdraw its support. Leadership also plays a role in garnering the public's support for taking casualties. The more united the leadership is, the more likely public support is to be strong; the more divided the leadership, the weaker the public support.[43] Objectives also matter: the public is most willing to support the use of force to stop interstate aggression. It is most skeptical of military interventions whose purpose it is to reconstruct nations because it rightly sees that as a long-term and difficult task. It is prepared, however, if the case is made, to back humanitarian interventions to save lives, especially when large numbers of people are at risk.[44] In sum, the American public is neither wholeheartedly opposed to using force and suffering casualties, nor blindly willing to follow its leaders wherever they want to go. If the case is strong, if leaders present the case publicly, and if the operation looks as if it is going to be successful, then the American public will give its support. The belief that the American people are gun-shy is more an image in the minds of the foreign policy elite than it is an accurate depiction of the American public's views.

These four attributes describe key features of American public opinion on foreign affairs, and we can draw guidelines from them for the policy makers who must implement selective engagement. If the United States appears to be taking on the world policeman role, the American public will quickly tire of it and will likely balk at doing those things that must be done. Lesson number one, therefore, is that the United States should be prudent in the choice of objectives and should avoid excessive ambition. Lesson number two is that the United States should avoid excessive unilateralism that makes it look as if it is bearing more than its fair share of the burden.

The corollary is that the United States should embrace multilateralism. This is the best way to diminish the appearance that the United States is doing more than its share (although this is, in fact, often the case), because multilateralism looks like burden sharing. Lesson number three is that U.S. leaders should make a clear and compelling case to the public for the use of military power when that is deemed necessary, which means that there must be a good case to be made. The public will follow its leaders and will support success; it will penalize them for their failures.

The final guideline is to remember that the American public is not stupid. While it may not be intimately familiar with all the details, the nuances, and the intricacies of each and every foreign policy issue confronting the country, the same is no less true for many domestic issues facing the nation. A public that lacks knowledge about the details of foreign policy can still make informed decisions about its major contours and basic direction, just as it can for domestic issues. Moreover, most of the goals of selective engagement presently have broad public support. There is no reason why the public will not continue to support these goals, and to support the use of force both in peacetime and in wartime to back them up, when the case is made clearly, when excessive ambition and unilateralism are avoided, and when the United States appears to be acting in concert with its allies and other friends. In the end, what works to sustain international support for the strategy of selective engagement will also work to sustain domestic support.

THE FUTURE OF SELECTIVE ENGAGEMENT

Three final questions must be addressed, but the answers must, of necessity, be speculative. How long can selective engagement be pursued? How long should it be pursued? What comes after selective engagement?

How Long Can Selective Engagement Be Pursued?

The first question is the easiest to answer: the United States can persevere with selective engagement as long as the American public supports the policy, as long as America's friends and allies back the policy, as long as its leaders follow the political policies required to facilitate it, and as long as the United States maintains sufficient economic and military power to implement it. The first three factors are, to a large degree, matters of political choice and political wisdom. The last factor, however, is only partially under America's control: maintenance of sufficient power to sustain selective engagement depends not only on what the United States does but also on what others do. Selective engagement does not require that the United States be as militarily dominant as it now is, but America's military power, relative to other great powers, must remain formidable. The United States cannot play the reassuring, deterring, and war-waging roles that selective engagement requires if its military power becomes inferior to that of any other great power, or could easily be checked by a hostile combination of other powers. Primacy does not require overwhelming dominance, but it does require a military edge something like what the British maintained with the Royal Navy in the late nineteenth century: preservation of naval power at least equal, and preferably superior, to the next two powers combined. The United States today is, in effect, following something between a nine-power standard and a fifteen-power standard, measured in budgetary and qualitative terms. Selective engagement does not require such a large margin of superiority, but it does require a healthy one: perhaps a three-to-five-power standard would be the minimum for the future.

America's military must be measured against those of its potential military competitors: the European Union, Russia, and China. The European Union is best placed to challenge the United States militarily in the near term. Its GDP is the closest to that of America and it has an edge in population. (In 2001, the European Union's GDP was $7.9 trillion, and that of the United States, $10.2 trillion.)[45] Both its population and GDP will grow as the Union expands from fifteen to perhaps as many as twenty-six members. The Achilles heel of the European Union is not its economic, technological, and population strength, but its political cohesiveness. Europe is a pluralistic security community, but it is one that is still being underwritten by America's military power.

We can guess at Europe's future by looking at the history of the most prominent western multi-state security communities. They began as confederations, but ultimately federated because the confederal solution proved unstable. The Swiss Confederation, born in 1291 as a mutual defense treaty among three cantons, ultimately federated in 1847 after a brief civil war among its members. America's experiment with the Articles of Confederation came into force in 1781 and ended in 1789, in good measure because the founders of the union concluded that the confederal solution was too dangerous: it would be too weak to withstand foreign machinations against it and too unstable to avoid war among its members. The German Confederation of 1815–1866 was explicitly designed as a collective defense organization with a single army under unified command, but the proposed federal army was never organized. The confederation was rent by conflicting objectives among its members; Prussia and Austria vied for domination within it, and Prussia ultimately won and created a federal solution through war.[46]

The European Union today is something between a confederal and a federal model, or between intergovernmentalist and supranationalist models. The chances are high that Europe will remain between the two models for a long time to come. If so, the prospects are not imminent for a truly effective common foreign and security policy or for a more powerful and cohesive European defense force. Germany may be the most willing of the large states to submerge its identity into a federal solution; France and Britain are not, especially in foreign and defense affairs. These are proud nations with a long history of glory and independence in foreign affairs; those traditions will die slowly, if at all. Moreover, expansion of the Union will lead to greater difficulty in decision making: states will be concerned about the effects of majority voting as the number of members becomes larger, and they will want to design safeguards against it, which would make cohesive action even more difficult than it now is. In the defense area, the European Union explicitly intends its rapid reaction force to be a complement to NATO, not a substitute for it, but most observers believe that it will not attain its intended capabilities until perhaps 2012 at the earliest. Over time, the military capability of the European Union will increase, but it will be a slow process, and the ultimate destination of Europe is not clear. The American transition from confederation to federation was rapid, but the Swiss and German ones were not. Whether Europe moves to a federal solution, and how quickly, cannot now be known, but such a transition is likely to take a long time if it happens. More likely, the Union will become, in French president Jacques Chirac's words, "a united Europe of states rather than a United States of Europe."[47] Either way, Europe is no imminent challenger to America's military predominance.

While Europe has the resources to challenge America's military preeminence, but not yet the political cohesiveness, Russia has the political will, but not yet the economic capability. Although it possesses a formidable nuclear force, its other military capabilities are in disrepair. Reconstructing Russia and its economy is a generation's work. Russia will become a great power again one day, but this will take several decades to accomplish, and it will not be a military challenger to the United States for quite some time.

China has both the will and the potential resources to challenge America's military preeminence. The critical questions are whether China will overtake the United States in overall power and, if so, when. The Chinese themselves have given some answers to these questions. The China Institute for Contemporary International Relations (roughly equivalent to the analytical division of the U.S. Central Intelligence Agency) completed a study in the fall of 2000 on "comprehensive national power" (CNP). In China's lexicon, comprehensive national power is made up of economic, military, technological, scientific, educational, natural resource, and social stability components.[48] The Institute's study assumed that America's comprehensive national power would continue to grow at an annual rate of 3 percent; it then looked at various rates of annual growth in China's comprehensive national power to calculate when it would catch up with America's. The study concluded that if China's CNP grew at a 7 percent annual rate, it would match America's in

2033; if it grew at a 6 percent rate, it would do so in 2043; but if it grew at 5 percent, it would never catch up with America's CNP.[49]

Central to estimates of future comprehensive national power are growth rates in gross domestic product (GDP). According the Organization for Economic Cooperation and Development (OECD), the American economy grew at an average annual rate of 4 percent between 1950 and 1973, and at a slightly slower 3 percent between 1973 and 1998. In the same periods, China's economy grew annually at 5 percent and 6.9 percent, respectively. (For comparison, Germany's economy grew at an annual rate of 5.7 percent from 1950 to 1973, the height of its economic miracle, but at only 1.8 percent between 1973 to 1998; in the same periods, Japan's GDP grew at 9.3 percent, then slowed to 3 percent annually.)[50] Based on these statistics, it would appear that a growth rate in GDP of at least 3 percent is feasible for the United States to sustain. If the American economy underwent a real change in its underlying productivity rate in the late 1990s, a slightly higher rate may be possible. The case is not so clear-cut for China. Whether it can sustain 7 percent growth rates in its GDP for the next several decades will depend heavily on political reform.[51] China will need to institute transparency and accountability to continue to attract financial capital from abroad and to retain intellectual capital at home. It will also need to extend modernization into its interior if it is to maintain the social and political stability essential to continued economic growth. If it does all of these things, China may be able to sustain a high growth rate in its GDP because of its huge size, its ability to reallocate resources, and its wealth of talent.[52] If so, China's GDP might equal that of the United States by 2015 or 2020.[53]

Equality in GDP, however, does not automatically produce equality in military power: for a state to be able to extract economic resources from its society, per-capita GDP is also important. When China's GDP is equal to America's, its per-capita GDP, and hence its average standard of living, will still be only one-quarter that of the United States, because China has four times as many people. Indeed, assuming a growth rate of 2 percent for America's GDP and 6 percent for China's, the latter's per-capita income would not equal that of the United States until sometime between 2056 and 2095.[54] Per-capita income is at least as important as total GDP for extracting economic resources to channel them into military power. All other things being equal, if two societies have the same GDP, the state with the higher per-capita income can extract more discretionary income from its populace and divert it to such uses as military power.

In sum, it seems reasonable to argue that until at least 2033, China will not be in a position to generate the military resources and the other components of comprehensive national power necessary to challenge America's global military predominance, even if it were to achieve GDP parity with the United States a decade or two earlier. By 2033, of course, the United States will have continued to invest heavily in its military, building up a lead, especially in air and naval power so central to global influence, that will be hard for China to surmount quickly. If China is the actor best positioned to challenge America's military preeminence, then even under the most favorable scenario for China this could not happen for another thirty years.[55]

How Long Should Selective Engagement Be Pursued?

If the United States can sustain the military edge it needs to implement selective engagement for thirty more years, will it need to? Here matters become even more speculative. A simple answer, based on an extrapolation of current trends, is "yes." It is hard to envision changes in Europe, East Asia, and the Persian Gulf so dramatic as to cause the United States to withdraw entirely from these regions. The major challenge for East Asia over the next several decades will be to absorb China's growing power. America's deterrence and reassurance will continue to be important factors for the region's stability. Similarly, in the Persian Gulf, it is hard to envision changes that would obviate the need for an American military presence during the next several decades. The world will depend heavily on oil and natural gas for a long time to come, no matter how quickly it addresses the challenge of climate change. The Persian Gulf sheikdoms may begin to liberalize politically, but that could well be a dangerous process in the short term. Forecasting the future political complexion of Iran and Iraq is particularly difficult, but both are proud countries and potential regional hegemons. If genuine democracy ultimately comes to either of them, it will likely be a gradual process, short of American conquest. For as long as it takes for the Persian Gulf to make a transition to a more stable region, America's presence there will be important for stability. America's troops might leave Europe, but here, again, the timing of their departure would depend in part on the rate at which Europe develops greater political and military cohesion and greater military capability. America's presence there, ironically, slows that process. The most likely scenario is for a gradual drawdown of American troops from Europe and their relocation to East Asia, the Persian Gulf, or the United States, or their demobilization, if for no other reason than to prod along Europe's efforts to develop its rapid reaction force.

The reasons for an American presence in Europe, East Asia, and the Persian Gulf are structural, not ephemeral. They depend on durable underlying international factors, especially on America's economic and military preeminence, and also on deeply rooted American interests. It seems reasonable to assume that the need for selective engagement could well last as long as America's ability to sustain it.

What Comes after Selective Engagement?

Nothing lasts indefinitely; selective engagement's time will eventually pass. What happens then will depend on why its time has ended. In an ideal world, selective engagement would end because it contained the seeds of its own destruction: it did the job that America's overseas presence was meant to accomplish. When all of Eurasia's great powers are ultra-stable democracies, when all of their territorial disputes have been solved, when grand terrorism and NBC spread are no longer worries, when the world no longer relies so heavily on fossil fuels for its energy needs, when economic interdependence and political integration have proceeded to the point that war is as inconceivable in the other parts of Eurasia as it is in western Europe, when democratic consolidation is proceeding well in other parts of the world— then America's job is finished and the United States can safely go home.

In another and darker scenario, the United States leaves Eurasia because it is no longer welcome there and because it faces simultaneous military challenges in several regions that undercut its ability to play its deterrent and reassurance roles in any of them.

In a third scenario, selective engagement does not achieve all of its ends, but works well enough that the United States is no worse off several decades from now, and is perhaps even better off because the strategy will have produced some tangible progress for the better in Eurasia and elsewhere. Under this scenario, the United States does not leave Eurasia entirely, but retains a sufficient presence to play the role of "balancer of last resort." It still remains a powerful military actor in these regions, but not the overwhelmingly dominant one that it is now. Under this scenario, selective engagement will wither, to a degree, but it will not die.

Of these three scenarios, the first is the least likely. Such a radical transformation of the world in a few decades is unlikely. Which of the other two scenarios materializes depends on how much, and on how quickly, the international balance of power changes, and also on how multilateral or unilateral America's policies are. If history is a reliable guide, challenges to America's preeminence will eventually materialize even if the United States follows a generally multilateral approach, but these challenges are likely to materialize more quickly and be more damaging to America's position if the United States follows a highly unilateralist line. Because the first scenario is not attainable over the next several decades, and because the second scenario is not desirable, it should be America's policy to aim for the third scenario once selective engagement's day has passed.

This will require that the United States maintain its military strength and then take the political steps necessary to make the transition to another grand strategy. The central thrust of such a transition should be to create regional multilateral security structures that can persist as America's relative power wanes. These structures would be organizations to manage regional security relations, not regional collective security organizations (which do not work, as I explained in Chapter 3). Such organizations must be based, first and foremost, on stable regional balances of power, second, on

American participation in those balances, and third, on some degree of insti-tutionalization to regularize contact and create transparency among the member states.

Several broad guidelines can be offered as to how to create these multi-lateral security structures. The first guideline is to repeat an earlier message: the United States must take into account the interests and opinions of the other influential regional actors with which it is allied, and should fashion these structures in close partnership with them. It should also reach out to include others who are not yet in and who wish to cooperate. Institutional structures created with the voluntary involvement of all participants are more likely to persist than those imposed by the dictates of a powerful actor.

A second guideline is that the United States must shift some of the burden of security management and defense to its regional partners. This should not be a sudden shift in burden sharing but a planned, gradual shift. Such an approach is more likely to create the stable regional balances of power that are essential if the United States is to lower its regional profile as its relative power wanes.

Third, the United States should seek to embed these multilateral regional security structures into America's alliance structures. This process is already advanced in Europe, where the NATO alliance has added regional security management to NATO's traditional collective defense function. In East Asia, America's alliances are bilateral and there is, as yet, no multilateral forum. This is not likely to be a stable solution over the long term, and work should begin now to shape the four most important U.S. bilateral alliances—those with South Korea, Japan, the Philippines, and Australia—into some sort of multilateral mechanism that can retain the collective defense functions of each alliance and can also begin to develop structures for regional security management. If this approach works, then this "East Asian NATO" may be able to reach out to China the way that NATO has reached out to Russia. Multilateral approaches are even more difficult to imagine for the Persian Gulf region than for East Asia, but some thought should be given to devel-oping a multilateral mechanism from America's de facto alliances with the individual Persian Gulf sheikdoms, perhaps in some form of cooperation with the Gulf Cooperation Council. This institution could eventually reach out to Iraq and Iran when they have become less radical, less intransigent, less aggressive, and more open to international cooperation.

Following these three guidelines would not guarantee a stable transition to another grand strategy, but they would assist in any such transition. Equally important, they can be helpful in sustaining selective engagement in its current form. A multilateral approach, because it takes into account the interests of key regional actors, would diminish resentment toward the United States. A greater sharing of security burdens would make the United States loom less large. An approach that utilizes America's alliances as building blocks for the creation of regional security structures would provide the reassurance needed to move to a new set of security arrangements. If the measures that the United States takes to ease the transition to a successor strategy can also help the United States in implementing selective engagement, then it makes sense to begin to develop these policies now. This means that if the United States now begins to plan for the day when its preeminence fades, it is more likely not only to engineer a soft landing but also to extend the useful life of selective engagement.

To the final question—"after selective engagement, what then?"—I think that the most likely picture is one of an America still engaged militarily abroad in some or all of the multilateral regional security structures that it helped to create and strengthen, but much less dominant than it now is. Its role will still count, because it will remain the world's most powerful actor, and its role will be welcomed, if it plays its cards right, because it is best positioned to be the most disinterested of the regional actors. As long as the United States remains a militarily powerful state, as long as it has global interests, and as long as it can play the role of most unbiased regional actor, then there is a political case to be made for some type of military presence abroad, even if it is only a residual one. When the day for a new strategy comes, then the United States will have moved from a robust form of selective engagement to a more modest one.

CONCLUSION

The United States needs a thoughtful and coherent grand strategy as much as it ever has in its history, perhaps more. The unipolar moment is now unfolding: no state in history has had as much global power as the United States possesses and, for better or worse, the United States will be the world's only superpower for the next several decades. Even those who dislike this fact must acknowledge its reality. An American foreign policy that blunders mindlessly, heedless of the adverse effects of our might on the rest of the world, risks disaster, both for ourselves and for others. However, an American foreign policy that disciplines the use of its power, especially its military power, offers an unparalleled opportunity both to protect U.S. security and prosperity and to improve, even if only to a degree, the security, health, prosperity, and human rights of the rest of the world. This is a mission we should not avoid, so we had better do it right. For all of the reasons set forth in this book, selective engagement is the best approach.

APPENDIX A
Civil Wars Active between 1991 and 2000

Civil wars by region	Year war began	Total deaths (estimates by source)			
		SIPRI estimate	V&H low estimate	V&H high estimate	Defense monitor estimate
AFRICA					
Morocco vs. Saharawis	1973	10,000	9,000	13,000	16,000
Ethiopia vs. Eritreans	1974	—	350,000	650,000	—
Senegal vs. MFDC (Mouvement Forces Democratiques Casamances)	1982	1,000	—	—	—
Sudan	1983	80,000	1,500,000	2,000,000	1,000,000
South Africa vs. various opponents	1984	18,900	5,200	8,300	—
Mozambique	1985	10,000	400,000	900,000	—
Chad vs. various opponents	1989	—	—	—	50,000
Rwanda	1990	5,500	500,000	800,000	1,000,000
Burundi	1991	—	150,000	200,000	170,000
Sierra Leone/ECOMOG vs. RUF (Revolutionary United Front)	1991	5,000	40,000	50,000	30,000
Liberia	1992	20,000	20,000	40,000	150,000
Kenya	1992	—	—	—	1,500
Algeria vs. FIS/GIA (Islamist Salvation Front/Armed Islamic Group)	1992	100,000	80,000	120,000	75,000
Somalia	1992	—	100,000	500,000	350,000
Angola	1992	40,000	300,000	400,000	750,000
Uganda vs. LRA/ADF (Lord's Resistance Army/Allied Democratic Forces)	1993	2,000	—	—	—

APPENDIX A (*continued*)

Civil wars by region	Year war began	Total deaths (estimates by source)			
		SIPRI estimate	V&H low estimate	V&H high estimate	Defense monitor estimate
Burundi vs. CNDD/Palipehutu (Natl. Council for Defense of Democracy)	1994	200,000	—	—	—
Zaire vs. ADFL/Rwanda (Alliance of Democratic Forces for the Liberation of Congo-Zaire)	1996	4,000	1,700,000	2,500,000	250,000
Rwanda	1997	—	—	—	—
Congo (Brazzaville) vs. FDU (United Democratic Forces)	1997	4,000	16,000	27,000	100
EUROPE					
UK vs. IRA (Irish Republican Army)	1969	1,500	—	—	3,200
Georgia vs. Abkhazia/Ossetia	1991	2,500	4,000	12,000	6,000
Russia/USSR vs. Nagarno-Karabakh	1991	—	18,000	25,000	—
Yugoslavia vs. Slovenia/Croatia	1991	6,000	10,500	25,800	—
Turkey vs. PKK (Kurdistan Workers Party)	1991	30,000	15,000	25,000	—
Tajikistan	1992	20,000	30,000	50,000	50,000
Bosnia vs. Serbian Rebellion	1992	25,000	150,000	200,000	—
Russia vs. Chechens	1994	70,000	61,400	68,600	50,000
Uzbekistan vs. Islamic militants	1997	—	—	—	—
Yugoslavia vs. KLA (Kosovo Liberation Army)	1998	1,000	9,000	18,000	—
Kyrgyzstan vs. Islamic militants	1999	—	—	—	—
FAR EAST					
China vs. Tibet (1949)/Uighur (1996)	1949	—	—	—	—
Indonesia vs. various opponents	1963	15,000	—	—	150,000
Philippines vs. various opponents	1972	27,000	135,000	205,000	75,000
Cambodia	1979	25,500	65,000	75,000	25,000
Myanmar	1983	8,000	18,000	60,000	21,000

LATIN AMERICA

Guatemala vs. URNG (Unidad Revolucionaria Nacional Guatemalteca)	1968	2,800	105,500	212,000	140,000
El Salvador	1979	77,000	80,000	100,000	—
Peru vs. Sendero Luminoso	1982	28,000	25,000	30,000	35,000
Colombia vs. FARC/ELN (Revolutionary Armed Forces of Colombia/National Liberation Army)	1984	30,000	30,000	50,000	45,000
Haiti	1991	—	—	—	3,000
MIDDLE EAST					
Israel vs. Palestinians	1948	13,000	—	—	125,000
Lebanon: factions	1978	—	—	—	—
Iran vs. Kurds	1979	—	—	—	—
Iraq vs. Kurdistan Front/SAIRI (Supreme Assembly of the Islamic Revolution in Iraq)	1985	—	35,000	45,000	—
Israel vs. Palestinians	2000	—	—	—	125,000
SOUTH ASIA					
Bangladesh vs. JSS/SB (Jana Sanghati Samiti/Shantih Bahini)	1971	3,500	—	—	3,000
Afghanistan vs. various opponents	1979	20,000	1,125,000	1,620,000	1,550,000
India vs. Jammu/Kashmir, Punjab	1985	20,000	29,500	35,000	40,000
Sri Lanka vs. Tamil Tigers	1987	50,000	40,000	70,000	50,000

Author's calculations based on data from: SIPRI: Stockholm International Peace Research Institute, *SIPRI Yearbook: Armaments, Disarmament, and International Security* (Oxford: Oxford University Press, various years); *Defense Monitor* (1991–2000), Washington, D.C., Center for Defense Information, <www.cdi.org/dm/>, information downloaded August 17, 2001 (hard copy on file with the author); V&H: Benjamin A. Valentino, Paul Huth, and Dylan Balch-Lindsay, *Draining the Sea: Mass Killing, Genocide, and Guerilla Warfare* (paper prepared for the Annual Meeting of the APSA, August 31, 2001).

APPENDIX B
International Wars Active between 1991 and 2000

International war by region	Year war began	Total deaths (estimates by source)			
		SIPRI estimate	V&H low estimate	V&H high estimate	Defense monitor estimate
AFRICA					
Dem. Rep. Congo vs. Rwanda/Uganda/Rebels	1998	—	1,700,000	2,500,000	—
Guinea-Bissau/Senegal/Guinea vs. Rebels	1998	1,000	—	—	—
Eritrea vs. Ethiopia	1998	100,000	100,000	100,000	—
EUROPE					
Azerbaijan vs. Armenia	1991	10,000	—	—	20,000
Moldova vs. Russia/Dniestr Separatists	1992	—	—	—	1,000
Serbia vs. Kosovo/UN	1998	—	—	—	—
FAR EAST					
LATIN AMERICA					
MIDDLE EAST					
Gulf War	1991	—	45,000	60,000	—
Iraq vs. U.S./UK	1991	—	—	—	—
Yemen vs. Dem. Rep. of Yemen	1994	1,500	931	7,000	—
SOUTH ASIA					
India vs. Kashmiris/Pakistan*	1989	20,000	20,000	26,000	35,000

Notes: International wars includes imperial, colonial, and interstate conflicts. *The Indians and Pakistanis fought an intense engagement at Kargil in 1999 and, according to news reports, at least 1000 battle deaths occurred, making this qualify as a war.
Sources: Author's calculations based on data from: SIPRI: Stockholm International Peace Research Institute, *SIPRI Yearbook: Armaments, Disarmament, and International Security* (Oxford: Oxford University Press, various years); *Defense Monitor* (1991–2000), Washington, D.C., Center for Defense Information, <www.cdi.org/dm/>, information downloaded August 17, 2001 (hard copy on file with the author); V&H: Benjamin A. Valentino, Paul Huth, and Dylan Balch-Lindsay, *Draining the Sea: Mass Killing, Genocide, and Guerilla Warfare* (paper prepared for the Annual Meeting of the APSA, August 31, 2001).

Notes

Introduction

1. Thomas Schelling coined the term compellence and was the first to lay out the differences between deterrence and compellence. Thomas C. Schelling, *Arms and Influence* (New Haven: Yale University Press, 1966), pp. 69–91. Also see Robert J. Art, "To What Ends Military Power?" *International Security*, Vol. 4, No. 4 (Spring 1980), pp. 4–14.

2. Defensive preparations can have dissuasion value. If the defender can convince a potential attacker that it has the capability to deny the attacker its goals, then the attacker may be dissuaded from attacking. Some analysts refer to this as the deterrent value of defense, but I prefer to call it the dissuasion value of defense so as not to conflate defense with deterrence.

3. I have drawn this list partially from Richard N. Haass, *Intervention: The Use of American Military Force in the Post–Cold War World* (Washington, D.C.: Carnegie Endowment for International Peace, 1994), chap. 3.

4. What I have said about the use of military power also holds for the other instruments of statecraft. Consider, for example, the use of state A's economic power to obtain B's cooperation on some matter. State A can use whatever economic leverage it possesses over B to get B to continue to cooperate (deter B from stopping its cooperation); compel B to cooperate (change B's behavior from non-cooperation to cooperation); or protect itself by taking counter-measures against the effects of B's decision to cease cooperation (defend against B's defection from cooperation). Actions whose aim is to produce cooperation can thus also be understood in the three basic categories of result.

One: The International Setting

1. Secretary of Defense William S. Cohen, *Annual Report to the President and the Congress* (Washington, D.C.: Office of the Secretary of Defense, 1998), p. 3; and Secretary of Defense William S. Cohen, *Annual Report to the President and the Congress* (Washington, D.C.: Office of the Secretary of Defense, 2001), p. 3. Both available at <www.defenselink.mil>. The 1998 report (p. 3) also noted: "it is likely that no regional power or coalition will amass sufficient conventional military strength in the next 10 to 15 years to defeat the U.S. and allied armed forces, once the full military potential of the United States and its coalition partners are [sic] mobilized and deployed to the region of conflict." Also see William C. Wohlforth, "The Stability of a Unipolar World," *International Security*, Vol. 24, No. 1 (Summer 1999), pp. 5–42; and William C. Wohlforth, "U.S. Strategy in a Unipolar World," in G. John Ikenberry, ed., *America Unrivaled: The Future of the Balance of Power* (Ithaca, N.Y.: Cornell University Press, 2002), pp. 98–118.

2. Carl Conetta, *America's New Deal with Europe: NATO Primacy and "Double Expansion"* (Cambridge, Mass.: Commonwealth Institute, January 1998), p. 10.

3. "Russian Air Force No Longer Effective," *China Daily*, August 7, 2001 <www.chinadaily.com.cn/news/wn2001-08-07/24898.html>.

4. Sources for these statements are: Secretary of Defense William S. Cohen, *Report of the Quadrennial Defense Review* (Washington, D.C.: Office of the Secretary of Defense, May 1997), p. 5; The International Institute for Strategic Studies (IISS), *The Military Balance 1997–1998* (Oxford: Oxford University Press, 1997), p. 102; IISS, *The Military Balance 2001–2002* (Oxford: Oxford University Press, 2001), p. 105; and Alexei G. Arbatov, "Military Reform in Russia: Dilemmas, Obstacles, and Prospects," *International Security*, Vol. 22, No. 4 (Spring 1998), pp. 105 and 108.

5. IISS, *The Military Balance 1999–2000* (Oxford: Oxford University Press, 1999), p. 104.

6. IISS, *The Military Balance 2000–2001* (Oxford: Oxford University Press, 2000), p. 115; and IISS, *The Military Balance 2001–2002*, pp. 105–107.

7. William E. Odom, "Realism about Russia," *The National Interest*, No. 65, (Fall 2001), p. 64.

8. International Monetary Fund (IMF), September 2002 World Economic Outlook Database, available at <www.imf.org/externalpubs/ft/weo/2002/02/data/index.htm>.

9. Avery Goldstein, "Great Expectations: Interpreting China's Arrival," *International Security*, Vol. 22, No. 3 (Winter 1997/98), p. 44.

10. David Shambaugh, "Sino-American Strategic Relations: From Partners to Competitors," *Survival*, Vol. 42, No. 1 (Spring 2000), p. 104; IISS, *The Military Balance 1997–1998*, p. 164; IISS, *The Military Balance 2000–2001*, pp. 180–181; and Admiral Dennis Blair, Chief of America's Pacific forces, quoted in Bates Gill and Michael O'Hanlon, "China's Hollow Military," *The National Interest*, No. 56 (Summer 1999), p. 56. For another short and useful analysis of China's current and projected military capabilities, see Andrew J. Nathan and Robert S. Ross, *The Great Wall and the Empty Fortress: China's Search for Security* (New York: W.W. Norton, 1997), chap. 8.

11. See Robert S. Ross, "The Stability of Deterrence in the Taiwan Strait," *The National Interest*, No. 65 (Fall 2001), p. 71. Also see Robert S. Ross, "Deterrence, Escalation Dominance, and Stability in the Taiwan Strait," *International Security*, Vol. 27, No. 2 (Fall 2002), pp. 48–85.

12. IISS, *The Military Balance 2001–2002*, p. 291.

13. The 2000 defense budgets of the top ten are (in constant 1999, rounded dollars): the United States, $295 billion; Russia, $59 billion; Japan, $44 billion; China, $41 billion; France, $34 billion; Britain, $34 billion; Germany, $28 billion; Italy, $21 billion; Saudi Arabia, $18 billion; and India, $14 billion. See IISS, *The Military Balance 1997–1998*, Table 53, pp. 293–295; IISS, *The Military Balance 2000–2001*, Table 38, pp. 297–299; and IISS, *The Military Balance 2001–2002*, Table 37, pp. 299–301.

14. Three thousand is the figure estimated by the State Department for the number of people killed at the World Trade Center; it does not include the 189 killed at the Pentagon, including those on board the hijacked plane, nor the 45 people killed on the hijacked plane that crashed in Pennsylvania. See United States Department of State, *Patterns of Global Terrorism 2001*, May 2002, pp. xx and 1, available at <www.state.gov>.

15. Brian Jenkins, "International Terrorism," in David Carlton and Carlo Schaerf, eds., *International Terrorism and World Security*, reprinted in Robert J. Art and Kenneth N. Waltz, eds., *The Use of Force*, 5th ed. (Boulder, Colo.: Rowman and Littlefield, 1999), p. 72.

16. These figures have been calculated by Audrey Cronin and are based on the data compiled by Cronin from the State Department's annual *Patterns of Global Terrorism* for the years 1968–2000. See Audrey Kurth Cronin, "Rethinking Sovereignty in the Age of Terrorism," *Survival*, Vol. 44, No. 2 (Summer 2002), Figure 3, p. 128.

17. Brian M. Jenkins, "The Organization Men: Anatomy of a Terrorist Attack," in James F. Hoge, Jr., and Gideon Rose, eds., *How Did This Happen? Terrorism and the New War* (New York: Public Affairs, 2001), pp. 4–5. Prior to the 1998 bombing of American embassies in two African countries that killed many people (an event that was not included in his data), Richard Falkenrath counted only twelve terrorist attacks in the entire twentieth century in which more than 100 people were killed. See Richard A. Falkenrath, "Confronting Nuclear, Biological, and Chemical Terrorism," *Survival*, Vol. 40, No. 3 (Autumn 1998), Table 1, p. 52.

18. United States Department of State, *Patterns of Global Terrorism, 2000*, April 2001, p. 1.

19. Thomas C. Schelling, "What Purposes Can 'International Terrorism' Serve?" in R.G. Frey and Christopher W. Morris, *Violence, Terrorism and Justice* (Cambridge: Cambridge University Press, 1991), p. 19.

20. Kurth, "Rethinking Sovereignty in the Age of Terrorism," Figure 1, p. 124. See also Paul R. Pillar, *Terrorism and U.S. Foreign Policy* (Washington, D.C.: Brookings, 2001), p. 57; Bruce Hoffman, "Terrorism Trends and Prospects," in Ian O. Lesser, ed., *Countering the New Terrorism* (Santa Monica: RAND, 1999), p. 19; and Judith Miller and Don Van Natta, Jr., "In Years of Plots and Clues, Scope of Qaeda Eluded U.S.," *New York Times*, June 9, 2002, p. 27.

21. In 1995, there were 6,454 casualties worldwide, 738 for the United States; in 1996, 3,226 worldwide, 533 for the United States; and in 1998, 6,693 worldwide, 4,798 for the United States. See Kurth, "Rethinking Sovereignty in the Age of Terrorism," Figure 2, p. 126. Kurth's casualty figures for the United States are "U.S. and U.S.-related," which explains why the 1998 figure is so large: it includes non-Americans who were working in the two American embassies in Kenya and Tanzania that were bombed by al Qaeda. Those bombings killed 257 people, of whom 11 were Americans.

22. U.S. State Department, *Patterns of Global Terrorism 2001*, p. 2.

23. Pillar, *Terrorism and U.S. Foreign Policy*, p. 57. This paragraph relies heavily on Pillar's analysis on pp. 57–69.

24. Ibid., pp. 58–59; and IISS, *Strategic Survey 2001/2002* (Oxford: Oxford University Press, 2002), p. 40.

25. Testimony of Brian M. Jenkins, senior advisor to the President of the RAND Corporation, before the United States Senate, Armed Services Committee, *Hearings before the Subcommittee on Emerging Threats and Capabilities*, 107th Cong., 1st Sess., November 15, 2001, available through Lexis-Nexis "Congressional Universe."

26. Hoffman, "Terrorism Trends and Prospects," pp. 13–28.

27. Ibid., pp. 16–17.

28. Bruce Hoffman, *Inside Terrorism* (New York: Columbia University Press, 1998), pp. 94–95. For more on religious terrorism, see David C. Rapoport, "Sacred Terror: A Contemporary Example from Islam," in Walter Reich, ed., *Terrorism: Psychologies, Ideologies, Theologies, States of Mind* (Washington, D.C.: Woodrow Wilson Center Press, 1998), pp. 103–131.

29. Huntington's view is this: "The underlying problem for the West is not Islamic fundamentalism. It is Islam, a different civilization whose people are convinced of the superiority of their culture and are obsessed with the inferiority of their power. The problem for Islam is not the CIA or the U.S. Department of Defense. It is the West, a different civilization whose people are convinced of the universality of their culture and believe that their superior, if declining, power imposes on them the obligation to extend that culture throughout the world. These are the basic ingredients that fuel conflict between Islam and the West." See Samuel P. Huntington, *The Clash of Civilizations and the Remaking of World Order* (New York: Simon and Schuster, 1996), pp. 219–220.

30. For a range of views, see Bernard Lewis, *What Went Wrong? Western Impact and Middle Eastern Response* (Oxford: Oxford University Press, 1992); John L. Esposito, *Unholy War: Terror in the Name of Islam* (Oxford: Oxford University Press, 2002); Gilles Kepel, *Jihad: The Trail of Political Islam* (Cambridge, Mass.: Harvard University Press, 2002); Olivier Roy, *The Failure of Political Islam* (Cambridge, Mass.: Harvard University Press, 1994); and Michael Doran, "Understanding the Enemy," *Foreign Affairs*, Vol. 81, No. 1 (January/February 2002), pp. 22–43.

31. Pillar, *Terrorism and U.S. Foreign Policy*, p. 46.

32. See Roland Jacquard, *In the Name of Osama bin Laden: Global Terrorism and the bin Laden Brotherhood* (Durham, N.C.: Duke University Press, 2002), chaps. 2–4.

33. Kepel, *Jihad*, p. 300.

34. There is circumstantial evidence that al Qaeda tried as early as 1993 to execute a grand terror attack against the United States, with the bombing of the World Trade Towers. The mastermind behind that attack, Ramzi Yousef, spent a lot of time in a guest house in Peshawar, Pakistan, between 1992 and 1995 that was financed by bin Laden. Khalid Shaikh Mohammed, who played an important role in the September 11 attacks, may be a relative of

Yousef. According to Yousef's interviews with the FBI, he aimed to kill 250,000 people in the 1993 attack by causing one of the trade towers to topple and fall into the other. See Miller and Natta, "In Years of Plots and Clues, Scope of Qaeda Eluded U.S.," p. 26.

35. For more details on al Qaeda and other global terrorist organizations, see Paul R. Pillar, "Terrorism Goes Global," *Brookings Review*, Vol. 19, No. 4 (Fall 2001), pp. 34–37; and Olivier Roy, "Kriegsziel erreicht? Bin Laden bewirkt den Untergang der Taliban" ("Bin Laden: An apocalyptic sect severed from political Islam"), *Internationale Politik*, Vol. 56, No. 12 (December 2001), pp. 55–60.

36. Pillar, *Terrorism and U.S. Foreign Policy*, p. 48; Hoffman, *Inside Terrorism*, p. 92.

37. Pillar, *Terrorism and U.S. Foreign Policy*, p. 72.

38. The most comprehensive analysis of interdependence can be found in David Held and Anthony McGrew, David Goldblatt and Jonathan Perraton, *Global Transformations: Politics, Economics, Culture* (Stanford: Stanford University Press, 1999). The best critiques of interdependence and globalization are found in Robert Wade, "Globalization and Its Limits: Reports of the Death of the National Economy Are Greatly Exaggerated," in Suzanne Berger and Ronald Dore, eds., *National Diversity and Global Capitalism* (Ithaca, N.Y.: Cornell University Press, 1996), pp. 60–89; and Paul Hirst and Grahame Thompson, *Globalization in Question*, 2d ed. (Cambridge, UK: Polity Press, 1999). Also see Vincent Cable, "The Diminished Nation-State: A Study in the Loss of Economic Power," *Daedalus*, Vol. 124, No. 2 (Spring 1995), pp. 22–53; Jeffrey G. Williamson, "Globalization, Convergence, and History," *The Journal of Economic History*, Vol. 56, No. 2 (June 1996), pp. 277–306; and International Monetary Fund (IMF) Staff Survey, *World Economic Outlook* (Washington, D.C.: IMF, May 1997).

39. For different definitions and analyses of interdependence, see Richard Rosecrance and Arthur Stein, "Interdependence: Myth or Reality?" *World Politics*, Vol. 24, No. 1 (October 1973), pp. 1–28; Peter J. Katzenstein, "International Interdependence: Some Long-Term Trends and Recent Changes," *International Organization*, Vol. 29, No. 4 (Autumn 1975), pp. 1021–1035; R. Rosecrance, A. Alexandroff, W. Koehler, J. Kroll, S. Laqueur, and J. Stocker, "Whither Interdependence?" *International Organization*, Vol. 31, No. 3 (Summer 1977), pp. 425–473; Kenneth N. Waltz, "The Myth of National Interdependence," in Charles Kindleberger, ed., *The International Corporation* (Cambridge, Mass.: MIT Press, 1970), pp. 205–227; Kenneth N. Waltz, "Structural Realism after the Cold War," *International Security*, Vol. 25, No. 1 (Summer 2000), pp. 14–18; and Robert Gilpin, "Economic Interdependence and National Security in Historical Perspective," in Klaus Knorr and Frank N. Trager, eds., *Economic Issues and National Security* (Lawrence, Kansas: Allen Press, 1977), pp. 19–67.

40. Stephan Haggard uses the term "deep integration" for "the fundamentally political process of policy coordination and adjustment designed to facilitate closer economic interdependence and to manage the externalities that arise from it." High levels of interdependence would give rise to the need to coordinate, adjust, and cope with its externalities. See Stephan Haggard, *Developing Nations and the Politics of Global Integration* (Washington, D.C.: Brookings, 1995), p. 2.

41. Dale Copeland stresses the role that expectations about future trade play in enhancing or mitigating conflict. If future expectations are positive, war is less likely; if they are negative, war is more likely. See Dale C. Copeland, "Economic Interdependence and War: A Theory of Trade Expectations," *International Security*, Vol. 20, No. 4 (Spring 1996), pp. 5–42. In his quantitative study, Mark Gasiorowski found that beneficial trade reduced conflict among states. See Mark J. Gasiorowski, "Economic Interdependence and International Conflict: Some Cross-National Evidence," *International Studies Quarterly*, Vol. 30, No. 1 (March 1986), pp. 23–39.

42. A similarly high level of economic interdependence was reached between 1870 and 1914. Then, as now, the industrializing powers exported a high percentage of their products. Then, as now, world trade grew rapidly and outstripped the growth rate of gross world product (GWP). Then, as now, international capital movements were of considerable size. Nevertheless, there are strong reasons to believe that the current era of interdependence is stronger and deeper than the previous one, if for no other reason than that the ratio of world exports

to GWP is more than twice as large today as it was in 1914. For arguments as to why this era is different than the previous one, see Robert J. Art, "A Defensible Defense: America's Grand Strategy After the Cold War," *International Security*, Vol. 15, No. 4 (Spring 1991), pp. 36–39; Richard E. Baldwin and Philippe Martin, *Two Waves of Globalization: Superficial Similarities, Fundamental Differences*, National Bureau of Economic Research Working Paper 6904, January 1999, available at <www.nber.org/papers/26904>; and Held, et al., *Global Transformations*, "Conclusion." For arguments that stress the similarity between the earlier period and now, see Waltz, "The Myth of Interdependence"; Kenneth N. Waltz, *Theory of International Politics* (Reading: Addison-Wesley, 1979), chap. 7 and the Appendix; Stephen D. Krasner, "State Power and the Structure of International Trade," *World Politics*, Vol. 28, No. 3 (April 1976), pp. 327, 328; and Janice E. Thomson and Stephen D. Krasner, "Global Transactions and the Consolidation of Sovereignty," in Ernst-Otto Czempiel and James N. Rosenau, eds., *Global Changes and Theoretical Challenges* (New York: Macmillan, 1989), pp. 198–206.

43. For data on cross-border transactions in bonds and equities from 1970–1996 and on direct foreign and portfolio investment in Western Europe, Japan, and the United States, see International Monetary Fund, IMF Staff Survey, *World Economic Outlook*, p. 60.

44. Comparing direct investment flows in these years with the pre-1914 period is difficult because of lack of complete data. Thomson and Krasner (see the sources cited in Figure 1.1) show that foreign investment as a percentage of GNP in Germany, Belgium, France, Sweden, Switzerland, the United Kingdom, and Holland reached the following levels: 1840, 0.19 percent; 1870, 0.57 percent; 1900, 1.02 percent; and 1913, 1.08 percent. These were the richest countries then and the most important net capital exporters. These pre-1913 figures are hard to compare to those in Table 1.2 because the latter include GWP and therefore a bigger denominator, which would make the percentages lower.

45. Peter F. Drucker, "The Changed World Economy," *Foreign Affairs*, Vol. 64, No. 4 (Spring 1986), p. 782.

46. Kathryn M. Dominguez and Jeffrey A. Frankel, *Does Foreign Exchange Intervention Work?* (Washington, D.C.: Institute of International Economics, 1994), pp. 88–89.

47. Quoted in Joseph S. Nye, Jr., *Bound to Lead: The Changing Nature of American Power* (New York: Basic Books, 1990), p. 183.

48. See Robert Gilpin, *The Political Economy of International Relations* (Princeton: Princeton University Press, 1987), pp. 122–127. As Gilpin puts it (p. 124): "The integration of national monetary systems with the London financial market endowed Great Britain with the ability to control to a considerable degree the world's money supply. By lowering and raising its discount rate, the Bank of England manipulated the flow of gold internationally and in effect managed world monetary policy." For an opposing view of the role of the London financial market, see Giulio M. Gallarotti, *The Anatomy of an International Monetary Regime* (New York: Oxford University Press, 1995). Gallarotti argues: "Not only can we say that the Bank [of England] did not manage the international monetary system, but it is questionable whether it even managed the British monetary system. . . . The Bank was even less of an international than a domestic central banker" (p. 8).

49. See Bruce G. Resnick, "The Globalization of World Financial Markets," *Business Horizons*, Vol. 32, No. 6 (November–December 1989), pp. 34–42.

50. See Paul Krugman, *Peddling Prosperity: Economic Sense and Nonsense in the Age of Diminished Expectations* (New York: W.W. Norton, 1994), p. 231.

51. Wade, "Globalization and Its Limits," p. 70; and Baldwin and Martin, *Two Waves of Globalization*, p. 19.

52. Figures are from Krugman, *Peddling Prosperity*, pp. 47 and 49.

53. Growing interdependence among the rich nations is not yet globalization, if that term means the truly free movement of goods and services among states, stateless corporations, and a single global capital market. Although goods flow more freely now than ever before, non-tariff barriers have replaced tariffs, and international trade in services is just beginning to burgeon. Most transnational corporations still concentrate their strategic decision making, research and development innovation, and assets and share-holding in their home country,

and they still retain a national outlook and national loyalties. Wade, "Globalization and Its Limits," pp. 78–82. Capital markets have become more integrated, but have not transmuted into a single global market. For example, domestic investment is still financed mostly by domestic savings, and real interest rate parity among countries has not been achieved. On service trade and capital markets, see IMF Staff Survey, *World Economic Outlook*, pp. 53–56 and 59–65.

54. The three best books on the spread of democracy since the mid-1970s are Samuel P. Huntington, *The Third Wave: Democratization in the Late Twentieth Century* (Norman: University of Oklahoma Press, 1991); Larry Diamond, *Developing Democracy: Toward Consolidation* (Baltimore: Johns Hopkins University Press, 1999; and Adam Przeworski, Michael E. Alvarez, Jose Antonio Cheibub, and Fernando Limongi, *Democracy and Development: Political Institutions and Well-Being in the World, 1950–1990* (Cambridge: Cambridge University Press, 2000).

55. Huntington, *The Third Wave*, p. 7. As Huntington explains (ibid., p. 6), in *Capitalism, Socialism, and Democracy*, Schumpeter rejected "the will of the people" and "the common good" as criteria for defining democracy, instead arguing that "the democratic method is that institutional arrangement for arriving at political decisions in which individuals acquire the power to decide by means of a competitive struggle for the people's vote."

56. Ibid., pp. 26 and 294. That 45 percent of the states with populations greater than one million are democratic is not unprecedented, as Huntington reminds us. In 1922, twenty-nine of the sixty-four states (45.3 percent) with populations greater than one million were democratic. Democracy, argues Huntington, comes in waves, with peaks and troughs. After the peak of its first long wave of advance (1828–1926), the number of democratic states fell to a trough of only twelve in 1942. In the second short wave (1943–1962), the number of democracies reached thirty-six out of 111 states (32.4 percent) and then fell back to thirty in 1973. The third wave began in 1974. It is not clear whether it has peaked. See ibid., Chapter 1.

57. See Freedom House, *Freedom in the World: The Annual Survey of Political Rights and Civil Liberties, 2000–2001*, Table 11, available at <www.freedomhouse.org>; and Diamond, *Developing Democracy*, p. 24.

58. Fareed Zakaria, "The Rise of Illiberal Democracy," *Foreign Affairs*, Vol. 76, No. 6 (November/December 1997), pp. 22–43. Applying the distinction between electoral and liberal democracies, Diamond concluded that 57 electoral and 28 liberal democracies were born during the third wave of democratization from 1974–1997. See Diamond, *Developing Democracy*, pp, 8–13 and 60–61.

59. Freedom House, *Freedom in the World*, Tables 9, 11, and 4. Percentages are rounded to the nearest whole number.

60. For an analysis of why democracy is now firmly rooted in Germany, see Stephen Van Evera, "Primed for Peace: Europe after the Cold War," *International Security*, Vol. 15, No. 3 (Winter 1990/91), pp. 41–43. For an analysis of why anti-militarism is strong in Japan, see Thomas U. Berger, "From Sword to Chrysanthemum: Japan's Culture of Anti-militarism," *International Security*, Vol. 17, No. 4 (Spring 1993), pp. 119–151.

61. Huntington, *The Third Wave*, pp. 40 and 164.

62. Ibid., pp. 45–46.

63. Ibid., pp. 61–62.

64. Samuel P. Huntington, "Democracy's Third Wave," *Journal of Democracy*, Vol. 2, No. 2 (Spring 1991), p. 33.

65. Seymour Lipset first pointed this out in 1959. See Seymour Martin Lipset, *Political Man: The Social Bases of Politics*, exp. and updated ed. (Baltimore: Johns Hopkins University Press, 1981), chap. 2. For a comprehensive review of subsequent studies of the link between economic growth and democracy, see Larry Diamond, "Economic Development and Democracy Reconsidered," *American Behavioral Scientist*, Vol. 35, No. 4/5 (March/June 1992), pp. 450–499. For a recent reconfirmation that economic growth alone does not necessarily lead to democracy, see Adam Przeworski and Fernando Limongi, "Modernization: Theories and Facts," *World Politics*, Vol. 49, No. 2 (January 1997), pp. 155–184; and Przeworski, Alvarez, Cheibub, and Limongi, *Democracy and Development*, pp. 88–89, 137, and 92–117. A short argu-

ment that democracy promotes economic growth is, "Democracy and Growth: Why Voting Is Good for You," *The Economist*, Vol. 332, No. 7878 (August 27, 1994), pp. 15–17.

66. For this discussion, I have borrowed from Robert A. Dahl, *Polyarchy: Participation and Opposition* (New Haven: Yale University Press, 1971), pp. 76–78 and 82–88.

67. Ibid., pp. 76 and 78. Emphasis in original.

68. Diamond, "Economic Development and Democracy Reconsidered," p. 488.

69. An excellent review of international environmental agreements is to be found in Peter M. Haas with John Sundgren, "Evolving International Environmental Law and Changing Practices of National Sovereignty," in Nazli Choucri, ed., *Global Accord: Environmental Challenges and International Responses* (Cambridge, Mass.: MIT Press, 1993), pp. 401–429. See also David Victor, Kal Raustiala, and Eugene B. Skolnikoff, eds., *The Implementation and Effectiveness of International Environmental Agreements: Theory and Practice* (Cambridge, Mass.: MIT Press, 1998).

70. For analyses of how environmental matters rose to prominence on the international agenda, see Tony Brenton, *The Greening of Machiavelli: The Evolution of International Environmental Politics* (London: Earthscan, 1994), chaps. 3–6; and Paul Wapner, "Politics Beyond the State: Environmental Activism and World Civic Politics," *World Politics*, Vol. 47, No. 3 (April 1995), pp. 311–341. A good overview of the environmental accords reached (and not reached) at Rio, as well as an account of the negotiations, is Michael Grubb, et al., *The Earth Summit Agreements: A Guide and Assessment* (London: Earthscan, 1993), chap. 6; and Irving M. Mintzer and J.A. Leonard, *Negotiating Climate Change: The Inside Story of the Rio Convention* (Cambridge: Cambridge University Press, 1994).

71. For a comprehensive catalogue of the world's environmental degradation, see The World Commission on Environment and Development, *Our Common Future* (Oxford: Oxford University Press, 1987); World Resources Institute, *World Resources, 1994–95: A Guide to the Global Environment* (Oxford: Oxford University Press, 1994), chaps. 2 and 6–11; and Paul Harrison, *The Third Revolution: Population, Environment and a Sustainable World* (London: Penguin Books, 1993), chaps. 3–15.

72. For the likelihood and nature of political conflicts produced by environmental degradation and resource shortages, see Peter H. Gleick, "Water and Conflict: Fresh Water Resources and International Security," *International Security*, Vol. 18, No. 1 (Summer 1993), pp. 79–113; Thomas F. Homer-Dixon, "Environmental Scarcities and Violent Conflict: Evidence from Cases," *International Security*, Vol. 19, No. 1 (Summer 1994), pp. 5–41; Arthur H. Westing, *Global Resources and International Conflict: Environmental Factors in Strategic Policy and Action* (Oxford: Oxford University Press, 1986); and The Woodrow Wilson Center, *Environmental Change and Security Project Report*, No. 3 (Washington, D.C.: The Woodrow Wilson Center, Spring 1997).

73. See Marc A. Levy, "Is the Environment a National Security Issue?" *International Security*, Vol. 20, No. 2 (Fall 1995), pp. 35–63.

74. The classic article on how the shared or "commons" nature of the environment tends to result in its overuse and eventual degradation is Garrett Hardin, "The Tragedy of the Commons," *Science*, Vol. 162 (December 13, 1968), pp. 1243–1248. For another good analysis of the commons issue, see Per Magnus Wijkman, "Managing the Global Commons," *International Organization*, Vol. 36, No. 3 (Summer 1982), pp. 511–536.

75. The best account of how the international community reached agreement on an ozone regime is by the U.S. negotiator to the ozone negotiations, Richard Elliot Benedict, *Ozone Diplomacy: New Directions in Safeguarding the Planet* (Cambridge, Mass.: Harvard University Press, 1991). Also see Karen Lifton, *Ozone Discourses: Science and Politics in Global Environmental Cooperation* (New York: Columbia University Press, 1994).

76. The definitive scientific assessments are to be found in volumes published by the Intergovernmental Panel on Climate Change (the IPCC), a body created by the World Meteorological Organization and the United Nations Environment Programme: J.T. Houghton, G.J. Jenkins, and J.J. Ephraums, eds., *Scientific Assessment of Climate Change: Report of Working Group I* (Cambridge: Cambridge University Press, 1990); J.T. Houghton, et al., *Climate Change 1995: The Science of Climate Change* (Cambridge: Cambridge University Press, 1996); and J.T.

Houghton, et al., *Climate Change 2001: The Scientific Basis* (Cambridge: Cambridge University Press, 2001), all available at <www.ipcc.ch/pub/reports.htm#sprep>. For assessments of how global warming will affect the United States, see U.S. Environmental Protection Agency, *Policy Options for Stabilizing Global Climate*, Draft Report to Congress, 2 vols., February 1989. Two useful overviews of the international politics of global warming are Matthew Paterson, *Global Warming and Global Politics* (New York: Routledge, 1996); and Ross Gelbspan, *The Heat Is On: The High Stakes Battle Over the Earth's Threatened Climate* (Reading, Mass.: Addison-Wesley, 1997).

77. In fact, there is no "average global temperature" because temperatures vary by region. Average global temperature is a scientific convention used to simplify the task of estimating the effects of global warming; it is a computed average surface temperature for the entire globe. Under various global warming scenarios, there will not be a uniform increase in regional temperatures. Some regions may actually become cooler, but most regions will experience warmer temperatures, a larger number of warm days, and more extremes in weather.

78. Houghton, et al., *Climate Change 1995*, pp. 15, 61, and 466–468; and *Summary for Policymakers: A Report of Working Group I of the Intergovernmental Panel on Climate Change* (The IPCC's Third Assessment Report), p. 2, at <www.ipcc.ch/pub/spm22-01.pdf>. From pre-industrial days to 1994, concentrations of carbon dioxide have increased from 280 to 358 parts per million volume (ppmv); methane from 700 to 1720 parts per billion (ppbv); and nitrous oxide from 275 to 312 ppbv. The lifetimes of these gases in the atmosphere are estimated at 50–150 years for carbon dioxide; 12 for methane; and 120 for nitrous oxide.

79. The statistics in this paragraph come from World Resources Institute, *World Resources 1990–91* (New York: Oxford University Press, 1990), pp. 14–15.

80. Ibid., pp. 15, 17, 349.

81. International Energy Agency, *CO_2 Emissions from Fuel Combustion: 1977–1998* (Paris: Organization for Economic Cooperation and Development, 2000), p. xix. Figures are rounded.

82. The first estimate by the IPCC gave a range of increase of 1.0 to 3.5 degrees centigrade. More recently it has estimated an increase of 1.4–5.8 degrees centigrade. See IPCC, *Summary for Policymakers* (Working Group 1), p. 13. Also see Houghton, et al., *Climate Change 1995*, pp. 5,6, and 323; Statement of Timothy E. Wirth, Undersecretary of State for Global Affairs, before the Subcommittee on Energy and Power, Committee on Commerce, U.S. House of Representatives, July 15, 1997, <gep-ed@igc.apc.org>; John Lanchbery and David Victor, "The Role of Science in the Global Climate Negotiations," in Helge Ole Bergesen and Georg Parmann, eds., *Green Globe Yearbook of International Cooperation and Development, 1995* (Oxford: Oxford University Press, 1995), p. 30; Thomas J. Crowley, "Causes of Climate Change Over the Past 1000 Years," *Science*, Vol. 289 (July 14, 2000), pp. 270–277; and William K. Stevens, "If Climate Changes, It May Change Quickly," *New York Times*, January 27, 1998, pp. C1–2.

83. For recent scientific evidence on the magnitude and swiftness of past climate changes triggered by small changes in average global temperature, see Jeffrey P. Severinghaus, et al., "Timing of Abrupt Climate Change at the End of the Younger Dryas Interval from Thermally Fractionated Gases in Polar Ice," *Nature*, Vol. 319 (January 8, 1998), pp. 144.

84. On these points, see Mikael Eriksson, Margareta Sollenberg, and Peter Wallensteen, "Armed Conflict 1946–1999: A New Dataset," pp. 9–10, paper prepared for a conference on identifying wars, Uppsala University, June 8–9, 2001, available at <www.pcr.uu.se>; Ted Robert Gurr, "Ethnic Warfare on the Wane," *Foreign Affairs*, Vol. 79, No. 3 (May/June 2000), pp. 52–65; and Ted Robert Gurr, Monty G. Marshall, and Deepa Khosla, *Peace and Conflict 2001: A Global Survey of Armed Conflicts, Self-Determination Movements, and Democracy* (College Park, Md.: Center for International Development and Conflict Management, University of Maryland, 2001), pp. 8–9.

85. See Benjamin Valentino, Paul Huth, and Dylan Balch-Lindsay, "Draining the Sea: Mass Killing, Genocide, and Guerilla Warfare," paper delivered at the Annual Meeting of the American Political Science Association, August 31, 2001. I adopt Benjamin Valentino's definition of mass killing: the intentional killing of 50,000 or more non-combatants within a five-

year period. See Benjamin A. Valentino, *Final Solutions: Mass Killing and Genocide in the 20ᵗʰ Century* (Ithaca, N.Y.: Cornell University Press, 2003), chap. 1.

Two: America's National Interests

1. I avoid the "vital-desirable" dichotomy that is more commonly used because those who employ it usually argue that a state's military power should almost never be used except to defend its vital interests. Desirable interests may be worth having, according to this view, but military force should not be employed to secure them. Accordingly, "desirable" connotes something that is expendable—something "nice to have but not worth paying much of a price to get." If we followed the vital-desirable distinction, the United States would use military force for homeland defense and perhaps for cutting down an emerging Eurasian hegemon, but for little or nothing else. In my judgment, this is far too restrictive.

2. For an assessment of the current and future cruise missile threat, see Dennis M. Gormley, "Hedging Against the Cruise-Missile Threat," *Survival*, Vol. 40, No. 1 (Spring 1998), pp. 92–112.

3. Among the best sources on the NBC rogue-regime and fanatical-terrorist threats are Richard A. Falkenrath, Robert D. Newman, and Bradley A. Thayer, *America's Achilles' Heel: Nuclear, Biological, and Chemical Terrorism and Covert Attack* (Cambridge, Mass.: MIT Press, 1998); Bruce Hoffman, *Responding to Terrorism across the Technological Spectrum*, P-7874 (Santa Monica, Calif.: RAND, 1994); Bruce Hoffman, *Inside Terrorism* (London: Macmillan, 1998); Jessica Stern, *The Ultimate Terrorists* (Cambridge, Mass.: Harvard University Press, 1999); Jonathan B. Tucker, ed., *Toxic Terror: Assessing Terrorist Use of Chemical and Biological Weapons* (Cambridge, Mass.: MIT Press, 2000); and Joshua Lederberg, ed., *Biological Weapons: Limiting the Threat* (Cambridge, Mass.: MIT Press, 1999).

4. I have borrowed this list of traits from Stephen Van Evera, *The Causes of War: Power and the Roots of Conflict* (Ithaca: Cornell University Press, 1999), pp. 247–250. For useful surveys of America's policy toward present-day states of concern, see Raymond Tanter, *Rogue Regimes: Terrorism and Proliferation* (New York: St. Martins Press, 1998); and Robert S. Litwak, *Rogue States and U.S. Foreign Policy: Containment after the Cold War* (Washington, D.C.: Woodrow Wilson Center Press, 2000).

5. Barry Posen makes this argument persuasively. See Barry R. Posen, "U.S. Security in a Nuclear-Armed World (Or What If Iraq Had Had Nuclear Weapons?)," *Security Studies*, Vol. 6, No. 3 (Spring 1997), pp. 1–32.

6. Kenneth N. Waltz, "Peace, Stability, and Nuclear Weapons," in Robert J. Art and Robert Jervis, eds., *International Politics: Enduring Concepts and Contemporary Issues* (New York: Longman, 2000), p. 471.

7. See Falkenrath, *America's Achilles' Heel*, p. 91.

8. The Iran-Iraq war of 1980–1988 may be a second case. Iraq used chemical weapons against the Iranians as early as 1983, when independent sources verified their use. Iran may also have used chemical weapons against Iraqi troops in the late stages of the war, but we lack independent verification of Iranian use. See ibid., pp. 226–227; and Kenneth M. Pollack, *The Threatening Storm: The Case for Invading Iraq* (New York: Random House, 2002), p. 260.

9. Both quotations are from Scott D. Sagan, "The Commitment Trap: Why the United States Should Not Use Nuclear Threats to Deter Biological and Chemical Weapons Attacks," *International Security*, Vol. 24, No. 4 (Spring 2000), pp. 93, 95.

10. Kenneth M. Pollack, "Why Iraq Can't Be Deterred," *New York Times*, September 26, 2002, p. A31. Also see Kenneth M. Pollack, *The Threatening Storm*, chap. 8.

11. Sagan, "The Commitment Trap," p. 93.

12. See John J. Fialka, "U.S. Nuclear Plants Face Security Gaps Since Sept. 11 Raids," *The Wall Street Journal*, July 3, 2002, p. A4. I am indebted to Ted Postol of MIT's Security Studies Program for walking me through the reactor-meltdown and chemical plant scenarios.

13. See William J. Broad, "How Japan Germ Terror Alerted World," *New York Times*, May 26, 1998, p. A1. For good analyses of the Tokyo sarin attack, see Jessica Stern, "Terrorist Motivations and WMD," in Peter Lavoy, Scott D. Sagan, and James Wirtz, eds., *Planning the Unthinkable: Military Doctrines for the Use of Weapons of Mass Destruction* (Ithaca, N.Y.: Cornell University Press, 2000), pp. 202–230; Falkenrath, et al., *America's Achilles' Heel*, Box 1, pp. 19–26.

14. See Falkenrath, et al., *America's Achilles' Heel*, pp. 170–178 and xxiii. The authors made this clear in a 1996 seminar briefing at the Belfer Center for Science and International Affairs, Harvard University, on the preliminary results of their research. See also Stern, *The Ultimate Terrorists*, chap. 4.

15. David E. Kaplan, "Aum Shinrikyo (1995)," in Tucker, *Toxic Terror*, pp. 216–221.

16. See Benjamin Weiser, "Informer Tells Jury of His Break From bin Laden and Path to U.S.," *New York Times*, February 8, 2001, p. A1; Colum Lynch, "Bin Laden Sought Uranium, Jury Told," *The Washington Post*, February 8, 2001, p. A2; and John Deutch, Director of Central Intelligence, "The Threat of Nuclear Diversion," Statement for the Record to the Permanent Subcommittee on Investigations of the Senate Committee on Government Affairs, March 20, 1996 (mimeo), p. 7.

17. Matthew Bunn reports that there were a "number of documented cases of theft of substantial quantities of weapon-usable nuclear materials" from Russia in the 1990s. See Matthew Bunn, *The Next Wave: Urgently Needed New Steps to Control Warhead and Fissile Material* (Cambridge, Mass., and Washington, D.C.: Harvard University Belfer Center for Science and International Affairs and the Carnegie Endowment for International Peace, April 2000), p. 16, available at <ksgnotes1.harvard.edu/bcsia/library.nsf/pubs/nextwave>. Also see David William and Alan C. Miller, "Nuclear Threat Is Real, Experts Warn," *Los Angeles Times*, November 11, 2001, at <www.latimes.com>.

18. John V. Parachini, "The World Trade Center Bombers (1993)," in Tucker, *Toxic Terror*, p. 202; Stern, "Terrorists Motivations and WMD," pp. 4–5; and Bruce Hoffman, "Terrorism Trends and Prospects," in Ian O. Lesser, et al., *Countering the New Terrorism* (Washington, D.C.: RAND, 1999), p. 17. Early analysis of the attack suggested that it was also meant to be a chemical weapons attack, but later analysis showed that there was no proof of use of sodium cyanide. That should not be cause for comfort. The mastermind, Ramzi Yousef, stated that he had considered using the poison, and had the capability to do so, but had decided not to because "it was going to be too expensive to implement." Quoted in Parachini, "World Trade Center Bombers (1993)," p. 200.

19. For greater detail on these groups, see Hoffman, *Inside Terrorism*, chaps. 4 and 7; Stern, *The Ultimate Terrorists*, chap. 5; and Falkenrath, et al., *America's Achilles' Heel*, pp. 179–202.

20. The "loose nukes" problem in Russia is truly frightening: after more than a decade of American efforts to help Russia safeguard the nuclear weapons and fissile material of the former Soviet Union, we cannot feel confident that more than 30–40 percent of the problem has been dealt with. See Bunn, *The Next Wave*; and Jon Brook Wolfsthal, Cristina-Astrid Chuen, and Emily Ewell Daughtry, eds., *Nuclear Status Report: Nuclear Weapons, Fissile Material, and Export Controls in the Former Soviet Union* (Monterey, Calif., and Washington, D.C.: The Monterey Institute of International Studies and the Carnegie Endowment for International Peace, June 2001).

21. Thomas A. Keaney and Eliot A. Cohen, *Revolution in Warfare? Air Power in the Persian Gulf* (Annapolis, Md.: Naval Institute Press, 1995), pp. 107–108.

22. Jonathan B. Tucker, "Bioterrorism: Threats and Responses," in Lederberg, *Biological Weapons*, p. 288.

23. As the British historian E.H. Carr put it: "The science of economics presupposes a given political order, and cannot be profitably studied in isolation from politics." See E.H. Carr, *The Twenty Years' Crisis, 1919–1939*, 2nd ed. (London: Macmillan, 1961), p. 117.

24. The dampening effects of security competitions on trade are not an iron law; the former do not invariably reduce the latter. Peter Liberman has published the best research to date on the relation between security competitions and trade, showing that there are important exceptions to the dampening effect. In the first of his two cases, French, Russian, and British trade with Germany increased, rather than decreased, in the decade before 1914, even

though all three states were engaged in a security competition with Germany. In the second case, he found that the United States was reluctant to curtail trade with Japan before 1941 for fear of pushing Japan towards war, even though the two were engaged in political conflict over Japan's aggression in China since 1931. My research, however, has thus far yielded different results: intense security competitions can reduce trade, and basically caused it to dry up in three cases. In the first, trade between Japan and the United States declined sharply after the two entered the intense phase of their security competition in the late spring of 1940. In the second case, after the Sino-Soviet split materialized in 1960, making China and the Soviet Union political, military, and ideological competitors, Sino-Soviet trade dried up. In the third case, that of the U.S.-Soviet Cold War rivalry, the two states' intense security competition prevented trade between them from developing at all, rather than causing a once-flourishing trade to dry up. Liberman (following Joanne Gowa) attributes the varying effects of security competitions on trade to systems structure: security and trade are delinked in multipolar worlds and linked in bipolar worlds. I find this explanation unpersuasive. After all, the world was not bipolar in 1940 when American-Japanese trade dried up, and during the bipolar era of the Cold War, Communist China did not become a quasi-ally of the United States until 1980, twenty years after Sino-Soviet trade dried up. It is therefore the pre-1914 cases that stand out as the anomaly. More research is thus needed to determine the underlying conditions that cause security and trade to be tightly or loosely linked. See Peter Liberman, "Trading with the Enemy: Security and Relative Economic Gains," *International Security*, Vol. 21, No. 1 (Summer 1996), pp. 147–176; Joanne Gowa, *Allies, Adversaries, and International Trade* (Princeton, N.J.: Princeton University Press, 1994), chaps. 3–5; and Robert J. Art, "Security Competitions in Historical Perspective," unpublished ms.

25. For the reasons why a Eurasian hegemon is no longer the threat it once was to America's security, see Robert J. Art, "A Defensible Defense: America's Grand Strategy after the Cold War," *International Security*, Vol. 15, No. 4 (Spring 1991), pp. 10–23.

26. For example, see Richard K. Betts, *Nuclear Blackmail and Nuclear Balance* (Washington, D.C.: The Brookings Institution, 1987); Richard Ned Lebow and Janice Gross Stein, *We All Lost the Cold War* (Princeton, N.J.: Princeton University Press, 1994); and Devin T. Hagerty, "Nuclear Deterrence in South Asia: The 1990 Indo-Pakistani Crisis," *International Security*, Vol. 21, No. 3 (Winter 1995/1996), pp. 79–115. War was averted in the 1990 India-Pakistani crisis, but a limited war broke out in the 1999 Kargil crisis. In the 2002 crisis, war appears to have been averted in part because of America's mediation and intense pressure on both. See Stewart Bell, "U.S. Averted Kashmir War, India Says," *National Post*, June 18, 2002, at <www.nationalpost.com>; and Celia W. Dugger, "The Kashmir Brink," *New York Times*, June 20, 2002, p. A14.

27. For an analysis of the effects of the American military presence in Western Europe during the critical years 1990–1996, see Robert J. Art, "Why Western Europe Needs the United States and NATO," *Political Science Quarterly*, Vol. 111, No. 1 (Spring 1996), pp. 1–39. For analyses of its neighbors' worries about China and the role that the United States plays in lessening those worries, see the various essays in Alistair Ian Johnston and Robert S. Ross, eds., *Engaging China: The Management of a Rising Power* (New York: Routledge, 1999); and Steve Glain, "New Arms Race: Fearing China's Plans and a U.S. Departure, Asians Rebuild Forces," *Wall Street Journal*, November 13, 1997, p. A1.

28. By periodically lowering oil prices, oil suppliers can easily disrupt the efforts of oil consumers to conserve and to find alternatives. I favor oil prices that are high enough to encourage conservation and that make alternative sources of energy competitive. For the United States, this requires a higher tax on oil and especially on gasoline than is now the case.

29. Daily figures come from the Energy Information Administration, Department of Energy, at <www.eia.doe.gov/pub/pdf/multi.fuel/aer1999/sec5_5.pdf>, Table 5.1. The 70 percent estimate comes from Rick Wartzman and Anne Reifenberg, "Big Energy Imports are Less of a Threat than They Appear," *Wall Street Journal*, August 17, 1995, p. A6.

30. For the earlier estimates, see American Petroleum Institute, *Basic Petroleum Data Book*, Vol. 14, No. 2 (Washington, D.C.: American Petroleum Institute, May 1994), Section 2, Table 4; and Geoffrey Kemp and Robert E. Harkavy, *Strategic Geography and the Changing Middle East*

(Washington, D.C.: Brookings Institution Press, 1997), p. 111. For recent estimates, see U.S. Energy Information Administration, "Persian Gulf Oil Export Fact Sheet," June 2000, p. 1, at <www.eia.doe.gov/emeu/cabs/pgulf.html>; British Petroleum, *BP Statistical Review of World Energy, June 2001*, pp. 4 and 20, at <www.bp.com/centres/energy/>; and Charles Fairbanks, et al., *A Strategic Assessment of Central Eurasia*, a study prepared for the Middle East Division, J-5, Joint Chiefs of Staff, by the Atlantic Council of the United States and the Central Asia–Caucasus Institute of the Nitze School of Advanced International Studies (Washington, D.C.: Johns Hopkins University, January 2001), p. 8.

31. Energy Information Administration, <www.eia.doe.gov/emeu/aer/contents.html>, Tables 5.12A and B. World oil production capacity refers to the total possible daily world production in millions of barrels per day. See Energy Information Administration, <www.eia.doe.gov/oiaf/ieo97/appa7.html>, Table A40. For a useful survey of the hydrocarbon alternatives to Gulf and Caspian Sea reserves, see Kemp and Harkavy, *Strategic Geography*, Appendix 1.

32. Daily American import figures come from the Energy Information Administration, at <www.eia.doe.gov/emeu/aer/petro.html>, Table 5.4. Figures are rounded.

33. For an exchange on the pros and cons of this point, see Joseph S. Nye, Jr., "Why the Gulf War Served the National Interest"; and Christopher Layne, "Why the Gulf War Was Not in the National Interest," both in *The Atlantic Monthly*, Vol. 268, No. 1 (July 1991), pp. 54–81.

34. This discussion is based on the following sources: Paul R. Krugman and Maurice Obstfeld, *International Economics: Theory and Practice*, 3d ed. (New York: HarperCollins, 1994), chap. 10; Mordechai E. Kreinin, *International Economics: A Policy Approach*, 6th ed. (New York: Harcourt Brace Jovanovich, 1991), chap. 11; Paul Krugman, *The Age of Diminished Expectations: U.S. Economic Policy in the 1990s* (Cambridge, Mass.: MIT Press, 1990), chap. 4; Paul Krugman, *Peddling Prosperity: Economic Sense and Nonsense in the Age of Diminished Expectations* (New York: W.W. Norton, 1994), chaps. 9–10; and Paul Krugman, "Competitiveness: A Dangerous Obsession," *Foreign Affairs*, Vol. 73, No. 2 (March/April 1994), pp. 28–45.

35. Economist Paul Krugman gave one estimate, now dated, of the static gains from trade. Measured in terms of the cost of protectionist measures for the American economy in the late 1980s, static gains ran about three-quarters of a percent of America's gross domestic product, or about $75 billion in 2002 dollars. Krugman, *The Age of Diminished Expectations*, p. 104.

36. For a large nation and a big economy such as the United States, both the static and dynamic gains from trade are less than they would be for a small state. There are some states, such as Canada, that are large and rich in natural resources but have small economies; there are others, such as Japan, that are small and poor in natural resources but have large economies. Then there are a few nations such as the United States that are doubly blessed both with an abundance of natural resources, and hence less of a need than small states to trade to get them, and with a market big enough to generate substantial efficiency gains from their own internal trade. For both reasons—fewer natural resources and smaller markets—smaller states have historically had to trade more and have therefore reaped more benefits from international trade than larger ones.

37. McKinsey Global Institute, *Manufacturing Productivity* (Washington, D.C.: McKinsey and Company, October 1993), chap. 3, pp. 3 and 1. Based on a weighted average of the nine industries studied, Germany's productivity is 86 percent of the American average, and Japan's, 78 percent. This study is the second of three done by McKinsey. The first, done a year earlier, assessed five service industries and found the United States to be the most competitive compared to Japan, Germany, France, and the United Kingdom. Although it did not argue this was due to global competition, the study did conclude that "competitive pressures on companies operating in the U.S. are greater than in the other countries" and that it was competition, not economies of scale, that made the United States the most productive. See McKinsey Global Institute, *Service Sector Productivity* (Washington, D.C.: McKinsey and Company, October 1992), introduction, summary, and chap. 3. The third study, published in 1996, assessed capital productivity in Germany, Japan, and the United States, and concluded that capital productivity in Germany is 65 percent and in Japan is 63 percent of that in the United States. The United States has lower savings and investment rates than these two, but its higher capital

productivity more than compensates by producing higher financial returns. (Capital productivity is defined as "the measure of how well physical capital is used in providing goods and services.") See McKinsey Global Institute, *Capital Productivity* (Washington, D.C.: McKinsey Global Institute, June 1996), pp. 1–7.

38. There is a third gain from trade that is nearly impossible to quantify. Free trade can act as a merciless (and hence effective) corrective to faulty or misguided governmental economic policies. Free trade keeps governments more efficient in their macroeconomic policies than they might otherwise be, because the discipline of the market makes the cost of unproductive policies felt more quickly in trade and direct foreign investment than under a protected regime.

39. See J. David Richardson and Karin Rindal, *Why Exports Really Matter* (Washington, D.C.: The Institute for International Economics and the Manufacturing Institute, July 1995); and J. David Richardson and Karin Rindal, *Why Exports Matter: More!* (Washington, D.C.: The Institute for International Economics and the Manufacturing Institute, February 1996). Also see Richard N. Cooper, *Is Growth in Developing Countries Beneficial to Developed Countries?* Working Paper No. 95-9 (Cambridge, Mass.: Center for International Affairs, Harvard University, July 1995).

40. See the World Bank Group, *Assessing Globalization*, Part 2, pp. 3–4, and Part 3, p. 2, at <www.worldbank.org/html/extdr/pb/globalization/paper2.htm>. Also see David Dollar and Aart Kraay, "Growth Is Good for the Poor," Development Research Group, the World Bank, March 2001; and David Dollar and Aart Kraay, "Trade, Growth, and Poverty," Development Research Group, World Bank, March 2001. Also see the A.T. Kearney/*Foreign Policy Magazine* Globalization Index, "Measuring Globalization," *Foreign Policy*, No. 122 (January/February 2001), pp. 56–65. This study concludes that: "With some exceptions, countries scoring high in the Globalization Index enjoy more egalitarian income patterns, while the nations that are less integrated with the rest of the world display more skewed distributions of income." This relation holds for both mature economies and the emerging-market economies (ibid., pp. 62 and 64). For the view that globalization is not a sure path to prosperity, see Dani Rodrik, "Trading in Illusions," *Foreign Policy*, No. 123 (March/April 2001), pp. 54–64.

41. A.T. Kearney, Inc., *Globalization Ledger* (Cambridge, Mass.: Global Business Policy Council, 2000), p. 1.

42. Lack of openness also appears to increase inequality within states. A.T. Kearney found that the higher a country scored on the Kearney globalization index, the more egalitarian were its incomes, and the lower it scored, the more skewed were its incomes. See A.T. Kearney/*Foreign Policy* Magazine, "Measuring Globalization," pp. 62–64.

43. "Trade Expansion Remains the Engine of Growth," *Financial Times Survey World Trade*, November 29, 1999, p. I.

44. For the argument that interdependence promotes peace, see John R. Oneal and Bruce M. Russett, "The Classical Liberals Were Right: Democracy, Interdependence, and Conflict, 1950–1985," *International Studies Quarterly*, Vol. 41, No. 2 (June 1997), pp. 267–294; Bruce Russett and John R. Oneal, *Triangulating Peace: Democracy, Interdependence, and International Organization* (New York: W.W. Norton, 2001), chap. 4; Edward D. Mansfield and Jon C. Pevehouse, "Trade Blocs, Trade Flows, and International Conflict," *International Organization*, Vol. 54, No. 4 (Autumn 2000), pp. 775–809; Solomon William Polachek, "Conflict and Trade," *Journal of Conflict Resolution*, Vol. 24, No. 1 (March 1980), pp. 55–78; and Erik Gartzke, Quan Li, and Charles Boehmer, "Investing in the Peace: Economic Interdependence and International Conflict," *International Organization*, Vol. 55, No. 2 (Spring 2001), pp. 429. For evidence that interdependence can enhance conflict and does not inhibit war, see Mark J. Gasiorowski, "Economic Interdependence and International Conflict: Some Cross-National Evidence," *International Studies Quarterly*, Vol. 30 (1986), pp. 23–38; and Norrin M. Ripsman and Jean-Marc F. Blanchard, "Commercial Liberalism under Fire: Evidence from 1914 and 1936," *Security Studies*, Vol. 6, No. 2 (Winter 1996–97), pp. 4–50. For a good review of arguments on both sides of the issue, see Dale C. Copeland, "Economic Interdependence and War: A Theory of Trade Expectations," *International Security*, Vol. 20, No. 4 (Spring 1996), pp. 5–42.

45. This theme runs through Robert Gilpin, *The Political Economy of International Relations* (Princeton, N.J.: Princeton University Press, 1987).

46. Quoted in Richard N. Gardner, *Sterling-Dollar Diplomacy in Current Perspective: The Origins and the Prospects of Our International Economic Order*, exp. ed. (New York: Columbia, 1980), pp. 8–9.

47. For an analysis of the first condition, see Richard Rosecrance, *The Rise of the Trading State: Commerce and Conquest in the Modern World* (New York: Basic Books, 1986). For a formal demonstration of the second condition, see Robert Powell, "Absolute and Relative Gains in International Relations Theory," *American Political Science Review*, Vol. 85, No. 4 (December 1991), pp. 1303–1320.

48. Shorn of the three conditions I specify, this is, in essence, Schumpeter's argument. He argued that capitalists are inherently pacific, not warlike as Lenin claimed. In Schumpeter's view, capitalists oppose war because it disrupts trade. The capitalist motto is: make trade, not war. For these reasons Schumpeter believed that when capitalists fully ran states, they would be at peace with one another. See Joseph Schumpeter, *Imperialism and Social Classes* (New York: Meridian, 1951).

49. For policy prescriptions on how the United States can and should use its leverage to lower the trade barriers of others, including the strategic use of subsidies when called for, see Laura D'Andrea Tyson, *Who's Bashing Whom? Trade Conflict in High-Technology Industries* (Washington, D.C.: Institute for International Economics, 1992), chaps. 1 and 7.

50. See Krugman, *The Age of Diminished Expectations*, chap. 1.

51. Figures in this paragraph are from Paul Krugman and Robert Lawrence, "Trade, Jobs and Wages," *Scientific American*, Vol. 270, No. 4 (April 1994), p. 45.

52. The assertion about the causes of the decline in the wages of low-skilled workers is based on the following sources: Albert Fishlow and Karen Parker, eds., *Growing Apart: The Causes and Consequences of Global Wage Inequality* (New York: Council on Foreign Relations Press, 1999), pp. 1–21; Susan M. Collins, ed., *Imports, Exports, and the American Worker* (Washington, D.C.: The Brookings Institution Press, 1998), pp. 3–49; Richard B. Freeman, "Are Your Wages Set in Beijing?" *Journal of Economic Perspectives*, Vol. 9, No. 3 (Summer 1995), pp. 15–32; J. David Richardson, "Income Inequality and Trade: How to Think, What to Conclude?" *Journal of Economic Perspectives*, Vol. 9, No. 3 (Summer 1995), pp. 35–55; Krugman and Lawrence, "Trade, Jobs, and Wages," pp. 44–49; Matthew Slaughter and Phillip Swagel, *The Effect of Globalization on Wages in the Advanced Economies*, IMF Working Paper 97/43, International Monetary Fund, April 1997; Robert Z. Lawrence and Matthew J. Slaughter, "International Trade and American Wages in the 1980s: Giant Sucking Sound or Small Hiccup?" in Martin Neil Baily, Peter C. Reiss, and Clifford Winton, eds., *Brookings Papers on Economic Activity* (Washington, D.C.: The Brookings Institution, 1993), pp. 161–226; and William R. Cline, *Trade and Income Distribution* (Washington, D.C.: Institute for International Economics, 1997). For a dissenting view that attributes a much larger share of the decline in unskilled labor in the United States to imports from low-wage countries, see Adrian Wood, *North-South Trade, Employment and Inequality: Changing Fortunes in a Skill-Driven World* (Oxford, U.K.: Clarendon Press, 1994).

53. See Paul Kennedy, *The Rise and Fall of the Great Powers: Economic Change and Military Conflict from 1500 to 2000* (New York: Random House, 1987).

54. For good analyses of the causes of economic and national decline, see Robert Gilpin, *War and Change in World Politics* (Cambridge: Cambridge University Press, 1981); Carlo M. Cipolla, ed., *The Economic Decline of Empires* (London: Methuen, 1970); and Aaron Friedberg, *The Weary Titan: Britain and the Experience of Relative Decline, 1895–1905* (Princeton, N.J.: Princeton University Press, 1988).

55. See, for example, Tony Smith, *America's Mission: The United States and the Worldwide Struggle for Democracy in the Twentieth Century* (Princeton, N.J.: Princeton University Press, 1994).

56. R.J. Rummel, *Power Kills: Democracy as a Method of Nonviolence* (New Brunswick, N.J.: Transaction Publishers, 1997), chaps. 5 and 6.

57. For example, see Håvard Hegre, Tanja Ellingsen, Scott Gates, and Nils Petter Gleditsch, "Towards a Democratic Civil Peace? Democracy, Political Change, and Civil War,

1816-1992," *American Political Science Review*, Vol. 95, No. 1 (March 2001), pp. 33-48; Michelle Benson and Jacek Kugler, "Power Parity, Democracy, and the Severity of Internal Violence," *Journal of Conflict Resolution*, Vol. 42, No. 2 (April 1998), pp. 196-209); and Matthew Krain and Marissa Meyers, "Democracy and Civil War: A Note on the Democratic Peace Proposition," *International Interactions*, Vol. 23, No. 1 (June 1997), pp. 109-118.

58. Eva A. Paus, "Economic Growth through Neoliberal Restructuring? Insights from the Chilean Experience," *The Journal of Developing Areas*, Vol. 28, No. 1 (October 1994), p. 35.

59. John Mueller argues that capitalism and democracy are independent and that each can exist without the other, and historically have done so. Even Mueller, however, agrees that democracy is beneficial to economic growth. See John Mueller, *Capitalism, Democracy, and Ralph's Pretty Good Grocery* (Princeton, N.J.: Princeton University Press, 1999), pp. 231 and 235-238.

60. Freedom House, *Freedom in the World 2001*, Table 13 (Combined Average Freedom Rating and GDP Growth) and Table 14 (Freedom and Prosperity) at <www.freedomhouse.org/research/freeworld/2001/tables.htm>. Also see United Nations Development Program, *Human Development Report 2000* (Oxford, U.K.: Oxford University Press, 2000), pp. 202-205. The Freedom House study contradicts the conclusions reached by Adam Przeworski and his colleagues in what is probably the most authoritative study of the relation between economic development and growth, on the one hand, and regime type, on the other, for the forty years prior to the Freedom House study. Przeworski and his associates found no difference in overall economic growth rates between democracies and non-democracies for the 1950-1990 period. They did find, however, that per-capita income in democracies grew faster than in dictatorships, because the former had lower rates of population growth than did the latter, and they hypothesize that this difference in population growth rate was due to the democratic-dictatorship difference. If the Freedom House study is somehow biased by the favorable economic conditions of the 1990s, then at the minimum we can conclude from the Przeworski study that individuals are better off economically in democracies because their per-capita incomes grow faster. If the Freedom House study shows the pattern for the future, then we can conclude that individuals are better off economically in democracies than in non-democracies because both overall economic growth and per-capita growth are better in democracies. Either way, democracies do better than non-democracies. See Adam Przeworski, Michael E. Alvarez, Jose Antonio Cheibub, and Fernando Limongi, *Democracy and Development: Political Institutions and Well-Being in the World, 1950-1990* (Cambridge: Cambridge University Press, 2000), p. 271 and chaps. 2 and 3.

61. For arguments in favor of the democratic peace theory, see Michael W. Doyle, "Kant, Liberal Legacies, and Foreign Affairs," Parts I and II, *Philosophy and Public Affairs*, Vol. 12, Nos. 2 and 3 (Summer and Fall 1983), pp. 205-235 and 323-353; Bruce M. Russett, *Grasping the Democratic Peace: Principles for a Post-Cold War World* (Princeton, N.J.: Princeton University Press, 1993); Russett and Oneal, *Triangulating Peace*, chap. 3; Bruce Bueno de Mesquita and David Lalman, *War and Reason: Domestic and International Imperatives* (New Haven: Yale University Press, 1992), chap. 5; John M. Owen, "How Liberalism Produces Democratic Peace," *International Security*, Vol. 19, No. 2 (Fall 1994), pp. 87-126; John M. Owen, *Liberal Peace, Liberal War: American Politics and International Security* (Ithaca: Cornell University Press, 1997); William J. Dixon, "Democracy and the Management of International Conflict," *Journal of Conflict Resolution*, Vol. 37, No. 1 (March 1993), pp. 42-68; David Lake, "Powerful Pacifists: Democratic States and War," *American Political Science Review*, Vol. 87, No. 1 (March 1992), pp. 2-37; Zeev Maoz, "Realist and Cultural Critiques of the Democratic Peace: A Theoretical and Empirical Re-Assessment," *International Interactions*, Vol. 24, No. 1 (1998), pp. 3-89; Michael D. Ward and Kristian S. Gleditsch, "Democratizing for Peace," *American Political Science Review*, Vol. 92, No. 1 (March 1998), pp. 51-61; Randall L. Schweller, "Domestic Structure and Preventive War: Are Democracies More Pacific?" *World Politics*, Vol. 44, No. 2 (January 1992), pp. 235-270; and James Lee Ray, *Democracy and International Conflict: An Evaluation of the Democratic Peace Proposition* (Columbia: University of South Carolina Press, 1995).

62. For a dissenting opinion that military dictatorships are not warlike, see Stanislav Andreski, "On the Peaceful Disposition of Military Dictatorships," *Journal of Strategic Studies*, Vol. 3, No. 3 (December 1980), pp. 3–10.

63. Support of democracy is embraced by both liberal internationalists and conservatives. The Clinton Administration adopted it, too. See The White House, *A National Security Strategy of Engagement and Enlargement*, February 1995, pp. 22–25; Anthony Lake, Assistant to the President for National Security Affairs, "From Containment to Enlargement," Address at Johns Hopkins University, September 21, 1993, in U.S. State Department, Bureau of Public Affairs, *Dispatch*, Vol. 4, No. 39 (September 27, 1993), pp. 658–665; and James A. Baker, *The Politics of Diplomacy: Revolution, War, and Peace 1989–1992* (New York: Putnam, 1995), p. 654.

64. These criticisms draw from the following sources: Miriam Fendius Elman, "Introduction: The Need for a Qualitative Test of the Democratic Peace Theory," in Miriam Fendius Elman, ed., *Paths to Peace: Is Democracy the Answer?* (Cambridge, Mass.: MIT Press, 1997), pp. 1–59; Christopher Layne, "Kant or Cant: The Myth of the Democratic Peace," *International Security*, Vol. 19, No. 2 (Fall 1994), pp. 5–50; David E. Spiro, "The Insignificance of the Liberal Peace," *International Security*, Vol. 19, No. 2 (Fall 1994), pp. 50–87; Joanne Gowa, "Democratic States and International Disputes," *International Organization*, Vol. 49, No. 3 (Summer 1995), pp. 511–523; Henry S. Farber and Joanne Gowa, *Common Interests or Common Polities: Reinterpreting the Democratic Peace* (Cambridge, Mass.: National Bureau of Economic Research, February 1995); Ido Oren, "The Subjectivity of the 'Democratic' Peace: Changing U.S. Perceptions of Imperial Germany," *International Security*, Vol. 20, No. 2 (Fall 1995), pp. 147–184; Edward D. Mansfield and Jack Snyder, "Democratization and the Danger of War," *International Security*, Vol. 20, No. 1 (Summer 1995), pp. 5–39; Jack Snyder, *From Voting to Violence: Democratization and Nationalist Conflict* (New York: W.W. Norton, 2000), pp. 31–39; and Edward D. Mansfield and Jack Snyder, "Democratic Transitions, Institutional Strength, and War," *International Organization*, Vol. 56, No. 2 (Spring 2002), pp. 297–339.

65. Spiro, "The Insignificance of the Liberal Peace." pp. 68 and 76. John Mearsheimer first made this argument in 1990. See John Mearsheimer, "Back to the Future: Instability in Europe After the Cold War," *International Security*, Vol. 15, No. 1 (Summer 1990), pp. 50–51. Spiro demonstrated the point more rigorously by comparing the democratic peace theory with the null hypothesis that random chance also explains the absence of war among democracies. He found random chance a better predictor, thus casting doubt on the theory.

66. See Layne, "Kant or Cant," pp. 14–37. Layne investigated four near misses: the 1861 *Trent* affair between the United States and England; the 1895 Venezuelan crisis between the United States and England; the 1898 Fashoda crisis between England and France; and the 1923 Ruhr crisis between Germany and France. I find his case strong for the last two crises, incomplete for the first, and reasonable for the second.

67. Between 1943 and 1975, the number of democracies, according to Huntington's calculations, varied between twenty-nine and fifty-one. Fifteen of them were allied with the United States in NATO; Australia and New Zealand were allied with it in ANZUS; Japan was allied with it in the American-Japanese alliance. Sweden and Austria were formally neutral but were de facto allied with the United States; Ireland and Israel were in tacit alliance with it. Most of the countries of Latin America, when they were democratic, were in the American orbit. Therefore, for at least thirty of the fifty years of the Cold War, somewhere between twenty-three and thirty, or 60–66 percent, of the world's democracies were allied with the United States against the Soviet Union. See Samuel P. Huntington, *The Third Wave: Democratization in the Late Twentieth Century* (Norman, Oklahoma: University of Oklahoma Press, 1991), pp. 3–26.

68. Russett and Oneal, *Triangulating Peace*, p. 94.

69. See Zeev Maoz and Nasrin Abdolali, "Regime Types and International Conflict, 1816–1976," *Journal of Conflict Resolution*, Vol. 33, No. 1 (March 1989), pp. 21–24; Russett and Oneal, *Triangulating Peace*, pp. 95–96, 109–110, and 114; Gregory Raymond, "Democracies, Disputes, and Third-Party Intermediaries," *Journal of Conflict Resolution*, Vol. 38, No. 1 (March 1994), pp. 24–42; William J. Dixon, "Democracy and the Management of International Conflict," *Journal of Conflict Resolution*, Vol. 37, No. 1 (March 1993), pp. 42–68; William

J. Dixon, "Democracy and the Peaceful Settlement of International Conflict," *American Political Science Review*, Vol. 88, No. 1 (March 1994), pp. 14–32; David L. Rousseau, Christopher Gelpi, Dan Reiter, and Paul K. Huth, "Assessing the Dyadic Nature of the Democratic Peace, 1918–1988," *American Political Science Review*, Vol. 90, No. 3 (September 1996), pp. 512–533; and Paul Huth and Todd Allee, *The Democratic Peace and Territorial Conflict in the Twentieth Century* (Cambridge: Cambridge University Press, 2002), chaps. 7–9. Also see Joanne Gowa, *Ballots and Bullets: The Elusive Democratic Peace* (Princeton, N.J.: Princeton University Press, 1999), pp. 64–67 and 96; and Lars-Erik Cederman, "Back to Kant: Reinterpreting the Democratic Peace as a Macrohistorical Learning Process," *American Political Science Review*, Vol. 95, No. 1 (March 2001), pp. 15–31.

70. For a summary of the regional impacts of climate change, including those for the United States, see Robert T. Watson, et al., eds., *The Regional Impacts of Climate Change: An Assessment of Vulnerability—Summary for Policymakers*, a special report of the Intergovernmental Panel on Climate Change (IPCC) Working Group II, November 1997, at <www.ipcc.ch/pub/regional(E).pdf>; J.T. Houghton, et al., eds., *Climate Change 1995: The Science of Climate Change* (Cambridge: Cambridge University Press, 1996), pp. 336–345; U.S. Environmental Protection Agency, *U.S. Climate Action Report—2002*, chap. 6, at <www.epa.gov/globalwarming/publications/car/index.html>; and The National Assessment Synthesis Team, *Climate Change Impacts on the United States: The Potential Consequences of Climate Variability and Change*, U.S. Global Change Research Program, Washington, D.C., 2000, available at <www.gcrio.org/NationalAssessment> and also published by Cambridge University Press. See especially pp. 6–12 and 120–124 for an overview of climate change effects on the United States.

71. The figures and effects in this paragraph are taken from The National Assessment Synthesis Team, *Climate Change Impacts*, p. 10; William Cline, *The Economics of Global Warming* (Washington, D.C.: Institute of International Economics, 1992), pp. 87–127; and Committee on the Science of Climate Change, National Research Council, *Climate Change Science: An Analysis of Some Key Questions* (Washington, D.C.: National Academy Press, 2001), chap. 6. For other assessments of climate change damage, see J. Bruce, Hoesung Lee, and E. Haites, eds., *Climate Change 1995: Economic and Social Dimensions of Climate Change* (Cambridge: Cambridge University Press, 1996); Kenneth M. Strzepek and Joel B. Smith, *As Climate Changes: International Impacts and Implications* (Cambridge: Cambridge University Press, 1995); and Joel B. Smith, et al., *Adapting to Climate Change: Assessments and Issues* (New York: Springer, 1996).

72. The National Assessment Synthesis Team, *Climate Change Impacts*, pp. 8 and 7.

73. Cline, *The Economics of Global Warming*, p. 131. Economist William Nordhaus estimates a lower level of damage that would cost between .28 and 2 percent of U.S. GNP. See Robert U. Ayres, "Assessing Regional Damage Costs from Global Warming," in Jurgen Schmandt and Judith Clarkson, eds., *The Regions and Global Warming: Impacts and Response Strategies* (New York: Oxford University Press, 1992), p. 187.

74. Cline, *The Economics of Global Warming*, pp. 75 and 213.

75. Ibid., pp. 8 and 232.

76. See Executive Summary, *Economic Effects of Global Climate Change Policies*, Results of the Research Efforts of the Interagency Analytical Team, June 1997, p. 1, available at <www.weathervane.rff.org/features/features/007.html#report>.

77. Jason Shogren and Michael Toman, *Climate Change Policy* (Washington, D.C.: Resources for the Future, 2000), p. 21, available at <www.rff.org>; and IPCC, *Summary for Policymakers: Climate Change 2001: Mitigation (A Report of Working Group III of the IPCC)*, March 2001, p. 8, available at <www.ipcc.ch/pub/wg3spm.pdf>.

78. Cline, *The Economics of Global Warming*, p. 133.

79. For an analysis of long-term warming, see ibid., chap. 2.

80. See IPCC, *Summary for Policymakers: A Report of Working Group I of the Intergovernmental Panel on Climate Change* (The Scientific Basis Working Group), January 2001, p. 17, at <www.ipcc/ch/pub/spm22-01.pdf> (this is the Third Assessment Report).

81. For a dissenting view, that large reductions in greenhouse gas emissions make little sense and that the money required to achieve those reductions is better spent elsewhere, see

Thomas C. Schelling, "Some Economics of Global Warming," *American Economic Review*, Vol. 82, No. 1 (March 1992), pp. 1–14; Thomas C. Schelling, "The Cost of Combating Global Warming: Facing the Tradeoffs," *Foreign Affairs*, Vol. 76, No. 6 (November/December, 1997), pp. 8–14; and Wilfred Beckerman, "Global Warming and International Action: An Economic Perspective," in Andrew Hurrell and Benedict Kingsbury, eds., *The International Politics of the Environment* (Oxford: Oxford University Press, 1992), pp. 253–290.

82. Integrated assessment models combine physical and economic effects into one integrated system or model. See Shogren and Toman, *Climate Change Policy*, pp. 17–20.

83. Estimates of the impact of abatement on America's GDP range from a 5 percent increase to an 8 percent decline, depending on the models used and the assumptions made. For an analysis of these predictions, see Robert Repetto and Duncan Austin, *The Costs of Climate Protection: A Guide for the Perplexed* (Washington, D.C.: World Resources Institute, 1997).

84. Tradable permits and joint implementation are two efficient mechanisms to implement carbon taxes so as to reduce greenhouse gas emissions. A tradable permit regime creates a market in permits to emit greenhouse gases. It enables emitters with a high marginal cost of control (those who could achieve only a low reduction in emissions per dollar spent) to buy permits to emit from those emitters with a low marginal cost of control (those who could achieve a large reduction in emissions per dollar spent). A tradable permit regime is efficient because it achieves an equalization in the marginal cost of control among all emitters, a point that represents the least-cost solution to a specified overall reduction in emissions. "Joint implementation" is a system that enables an emitter in one country that has a high marginal cost of control to pay for a program to reduce the emissions of an emitter in another country that has a low marginal cost of control, and that credits the high-cost emitter for an emissions reduction in its own country. Because the low-marginal-cost emitter achieves a greater reduction in emissions amounts for the specified sum spent than the high marginal cost emitter would have, this mechanism, although it does not necessarily equalize the marginal costs of control of the two emitters, nevertheless does send dollars to the emitter that produces the larger reduction in emissions for the given sums spent. Thus, both tradable permits and joint implementation work in a manner that brings the largest reduction in greenhouse gas emissions per dollar spent. Neither will achieve their full efficiencies, however, unless states have set binding emissions targets and allocated their permits or imposed their carbon taxes. For a good summary of how a tradable permit regime works, see Tom Teitenberg, *Environmental and Natural Resource Economics*, 3rd ed. (New York: HarperCollins, 1992), pp. 372–377.

85. See "Testimony of Dr. Janet Yellen, Chair, White House Council of Economic Advisors, before the House Commerce Subcommittee on Energy and Power on the Economics of the Kyoto Conference," March 4, 1998, pp. 22 and 24, <www.weathervane.rff.org/refdocs/yellen2.html>. The $14–23 per ton estimate was based on the use of tradable permits among the industrial countries (referred to as "Annex I" states), joint implementation among the Annex I states, and "Clean Development" between developed and developing countries. Clean Development is the name given to joint implementation between Annex I and developing states.

86. Still other models show that when the improvements in air quality that would ensue from greenhouse gas reductions are factored into abatement costs, a net positive increase in GNP is produced by emissions reductions. See Repetto and Austin, *The Costs of Climate Protection*, pp. 15–16.

87. IPCC, *Summary for Policymakers* (Working Group 1), pp. 13 and 7.

88. For recent evidence about climate triggers and the swiftness of climate changes, see Jeffrey P. Severinghaus, et al., "Timing of Abrupt Climate Change at the End of the Younger Dryas Interval from Thermally Fractionated Gases in Polar Ice," *Nature*, Vol. 19 (January 8, 1998), pp. 141–146; and Houghton, et al., *Climate Change 1995*, pp. 177–179.

89. For the analysis in this paragraph, I have relied on Ross Gelbspan, *The Heat Is On: The High Stakes Battle Over the Earth's Threatened Climate* (Reading, Mass.: Addison-Wesley, 1997), pp. 27–32; Houghton, et al., *Climate Change 1995*, pp. 7, 45, 46, and 62; IPCC, *Summary for Policy Makers* (Working Group 1), p. 17; and IPCC, *Summary for Policy Makers: Climate Change*

2001: Impacts, Adaptation, and Vulnerability: A Report of Working Group II of the IPCC, February 2001, p. 6, available at <www.ipcc.ch/pub/wg2spmfinal.pdf>.

90. For arguments against an emissions trading regime, see Thomas C. Schelling, "What Makes Greenhouse Sense," *Foreign Affairs,* Vol. 81, No. 3 (May/June, 2002), pp. 2–10.

Three: Dominion, Collective Security, and Containment

1. My discussion of these strategies has benefited from the following sources: Barry R. Posen and Andrew L. Ross, "Competing U.S. Grand Strategies," in Robert L. Lieber, ed., *Eagle Without a Cause* (New York: HarperCollins, 1996), pp. 100–134; Barry R. Posen and Andrew L. Ross, "Competing Visions for U.S. Grand Strategy," *International Security,* Vol. 21, No. 3 (Winter 1996–97), pp. 5–54; Ronald D. Asmus, *The New U.S. Strategic Debate* (Santa Monica: RAND, 1993); Stanley R. Sloan, *The U.S. Role in the Post–Cold War World: Issues for a New Great Debate,* No. 92-308 S (Washington, D.C.: Congressional Research Service , March 24, 1992); Christopher Layne, "From Preponderance to Offshore Balancing: America's Future Grand Strategy," *International Security,* Vol. 22, No. 1 (Summer 1997), pp. 1–39; and John J. Mearsheimer, *The Tragedy of Great Power Politics* (New York: W.W. Norton, 2001), chap. 7.

2. Both quotations are from James Burnham, *Containment or Liberation? An Inquiry Into the Aims of United States Foreign Policy* (New York: John Day, 1953), p. 221. I am indebted to Stephen Van Evera for calling my attention to Burnham's book. Also see the discussion of rollback in Colin S. Gray, *The Geopolitics of Super Power* (Lexington: University Press of Kentucky, 1988), chap. 13.

3. For a comprehensive analysis of these activities, see Gregory Mitrovich, *Undermining the Kremlin: America's Strategy to Subvert the Soviet Bloc, 1947–1956* (Ithaca, N.Y.: Cornell University Press, 2000). Mitrovich's important book is based on a careful review of recently declassified documents and shows that the early years of America's Cold War foreign policy were much more aggressive than heretofore thought.

4. For good analyses of all these activities, see Seyom Brown, *The Faces of Power,* 2d ed. (New York: Columbia University Press, 1994), chaps. 22–26; Joshua Muravchik, *Exporting Democracy: Fulfilling America's Destiny* (Washington, D.C.: AEI Press, 1991), chap. 13; Peter J. Schraeder, "Paramilitary Intervention," in Peter J. Schraeder, ed., *Intervention into the 1990s,* 2d ed. (Boulder: Lynn Rienner, 1992), pp. 131–151; and Tony Smith, *America's Mission: The United States and the Worldwide Struggle for Democracy in the Twentieth Century* (Princeton, N.J.: Princeton University Press, 1994), chap. 10.

5. Quotations are from: "Excerpts from Pentagon's Plan: Prevent the Re-emergence of a New Rival," *New York Times,* March 8, 1992, p. 14; and Patrick E. Tyler, "U.S. Strategy Plan Calls for Insuring No Rivals Develop," *New York Times,* March 8, 1992, p. 14.

6. For a critique of reconstitution, see Robert J. Art, "A U.S. Military Strategy for the 1990s: Reassurance Without Dominance," *Survival,* Vol. 34, No. 4 (Winter 1992–93), pp. 18–20.

7. Shades of dominion appeared briefly during the 1996 campaign, when two Republican intellectuals called for a dramatic increase in the American defense budget and for the unabashed exercise of a benevolent American hegemony. See William Kristol and Robert Kagan, "Toward a Neo-Reaganite Foreign Policy," *Foreign Affairs,* Vol. 75, No. 4 (July/August 1996), pp. 18–33. See also Robert Kagan and William Kristol, eds., *Present Dangers: Crisis and Opportunity in American Foreign and Defense Policy* (San Francisco: Encounter Books, 2000), esp. pp. 3–25 and 307–337.

8. The quotation is from The White House, *The National Security Strategy of the United States,* 2002, Part 9, available at <www.whitehouse.gov/nsc/nssall.html>. See Part 5 of this document for a discussion of the rationale for preemption. The preemptive aspect of the national security strategy was previewed in President Bush's January 2002 State of the Union address (in which he used the phrase "axis of evil" to refer to North Korea, Iraq, and Iran): "I will not wait on events, while dangers gather." He reiterated this preemptive theme in a speech in June 2002 to the graduating seniors at West Point: "Deterrence—the promise of massive

retaliation against nations—means nothing against shadowy networks with no nation or citizens to defend. Containment is not possible when unbalanced dictators with weapons of mass destruction can deliver those weapons on missiles or secretly provide them to terrorist allies." Both at <www.whitehouse.gov>.

9. For critiques of primacy, see Robert Jervis, "International Primacy: Is the Game Worth the Candle?" *International Security*, Vol. 17, No. 4 (Spring 1993), pp. 52–568; David Callahan, *Between Two Worlds: Realism, Idealism and American Foreign Policy after the Cold War* (New York: HarperCollins, 1994), chap. 7; Posen and Ross, "Competing Visions for U.S. Grand Strategy" pp. 42–43; and Cindy Williams, "Defense Policy for the Twenty-First Century," in Robert Lieber, ed., *Eagle Rules? Foreign Policy and American Primacy in the Twenty-First Century* (New York: Prentice Hall, 2001), pp. 241–266. For a defense of primacy, see Samuel P. Huntington, "Why International Primacy Matters," *International Security*, Vol. 17, No. 4 (Spring 1993), pp. 68–84.

10. Hans J. Morgenthau, *Politics Among Nations: The Struggle for Power and Peace*, 3d ed. (New York: Alfred A. Knopf, 1964), p. 238.

11. The best descriptions of the logic of collective security can be found in Morgenthau, *Politics Among Nations*, pp. 412–418; Inis L. Claude, Jr., *Swords Into Plowshares: The Problems and Progress of International Organization*, 4th ed. (New York: Random House, 1971), chap. 12; Inis L. Claude, Jr., *Power and International Relations* (New York: Random House, 1962), chap. 4; Arnold Wolfers, *Discord and Collaboration: Essays on International Politics* (Baltimore: Johns Hopkins University Press, 1962), chap. 12; Charles A. Kupchan, "The Case for Collective Security," in George W. Downs, ed., *Collective Security beyond the Cold War* (Ann Arbor: University of Michigan Press, 1994), pp. 41–69; and Jerome Slater, *A Reevaluation of Collective Security: The OAS in Action*, Mershon Center Pamphlet Series, No. 1 (Columbus: Ohio State University Press, 1965), chap. 1.

12. The speech was delivered to the League Assembly on October 10, 1935, and is quoted in F.P. Walters, *A History of the League of Nations* (London: Oxford University Press, 1967), p. 653. Nemours and Maxim Litvinov, the Soviet delegate to the League, were the only two delegates to raise serious criticisms of Italy's claims against Ethiopia. Nemours gave two speeches on the subject to the League Assembly, and Walters says, "No more remarkable oration is to be found in the annals of the Assembly than the second of these speeches" (p. 653).

13. Claude, *Swords into Plowshares*, p. 252 (emphasis in original).

14. Many analysts miss this simple but fundamental point. For example, George Downs and Keisuke Iida argue that: "there are different kinds of collective security systems. These will generate different amounts of security in the same way that different alliances might do so or in the same way various oligopolies will have different impacts on production levels or prices." An arrangement either is a genuine collective security system or it is not; there cannot be "degrees of collective security." George W. Downs and Keisuke Iida, "Assessing the Theoretical Case against Collective Security," in Downs, *Collective Security Beyond the Cold War*, p. 17.

15. Critiques of collective security are legion. Among the best are: Morgenthau, *Politics Among Nations*, pp. 412–418; Claude, *Power and International Relations*, chap. 5; Josef Joffe, "Collective Security and the Future of Europe," *Survival*, Vol. 34, No. 1 (Spring 1992), pp. 36–51; Richard K. Betts, "Systems for Peace or Causes of War? Collective Security, Arms Control, and the New Europe," *International Security*, Vol. 17, No. 1 (Summer 1992), pp. 5–44; and John J. Mearsheimer, "The False Promise of International Institutions," *International Security*, Vol. 19, No. 3 (Winter 1994–95), pp. 26–37.

16. Morgenthau, *Politics Among Nations*, p. 518.

17. For this analysis, I have relied on Morgenthau's excellent discussion, which, fifty years after he first made it, still stands as the best and most succinct analysis of the reasons why the League, and later the UN, failed to collectivize security. Ibid., pp. 298–311.

18. Article 16 has four parts; Parts 1 and 2 are the important sections. The text of Part 1 reads (in part): "Should any Member of the League resort to war in disregard of its covenants under Articles 12, 13, or 15, it shall *ipso facto* be deemed to have committed an act of war against all other Members of the League, which hereby undertake immediately to subject it to the severance of all trade or financial relations." Part 2 reads (in full): "It shall be the duty of the Council in such case to recommend to the several Governments concerned what effec-

tive military, naval or air force the Members of the League shall severally contribute to the armed forces to protect the covenants of the League." The Covenant of the League of Nations can be found in Claude, *Swords into Plowshares*, pp. 453–462.

19. Morgenthau, *Politics Among Nations*, p. 301, footnote 7.

20. Paragraph 7 of Article 15 provided that members of the League could take action against a state should the Council fail to reach a unanimous decision.

21. Article 39 of Chapter 7 of the UN charter reads as follows (in full): "The Security Council shall determine the existence of any threat to the peace, breach of the peace, or act of aggression and shall make recommendations, or decide what measures shall be taken in accordance with Articles 41 and 42, to maintain or restore international peace and security." Article 43, Part 1, says: "All Members of the United Nations . . . undertake to make available to the Security Council, on its call and in accordance with a special agreement or agreements, armed forces, assistance, and facilities, including rights of passage, necessary for the purpose of maintaining international peace and security." The Charter of the United Nations can be found in Claude, *Swords into Plowshares*, pp. 463–489.

22. Morgenthau, *Politics Among Nations*, p. 305. The full text of Article 106 reads: "Pending coming into force of such special agreements referred to in Article 43 as in the opinion of the Security Council enable it to begin the exercise of its responsibilities under Article 42, the parties to the Four-Nation Declaration, signed at Moscow, October 30, 1941, and France, shall, in accordance with the provisions of paragraph 5 of that Declaration, consult with one another and as occasion requires with other Members of the United Nations with a view to such joint action on behalf of the Organization as may be necessary for the purpose of maintaining international peace and security."

23. "Excerpts from Communiqué: What the G-7 Decided," *New York Times*, July 17, 1991, p. A10.

24. The phrase quoted is from United Nations A/47/277, S/24111, "Agenda for Peace," June 17, 1992, p. 1 (mimeo).

25. Ibid., pp. 12–13 (emphasis added).

26. Eric Schmitt, "15 Nations Offer Troops for U.N. Force of 54,000," *New York Times*, April 13, 1994, p. A12.

27. Department of State, "The Clinton Administration's Policy on Reforming Multilateral Peace Operations, May 1994," mimeo.

28. For a comprehensive analysis of the history of these efforts in the 1990s, see Rosemary Righter, *Utopia Lost: The United Nations and World Order* (New York: The Twentieth Century Fund Press, 1995), chaps. 10 and 11. For two brief but useful histories and analyses of the UN standing force concept, see Adam Roberts, "Proposals for UN Standing Forces: History, Tasks, and Obstacles" in David Cox and Albert Legault, eds., *UN Rapid Reaction Capabilities: Requirements and Prospects* (Clementsport, Nova Scotia: Canadian Peacekeeping Press, 1995), pp. 49–67; and Alex Morrison, "Efforts to Establish UN Stand-By Arrangements: An Historical Account and Appraisal," in ibid., pp. 136–147.

29. F.H. Hinsley, *Power and the Pursuit of Peace: Theory and Practice in the History of Relations between States* (Cambridge: Cambridge University Press, 1967), p. 315.

30. An account of the League's successes in Europe in the 1920s and in Latin America in the early 1930s can be found in Walters, *A History of the League of Nations*, chaps. 14, 17, 26, and 43. (Walters was Deputy Secretary-General of the League.) A more concise review of the League's record is David W. Wainhouse, *International Peace Observation: A History and Forecast* (Baltimore: Johns Hopkins University Press, 1966), pp. 7–85. A convenient list and short description of UN peacekeeping efforts can be found in William J. Durch and Barry M. Blechman, *Keeping the Peace: The United Nations in the Emerging World Order* (Washington, D.C.: The Henry L. Stimson Center, March 1992), pp. 11 and 14. Concise summaries can also be found in the United Nations, *The Blue Helmets: A Review of United Nations Peace-keeping*, 2d ed. (New York: UN Department of Public Information, 1990). For comprehensive analyses of UN peacekeeping efforts, see William J. Durch, ed., *The Evolution of UN Peacekeeping: Case Studies and Comparative Analysis* (New York: St. Martin's Press, 1993); William J. Durch, *UN Peacekeeping, American Politics, and the Uncivil Wars of the 1990s* (New York: St. Martin's Press, 1996);

and Michael W. Doyle and Nicholas Sambanis, "International Peacebuilding: A Theoretical and Quantitative Analysis," *American Political Science Review*, Vol. 94, No. 4 (December 2000), pp. 779–801. For recent thinking about how to improve UN peacekeeping capabilities, see the Government of Canada, *Towards a Rapid Reaction Capability for the United Nations*, September 1995; and *Report of the Panel on United Nations Peace Operations* (the Brahimi Report), the United Nations (2000), <www.un.org/peace/reports/peace_operations/docs/part1.htm>.

31. J. David Singer and Melvin Small, *The Wages of War, 1816–1965: A Statistical Handbook* (New York: John Wiley and Sons, 1972), p. 38. This publication is part of what is known as the Correlates of War (COW) Project.

32. The figure of 29 interstate wars is based on the twenty-two wars that began between 1948 and 1992, as listed in the updated Correlates of War (COW) Project; the five international wars listed in Appendix B to this volume that began between 1993 and 2000; and the 1991 Gulf War and the 1992 Moldova-Dniestr war. (The COW data lists twenty-three wars that began between 1948 and 2000, but I have excluded the 1956 Soviet invasion of Hungary from the COW count of interstate wars, because Hungary was already a member of the Soviet bloc and militarily ruled by the Soviet Union. The COW data also excludes the Moldova-Dniestr war, but I have included it in Appendix B. Finally, the COW data counts the Iraqi invasion of Kuwait in 1990 and the United States attack on Iraq in 1991 as one war, whereas I count these as two separate wars (as shown in Appendix B). Updated COW data was released in April 1994 and is available from the Inter-university Consortium for Political and Social Research, P.O. Box 1248, Ann Arbor, MI 48106. Also useful is the comprehensive listing of international armed conflicts found in Herbert K. Tillema, *International Armed Conflict Since 1945: A Bibliographic Handbook of Wars and Military Interventions* (Boulder, Colo.: Westview Press, 1991), pp. 276–287.)

33. Some analysts might choose to add to the Ethiopian, Korean, and Iraqi cases discussed in the text, four others: the League's mediation of the Albanian border dispute in 1921; the UN insertion of a military force into Egypt in the 1956 Suez case; UN efforts in the Turkish-Greek War of 1974 over Cyprus; and the UN peace enforcement role in Bosnia in 1995–96. I choose not to include these four in the combined record of collective enforcement for the following reasons. The 1921 case is admittedly in a gray area. Yugoslavia withdrew its troops from Albania only after Britain threatened to go to the League and seek economic sanctions against it. Sanctions were not passed, nor was a proposal to impose them ever brought to the League, but the threat of sanctions apparently had an effect on Yugoslavia. In the Suez case, the United Nations provided a useful fig leaf for British and French withdrawal of their forces from Egypt when it inserted the United Nations Emergency Force (UNEF). UNEF, however, was a peacekeeping force, not a war-waging force. It was America's financial leverage over the British, and Eisenhower's threat to use it, that caused the British and the French to withdraw their forces from the Suez Canal. Eisenhower threatened not to back the pound with financial credits so that Britain could counter the run on the pound that had begun two months earlier. This would have caused the pound to collapse and would also have left Britain without the ability to import oil. With oil from the Mideast cut off, Britain would have had to buy oil from North and South America, but without dollar reserves provided by the United States (oil is paid for in dollars), the British could not have bought the oil they needed. Thus, without American financial backing, Britain would have no oil, and it would see the pound collapse. It was this pressure, not the United Nations, that ended the Suez fiasco. Therefore, in neither the Albanian nor Suez cases were sanctions or the use of force collectively applied. Thus, I do not include them in the record of twentieth century collective security enforcement. For the Albanian case, see Walters, *A History of the League of Nations*, pp. 158–161; and Wainhouse, *International Peace Observation*, pp. 29–33. For Suez, see Anthony Nutting, *No End of A Lesson: The Story of Suez* (New York: Clarkson N. Potter, 1967), esp. chaps. 12–18.

I did not count the Turko-Greek War over Cyprus in 1974 as an example of UN enforcement, because the United Nations force stationed there after the Cypriot civil war of 1963–64 stayed out of harm's way when Turkish troops invaded northern Cyprus in 1974, and because the United Nations played little role in the ceasefire that the British helped to arrange.

The Bosnian case is the toughest to classify and to exclude from the record of collective security enforcement. The United Nations played a peacekeeping role from 1992 to 1995, but did it badly and did not keep the peace among the warring parties in Bosnia (the Serbs, the Croats, and the Bosnians). It subcontracted its enforcement role to NATO, but retained control over when NATO could act militarily, did not allow NATO to operate freely, severely restricted NATO's use of force, and generally crippled NATO. Only when the United States pushed hard for air strikes in the late summer of 1995 did the Security Council and NATO take a hard military line. Under intense American pressure, NATO began to rain destruction from the air on Serbian forces, which helped bring the Serbs to the conference table. The United States then brokered a ceasefire among the three warring parties, and sent its forces and those of its NATO allies into Bosnia, together with forces of non-NATO members, as peacekeepers in late 1995. The 1995–96 Bosnian case was thus more a NATO than a UN operation, even though NATO was operating under the UN mandate as a regional security organization. In the late summer of 1995, however, the United States and NATO pushed the United Nations aside and took matters into their own hands. The Bosnia case is therefore one of a regional military alliance in action, not universal collective security.

34. The British were more inclined to go for an oil embargo than were the French, but they were not prepared to do so unless the United States went along. It could not, because Roosevelt and Secretary of State Cordell Hull had no legal authority to block American oil exports to Italy. They had persuaded the big American oil companies to go along with a "moral embargo" of oil to Italy, but the smaller ones chose not to do so in order to gain market share against the majors. As a consequence, U.S. oil exports to Italy were double their normal level in October (Mussolini had attacked in early October), and triple their normal level in November. See Robert Divine, *The Illusion of Neutrality* (Chicago: University of Chicago Press, 1962), pp. 122–134. For British and French actions, see Arnold Wolfers, *Britain and France between Two Wars: Conflicting Strategies of Peace from Versailles to World War II* (New York: W.W. Norton, 1966), chaps. 10 and 21.

35. Dean Acheson, *Present at the Creation: My Years in the State Department* (New York: W.W. Norton, 1969), p. 405.

36. Walter G. Hermes, *Truce Tent and Fighting Front* (Washington, D.C.: Office of the Chief of Military History, United States Army, 1966), Appendix A and Appendix A-2.

37. In fact, the United States committed itself to take military action before it went to the United Nations to seek a resolution that asked UN members to give such help as might be needed. See Acheson, *Present at the Creation*, pp. 407–408.

38. Why the Soviets were so stupid as to be absent that day has been a matter of much speculation. The most common explanation is that they were boycotting the Council's non-recognition of Communist China. Stalin did not believe that the United States would go to the United Nations in the Korean case, even though Gromyko warned him to send the Soviet delegate back to the Council as a precaution to block its taking action. See S.N. Goncharov, John W. Lewis, and Xue Litai, *Uncertain Partners: Stalin, Mao, and the Korean War* (Stanford: Stanford University Press, 1993), pp. 161–162.

39. There were two key Security Council resolutions authorizing action against Iraq. Resolution 665 authorized the blockade; Resolution 678 authorized the use of force (war). The first was passed on August 25, 1990, by a vote of 13–0, with China and Yemen abstaining. The second was passed on November 28, 1990, by a vote of 12–2, with China again abstaining, and with Cuba and Yemen voting "no." China abstained on both votes because it had conflicting interests, as I explain in the next note. An abstention by a permanent member, however, is as good as a "yes" vote. See Lawrence Freedman and Efraim Karsh, *The Gulf Conflict 1990–1991: Diplomacy and War in the New World Order* (Princeton, N.J.: Princeton University Press, 1993), pp. 150 and 234.

40. In France and especially Britain, the United States found generally loyal allies. Britain and France supported American-led initiatives for several reasons: because they were America's closest allies and especially because, with the ending of the Cold War, they wanted to preserve an American military presence in Europe; consequently, they had to demonstrate loyalty to the United States on a matter over which it was determined to take a tough line.

Even with France, however, there was not total harmony. French President Mitterrand tried several times to fly solo with Iraq. France had historically had close ties with Iraq. It tried everything possible, short of accepting the aggression, to avoid war with Iraq. See Freedman and Karsh, *The Gulf Conflict 1990–1991*, pp. 167 and 270–274. China was conflicted but ultimately supported tough action because it wanted to court the United States. Its role as America's strategic ally against the Soviet Union came to an abrupt halt in 1990 when the Cold War ended; absent the Soviet threat, the United States no longer required the weighty Chinese offset. To cope with this state of affairs, China backed rather than opposed the United States in its desire to be tough with Iraq. It calculated that through cooperation it could enhance its diminished status, demonstrate its importance as a strategic ally, and show that it was a global and not merely a regional power. Thus, strategic calculations, not simply a generalized opposition to aggression, pushed China to resolve its conflicting principles in favor of supporting the United States. Gorbachev gave his support both because of the Soviet Union's economic and political weakness at the time, and because his personal commitment to "new thinking" in foreign affairs. He needed Western economic aid to help him restructure the Soviet economy, and opposition to the West on such a clear-cut act of military aggression would endanger that aid. Moreover, in his search for new thinking, Gorbachev had been pushing Soviet-American détente, an end to the Cold War, eradication of the nuclear danger, respect for international law, and a revival of the United Nations. If Gorbachev had opposed Security Council action so soon after having urged greater respect for international law and greater use of the United Nations, he would have discredited his new foreign policy line, called into question his sincerity about putting Soviet-American relations on a more cooperative basis, and thus risked the future Western economic aid he needed. Thus, the four permanent members of the Security Council supported the United States in its tough line against Iraq, not simply because they saw the need to uphold the principle of collective security, but because they calculated that their respective interests would be well served if they did. Therefore, blatant military aggression was resisted and the sanctity of territorial borders upheld because each great power calculated it could gain from supporting the collective effort. Thus, in the Iraqi case, collective security was instrumental to other goals, not an end in itself.

41. See Tom J. Farer, "The Role of Regional Collective Security Arrangements," in Thomas G. Weiss, ed., *Collective Security in a Changing World* (Boulder, Colo.: Lynne Rienner, 1990), pp. 153–186; Charles A. Kupchan, "Reviving the West," *Foreign Affairs*, Vol. 75, No. 3 (May/June 1996), pp. 92–105; and Charles A. Kupchan, "Rethinking Europe," *The National Interest*, No. 56 (Summer 1999), pp. 73–81. Farer makes an abstract case for the viability of regional collective security, although he is vague on exactly what he means by it. Kupchan makes a concrete proposal for a European regional system. He prescribes what he calls an Atlantic Union, whose "commitments to collective security would be looser and less automatic than NATO's assurances" (p. 100) and whose membership could "expand at a steady pace not just to Central Europe, but also to Russia and the other states of the former Soviet Union" (p. 99). Granted, this union would continue to have the United States as a member, but how the United States could make such a system function with so many members, and how collective security could be provided by loose assurances, are not spelled out.

42. The first quotation is from Claude, *Power and International Relations*, p. 199; the second, from Claude, *Swords into Plowshares*, p. 274.

43. Morgenthau, *Politics Among Nations*, p. 415.

44. As MacFarlane and Weiss put it: "Their shared interest in the public good of regional stability is often accompanied by unilateral interests in obtaining specific favorable outcomes to the conflict in question." Neil MacFarlane and Thomas G. Weiss, "Regional Organizations and Regional Security," *Security Studies*, Vol. 2, No. 1 (Autumn 1992), pp. 29–30.

45. The Delian League of ancient Greece may be the first recorded attempt to construct a regional collective security system. Formed by Athens with some of the lesser city states in order to wage war against the Persians, it quickly became an instrument used by Athens to exact tribute from them and eventually mutated into the Athenian empire. Thus, if it was not a sphere-of-influence arrangement at the outset, it quickly became one. See Donald

Kagan, *On the Origins of War and the Preservation of Peace* (New York: Doubleday, 1995), pp. 24–27.

46. For a concise political history of the formation of the Rio Treaty and the Organization of American States (OAS), and a perceptive analysis of how both functioned through the mid-1960s, see Jerome Slater, *The OAS and United States Foreign Policy* (Columbus: Ohio State University Press, 1967), esp. chaps. 1, 2, and the conclusion; and Slater, *A Revaluation of Collective Security.*

47. These provisions are found in articles 3 and 7 of the Rio Treaty and articles 24 and 25 in the OAS Charter. The texts of both can be found in Senate Committee on Foreign Relations, *A Decade of American Foreign Policy; Basic Documents, 1941–1949,* 81st Cong., 1st sess. (Washington, D.C.: U.S. Government Printing Office, 1950), pp. 421–426 and 427–446, respectively.

48. The OAS has had a mixed record for peaceful mediation of disputes. Scheman finds that of 94 incidents that had the potential to escalate to armed conflict between 1948 and 1982, the OAS had a mediating role in 33 of them, or a record of involvement of 35 percent. For the disputes that escalated to armed conflict, however, its record was considerably better: the OAS was involved in mediating all five of them. See L. Ronald Scheman, *The Inter-American Dilemma: The Search for Inter-American Cooperation at the Centennial of the Inter-American System* (New York: Praeger, 1988), pp. 57 and 72 and Tables 3.1 and 3.3.

49. Ibid.; p. 56.

50. Ibid., pp. 17 and 80.

51. I have relied for the following analysis on two fine studies: Timothy Ireland, *Creating the Entangling Alliance: The Origins of the North Atlantic Treaty Organization* (Westport, Conn.: Greenwood Press, 1981), chaps. 2 and 3; and James McAllister, *No Exit: America and the German Problem, 1943–1954* (Ithaca, N.Y.: Cornell University Press, 2002).

52. The texts of the Washington and Brussels treaties can be found in John A. Reed, Jr., *Germany and NATO* (Washington, D.C.: National Defense University Press, 1987), Appendices A and B.

53. Quoted in Ireland, *Creating the Entangling Alliance,* p. 69.

54. The concept of cooperative security was first proposed in Ashton B. Carter, William J. Perry, and John D. Steinbruner, *A New Concept of Cooperative Security* (Washington, D.C.: The Brookings Institution, 1992). The concept was elaborated fully in Janne E. Nolan, ed., *Global Engagement: Cooperation and Security in the 21st Century* (Washington, D.C.: The Brookings Institution, 1994), esp. chaps. 1 and 2. Many analysts have adopted the phrase "cooperative security," but in the process the original meaning has often been lost. John Ruggie, for example, includes under its rubric "any joint measures by which potential adversaries prevent, resolve, reduce, contain, or counter threats that could lead to war among them." Although this definition may be useful for Ruggie's purposes, it is much broader than that of Carter, Perry, and Steinbruner. As used here, cooperative security embodies a collective security scheme that relies heavily on arms control measures to make offensive military campaigns militarily difficult to implement. In this regard, Carter and his colleagues recall Woodrow Wilson, who considered disarmament to be a crucial component of the League of Nations. See John Gerard Ruggie, *Winning the Peace: America and World Order in the New Era* (New York: Columbia University Press, 1996), p. 80; Posen and Ross, "Competing Visions for U.S. Grand Strategy," pp. 23–32; and Thomas J. Knock, *To End All Wars: Woodrow Wilson and the Quest for a New World Order* (New York: Oxford University Press, 1992), p. 127.

55. During the latter stages of the Cold War, certain military analysts and political actors, mostly those on the left and primarily in the United States and Western Europe, advocated making the offense militarily difficult. Their various plans went under the general rubric of "defensive defense."

56. Carter, Perry, and Steinbruner, *A New Concept of Cooperative Security,* p. 7.

57. Ibid., pp. 7–8.

58. Ibid., p. 24.

59. Ibid., p. 25.

60. Ibid., pp. 27–28.

61. This was certainly the case for one of the most successful arms control agreements of the twentieth century, the Treaty on Conventional Armed Forces in Europe (the CFE Treaty). The best study of this treaty is Richard A. Falkenrath, *Shaping Europe's Military Order: The Origins and Consequences of the CFE Treaty* (Cambridge, Mass.: MIT Press, 1995).

62. Collective defense and collective security are often conflated, but they are, in fact, two different things. See Wolfers, *Discord and Collaboration*, pp. 182–184.

63. Two excellent overviews of America's containment policy are John Lewis Gaddis, *Strategies of Containment: A Critical Appraisal of Postwar American National Security Policy* (New York: Oxford University Press, 1982); and Seyom Brown, *The Faces of Power: United States Foreign Policy from Truman to Clinton*, 2d ed. (New York: Columbia University Press, 1994).

64. See Michael Mastanduno, *Economic Containment: CoCom and the Politics of East-West Trade* (Ithaca, N.Y.: Cornell University Press, 1992), pp. 40–52.

65. See William E. Linglebach, "England and Neutral Trade," *Military Historian and Economist*, Vol. 2 (1917), pp. 153–178; Avner Offer, *The First World War: An Agrarian Interpretation* (Oxford: Clarendon Press, 1989); Charles Seymour, *American Diplomacy During the World War* (Hamden, Conn.: Archon Books, 1964; first published in 1934), chaps 2–3; Ernest R. May, *The World War and American Isolationism, 1914–1917* (Cambridge, Mass.: Harvard University Press, 1959), chaps. 3, 6, 7, 14, 15; W.M. Medlicott, *The Economic Blockade*, 2 vols. (London: HMSO, 1952 and 1959); Robert Pape, *Bombing to Win: Air Power and Coercion in War* (Ithaca, N.Y.: Cornell University Press, 1996), chap. 4; and Mancur Olson, Jr., *The Economics of the Wartime Shortage: A History of British Food Supplies in the Napoleonic War and in World Wars I and II* (Durham, N.C.: Duke University Press, 1963).

66. These nine cases constitute the complete record of America's compound containment efforts, but they do not include all the states against whom the United States has instituted military measures or economic denial since 1945. Indeed, the United States has had a myriad of goals in applying coercive measures against other states, ranging from ending apartheid to improving human rights to stopping drug smuggling. The nine cases selected, however, are the only ones in which the United States combined military force with economic denial for the purpose of containing territorial expansion and political subjugation. Because I treat the spread of communism as political subjugation, I have put Cuba and Nicaragua in the compound containment category. Cuba was seeking to export its revolution to Latin America; Nicaragua, its revolution to El Salvador. I have included Libya in the nine cases because it was exporting terrorism by harboring and training terrorists. Whether Qadaffi had designs for territorial expansion or political subjugation in his own region is not completely clear, although he aided rebel forces in neighboring Chad and the Sudan. I have excluded Syria from this list because, although the United States has applied sanctions against Syria for its support of terrorism, the American government has never used military force directly against Syrian territory. I have also included Iran, because the United States has imposed sanctions on it since the 1979 revolution, and because the United States convoyed Kuwaiti tankers against Iranian attacks in the late 1980s. For a complete list of all states against which the United States applied economic sanctions from 1945 through 1990, as well as an analysis of the purposes and efficacy of the sanctions, see Gary Clyde Hufbauer, Jeffrey J. Schott, and Kimberly Ann Elliot, *Economic Sanctions Reconsidered*, 2d ed. (Washington, D.C.: Institute for International Economics, 1990), Vol. 1, pp. 15–27, Appendix B, and all of Vol. 2. Their study is the most complete analysis of economic sanctions in the twentieth century. For the list of thirty-five countries against which the United States unilaterally imposed sanctions from 1993–1996, together with an analysis of the results, see *A Catalogue of New U.S. Unilateral Economic Sanctions for Foreign Policy Purposes, 1993–1996* (Washington, D.C.: National Association of Manufacturers, 1997). Also see Richard N. Haass, *Economic Sanctions and American Diplomacy* (New York: Council on Foreign Relations, 1998), especially the conclusion; Daniel W. Drezner, *The Sanctions Paradox: Economic Statecraft and International Relations* (Cambridge: Cambridge University Press, 1999); Margaret Doxey, *Economic Sanctions and International Enforcement* (New York: Oxford University Press, 1971); M.S. Daodi and M.S. Dajani, *Economic Sanctions: Ideals and Experience* (Boston: Routledge and Kegan Paul, 1983); Barry E. Carter, *International Economic Sanctions: Improving the Haphazard U.S. Legal Regime* (New York:

Cambridge University Press, 1988); and Thomas G. Weiss, et al., eds. *Political Gain and Civilian Pain: Humanitarian Impacts of Economic Sanctions* (Lanham, Md.: Rowman and Littlefield, 1997).

67. Welfare loss is the loss of consumer surplus, which is defined as "the reductions in gains that purchasers enjoy from engaging in market transactions." For the exact methodology by which welfare loss was calculated, see Hufbauer, Schott, and Elliot, *Economic Sanctions Reconsidered*, Vol. 1, Appendix A, pp. 120–122.

68. See ibid., Vol. 1, pp. 135, 150, 189, 297; and Vol. 2, pp. 107, 113, 140, 202, 583.

69. Ibid., Vol. 1, p. 191.

70. Mastanduno, *Economic Containment*, p. 325. CoCom was a multilateral export control regime of Western states, and its purpose was to monitor and control the export of both technology and other items that could be of military assistance to the Soviet Union during the Cold War.

71. See Kenneth M. Pollack, *The Threatening Storm: The Case for Invading Iraq* (New York: Random House, 2002), chap. 7, for a discussion of why the sanctions regime crumbled.

72. For the Soviet case, I have relied on Mastanduno, *Economic Containment*; Beverly Crawford, *Economic Vulnerability in International Relations: East-West Trade, Investment, and Finance* (New York: Columbia University Press, 1993); Committee on Science, Engineering, and Public Policy, National Academy of Sciences, *Finding Common Ground: U.S. Export Controls in a Changed Global Environment* (Washington D.C.: National Academy Press, 1991), chap. 4; and Douglas E. McDaniel, *United States Technology Export Control: An Assessment* (Westport, Conn.: Praeger, 1993). Mastanduno is best for the Soviet case. For the Iraqi case, I have relied on Alan Dowty, "Sanctioning Iraq," *The Washington Quarterly*, Vol. 17, No. 3 (Summer 1994), pp. 179–198; Kenneth R. Timmerman, *Iraq Rebuilds Its Military Industries*, Staff Report, House Foreign Affairs Committee, U.S. Congress, June 19, 1993; Patrick Clawson, *How Has Saddam Hussein Survived? Economic Sanctions, 1990–1993*, NcNair Paper No. 40 (Washington, D.C.: Institute for National Strategic Studies, National Defense University, 1993); and Phebe Marr, "Iraq and Sanctions: What Lies Ahead for the Future?" Testimony before the Senate Foreign Relations Subcommittee on Near East and South Asia, August 3, 1995 (mimeo). Timmerman and Marr are best for the Iraqi case.

73. Mastanduno, *Economic Containment*, p. 325. For the same conclusion, also see National Academy of Sciences, *Finding Common Ground*, p. 33. Crawford dissents from this conclusion and argues instead: "An examination of cases in which dual-use technology was transferred but made little difference to Soviet military potential could support the argument that it is the Soviets' lack of success in assimilating, diffusing, and using Western technology rather than the Western embargo that prevented Western vulnerability in the face of [the import of advanced technology into the Soviet Union]." See Crawford, *Economic Vulnerability in International Relations*, p. 132 and chap. 4. No one should underestimate the difficulty the Soviet Union had in absorbing advanced Western technology into its economy. See, for example, Joseph Berliner, *The Innovation Decision in Soviet Industry* (Cambridge, Mass.: MIT Press, 1976). But the Soviet military-industrial sector was much better at this than the civilian-service sector. And besides, if the Soviets could not make good use of advanced Western technology for their military, why did they expend such great resources over such a long period to acquire it? Crawford's argument is valid up to a point, but as Mastanduno points out, it strains credulity to argue that the Soviets would work so hard to acquire Western technology if they did not somehow make good use of it.

74. Timmerman, *Letter of Transmittal*, June 21, 1993, appended to *Iraq Rebuilds Its Military Industries*.

75. Marr, "Iraq and Sanctions," p. 5.

76. Dowty, "Sanctioning Iraq," p. 182.

77. Timmerman, *Iraq Rebuilds Its Military Industries*, pp. 9, 10, 22.

78. Quoted in *Iraq's Weapons of Mass Destruction: The Assessment of the British Government*, September 2002, p. 17, available at <www.pm.gov.uk>. Also see Director of Central Intelligence, *Iraq's Weapons of Mass Destruction Programs*, October 2002, pp. 1–2, available at <www.cia.gov>. For an assessment of what the United Nations weapons inspectors

accomplished from 1991 to 1998, see "Iraq: A Chronology of UN Inspections and an Assessment of Their Accomplishments," *Arms Control Today*, October 2002, available at <www.armscontrol.org/act/2002_10/iraqspecialocto2.asp?print>.

79. For CIA Director George Tenet's March 19, 2002, testimony, see <www.senate.gov/~armed_services/testimony.cfm?wit_id=193&id=192>.

80. *Iraq's Weapons of Mass Destruction*, pp. 24–25; and "Iraq: A Chronology of UN Inspections and as Assessment of Their Accomplishments," p. 1.

81. *Iraq's Weapons of Mass Destruction*, pp. 26–27.

82. In his famous "Sources of Soviet Conduct" article of the late 1940s, George Kennan predicted that the nature of the Soviet regime would change by becoming mellower, or else it would break up, if the United States pursued vigilant containment. Even though he did not fully argue the case, Kennan postulated that frustration of its expansionist urges would cause the Soviet system to change for the better. "But the United States has it in its power to increase enormously the strains under which Soviet policy must operate, to force upon the Kremlin a far greater degree of moderation and circumspection than it has had to observe in recent years, and in this way to promote tendencies which must eventually find their outlet in either the breakup or the gradual mellowing of Soviet power. For no mystical, Messianic movement — and particularly not that of the Kremlin — can face frustration indefinitely without eventually adjusting itself in one way or another to the logic of that state of affairs." George F. Kennan, *American Diplomacy 1900–1950* (New York: New American Library, 1962), pp. 105–106.

83. As late as February 20, 1989, five days before Nicaragua's elections, an American poll showed that the Sandinista candidate Daniel Ortega led the opposition candidate Violetta Chamorro by 16 points (48 percent to 32 percent). Bush National Security Advisor Brent Scowcroft thought that, "the Sandinistas were going to win. The only question is how brazen they will be." The Sandinistas agreed to elections not only because they were confident they would win, but also because the Americans agreed, as part of the bargain, to stop backing the Contras, which would be disbanded. Elections would thus end the American-backed military threat and legitimize the Sandinista rule. I do not deny the importance of the Contra effort to changing the Nicaraguan government, but the case that American pressure was wholly responsible for changing the Nicaraguan government is not clear-cut. Sandinista miscalculation also played a crucial role. See Robert Kagan, *A Twilight Struggle: American Power and Nicaragua, 1977–1990* (New York: The Free Press, 1996), p. 707, for the polls and Scowcroft quotation, and pp. 57–63, for a full analysis of Sandinista thinking in the fall and winter of 1989 and early 1990.

84. See Hufbauer, Schott, and Elliot, *Economic Sanctions Reconsidered*, pp. 92–93.

85. Elizabeth Rogers has cogently argued that "the main risk to sanctions' success lies as much in the failure to fully commit as it does in the weakness of the sanctions instrument itself." Elizabeth S. Rogers, "U.S. Use of Economic Sanctions to Control Regional Conflicts," *Security Studies*, Vol. 5, No. 4 (Summer, 1996), p. 43–72. Rogers argues that Hufbauer, Schott, and Elliot understate how effective sanctions can be because their data does not discriminate among cases according to how the sanctions were applied. Had they separated the cases where sanctions were applied broadly, with full force, and all at once from cases where sanctions were applied narrowly, imposed incrementally, and leaked badly, they would have discovered that sanctions work well under the former conditions and badly under the latter.

86. Hufbauer, Schott, and Elliot categorized the 115 sanctions cases from 1914 to 1990 according to the type of political objective sought: modest change in the targeted state's policy, disrupting its military adventures (other than major war), impairing its military potential, major changes in its policy, and destabilizing its government. The success rates for these five, respectively, were: 33 percent, 33 percent, little success, 24 percent, and 50 percent. Destabilization had the highest success rate because, they appear to argue, covert and quasi-military actions also played important roles in them. Pape reclassified the Hufbauer data and argued that of the forty cases out of 115 where sanctions were successful, only four were clear successes for sanctions. Eighteen successes were cases where the use of force also played a large role. See Hufbauer, Schott, and Elliot, *Economic Sanctions Reconsidered*, chapter 3 and

especially the tables on pp. 56–62; and Robert Pape, "Why Economic Sanctions Still Don't Work," *International Security*, Vol. 22, No. 2 (Fall 1997), pp. 90–136.

Four: Selective Engagement

1. See Jeffrey E. Garten, *The Big Ten: The Big Emerging Markets and How They Will Change Our Lives* (New York: Basic Books, 1997), p. 16.

2. Even though it is still smaller in magnitude than merchandise trade, America's service trade has grown recently. Taking 1998 figures for an example, world merchandise trade totaled $5.2 trillion, and services trade, $1.3 trillion. Of that total, U.S. merchandise exports were 13 percent ($683 billion) of the world's total, while its service exports were 18 percent (at $233.6 billion) of the world's total. U.S. imports of merchandise (at $944.6 billion) were 17 percent of the world's total, and its imports of services (at $161.5 billion) were 12.5 percent of the world's total. Put another way, in 1998, America's service exports totaled 25.5 percent of its combined exports of merchandise and services, and its service imports totaled 14.4 percent of its combined imports. World Trade Organization figures, <www.WTO.org>.

3. See U.S. Census Bureau, *Statistical Abstract of the United States, 2001*, at <www.census.gov/prod/2001pubs/statab/sec28.pdf> from Table No. 1283, "Private Services Transaction by Type of Service and Country, 1990 to 1999." Service trade is harder to track than merchandise trade, and the data typically lag several years behind the current calendar year.

4. U.S. direct foreign investment refers to investments made in a business, company, plant, or facility in another country by a U.S.-owned and based company, and that yield either ownership or substantial control of that foreign-based entity. For instance, General Motors could set up its own manufacturing plant in Germany, or it could take a 50 percent stake in Volkswagen based in Germany. Both would fall into the DFI category. Direct foreign investment differs from portfolio investment. Whereas DFI implies the ability to influence or control the operations of a foreign-based business entity through a significant investment in that entity, portfolio investment is the purchase of stock or debt of a foreign company that yields no significant operational influence. The United States government uses 10 percent ownership of a foreign-based entity as the baseline for defining DFI.

5. The figures refer to the cumulative stock of DFI, not annual flows, and because they are calculated on book value at the time of purchase, the figures understate the value of earlier purchases, thereby inflating the more recent purchases artificially. This has the effect of overstating the relative importance of investments in East Asia since 1990.

6. For a more comprehensive analysis of the American-European economic relationship, see Robin Gaster and Clyde V. Prestowitz, Jr., *Shrinking the Atlantic: Europe and the American Economy* (Washington, D.C.: North Atlantic Research Group and Economic Strategy Institute, June 1994).

7. For the world as a whole, trade patterns involving developing states have changed as follows: comparing figures for 1913 and 1999, trade among developed states in both years was 43 percent; trade between developed and developing states declined from 52 percent to 37 percent; but trade among developing states, just 5 percent in 1913, was 16 percent by 1999. Investment patterns show a more marked change. In 1913, 76 percent of direct foreign investment was outside of North America and Europe because most of it was directed to the exploitation of natural resources. By 1993, that situation had changed dramatically. Only 11 percent of DFI was resource-based, and 70 percent of world DFI was either in North America (27 percent) or Western Europe (43 percent). Sources for these figures are: International Monetary Fund, *Direction of Trade Statistics Yearbook, 2000*; Geoffrey Jones, *The Evolution of International Business* (London: Routledge, 1966), p. 31; and David Held and Anthony McGrew, David Goldblatt and Jonathan Perraton, *Global Transformations: Politics, Economic, and Culture* (Stanford: Stanford University Press, 1999), p. 156. I thank Stephen Brooks for his careful eye on these statistics.

8. See Garten, *The Big Ten*, chap. 1.

9. The figures in this paragraph come from The International Institute for Strategic Studies (IISS), *The Military Balance, 2000–2001* (Oxford: IISS/Oxford University Press, 2002), Table 26, pp. 332–337. Figures rounded from data in *The Military Balance*.

10. Ibid.

11. Based on this principle, the United States should avoid a permanent peacetime presence in Central Asia and remove its troops from Afghanistan and neighboring countries once the war in Afghanistan is over and the country is stabilized. This is the intention of the Bush Administration, according to General Tommy Franks, head of Central Command, who said in a press conference on June 24, 2002: "we do not anticipate a permanent presence in any of the countries in the region." A transcript of the press conference is available at <www.centcom.mil/news/transcripts/CINC%20in%20Uzbekistan%2024%20Jan%2002.html>.

12. The "Guidelines for Japan-U.S. Cooperation" are at <www.mofa.go.jp/region/n-america/us/security/guideline2.html>. See also "Japan-U.S. Joint Declaration on Security—Alliance for the 21st Century," April 17, 1996, <www.mofa.go.jp/region/n-america/us/security/security.html>.

13. The differences that do exist between the United States, on the one hand, and Kuwait and especially Saudi Arabia, on the other, have not been over whether the United States has extended its military umbrella over them, but instead over how large and visible the American military presence should be in these two states and how tight the restrictions should be on American use of forces based there.

14. For the details of the negotiations between the United States and China, on the one hand, and between the Carter Administration and Congress, on the other, concerning the normalization of relations with China and the passage of the Taiwan Relations Act, see Harry Harding, *The Fragile Relationship: The United States and China Since 1972* (Washington, D.C.: The Brookings Institution, 1992), pp. 75–87.

15. This was in fact the position reached by the U.S. government under Clinton and communicated by National Security Advisor Samuel Berger on a trip to Beijing and Taipei after the 1996 Taiwan Straits crisis. Interview on November 6, 2000, with a high-level official who dealt with East Asia. See also Thomas J. Christensen, "Posing Problems without Catching Up: China's Rise and Challenges for U.S. Security Policy," *International Security*, Vol. 25, No. 4 (Spring 2001), p. 37.

16. Department of Defense, Washington Headquarters Services, Directorate for Information Operations and Reports, "Active Duty Military Personnel Strengths by Regional Area and by Country," September 30, 2001, <web1.whs.osd.mil/mmid/military/miltop.htm>. Figures are rounded from that data.

17. The effectiveness of extended deterrence—that is, the ability of one state to dissuade a third party from attacking its ally—has been subjected to careful scholarly analysis. Paul Huth and Bruce Russett found that extended deterrence worked 57 percent of the time in the fifty-four cases they identified between 1900 and 1980. James Fearon reanalyzed the Huth-Russett data and found that America's extended deterrence during the Cold War had a significant effect in preventing an adversary's limited challenge against U.S. allies from succeeding. He concluded that America's nuclear umbrella worked in six of the seven cases of immediate extended-deterrence failure (a limited challenge to the status quo), or 86 percent of the time, keeping the conflict limited and protecting its ally. Thus, if the past is a reliable guide, the United States, by extending its nuclear umbrella over its allies, can help reduce many, although not all, of the challenges to the status quo, or keep them from escalating to full-scale war. See Paul Huth and Bruce Russett, "What Makes Deterrence Work? Cases from 1900 to 1980," *World Politics*, Vol. 36, No. 4 (July 1984), p. 505; and James D. Fearon, "Signaling versus the Balance of Power and Interests," *Journal of Conflict Resolution*, Vol. 38, No. 2 (June 1994), p. 256, Table 4.

18. For the contrary view—that the United States could not have deterred an Iraqi attack—see Janice Gross Stein, "Deterrence and Compellence in the Gulf, 1990–1991," *International Security*, Vol. 17, No. 2 (Fall 1992), pp. 147–180. Stein's argument is not persuasive, mainly because she argues (pp. 167–168) that Saddam's decision to occupy all of Kuwait, not

just the part that held the disputed oil field, came after he was told that Kuwait intended to invite the United States in to establish bases in the unoccupied part of the country after his partial invasion. According to Stein, this information pushed Saddam to occupy all of Kuwait for two reasons: total occupation would deny the Americans bases there, and he believed that the Saudis would deny the Americans bases from which to launch a counterattack. This line of argument begs the question of what Saddam would have done had the United States concluded a defensive treaty with Kuwait and perhaps stationed American troops along the Iraqi-Kuwaiti border. Such a deterrent posture would have confronted Saddam unequivocally with the prospect that an attack on Kuwait, even if limited, meant attacking American forces and thus provoking a war with the United States.

19. Interview in Boston on March 3, 2000.

20. The attitudes described here are based upon 130 interviews conducted from January 1992 through December 1993 in London, Brussels, Paris, Bonn, Warsaw, Prague, Budapest, and Washington, and a second round of 34 interviews in Berlin, Paris, Brussels, and London in June 2000. Interviewed were officials in ministries of defense and foreign affairs, legislative officials, academic specialists, and individuals at high political levels. For a more comprehensive analysis of these points, see Robert J. Art, "Why Western Europe Needs the United States and NATO," *Political Science Quarterly*, Vol. 111, No. 1 (Spring 1996), pp. 1–41.

21. Interview with a Western European ambassador to NATO, Brussels, January 10, 1992.

22. Kim Dae-jung, quoted in John Burton, "Unification may take 30 years, says South Korea leader," *Financial Times*, July 17, 2000, p. 1.

23. Kim, quoted in Jane Perlez, "South Korean Says North Agrees U.S. Troops Should Stay," *New York Times*, September 11, 2000, p. A3. China's English-language *Beijing Review* also reported on July 26, 2000, that North Korea was willing to tolerate the long-term presence of American troops on the Korean peninsula. See <www.stratfor.com/asia/commentary/0007280105.htm>.

24. George Yeo, Singapore's Trade and Industry Minister, said of the Changi naval base: "We built it at our own expense to facilitate the deployment of the U.S. 7th Fleet in Southeast Asian waters. At a time when the region is going through dramatic political change, the presence of these ships has a stabilizing effect." Quoted in *Far Eastern Economic Review* (May 17, 2001), <www.feer.com/_0105_17/po21region.html>.

25. A Vietnamese economist quoted in Seth Mydans, "Vietnam Finds an Old Foe Has New Allure," *New York Times*, April 13, 2000, p. A14.

26. For good analyses of the buffering role that the United States plays in East Asia, see Thomas J. Christensen, "China, the U.S.-Japan Alliance, and the Security Dilemma in East Asia," *International* Security, Vol. 23, No. 4 (Spring 1999), p. 74–80; and Robert S. Ross, "The Geography of the Peace: East Asia in the Twenty-First Century," ibid., pp. 114–116.

27. This paragraph is based on an interview with an official at the National Security Council, Washington, D.C., June 29, 2000, and discussions with Gary Sick of Columbia University.

28. For the account of how the United States persuaded Gorbachev that the Soviet Union's interests would be best served if a reunited Germany were in NATO, see Philip Zelikow and Condoleezza Rice, *Germany Unified and Europe Transformed: A Study in Statecraft* (Cambridge, Mass.: Harvard University Press, 1995), chap. 7; and George Bush and Brent Scowcroft, *A World Transformed* (New York: Alfred A. Knopf, 1998), chaps. 10–12.

29. See "NATO-Russian Relations: A New Quality," Declaration by the Heads of State and Government of NATO Member States and the Russian Federation, May 28, 2002, at <www.natodoc@hq.nato.int>. For analysis of the meaning of the NATO-Russia Council, see *Russia Watch*, No. 8 (April 2002), at <www.ksg.harvard.edu/bcsia/sdi>.

30. This paragraph has benefited from conversations with Andrei Kortunov of the Open Society Institute in Moscow; William Wohlforth of Dartmouth College; Celeste Wallander of the Center for Strategic and International Studies; and an interview on January 8, 2001, with an official on the National Security Council.

31. The observations in this paragraph and the next are based on the following sources. In the summer of 1992, I conducted interviews in Beijing with about twenty analysts who

worked in think tanks well-connected to government sources. The think tanks included those most important in military and foreign policy, including China's National War College. At that time, governmental officials would not talk openly about these matters, but the think tank analysts would. Other sources are: an interview with a high-level American official who has dealt with East Asian affairs for a long time, Washington, D.C., November 6, 2000; Thomas J. Christensen, "Chinese Realpolitik," *Foreign Affairs*, Vol. 75, No. 5 (September/October 1996), pp. 37–53; Christensen, "China, the U.S.-Japan Alliance, and the Security Dilemma in East Asia"; David Shambaugh, "China's Military Views the World: Ambivalent Security," *International Security*, Vol. 24, No. 3 (Winter 1999/2000), pp. 52–80; David Shambaugh, "Sino-American Strategic Relations: From Partners to Competitors," *Survival*, Vol. 42, No. 1 (Spring 2000), pp. 97–116; James Miles, "Chinese Nationalism, U.S. Policy, and Asian Security," *Survival*, Vol. 42, No. 4 (Winter 2000–01), pp. 51–73; "China Accepts U.S. Presence in Asia?" (28 July 2000), at <www.stratfor.com/asia/commentary/0007280105.htm>; and "China's Policy of Distraction Involves Japan," December 13, 2000, at <www.stratfor.com/home/giu/archive/121300.asp>. I have also benefited from discussions with Richard Samuels of MIT, Robert Ross of Boston College, and Thomas Christensen of MIT.

32. For a careful analysis of the effects of the 1996 crisis on Chinese and American thinking, see Robert S. Ross, "The 1995–96 Taiwan Strait Confrontation: Coercion, Credibility, and the Use of Force," *International Security*, Vol. 25, No. 2 (Fall 2000), pp. 87–124. Also see "Guidelines for Japan-U.S. Cooperation"; "Japan-U.S. Joint Declaration on Security—Alliance for the 21st Century."

33. Erik Eckholm with Joseph Kahn, "Asia Worries About Growth of China's Economic Power," *The New York Times*, November 24, 2002, p. 6.

34. For analyses of the institutional effects that alliances can produce on state behavior, see Celeste A. Wallander and Robert O. Keohane, "When Threats Decline, Why Do Alliances Persist? An Institutional Approach," paper presented at the second Conference on Security Institutions, Cambridge, March 16–19, 1997, hosted by the Center on Foreign and Security Policy Research, The Free University of Berlin, and the Weatherhead Center for International Affairs, Harvard University; Celeste A. Wallander, *Balancing Acts: Security, Institutions, and German-Russian Relations after the Cold War* (Ithaca, N.Y.: Cornell University Press, 1999), chap. 2; and Helga Haftendorn, Robert O. Keohane, and Celeste A. Wallander, eds., *Imperfect Unions: Security Institutions over Time and Space* (Oxford: Oxford University Press, 1999), esp. "Introduction" and "Conclusion."

35. See Paul W. Schroeder, "Alliances, 1815–1945: Weapons of Power and Tools of Management," in Klaus Knorr, ed., *Historical Dimensions of National Security Problems* (Lawrence: University Press of Kansas, 1976), pp. 227–262. See also Patricia A. Weitsman, "Intimate Enemies: The Politics of Peacetime Alliances," *Security Studies*, Vol. 7, No. 1 (Autumn 1997), pp. 156–194.

36. Christopher Gelpi, "Alliances as Instruments of Intra-Allied Control," in Haftendorn, Keohane, and Wallander, *Imperfect Unions*, p. 132. For the difficulties of alliance management, see Glenn H. Snyder, *Alliance Politics* (Ithaca, N.Y.: Cornell University Press, 1997), chaps. 6 and 9.

37. In January 1996, Greece and Turkey were on the verge of military hostilities over a twelve-acre Aegean island, called Imia by the Greeks and Kardak by the Turks. The island, located four miles off the coast of Turkey and inhabited at the time only by twelve goats, was claimed by both states. Only the personal intervention of President Clinton and his top national security advisors averted a military clash between the two states. See Stephen Engelberg, "U.S. Brokers Peace Accord in the Aegean," *New York Times*, January 31, 1995; and editorial, "Aegean Tantrum," *New York Times*, February 3, 1996, both found in the archives of the *New York Times* at <www.nytimes.com>. During the Kargil crisis in the spring of 1999, President Clinton gave Pakistan's Sharif a face-saving way to back down in Kargil, but told him that he could not come to Washington to exercise it unless he withdrew Pakistani troops back across the line of control in Kashmir. Scott D. Sagan, "The Perils of Proliferation in South Asia," *Asian Survey*, Vol. 41, No. 6 (November/December 2001), pp. 1071–1072. In late spring

2002, India and Pakistan had nearly 1,000,000 troops on a high state of alert on their border. The intervention of President Bush, and especially the pressure put on General Musharraf to stop the infiltration of terrorists into Indian-held Kashmir and India itself, was by nearly all accounts crucial in deescalating the pressures towards war. Celia W. Dugger, "The Kashmir Brink," *New York Times*, June 20, 2002, p. A14; and Edward Luce, "An Indian Summer," *Financial Times*, July 2, 2002, p. 14.

38. Barry Schneider has established a checklist of eleven principles to guide decision makers on whether to try to disarm such a regime. See Barry R. Schneider, *Radical Responses to Radical Regimes: Evaluating Preemptive Counter-Proliferation*, McNair Paper 41 (Washington, D.C.: National Defense University, May 1995), pp. 23–27.

39. Ivo H. Daalder and Michael E. O'Hanlon, *Winning Ugly: NATO's War to Save Kosovo* (Washington, D.C.: The Brookings Institution, 2000), pp. 133–134.

40. There are those who argue that American military intervention can, in fact, advance the cause of democracy by bringing about more political liberalization in a target state than would otherwise be the case. For example, Margaret Hermann and Charles Kegley concluded, from their survey of three datasets that encompassed sixty-four U.S. military interventions between 1945 and 1991, that: "U.S. policymakers can use military intervention as a tool for engineering social reforms. . . . [because] past U.S. interventions have more often worked toward enlarging, rather than restricting, the liberal democratic community." Margaret G. Hermann and Charles W. Kegley, Jr., "The U.S. Use of Military Intervention to Promote Democracy: Evaluating the Record," *International Interactions*, Vol. 24, No. 2 (June 1998), pp. 107–108. The Hermann-Kegley data, however, do not give convincing evidence that the liberalizing effects of American military intervention are long-lasting. Of the sixty-four interventions, thirty-two, or half, involved repeated U.S. interventions in eight states (five each in South Korea, South Vietnam, Laos, and Panama; four in Lebanon; three each in Cambodia, and Thailand; and two in Liberia). See ibid., appendix, pp. 112–113. Today, only three can qualify as democracies—South Korea, Panama, and Thailand, of which South Korea, with over fifty years of American occupation, is the most solidly democratic. Other analysts, moreover, read the record of American intervention differently. For example, James Meernik analyzed twenty-seven cases of U.S. military intervention from 1950 to 1990 and concluded that, "U.S. military interventions generally do not leave behind more democratic regimes." James Meernik, "United States Military Intervention and the Promotion of Democracy," *Journal of Peace Research*, Vol. 33, No. 4 (November 1996), p. 396. See also Mark Peceny, "Two Paths to the Promotion of Democracy During U.S. Military Interventions," *International Studies Quarterly*, Vol. 39, No. 3 (September 1995), pp. 371–340. For a full listing of military interventions by all states from 1945 to 1985, see Herbert K. Tillema, "Foreign Overt Military Intervention in the Nuclear Age," *Journal of Peace Research*, Vol. 26, No. 2 (May 1989), pp. 179–195.

41. See Jack Snyder, *From Voting to Violence: Democratization and Nationalist Conflict* (New York: W.W. Norton, 2000), pp. 316–321.

42. Michael Mandelbaum and Richard Betts ably make these points. Michael Mandelbaum, "The Reluctance to Intervene," *Foreign Policy*, No. 95 (Summer 1994), pp. 3–19; Richard K. Betts, "The Delusion of Impartial Intervention," *Foreign Affairs*, Vol. 73, No. 6 (November/December 1994), pp. 20–33.

43. For an analysis of the military requirements of intervention in civil wars, see Barry R. Posen, "Military Responses to Refugee Disasters," *International Security*, Vol. 21, No. 6 (Summer 1996), pp. 72–111. By analyzing the Bosnian conflict and the Vietnam War, Posen calculates, for example, that it would take 6,000–8,000 troops to defend a single town surrounded by enemy forces or to create safe havens of a town-like size. This does not include airpower requirements, which could be considerable for resupply and combat needs. Ibid., pp. 103–104, notes 45 and 47.

44. See Larry Rohter, "U.N. Troops to Leave Haiti as Feeble as They Found It," *New York Times*, December 4, 1997, p. A1; David Gonzalez, "Haiti's Paralysis Spreads as U.S. Troops Pack Up," *New York Times*, November 10, 1999, p. A1; "U.N. Report Describes Somalia's Swift Descent into Anarchy," *New York Times*, August 19, 1999, and Ian Fisher, "With Warlords at Home, Somalis Talk Peace," *New York Times*, August 6, 2000, p. 3.

45. See Adam Przeworski, Michael Alvarez, Jose Antoia Cheibub, and Fernando Limongi, "What Makes Democracies Endure?" *Journal of Democracy*, Vol. 7, No. 1 (January, 1996), pp. 40–41. See also Stephan Haggard and Robert R. Kaufman, *The Political Economy of Democratic Transitions* (Princeton, N.J.: Princeton University Press, 1995), pp. 325–334. Great inequalities in income can also be a threat to the survival of democracy, as these authors argue at ibid., pp. 42–43. Also see Terry Lynn Karl, "Economic Inequality and Democratic Instability, " *Journal of Democracy*, Vol. 11, No. 1 (January 2000), pp. 149–156.

46. Quoted in Colin Nickerson, "Flight by U.S. Jets Fuels Philippine Debate on Bases," *The Boston Globe*, December 28, 1989, <available from Lexis-Nexis>.

47. See Benjamin Valentino, "Final Solutions: The Causes of Mass Killing and Genocide" (doctoral dissertation, MIT, 2000), chap. 1, pp. 8–9. My discussion of mass killing relies heavily on Valentino's excellent work.

48. Valentino finds six reasons for calculated mass murder: communization of a society; chauvinist mass killing, which means removing a religious, ethnic, or national group from society because of the threat it is thought to pose; territorial grabs; counter-guerilla operations, which take the form catching the "fish" (the terrorists) by draining the "sea" (their civilian supporters); terrorism, to bring a protracted civil war to an end; and imperial conquests. See Valentino, *Final Solutions*, chap. 2.

49. See Valentino, *Final Solutions*, chap. 3, Tables 2–7.

50. See Roy Licklider, "The Consequences of Negotiated Settlements in Civil Wars, 1945–1993," *American Political Science Review*, Vol. 89, No. 3 (September 1995), p. 686. Licklider compiled, from several datasets, data on ninety-one civil wars that took place between 1945 and 1993 (he excluded seven civil wars that began after 1990 in order to make several datasets comparable). He then asked how many of these civil wars involved large amounts of killing. Of the eighty-four wars that took place between 1945 and 1990, he classified fifty-nine as "identity wars" and twenty-five as "non–identity wars." Mass murder was termed "genocide" in the former (people killed because of their communal characteristics), and "politicide" in the latter (target populations defined by their political opposition to the regime). Twenty-five percent of the identity civil wars were associated with genocide; 20 percent of the non–identity civil wars were associated with politicide. If we combine Valentino's and Licklider's data, we find six to eight civil wars between 1900 and 1945 that involved mass killing; about nineteen between 1945 and 1990; and about five between 1991 and 1999. Through a different method of calculating noncombatant causalities, Valentino and his associates found that 24 percent of civil wars from 1945–1999 experienced mass murder. See Benjamin Valentino, Paul Huth, and Dylan Balch-Lindsay, "Draining the Sea: Mass Killing, Genocide, and Guerilla Warfare," paper delivered at the Annual Meeting of the American Political Science Association, August 31, 2001.

51. In thinking through this issue, I have benefited immensely from discussions with Kelly Greenhill, Alan Kuperman, Barry Posen, Taylor Seybolt, and Benjamin Valentino, and from the following sources: Kelly M. Greenhill, "Mission Impossible: Preventing Deadly Conflict in the African Great Lakes Region," *Security Studies*, Vol. 11, No. 1 (Autumn 2001), pp. 77–124; Taylor Seybolt, "Eyes Wide Open: Rwanda and the Difficulty of Worthy Military Intervention," unpublished ms.; Alan J. Kuperman, "Rwanda in Retrospect: Could the Genocide Have Been Stopped?" *Foreign Affairs*, Vol. 79, No. 1 (January/February 2000), pp. 94–119; Alan J. Kuperman, *The Limits of Humanitarian Intervention: Genocide in Rwanda* (Washington, D.C.: The Brookings Institution, 2001); Herbert Howe, "Lessons of Liberia: ECOMOG and Regional Peacekeeping," *International Security*, Vol. 21, No. 3 (Winter 1996/97), pp. 145–177; Jeremy Ginifer, "Refugees and Disarmament: Protecting Displaced Persons through Disarmament," *Survival*, Vol. 40, No. 2 (Summer 1998), pp. 161–177; and Michael O'Hanlon, *Saving Lives with Force: Military Criteria for Humanitarian Intervention* (Washington, D.C.: The Brookings Institution, 1997).

52. For an analysis of the critical role that outside intervenors with credible military power may play in civil war settlements, see Barbara F. Walter, "The Critical Barrier to Civil War Settlement," *International Organization*, Vol. 51, No. 3 (Summer 1997), pp. 335–364; and Barbara F. Walter, *Committing to Peace: The Successful Settlement of Civil Wars* (Princeton, N.J.: Princeton University Press, 2002).

53. As one Bosnian put it: "Everything good that has happened in the past five years has been imposed from the outside. It's too early [for NATO] to think about getting out." Quoted in Carla Anne Robbins, "Nation-Building Looms as a Policy Challenge for the New President," *Wall Street Journal*, November 3, 2000, p. A1.

54. I realize that preventive deployment to avert mass murder is easier to prescribe than to implement. For starters, the pool of targets for such a deployment is large. A few years ago, the CIA narrowed down the list of states likely to experience mass murder to about thirty, which is still too large for policymakers to act on if preventive deployment is being considered. (I thank Dan Byman for this bit of information.) Second, democracies find it hard to mobilize their citizens for such deployments until after the killing has started and horrific scenes of it are shown on national television. Third, if a preventive deployment did actually avert a mass murder somewhere, it could hurt future such efforts elsewhere, because if the mass murder did not take place, critics of such deployments could argue that it would not have taken place anyway, and that the preventive deployment was unnecessary. A success could beget future failure because arguing why something did not happen is always a tricky affair. I can think of no easy way out of these conundrums.

55. By these criteria, the United States was correct not to have intervened in Chechnya (which would have provoked a great-power war with Russia); correct not to have intervened in Algeria (where a well-armed military government faced a fundamentalist group also well armed and engaging in terror killings); and wrong not to have intervened in Rwanda, as I explain in the text. Bosnia was a case where American strategic interests were also at risk (discussed below), and therefore it was correct for the United States to intervene, although it should have done so earlier. Burundi would be a difficult case because, as Kelly Greenhill shows, a force of 25,000 Americans would be required simply to enforce a ceasefire that had been agreed to by both parties. If forcible entry were required, the number of troops required would increase dramatically, and so, too, would American casualties, especially if one or both belligerent parties resorted to guerilla warfare against American troops. See Greenhill, "Mission Impossible."

56. Gerard Prunier, *The Rwanda Crisis: History of a Genocide* (New York: Columbia University Press, 1995), is the definitive account of this sad episode. See also Bruce D. Jones, "Military Intervention in Rwanda's 'Two Wars': Partisanship and Indifference," in Barbara F. Walter and Jack Snyder, eds., *Civil Wars, Insecurity, and Intervention* (New York: Columbia University Press, 1999), pp. 116–146; and Astri Suhrke and Bruce Jones, "Preventive Diplomacy in Rwanda: Failure to Act or Failure of Actions?" in Bruce W. Jentleson, ed., *Opportunities Missed, Opportunities Seized: Preventive Diplomacy in the Post–Cold War World* (Lanham, Md.: Rowman and Littlefield, 2000), pp. 238–265.

57. The United Nations, *Report of the Independent Inquiry into the Actions of the United Nations during the 1994 Genocide in Rwanda*, December 15, 1999, p. 35, <www.un.org/News/ossg/rwanda_report.htm>. Alan Kuperman points out, however, that there had been many previous false alarms about a pending genocidal campaign, which is one of the reasons why officials in Western capitals discounted these warnings. Western officials also tended to discount the most proximate warnings because they believed that if the civil war in Rwanda started up again, the Hutus would devote their military resources to fighting the Tutsi invasion force, not to killing Tutsi civilians. Rwanda can be seen as a classic intelligence failure: the signals for pending genocide were there, but there were also reasonable grounds for discounting them. See Kuperman, *The Limits of Humanitarian Intervention*, chap. 9. For the argument that the United States was forewarned in early April that a lot of killing would happen, see Samantha Powers, "Bystanders to Genocide: Why the United States Let the Rwandan Tragedy Happen," *The Atlantic Monthly*, September 2001, <www.theatlantic.com/issues/2001/09/power.htm>; and declassified documents on Rwanda at the National Security Archive at <www.nsarchive.org/NSAEBB/NSAEBB53/press.html>.

58. Kuperman, "Rwanda in Retrospect," pp. 105–106 and 116; and Kuperman, *The Limits of Humanitarian Intervention*, p. 108. He takes issue with Scott Feil, who argues that if 5,000 troops had been sent sometime between April 7 and April 21, 1994, that would have been sufficient to have "stemmed the violence in and around the capital, prevented its spread to

the countryside, and created conditions conducive to the cessation of the civil war." See Scott R. Feil, *Preventing Genocide: How the Early Use of Force Might Have Succeeded in Rwanda* (New York: Carnegie Corporation, April 1998), p. 3. Kuperman points out that the killing was so rapid that most of the deaths would have occurred before such a force could have been deployed.

59. Valentino, *Final Solutions*, p. 270. In the other seven cases that Valentino studied in detail, ordinary civilians played little or no role in the mass killings. See also Valentino, "Final Solutions: The Causes of Mass Killing and Genocide," *Security Studies*, Vol. 9, No. 3 (Spring 2000), pp. 1–60.

60. Personal conversation with Alan Kuperman.

61. Seybolt argues that Rwanda would not have been an easy case, in large part because the Tutsi Rwandan Patriotic Front would have opposed the foreign intervention. See Seybolt, "Eyes Wide Open," pp. 4–12.

62. See John Mueller, "The Banality of 'Ethnic War'," *International Security*, Vol. 25, No. 1 (Summer 2000), pp. 42–71.

63. Seybolt, "Eyes Wide Open," pp. 12–19, explains why a decapitation strike against the leaders of the Rwandan genocide would have been an extremely difficult and dangerous operation.

64. A good short overview of U.S. and Western policy toward the breakup of Yugoslavia is found in Ivo H. Daalder, "Fear and Loathing in the Former Yugoslavia," in Michael E. Brown, ed., *The International Dimensions of Internal Conflict* (Cambridge, Mass.: MIT Press, 1996), pp. 35–69. Detailed histories can be found in Steven L. Burg and Paul S. Shoup, *The War in Bosnia-Herzegovina: Ethnic Conflict and International Intervention* (Armonk, N.Y.: M.E. Sharpe, 1999); Susan L. Woodward, *Balkan Tragedy: Chaos and Dissolution after the Cold War* (Washington, D.C.: The Brookings Institution, 1995), esp. chaps. 6, 9, and 11; and James Gow, *Triumph of the Lack of Will: International Diplomacy and the Yugoslav War* (New York: Columbia University Press, 1997).

65. Ivo H. Daalder, *Getting to Dayton* (Washington, D.C.: Brookings Institution Press, 2000), p. 164. Also see Richard Holbrooke, *To End A War* (New York: Random House, 1998), pp. 65–75 and 359–360.

66. For an account of American and NATO policy in the Kosovo war, see Daalder and O'Hanlon, *Winning Ugly*. For an insider's account of American decision making and American-European interactions on Kosovo in 1998–99, see James P. Rubin, "Kosovo: The Inside Story," *Financial Times Weekend*, Part 1, (September 30/October 1, 2000); and Part 2 (October 7/8, 2000).

67. The debate over globalization and its effects on state power is a charged one. Among those who argue that the state is losing out to the market and other forces, see Susan Strange, *The Retreat of the State: The Diffusion of Power in the World Economy* (Cambridge: Cambridge University Press, 1996); William Greider, *One World, Ready or Not: The Manic Logic of Global Capitalism* (New York: Simon and Schuster, 1997); and Thomas L. Friedman, *The Lexus and the Olive Tree: Understanding Globalization* (New York: Farrar Straus and Giroux, 1999). For the contrary view, see Robert Wade, "Globalization and Its Limits: Reports of the Death of the National Economy are Greatly Exaggerated," in Suzanne Berger and Ronald Dore, eds., *National Diversity and Global Capitalism* (Ithaca, N.Y.: Cornell University Press, 1996), pp. 60–89; Robert G. Gilpin, "No One Loves a Political Realist," *Security Studies*, Vol. 5, No. 3 (Spring 1996), pp. 3–26; Kenneth N. Waltz, "Globalization and Governance," *PS: Political Science and Politics*, Vol. 32, No. 4 (December 1999), pp. 693–701; Linda Weiss, *The Myth of the Powerless State* (Ithaca, N.Y.: Cornell University Press, 1998), esp. chaps. 6 and 7; and Paul Hirst and Grahame Thompson, *Globalization in Question: The International Economy and the Possibilities of Governance* (Cambridge, U.K.: Polity Press, 1996).

68. For the argument that global capitalism rests on political foundations and that these foundations have eroded since the end of the Cold War, see Robert Gilpin, *The Challenge of Global Capitalism: The World Economy in the 21st Century* (Princeton, N.J.: Princeton University Press, 2000).

69. See Samuel P. Huntington, *The Clash of Civilizations and the Remaking of World Order* (New York: Simon and Schuster, 1996). For a perceptive critique of Huntington's views, see

Stephen M. Walt, "Building Up New Bogeymen," *Foreign Policy*, No. 106 (Spring 1997), pp. 177–189.

70. Kenneth N. Waltz, *Theory of International Politics* (Reading, Mass.: Addison-Wesley, 1979), p. 210. Waltz was speaking of economic matters in this passage, but it is equally applicable to military and political matters. On the need for American leadership, also see Richard N. Haass, *The Reluctant Sheriff: The United States after the Cold War* (New York: Council on Foreign Relations, 1997).

71. Joseph S. Nye, Jr., "Redefining the National Interest," *Foreign Affairs*, Vol. 78, No. 4 (July/August 1999), pp. 27–28.

72. In hindsight, the outcome of World War II looks inevitable. It was not. For a superb analysis of why an allied loss was closer than commonly thought, see Richard Overy, *Why the Allies Won* (New York: W.W. Norton, 1995).

73. See Cindy Williams, ed., *Holding the Line: U.S. Defense Alternatives for the Early 21ˢᵗ Century*, (Cambridge, Mass.: MIT Press, 2001), "Introduction," especially pp. 14–15, "Conclusion," and Table 9.1, pp. 260–261; and Congressional Budget Office, *Budgeting for Defense: Maintaining Today's Forces* (Washington, D.C.: U.S. Government Printing Office, 2000), p. xiii and Summary Table 3 (p. xii).

74. A different sort of calculation would yield a smaller cost for selective engagement. America's forward-deployed forces constitute about 18 percent of its total active-duty forces. A simple calculation, then, is to take 18 percent of the FY 2000 defense budget of about $300 billion; this yields a cost of $54 billion to run a selective engagement strategy.

75. I am indebted to Cindy Williams for suggesting these points.

76. See Office of the Under Secretary of Defense (Comptroller), *National Defense Budget Estimates for Fiscal Year 2003*, March 2002, Table 7.7, p. 216, at <www.dtie.mil/comptroller/fy2001budget>.

77. This paragraph has benefited from Peter Liberman, "Will Germany and Japan Rely Too Much on the United States?" *Security Studies*, Vol. 10, No. 2 (Winter 2000/2001), pp. 98–139; Stephen M. Walt, "Why Alliances Endure or Collapse," *Survival*, Vol. 39, No. 1 (Spring 1997), pp. 156–180; Patricia A. Weitsman, "Intimate Enemies: The Politics of Peacetime Alliances," *Security Studies*, Vol. 7, No. 1 (Autumn 1997), pp. 156–194; and Glenn H. Snyder, *Alliance Politics*, chap. 9.

78. Snyder, *Alliance Politics*, p. 192.

79. For the view that commitments inevitably become open-ended, see Christopher Layne, "From Preponderance to Offshore Balancing: America's Future Grand Strategy," *International Security*, Vol. 22, No. 1 (Summer 1997), pp. 98–102.

80. Good analyses of the Somalia intervention can be found in John L. Hirsch and Robert B. Oakley, *Somalia and Operation Restore Hope: Reflections on Peacemaking and Peacekeeping* (Washington, D.C.: United States Institute of Peace Press, 1995); and Nora Bensahel, "The Coalition Paradox: The Politics of Military Cooperation," chap. 4 (Ph.D. Dissertation, Stanford University, August 1999); Nora Bensahel, "Humanitarian Relief and Nation Building in Somalia," in Robert J. Art and Patrick M. Cronin, eds., *The United States and Coercive Diplomacy* (Washington, D.C.: United States Institute of Peace Press, 2003); and Kenneth Menkhaus and Louis Ortmayer, "Somalia: Misread Crises and Missed Opportunities," in Bruce W. Jentleson, *Preventive Diplomacy in the Post–Cold War World* (Lanham, Md.: Rowman and Littlefield, 2000), pp. 211–238.

81. For an argument that states will not soon balance against the United States because its lead is too overwhelming, see William C. Wohlforth, "The Stability of a Unipolar World," *International Security*, Vol. 24, No. 1 (Summer 1999), pp. 5–41; and William C. Wohlforth, "U.S. Strategy in a Unipolar World," in John G. Ikenberry, ed., *American Unrivaled: The Future of the Balance of Power* (Ithaca, N.Y.: Cornell University Press, 2002), pp. 98–118. For the argument that other states already are balancing against the United States, see Kenneth N. Waltz, "Structural Realism after the Cold War," *International Security*, Vol. 24, No. 1 (Summer 2000), pp. 27–39.

82. For the pure structuralist view, see Waltz, *Theory of International Politics*, esp. chaps. 6–8; and John J. Mearsheimer, *The Tragedy of Great Power Politics* (New York: W.W. Norton, 2001),

esp. chaps. 2 and 3. For the qualified structuralist view, see Stephen M. Walt, *The Origins of Alliances* (Ithaca, N.Y.: Cornell University Press, 1987), esp. chap. 2. For a sensible analysis of the conditions under which power considerations matter a lot or only a little, see Joseph M. Grieco, "Understanding the Problem of International Cooperation: The Limits of Neoliberal Institutionalism and the Future of Realist Theory," in David A. Baldwin, ed., *Neoliberalism and Neorealism: The Contemporary Debate* (New York: Columbia University Press, 1993), pp. 312–328.

83. For a perceptive elaboration of this point, see Josef Joffe, "How America Does It," *Foreign Affairs*, Vol. 76, No. 5 (September/October 1997), pp. 1–28.

84. There are those who argue that the United States cannot muster a coherent grand strategy in the absence of a clear geostrategic threat of the kind constituted by the Soviet Union. See Robert Jervis, "U.S. Grand Strategy: Mission Impossible," *Naval War College Review*, Vol. 51, No. 3 (Summer 1998), pp. 22–36.

85. Quoted in Thucydides, *History of the Peloponnesian War*, trans. Rex Warner (New York: Penguin Books, 1972), p. 22 (Book One, paragraph 144). The full passage is as follows: "I could give you many other reasons why you should feel confident in ultimate victory, if only you will make up your minds not to add to the empire while the war is in progress, and not to go out of your way to involve yourselves in new perils. What I fear is not the enemy's strategy, but our own mistakes." Ibid.

Five: Isolationism and Offshore Balancing

1. For the intellectual origins of Washington's Farewell Address, see Felix Gilbert, *To the Farewell Address: Ideas of Early American Foreign Policy* (Princeton, N.J.: Princeton University Press, 1961), especially chap. 5. For the polarizing effects of foreign policy on domestic politics, see Joseph Charles, *The Origins of the American Party System* (New York: Harper and Row, 1961). For the Monroe Doctrine, see Samuel Flagg Bemis, *John Quincy Adams and the Foundations of American Foreign Policy* (New York: Knopf, 1949); and Ernest R. May, *The Making of the Monroe Doctrine* (Cambridge, Mass.: Harvard University Press 1975).

2. Good histories of isolationism in twentieth century are Selig Adler, *The Isolationist Impulse: Its Twentieth Century Reaction* (New York: Collier Books, 1961); and Manfred Jonas, *Isolationism in America, 1935–1941* (Ithaca, N.Y.: Cornell University Press, 1966). For Roosevelt's conception of the United Nations, see Alexander George, "Domestic Constraints on Regime Change in U.S. Foreign Policy: The Need for Legitimacy," in John G. Ikenberry, ed., *American Foreign Policy: Theoretical Essays* (Glenview, Ill.: Scott, Foresman, 1989), pp. 587–598; and Warren F. Kimball, *The Juggler: Franklin Roosevelt as Wartime Statesman* (Princeton, N.J.: Princeton University Press, 1991). For the Truman Administration's exaggeration of the threat, see Thomas J. Christensen, *Useful Adversaries: Grand Strategy, Domestic Mobilization, and Sino-American Conflict, 1947–1958* (Princeton, N.J.: Princeton University Press, 1996).

3. William Schneider, "The Old Politics and the New World Order," in Kenneth A. Oye, Robert J. Lieber, and Donald Rothchild, eds., *Eagle in a New World: American Grand Strategy in the Post–Cold War Era* (New York: HarperCollins, 1992), p. 40.

4. In the following discussion of isolationism's essence and assumptions, I have drawn from the works of those whom I consider to be the best representatives of the isolationist position. Listed in chronological order since 1945, they are: Senator Robert A. Taft, *A Foreign Policy for Americans* (Garden City: Doubleday, 1952); Robert W. Tucker, *A New Isolationism: Threat or Promise?* (New York: Universe Books, 1972); Eric A. Nordlinger, *Isolationism Reconfigured: American Foreign Policy for a New Century* (Princeton, N.J.: Princeton University Press, 1995); and Eugene Gholz, Daryl Press, and Harvey Sapolsky, "Come Home America: The Strategy of Restraint in the Face of Temptation," *International Security*, Vol. 21, No. 4 (Spring 1997), pp. 1–43. Gholz, Press, and Sapolsky are not pure isolationists; they accept the importance of secure access to Persian Gulf oil and are willing to have a small American military presence in the Gulf. I include them in the isolationist position because of the powerful arguments they offer in general support of it.

5. Taft, *A Foreign Policy for Americans*, p. 12 (emphasis added).

6. An isolationist strategy would not rule out the U.S. navy patrolling the seas and showing its presence around the world. It would, however, rule out a constant U.S. presence in any given place, and permanent overseas bases.

7. See Nordlinger, *Isolationism Reconfigured*, chap. 3.

8. Ibid., pp. 151–152. Although he is not an isolationist, Richard Betts makes the same point. See Richard K. Betts, "The New Threat of Mass Destruction," *Foreign Affairs*, Vol. 77, No. 1 (January/February 1998), p. 41.

9. On these points, see Nordlinger, *Isolationism Reconfigured*, chap. 11.

10. Although he not an isolationist but rather an offshore balancer, Layne makes this point forcefully. See Christopher Layne, "The Unipolar Illusion: Why New Great Powers Will Rise," *International Security*, Vol. 17, No. 4 (Spring 1993), pp. 41–51.

11. Taft, *A Foreign Policy for Americans*, especially chaps. 1 and 6. Nordlinger argues that the United States could have withdrawn its troops from Europe by the late 1950s, after Europe had regained its economic health; he thereby implicitly agrees that the United States needed to defend Europe from the Soviet Union before that time. Nordlinger, *Isolationism Reconfigured*, pp. 65 ff. Bruce Russett makes the strongest isolationist case when he argues that the United States did not need to fight in Europe in World War II because the Soviet Union and Nazi Germany would have fought one another to a stalemate and Germany would not have conquered Britain. All the United States had to do, Russett argues, was to continue to supply economic aid and military matériel to Britain and the Soviet Union. Bruce M. Russett, *No Clear and Present Danger: A Skeptical View of the U.S. Entry into World War II* (New York: Harper and Row, 1972), chaps. 2 and 4.

12. The best representatives of the offshore balancing strategy are Christopher Layne, Ted Carpenter, and John Mearsheimer. See Christopher Layne, "The Unipolar Illusion," pp. 5–52; Christopher Layne, "From Preponderance to Offshore Balancing: America's Future Grand Strategy," *International Security*, Vol. 22, No. 1 (Summer 1997), pp. 1–39; Ted Galen Carpenter, *A Search For Enemies: America's Alliances After the Cold War* (Washington, D.C.: Cato Institute, 1992); Ted Galen Carpenter, *Beyond NATO: Staying Out of Europe's Wars* (Washington, D.C.: Cato Institute, 1994); John J. Mearsheimer, "The Future of the American Pacifier," *Foreign Affairs*, Vol. 80, No. 5 (September/October 2001), pp. 46–61; and John J. Mearsheimer, *The Tragedy of Great Power Politics* (New York: W.W. Norton, 2001), chaps. 7 and 10.

13. Geopolitical analysis became popular at the turn of the twentieth century, especially in Germany, Great Britain, and the United States. Probably the most influential article on geopolitics ever written is Halford J. Mackinder, "The Geographical Pivot of History," *The Geographical Journal*, Vol. 23, No. 4 (April 1904), pp. 421–437. Mackinder did not invent geopolitics (the Swedish political scientist Rudolf Kjellén did), but Mackinder is its most famous exponent. For more about the geopolitical mode of analysis, see Paul Kennedy, *The Rise and Fall of the Great Powers: Economic Change and Military Conflict, 1500–2000* (New York: Random House, 1987), pp. 86–100; Paul Kennedy, "Mahan versus Mackinder: Two Interpretations of British Seapower," in Paul Kennedy, *Strategy and Diplomacy, 1870–1945* (London: Allen and Unwin/Fontana, 1984), pp. 41–87; Daniel Deudney, "Geopolitics and Change," in Michael W. Doyle and G. John Ikenberry, eds., *New Thinking in International Relations Theory* (Boulder, Colo.: Westview Press, 1997), pp. 91–124, especially 91–100; and Geoffrey Parker, *Western Geopolitical Thought in the Twentieth Century* (London: Croom Helm, 1985).

14. The best analyses of the geopolitical bases of American security in the pre-nuclear age are to be found in Nicholas J. Spykman, *America's Strategy in World Politics: The United States and the Balance of Power* (New York: Harcourt, Brace, 1942), especially chaps. 2, 3, 14 and 15; and Walter Lippmann, *U.S. Foreign Policy: Shield of the Republic* (Boston: Little, Brown, 1943), especially Part 1. For an excellent statement about the importance to America's security of the balance of power on the Eurasian land mass, see Stephen M. Walt, "The Case for Finite Containment: Analyzing U.S. Grand Strategy," *International Security*, Vol. 14, No. 1 (Summer 1989), pp. 5–49.

15. For American diplomacy during the early period, see Max Savelle, "Colonial Origins of American Diplomatic Principles," *Pacific Historical Review*, Vol. 3 (1934), pp. 334–350; Max

Savelle, *The Origins of American Diplomacy* (New York: Macmillan, 1967), chaps. 17–19; Gilbert, *To The Farewell Address;* Samuel Flagg Bemis, *A Diplomatic History of the United States,* 5th ed. (New York: Holt, Rinehart and Winston, 1965), chaps. 1, 7, 9, and 10.

16. The three exceptions are Spain's reincorporation of the Dominican Republic into the Spanish empire in 1861; Napoleon III's conquest of Mexico in the name of collecting debts that Mexico owed to France, Spain, and Britain; and Britain's temptation to back the South and thus permanently diminish America's power by helping divide it. These were all short-lived threats. The Spanish voluntarily withdrew in 1865 after the Dominicans revolted. The French agreed to withdraw their troops from Mexico in 1867 after General Grant sent General Sheridan with 50,000 troops to the Texas border. The British decided against recognition of the South as an independent nation after the North stalemated Lee's invasion of Maryland at the battle of Antietam Creek in September 1862. See Thomas A. Bailey, *A Diplomatic History of the American People,* 8th ed. (New York: Appleton-Century-Crofts, 1969), chaps. 22–24.

17. Kennedy, *The Rise and Fall of the Great Powers,* p. 202; and Jeffrey Madrick, *The End of Affluence: The Causes and Consequences of America's Economic Dilemma* (New York: Random House, 1995), pp. 40–41. America's economic growth between 1880 and 1913 was phenomenal: in 1880 it produced only 14.7 percent of the world's manufacturing output, but by 1913 it produced 32 percent, more than doubling its share in thirty-three years.

18. Figures are from the Correlates of War (COW) Project data base, April 1994 (ICPSR No. 9905), Inter-University Consortium for Political and Social Research (ICPSR), University of Michigan.

19. See Harold and Margaret Sprout, *The Rise of American Naval Power, 1776–1918* (Princeton, N.J.: Princeton University Press, 1967), p. 180.

20. For a full analysis of the nature of Britain's imperialism and its imperial grand strategy in the nineteenth century, see D.K. Fieldhouse, "Imperialism: An Historiographical Revision," *The Economic History Review,* Second Series, Vol. 14, No. 2 (1961), pp. 187–209; John Gallagher and Ronald Robinson, "The Imperialism of Free Trade," *The Economic History Review,* Second Series, Vol. 6, No. 1 (1953), pp. 1–15; Robinson and Gallagher, *Africa and the Victorians: The Official Mind of British Imperialism* (London: Macmillan, 1961); and C.J. Lowe, *The Reluctant Imperialists: British Foreign Policy, 1878–1902* (New York: Macmillan, 1969). For how British seapower protected the United States, see Spykman, *America's Strategy in World Politics,* pp. 68–89.

21. For British strategy at the end of the nineteenth century, see George Monger, *End of Isolation: British Foreign Policy, 1900–1907* (London: T. Nelson, 1963); and John A.S. Grenville, *Lord Salisbury and Foreign Policy* (London: Athlone Press, University of London, 1964).

22. Edward Rhodes, "Explaining Strategic Choices in the 1890s," *Security Studies,* Vol. 5, No. 4 (Summer 1996), pp. 79–82.

23. The figures on warship tonnage and number of ships come from Rhodes, "Explaining Strategic Choices in the 1890s," pp. 123–124; George T. Davis, *A Navy Second to None: The Development of Modern American Naval Policy* (New York: Harcourt, Brace, 1940), pp. 87, 251, and 268; Kennedy, *Rise and Fall of the Great Powers,* pp. 200–203, 243; and Paul Kennedy, *The Rise and Fall of British Naval Mastery* (New York: Scribners, 1976), p. 263.

24. Still the best book on the defensive nature of America's expansion during this period is John A.S. Grenville and George Berkeley Young, *Politics, Strategy, and American Diplomacy: Studies in Foreign Policy, 1873–1917* (New Haven: Yale University Press, 1966), especially chaps. 3, 4, 7, and 8. Also useful are J.A.S. Grenville, "Diplomacy and War Plans in the United States, 1890–1917," in Paul M. Kennedy, ed., *The War Plans of the Great Powers, 1880–1914* (Boston: Allen and Unwin, 1985), pp. 1–23; Davis, *A Navy Second to None,* esp. chaps. 4–7; Margaret Leech, *In the Days of McKinley* (New York: Harper and Row, 1959), chaps. 7, 9, and 11; Richard D. Challenger, *Admirals, Generals, and American Foreign Policy* (Princeton, N.J.: Princeton University Press, 1973); and Allan R. Millett and Peter Maslowski, *For the Common Defense: A Military History of the United States* (New York: Free Press, 1994), chap. 10.

25. Challenger, *Admirals, Generals, and American Foreign Policy,* pp. 68–69.

26. Grenville and Young, *Politics, Strategy, and American Diplomacy,* p. 7.

27. Ibid., pp. 7–8. This passage is taken from the *Congressional Record*, February 16, 1887.

28. For a good overview of why the United States worried about German designs in the Caribbean and Japanese designs on Hawaii, see Davis, *A Navy Second to None*, pp. 114–134. For good analyses of why the United States and Britain developed close relations after 1895 but why the United States and Germany did not, see Stephen R. Rock, *Why Peace Breaks Out: Great Power Rapprochement in Historical Perspective* (Chapel Hill: University of North Carolina Press, 1989); and Manfred Jonas, *The United States and Germany: A Diplomatic History* (Ithaca, N.Y.: Cornell University Press, 1984), chaps. 24.

29. The objective need for the United States to take defensive actions in the Caribbean and in Hawaii is subject to debate. Russell Weigley, Edward Rhodes, and Fareed Zakaria all downplay the threats. All three have valid points to make, but in my judgment they underestimate the preventive and defensive nature of America's actions in the Caribbean and towards Hawaii. The preventive motive was powerful in these two areas because, even if no threat was then objectively present, there is substantial evidence of perceptions of potential threats. The issue, moreover, was not the threat of an invading armada from Eurasia, but rather the fear that a militarily strong great power from outside the western hemisphere could establish military bases in former Spanish territories if the United States did not take them first. Similarly with Hawaii: it was thought better to seize it first than to allow a potentially hostile power to establish itself there and create a military base. At the deepest level, what was at work during this period within the United States was what had already saturated European politics and infected Japan: a highly competitive, Darwinist mode of thinking about international politics, which could and did justify territorial grabs and the building of large battle fleets for both defensive and offensive reasons. America's imperialism at this time exhibited both aspects: largely defensive in the Caribbean and Hawaii, and mostly offensive in the Philippines, Guam, and the China market. At root, America's imperialism at this time was a product of changes in material conditions (European imperialism and the building of large navies) and in what Rhodes and Zakaria both see as a changed understanding of the nature of the international game. Without the change in conditions, however, it is not evident that the understanding would have altered. See Russell F. Weigley, *The American Way of War: A History of United States Military Policy* (New York: Macmillan, 1973), p. 169; Rhodes, "Explaining Strategic Choices in the 1890s"; and Fareed Zakaria, *From Wealth to Power: The Unusual Origins of America's World Role* (Princeton, N.J.: Princeton University Press, 1998).

30. Wilson quoted in Daniel Patrick Moynihan, "The Peace Dividend," *The New York Review of Books*, June 18, 1990, p. 4 (emphasis added.) Wilson's sentiments in this speech presage the warnings about the military-industrial complex that President Eisenhower issued forty years later in his farewell address.

31. See, on the Cold War period, Aaron Friedberg, "Why Didn't the United States Become a Garrison State?" *International Security*, Vol. 16, No. 4 (Spring 1992), pp. 109–142.

32. The most comprehensive account of German-American interactions over submarine warfare can be found in Ernest R. May, *The World War and American Isolation, 1914–1917* (Cambridge, Mass.: Harvard University Press, 1959), especially chaps. 7, 9, 18–19. The best short overview of these interactions, as well as of Wilson's diplomacy before, during, and after the war, remains Arthur S. Link, *Woodrow Wilson—Revolution, War, and Peace* (Wheeling, Ill.: Harlan Davidson, 1979; first published in 1957).

33. Link, *Woodrow Wilson*, pp. 71 and 23.

34. Ibid., p. 75. Bismarck had seized Alsace-Lorraine from France after Prussia defeated it in the 1870 Franco-Prussian War, and thus Wilson's reference to a peace with "no Alsace-Lorraine in it" meant a peace that would not create a revanchist state that would seek to take back territory lost in war.

35. Wilson never used the phrase "collective security" in describing the deterrent function of the League of Nations, but spoke instead of "a community of power" to replace the balance of power. Good analyses of the origins of the League idea and Wilson's views on its functions are Edward H. Buehrig, *Woodrow Wilson and the Balance of Power* (Gloucester, Mass.: Peter Smith, 1968), pp. 170–211 and 260–275; and Thomas J. Knock, *To End All Wars:*

Woodrow Wilson and the Quest for a New World Order (New York: Oxford University Press, 1992), pp. 111–114, 127, and 152–153.

36. This scenario comes close to the provocative one presented in Russett, *No Clear and Present Danger,* chap. 2.

37. See Robert Dallek, *Franklin Roosevelt and American Foreign Policy, 1932–1945* (New York: Oxford University Press, 1979), p. 233. For a full analysis of Hitler's intentions towards the western hemisphere, see Alton Frye, *Nazi Germany and the American Hemisphere, 1933–1941* (New Haven: Yale University Press, 1967), pp. 168–186.

38. Walter Lippmann, *U.S. War Aims* (Boston: Little, Brown, 1944), p. 53.

39. See Spykman, *America's Strategy in World* Politics, chaps. 10–16, and the conclusion. In his day, Spykman was the most prominent American practitioner of the geopolitical school of analysis. For his predictions of the shape of the future when America's victory was no longer in doubt, see Nicholas John Spykman, *The Geography of the Peace* (New York: Harcourt, Brace, 1944).

40. A blockade prevents goods from either entering or leaving the state being blockaded and thus affects both the imports and exports of a given state. An embargo prevents goods from leaving other states if they are destined to go to the country in question; it is thus directed only against the given state's imports. Thus, under a blockade, goods are intercepted; under an embargo, no interception is necessary because the goods do not leave their point of origin.

41. See the maps following pp. 414 and 424 in Spykman, *America's Strategy in World Politics.*

42. Ibid., p. 412.

43. Spykman defined categories of raw materials, following the classification used by the Army-Navy Munitions Board in its 1939 report, as strategic, critical, and those neither strategic nor critical. Critical materials were those that, while essential to defense, were less important to the war effort and could be produced domestically, and for which conservation would help assure adequate supplies. The third category consisted of goods for which no supply problems were envisioned. See ibid., p. 293.

44. Ibid., p. 454.

45. Ibid., p. 456.

46. Retrospective analysis shows that Spykman was wrong: the United States could have mounted an indefinite defense of the quarter-sphere. The United States was self-sufficient at the time in food and energy. Thus, Spykman's case for economic strangulation rests on two points: first, that America lacked sufficient domestic reserves of the eleven minerals that the 1939 Army-Navy Munitions Board report termed strategic—those raw materials without which the war effort would have failed—and second, that there were insufficient amounts of them within the quarter-sphere. Careful calculations show that neither was the case at the time. Through a variety of measures—substitution, synthetic production, expanded domestic production, conservation, recycling, and imports from elsewhere in the quarter-sphere—the United States could have acquired sufficient amounts of these eleven raw materials to fuel a vast military machine indefinitely. The only potential exception may have been tin, but even here conservation, recycling, and substitution would probably have sufficed, as well as seizure and stockpiling of Bolivian tin before Bolivia fell to the Germans. For more detail on why the quarter-sphere would have been economically viable, see Robert J. Art, "Geopolitics Reconsidered: The United States and the Eurasian Balance of Power, 1890–1945," unpublished ms., June 1998.

47. Those who argue that Roosevelt provoked Japan to launch its surprise attack on Pearl Harbor in order to get the United States into the European war have the story wrong. They are correct as to the consequences of Pearl Harbor, but wrong about Roosevelt's preferences. For the view that Roosevelt deliberately provoked the Japanese attack, see Charles A. Beard, *President Roosevelt and the Coming of the War, 1941: A Study in Appearances and Realities* (New Haven: Yale University Press, 1948), esp. chap. 14; C.C. Tansill, *Back Door to War: The Roosevelt Foreign Policy, 1933–1941* (Chicago: H. Regnery, 1952); and Harry Elmer Barnes, ed., *Perpetual War for Perpetual Peace* (Caldwell, Id.: Caxton Printers, 1953).

48. For Japan's calculations about war with the United States, see Michael A. Barnhart, *Japan Prepares for Total War: The Search for Economic Security, 1919–1941* (Ithaca, N.Y.: Cornell University Press, 1987), chaps. 11–14. For Hitler's calculations about war with the United States, see Norman Rich, *Hitler's War Aims: Ideology, the Nazi State, and the Course of Expansion* (New York: W.W. Norton, 1973), chap. 20; and Gerhard L. Weinberg, *Germany, Hitler, and World War II* (Cambridge: Cambridge University Press, 1995), chap. 15.

49. By my count, the nine minor European wars among the great powers were: the Russo-Turkish War of 1806–1812, the Russo-Turkish War of 1828–29, the Roman Republic War of 1849, the War of Italian Unification (1859), the Second Schleswig-Holstein War (1864), the Seven Weeks War of 1866 (largely between Prussia and Austria-Hungary, although Italy fought with the former against the latter), the Franco-Prussian War of 1870–71, the Russo-Turkish War of 1877–78, and the Italo-Turkish War of 1911–1912. Some of the "small" great-power wars produced significant casualties: 285,000 in the 1877–78 Russo-Turkish War, comparable to 264,000 deaths in the Crimean War, the least destructive of the major great-power wars for which we have reliable records. The wars and their participants are found in data from the Correlates of War (COW) Project database, April 1994 (ICPSR No. 9905), Inter-University Consortium for Political and Social Research, University of Michigan; and Jack Levy, *War in the Modern Great Power System, 1495–1975* (Lexington: University of Kentucky Press, 1983), pp. 72–73. Battle deaths come from the COW data.

50. See Eugene Gholz and Daryl G. Press, "The Effects of Wars on Neutral Countries: Why It Doesn't Pay to Preserve The Peace," *Security Studies*, Vol. 10, No. 4 (Summer 2001), pp. 37–42. For America's involvement in the clash between Napoleon's continental system and the British continental blockade, see William E. Lingelbach, "England and Neutral Trade," *Military Historian and Economist*, Vol. 2 (1917), pp. 153–178; and Alfred W. Crosby, Jr., *America, Russia, Hemp, and Napoleon: American Trade with Russia and the Baltic, 1783–1812* (Columbus: Ohio State University Press, 1965). For World War I, the classic treatment is Charles A. Beard, *The Devil Theory of War: An Inquiry into the Nature of History and the Possibility of Keeping Out of War* (New York: Vanguard, 1936).

51. Press Conference, No. 537, April 8, 1939, cited in *Complete Presidential Press Conferences of Franklin D. Roosevelt* (New York: Da Capo Press, 1972), Vol. 13, pp. 258–262. William Clayton, a prominent member of the Roosevelt Administration, summarized the matter more succinctly: "Standing alone in a hostile world, with our foreign trade destroyed, with the colossal readjustments this would entail, and with the enormous sacrifice imposed by total defense, the strain on our traditional way of life would probably be too great." Quoted in Jonathan G. Utley, *Going to War with Japan, 1937–1941* (Knoxville: University of Tennessee Press, 1985), p. 87.

52. After World War II, America's next costliest interstate war was the Vietnam War, with 47,000 dead and 315,000 wounded. Figures are rounded and are from Millett and Maslowski, *For the Common Defense*, p. 653.

Six: Selective Engagement and the Free Hand Strategies

1. See, for example, Ted Galen Carpenter, "Closing the Nuclear Umbrella," *Foreign Affairs*, Vol. 73, No. 2 (March/April 1994), pp. 8–14. There is, of course an inconsistency between this view and the first one. If America's nuclear forces are sufficient to deter nuclear and other attacks on the continental United States, then involvement in regional conflicts should not put the American homeland at any additional risk. If nuclear deterrence works, then only those American forces in the region where there is war will be at risk.

2. Michael O'Hanlon, "A Flawed Masterpiece," *Foreign Affairs*, Vol. 81, No. 3 (May/June 2002), pp. 47–48.

3. Barry R. Posen, "The Struggle against Terrorism: Grand Strategy, Strategy, and Tactics," *International Security*, Vol. 26, No. 3 (Winter 2001/02), p. 43.

4. See Eric Nordlinger, *Isolationism Reconfigured: American Foreign Policy for a New Century* (Princeton, N.J.: Princeton University Press, 1995), pp. 151 ff; and Christopher Layne,

"Offshore Balancing Revisited," *The Washington Quarterly*, Vol. 25, No. 2 (Spring 2002), pp. 245–257.

5. Layne, "Offshore Balancing Revisited," p. 240.

6. Paul Pillar, *Terrorism and U.S. Foreign Policy* (Washington, D.C.: The Brookings Institution, 2001), p. 60 (emphasis in original).

7. Ibid., p. 62; and U.S. Department of State, *Patterns of Global Terrorism 2001*, May 2002, pp. xx and xxii.

8. See Mansoor Ijaz and R. James Woolsey, "How Secure Is Pakistan's Plutonium?" *New York Times*, November 28, 2001, p. A27.

9. The Central Command, with responsibility for the Middle East, has prepared what is described as "a sweeping contingency plan to move out of Saudi Arabia." The plan would relocate the advanced command and control center at Prince Sultan air base, along with dozens of fighter aircraft, at the Al Udeid air base in Qatar, which has "vast" hangar capacity and a 15,000-foot runway. See Elaine Sciolino with Eric Schmitt, "U.S. Rethinks Its Role in Saudi Arabia," *New York Times*, March 10, 2002, p. 10.

10. For a more comprehensive set of changes in American policy, see Stephen M. Walt, "Beyond Bin Laden: Reshaping U.S. Foreign Policy," *International Security*, Vol. 26, No. 3 (Winter 2001/02), pp. 64–77.

11. See Christopher Layne, "The Unipolar Illusion: Why New Great Powers Will Rise," *International Security*, Vol. 17, No. 4 (Spring 1993), pp. 47–49; Ted Galen Carpenter, *A Search for Enemies: America's Alliances after the Cold War* (Washington, D.C.: Cato Institute, 1992) p. 174; and John J. Mearsheimer, *The Tragedy of Great Power Politics* (New York: W. W. Norton, 2001), pp. 265–266 and 386–402.

12. See Eugene Gholz and Daryl G. Press, "The Effects of Wars on Neutral Countries: Why It Doesn't Pay to Preserve the Peace," *Security Studies*, Vol. 10, No. 4 (Summer 2001), pp. 1–60.

13. Ibid., pp. 32 and 41.

14. Ibid., pp. 52–53 and 55.

15. Gholz and Press calculate the cost of keeping Eurasia stable at $1.2 trillion dollars (2001 dollars) per decade, and the costs of a great-power war during such a decade at no more than $100 billion. The $1.2 trillion figure is based on their view that a defense budget that did not need to provide for forces to fight wars in Eurasia would cost $150 billion less than the 2001 defense budget, which was approximately $300 billion. Totaled over ten years, this amounts to the $1.2 trillion present net value figure, calculated with a 6 percent discount rate. Ibid., pp. 57–58. Their offshore balancing defense budget of $150 billion is $80–90 billion less than the budget I use, $230–240 billion as calculated both by Cindy Williams and by Barry Posen and Andrew Ross. See Cindy Williams, ed., *Holding the Line: U.S. Defense Alternatives for the Early 21ˢᵗ Century* (Cambridge, Mass.: MIT Press, 2000), pp. 14–15; Barry R. Posen and Andrew L. Ross, "Competing Visions for U.S. Grand Strategy," *International Security*, Vol. 21, No. 3 (Winter 1996/97), Table 2 (Force A and Force C), p. 10.

16. In an earlier draft of their article ("Economic Externalities of Foreign Wars"), Gholz and Press argued that the United States need not cease all trade with great-power belligerents in order to avoid being dragged into war, but that the goods sold to them should be carried on belligerents' ships, not American ships. In their view, what got the United States into World War I was not its trade with the British and the French per se, but rather the fact that the United States allowed goods bought by the British and French to be carried on American ships. Had the United States insisted that they carry the goods they had bought on their own ships, then the United States would not have come to blows with the Germans over their sinking of American ships. (In fact, however, as Ernest May records, "the largest part of America's expanding export trade continued to be carried in British and French ships." Ernest R. May, *The World War and American Isolationism, 1914–1917* [Cambridge, Mass.: Harvard University Press, 1959], p. 156.) Gholz and Press offer a logical and clever argument, but I remain dubious that it would be easy in any future great-power war to prevent American goods and American ships, or American aircraft, from being challenged, sunk, or

shot down by the belligerents. Not only would all American goods have to be shipped on belligerents' vessels, but American and other neutral ships and planes would have to stay well clear of the belligerents. This would not be as easy as Gholz and Press seem to think. During World War I, for example, the British resorted to disguising their ships as neutrals in an attempt to avoid German U-boat attacks, which is one of the reasons why the Germans attacked neutral shipping. See Charles Seymour, *American Neutrality during the World War* (Hamden, Conn.: Archon Books, 1964), pp. 59–60; and John W. Coogan, *The End of Neutrality: The United States, Britain, and Maritime Rights, 1899–1915* (Ithaca, N.Y.: Cornell University Press, 1981), p. 221. We could expect similar attempts by future belligerents, and no one could be certain that the ships flying American flags were truly neutral. Moreover, all American sea-borne trade would not cease, and therefore a belligerent could not know whether American goods would ultimately end up in its enemy's hands. Finally, belligerents, especially in an East Asian war scenario, would try to strike at one another's sea-borne energy supplies (oil). It does not take too much imagination to imagine that this could lead, for example, to clashes between the U.S. Seventh Fleet and belligerent navies in the South China Sea. Thus, one way or another, war-provoking incidents would occur, like those that occurred before World War I, when the United States tried to be neutral (in contrast to before World War II, when it was decidedly pro-British). The United States would not tolerate interference with freedom of the seas and its shipping. Although such incidents would not inevitably drag the United States into war, the point is that they could.

17. Gholz and Press dispute the analysis in this paragraph. See Gholz and Press, "The Effects of War on Neutral Countries," pp. 49–54.

18. The figure is actually somewhat less than this, because America's allies in Europe and East Asia have cost-sharing and offset agreements with the United States that, for example, amounted to $7.5 billion in 1998. See Report to the U.S. Congress by the Secretary of Defense, *Report on Allied Contributions to the Common Defense*, March 2000, p. III-27, available at <www.defenselink.gov>.

19. The Soviet Union ultimately fielded 900 MiG-15 fighters based in China against a U.S. force of 150 F-86s. The first U.S. combat with Soviet MiGs occurred on November 8, 1950, when Lt. Russell J. Brown shot down a MiG-15 in the first jet-fighter versus jet-fighter combat in history. See Walter J. Boyne, "The Forgotten War," *Air Force Magazine*, Vol. 83, No. 6 (June 2000), online.

20. Peter Lavoy cites reports from Pakistani and Indian journalists that each side lost more than 1,000 lives during the Kargil conflict. Peter Lavoy, "The Costs of Nuclear Weapons in South Asia," undated manuscript, p. 23, citing Raj Chengappa, "Kargil: Holding the Heights," *India Today*, August 16, 1999; and Rahul Bedi, "The Real Cost of Victory," *Asiaweek*, August 13, 1999. Information provided to me by Page Fortna of Columbia University cites a report from Agence France Press on May 30, 2000, which stated that more than 2,000 troops were killed in Kargil, and a report from Inter Press Service of January 26, 2000, that over 2,000 troops were killed in Kargil. See also Sumantra Bose, "Kashmir: Sources of Conflict, Dimensions of Peace," *Survival*, Vo. 41, No. 3 (Autumn 1999), p. 150; Waheguru Pal Singh Sindhu, "India's Nuclear Use Doctrine," in Peter R. Lavoy, Scott D. Sagan, and James J. Wirtz, *Planning the Unthinkable: How New Powers Will Use Nuclear, Biological, and Chemical Weapons* (Ithaca, N.Y.: Cornell University Press, 2000), pp. 142–145; Scott D. Sagan, "The Perils of Proliferation in South Asia," *Asian Survey*, Vol. 41, No. 6 (November/December 2001), pp. 1064–1086; and *The Kargil Committee Report—Executive Summary*, online at the Federation of American Scientists, at <www.fas.org/news/india/2000/25indi1.htm>.

21. See Bruce Riedel, *American Diplomacy and the 1999 Kargil Summit at Blair House* (Policy Paper Series, Center for the Advanced Study of India, University of Pennsylvania, 2000), pp. 9 and 12, at <www.sas.upenn.edu/casi/reports/RiedelPaper051302.pdf>.

22. See Marion Lloyd, "Soviets Close to Using A-Bomb in 1962 Crisis, Forum is Told," *Boston Globe*, October 13, 2002, reporting on the 2002 Havana conference on the Cuban Missile Crisis: "It was the most dangerous moment of the Cold War. At about 5 p.m. on Oct. 27, 1962, a Soviet submarine armed with a nuclear warhead found itself trapped and being

bombarded by a U.S. warship patrolling off Cuba. One of the Soviet captains gave the order to prepare to fire. But a cooler-headed officer persuaded him to wait for instructions from Moscow before unleashing a nuclear attack."

23. See Glenn H. Snyder, "The Balance of Power and the Balance of Terror," in Paul Seabury, ed., *The Balance of Power* (San Francisco: Chandler, 1965), pp. 198–199. Also see the discussion of the stability-instability paradox in Robert Jervis, *The Illogic of American Nuclear Strategy* (Ithaca, N.Y.: Cornell University Press, 1984), pp. 31–33 and 148–157.

24. Snyder, "The Balance of Power and the Balance of Terror," p. 199.

25. The first dynamic appears to have been in action during the Kargil crisis as viewed from Pakistan's vantage point. "Pakistani troops and Pakistan-supported guerillas were engaged in risky military actions in Kashmir during the Kargil conflict in summer of 1999 . . . . Pakistani officials appear to have calculated that the fear of nuclear war would dissuade India from escalating the conflict, thereby permitting Pakistan to make political, if not territorial, gains." Zafar Iqbal Cheema, "Pakistan's Nuclear Use Doctrine and Control," in Lavoy, Sagan, and Wirtz, *Planning the Unthinkable*, p. 160.

26. This paragraph draws from Yair Evron, *Israel's Nuclear Dilemma* (Ithaca, N.Y.: Cornell University Press, 1994), pp. 87–93; Michael Quinlan, "How Robust Is India-Pakistan Deterrence?" *Survival*, Vol. 42, No. 4 (Winter 2000–01), pp. 141–154; and Michael Krepon, "Nuclear Risk Reduction: Is the Cold War Experience Applicable to South Asia?" in Michael Krepon and Chris Gagne, eds., *The Stability-Instability Paradox: Nuclear Weapons and Brinksmanship in South Asia*, Report No. 38 (Washington, D.C.: The Stimson Center, June 2001), pp. 1–15, at <www.stimson.org>.

27. For Kenneth Waltz's argument that nuclear deterrence will work in the Indian-Pakistani case and that it worked to keep the Kargil conflict limited, see Scott D. Sagan and Kenneth N. Waltz, *The Spread of Nuclear Weapons: A Debate Renewed* (New York: W.W. Norton and Company, 2003), pp. 109–124.

28. China also refuses to recognize Sikkim as Indian. See David Gardner, "China, India Move to More Businesslike Ties," *Financial Times*, January 15, 2001, p. 2.

29. See Henry A. Kissinger, *White House Years* (Boston: Little, Brown, 1979), pp. 183–84; and Richard K. Betts, *Nuclear Blackmail and Nuclear Balance* (Washington, D.C.: The Brookings Institution, 1987), p. 81.

30. India declared general mobilization after Pakistan established military positions in Indian-held Kashmir, and the two were closer to general war at the time than was commonly known. Clinton was on the phone to both leaders, urging them to show restraint, and he is credited with helping defuse the situation. See John Lancaster, "War was Narrowly Averted; Kashmir Conflict Flared Dangerously," *Washington Post*, July 26, 1999; Jane Perlez, "U.S. is Expecting Kashmir Pullback By Pakistani Side," *New York Times*, July 5, 1999, online; and Judith Miller and James Risen, "United States is Worried about an Increased Threat of Nuclear Conflict over Kashmir," *New York Times*, August 8, 2000, online.

31. Arguing that Europe now constitutes a security community, although not that the United States should militarily withdraw from it, are Robert Jervis, "Theories of War in an Era of Leading-Power Peace," *American Political Science Review*, Vol. 96, No. 1 (March 2002), pp. 1–14; and Stephen Van Evera, "Primed for Peace: Europe after the Cold War," *International Security*, Vol. 15, No. 3 (Winter 1990/91), pp. 7–57.

32. See Karl W. Deutsch, et al., *Political Community and the North Atlantic Area: International Organization in the Light of Historical Experience* (New York: Greenwood Press, 1969; first published by Princeton University Press, 1957), p. 5. In studying the North Atlantic area (Europe and North America) from the late thirteenth to the mid-twentieth century, these researchers identified thirteen pluralistic security communities. Ten were bilateral; the three multi-state communities were the Swiss Confederation (1291–1848), the American Articles of Confederation (1781–1789), and the German Confederation (1815–1866). At the time Deutsch and his colleagues completed their study, the European Economic Community had just been formed and was therefore not yet considered to qualify as a security community, although it was thought to be on the road to becoming one. Ibid., pp. 29 and 65. Also see Emanuel Adler and Michael Barnett, eds., *Security Communities* (Cambridge: Cambridge

University Press, 1998); and Bruce Cronin, *Community under Anarchy: Transnational Identity and the Evolution of Cooperation* (New York: Columbia University Press, 1999).

33. Deutsch, et al., *Political Community and the North Atlantic Area*, p. 5. As defined by these researchers, a "pluralistic" security community is one of two types of security communities, the other being the "amalgamated" security community. The pluralistic form consists of at least two independent states; the amalgamated form denotes a set of states that have coalesced into a single state. Ibid., p. 6.

34. With the Rush-Bagot Treaty of 1817, the United States and Canada demilitarized their border. This did not mean, however, that military considerations were totally absent from their relations. Demilitarization rested for a time on a balance of power. The United States could have attacked Canada with its more powerful army, but Britain retained the ability to retaliate against American shipping and American ports with its more powerful navy. Gradually, a demilitarization based in part on the ability to retaliate grew into a state of affairs where the use of force between Canada and the United States became normatively unthinkable. See Deutsch, et al., *Political Community and the North Atlantic Area*, p. 84; and Sean M. Shore, "No Fences Make Good Neighbors: The Development of the U.S.-Canadian Security Community, 1871–1940," in Adler and Barnett, *Security Communities*, pp. 333–368.

35. Josef Joffe, "Europe's American Pacifier," *Foreign Policy*, No. 54 (Spring 1984), p. 74.

36. Among the other factors favoring European unification were the following: in the years immediately after World War II, the most powerful motive was the desire to avoid another devastating European war. Farsighted men such as Jean Monnet, Robert Schumann, and Konrad Adenauer, who were committed to Franco-German reconciliation, hit upon economic integration of their two economies as one promising path to avoid war between them. Multiple factors were again at work during the most recent stage in Europe's continuing integration, marked by the passage of the Single European Act in 1986, the formation of the European Union in 1991, and the consequent effort to create a European defense identity in 1999–2000. These included Europe's goal of making Europe equal in economic weight to the United States and Japan, as well as a technological competitor of both. Another reason was the desire of Germany's economic partners to wrest control of the Bundesbank away from its governors and to put it under the control of all of the West European states by creating a European central bank (former French president Valéry Giscard d'Estaing said, several years after the fact, "We need an organized Europe to escape German domination"; quoted in David March, "Final March of the Old Guard," *Financial Times*, April 25, 1994, p. 17). Germany also wanted to protect its exports to its European partners, by establishing a single European currency so as to avoid an over-valued mark that would hurt exports. Germany's partners aimed to strengthen the political ties of Western European institutions, the better to embed and entangle a unified Germany in them. Finally, Western Europe hoped to build a defense capability that would lessen its dependence on the United States. For the early period, see Ernst Haas, *The Uniting of Europe: Political, Social, and Economic Forces, 1950–1957* (Stanford: Stanford University Press, 1958); and Andrew Moravcsik, *The Choice for Europe: Social Purpose and State Power from Messina to Maastricht* (Ithaca, N.Y.: Cornell University Press, 1998), chap. 2. For the 1986–1999 period of European integration, see Alberta Sbragia, *Euro-Politics* (Washington, D.C.: The Brookings Institution, 1992); Joseph M. Grieco, "The Maastricht Treaty, Economic and Monetary Union, and the Neo-Realist Research Program," *Review of International Studies*, Vol. 21, No. 1 (January 1995), pp. 21–40; Wayne Sandholtz and John Zysman, "1992: Recasting the European Bargain," *World Politics*, Vol. 42, No. 1 (October 1989), pp. 95–129; Patrick McCarthy, "France Looks at Germany, or How to Become German (and European) while Remaining French," in Patrick McCarthy, ed., *France-Germany 1983–1993* (New York: St. Martin's, 1993), pp. 57–63; and Craig R. Whitney, "Military Posture of Europe to Turn More Independent," *New York Times*, December 13, 1999, p. A1.

37. The phrase is that of French analyst François Heisbourg. François Heisbourg, "The European-U.S. Alliance: Valedictory Reflections on Continental Drift in the Post–Cold War Era," *International Affairs*, Vol. 60 (April 1992), p. 669.

38. See Robert J. Art, "Why Western Europe Needs the United States and NATO," *Political Science Quarterly*, Vol. 111, No. 1 (Spring 1996), pp. 1–39.

39. The phrase "night watchman" is from John J. Mearsheimer, "Back to the Future: Instability in Europe after the Cold War," *International Security*, Vol. 15, No. 1, (Summer 1990), p. 47.

40. See, for example, Nordlinger, *Isolationism Reconfigured*, pp. 78–91, 39–140, and 218–229.

41. See Joanne Gowa, *Allies, Adversaries, and International Trade* (Princeton, N.J.: Princeton University Press, 1994), chaps. 3 and 4.

42. See Nordlinger, *Isolationism Reconfigured*, pp. 227–228.

43. Nordlinger ably makes this argument about the Cold War era. Ibid., pp. 223–226.

44. I base this conclusion on conversations with Richard Samuels of MIT and Michael Mastanduno of Dartmouth, both of whom are knowledgeable and astute observers of the Japanese-American relationship. Mastanduno reports that during a stint in the Office of the United States Trade Representative (USTR), he asked whether the defense linkage was ever "put on the table" when negotiating trade agreements with the Japanese. The USTR officials said "absolutely not," with evident frustration, because the State and Defense Departments would not allow it. In fact, the Defense Department sometimes had a representative in trade negotiations to make certain that no linkage was made between trade and defense.

45. Satoshi Isaka, "Japan Under Pressure to Take Sides on Trade Caucus," *Nikkei Weekly*, July 25, 1994, quoted in Joseph M. Grieco, "Realism and Regionalism: American Power and German and Japanese Institutional Strategies during and after the Cold War," in Ethan B. Kapstein and Michael Mastanduno, eds., *Unipolar Politics: Realism and State Strategies after the Cold War* (New York: Columbia University Press, 1999), p. 329.

46. Figures are rounded to the nearest billion. See International Monetary Fund, *Direction of Trade Statistics Yearbook* (Washington, D.C.: IMF, various years). Part of the change in trade patterns came from governmental awards of large contracts. In 1994 and 1995, for example, two large American firms won contracts from the Saudi government: a $4 billion AT&T telecommunications sale and a $6 billion Boeing–McDonnell Douglas commercial aircraft sale. With American governmental lobbying—and in the case of the commercial aircraft deal, through personal lobbying by President Clinton of King Fahd—the United States beat out, respectively, the Swedish firm Ericsson, which had expanded the Saudi telecommunications system in the 1970s and was the favored candidate for the new contract, and Airbus Industrie, which had the inside track on the commercial aviation deal. The U.S. government pushed the states in the region to buy American, and used its leverage, as the region's dominant outside political-military power, to extract big government-controlled contracts for U.S. companies. See Amy Docker Marcus, "A Different War—In the Middle East, the Newest Rivalry Is Over Cash, Not Arms," *Wall Street Journal*, December 18, 1999, pp. A1 and A10. For historical parallels where finance and trade were governed by diplomatic considerations, see Herbert Feis, *Europe, the World's Banker, 1870–1914* (New Haven: Yale University Press, 1930); and Eugene Staley, *War and the Private Investor* (Garden City, N.Y.: Doubleday, Doran, 1935).

47. Robert Gilpin, *The Challenge of Global Capitalism: The World Political Economy in the 21ˢᵗ Century* (Princeton, N.J.: Princeton University Press), pp. 50 and 348.

48. William Jefferson Clinton, "China's Opportunities, And Ours," *New York Times*, September 24, 2000, p. 15.

Seven: Implementing Selective Engagement

1. See Edward Rhodes, Jonathan DiCicco, Sarah Milburn Moore, and Tom Walker, "Forward Presence and Engagement: Historical Insights into the Problem of 'Shaping'," *Naval War College Review*, Vol. 53, No. 1 (Winter 2000), p. 45.

2. See Rachel L. Swarns with Norimitsu Onishi, "Africa Creeps Along Its Path to Democracy," *New York Times*, June 2, 2002, p. 8.

3. "U.S. Trade Policy Assailed as Latin Summit Opens," *International Herald Tribune*, July 27–28, 2002, p. 5.

4. Thomas L. Friedman, "Globalization, Alive and Well," *New York Times*, September 22, 2002, Section 4, p. 13.

5. The Pew Research Center for the People and the Press report that negative opinions of the United States have increased over the last two years, based on opinion polls conducted in forty-four countries. See Adam Clymer, "World Survey Says Negative Views of U.S. Are Rising," *The New York Times*, December 5, 2002, p. A11. The complete results of the poll can be found at <www.people-press.org>.

6. For more on how foreigners view American actions and motives differently than Americans do, see Chalmers Johnson, *Blowback: The Costs and Consequences of American Empire* (New York: Henry Holt, 2000).

7. These five are particularly useful: Cindy Williams, ed., *Holding the Line: U.S. Defense Alternatives for the Early 21st Century* (Cambridge, Mass.: MIT Press, 2001); Lawrence J. Korb, *Reshaping America's Defenses: Four Alternatives* (New York: Council on Foreign Relations, 2002), at <www.cfr.org/Public/publications/Defense_CPI.html>; Report of the National Defense Panel, *Transforming Defense: National Security in the 21st Century* (Arlington, Va.: December 1997); John C. Steinbruner, *Principles of Global Security* (Washington, D.C.: The Brookings Institution, 2000); and Michèle A. Flournoy, ed., *QDR 2001: Strategy-Driven Choices for America's Security* (Washington, D.C.: National Defense University Press, 2001).

8. The National Intelligence Council has stated that, "The Intelligence Community judges that U.S. territory is more likely to be attacked with WMD using nonmissile means" because these other methods are less expensive than ICBMs, are easier to develop and deploy covertly, are probably more reliable and accurate than ICBMs that have not been tested and validated, and are more effective for disseminating biological agents than ICBMs. See National Intelligence Council, Central Intelligence Agency, *Foreign Missile Developments and the Ballistic Missile Threat through 2015*, unclassified Summary of a National Intelligence Estimate, December 2001, at <www.cia.gov/nic/pubs/other_products/Unclassifiedballisticmissilefinal.htm>.

9. See, for example, Dexter Filkins, David Johnston, Eric Schmitt, and Thom Shanker, "F.B.I. and Military United in Pakistan to Hunt Al Qaeda," *New York Times*, July 14, 2002, p. 1.

10. Michael O'Hanlon, et al., *Protecting the American Homeland: A Preliminary Analysis* (Washington, D.C.: Brookings Institution Press, 2002), pp. 125–133. Also see Report of the Heritage Foundation Homeland Security Task Force, *Defending the American Homeland* (Washington, D.C.: The Heritage Foundation, January 2002); and Frank Cilluffo, et al., *Defending America in the 21st Century*, Executive Summary of Four CSIS Working Group Reports on Homeland Defense (Washington, D.C.: Center for Strategic and International Studies [CSIS], 2000).

11. O'Hanlon, *Protecting the American Homeland*, p. 131.

12. On the cruise missile threat, see Michael O'Hanlon, "Cruise Control: A Case for Missile Defense," *The National Interest*, No. 67 (Spring 2002), pp. 89–93.

13. Andrew M. Sessler, et al., *Countermeasures: A Technical Evaluation of the Operational Effectiveness of the Planned U.S. National Missile Defense System* (Union of Concerned Scientists and the MIT Security Studies Program, April 2000), available at <www.ucsusa.org/publication.cfm?publicationID=132>.

14. Personal communication with Ted Postol, June 2001.

15. Even James Lindsay and Michael O'Hanlon, two proponents of missile defense, agree that "basic physics argues strongly that decoys closely resembling real warheads simply cannot be distinguished from actual threats by the U.S. sensor systems now in development." See James M. Lindsay and Michael E. O'Hanlon, *Defending America: The Case for Limited National Missile Defense* (Washington, D.C.: The Brookings Institution Press, 2001), p. 94.

16. Thomas Friedman, "Who's Crazy Here?" *New York Times*, May 15, 2001, p. A25 (emphasis in the original).

17. See Barry R. Posen, "U.S. Security Policy in a Nuclear-Armed World (Or What If Iraq Had Had Nuclear Weapons?)," *Security Studies*, Vol. 6, No. 3 (Spring 1997), pp. 1–32.

18. Steven E. Miller, "The Flawed Case for Missile Defense," *Survival*, Vol. 43, No. 3 (Autumn 2001), pp. 105–106.

19. G. John Ikenberry, "America's Imperial Ambition," *Foreign Affairs*, Vol. 81, No. 5 (September/October 2002), pp. 56–59.

20. See *The National Security Strategy of the United States, 2002*, Section 5, at <www.nytimes.com/2002/09/20/international/20textfull.html>.

21. James T. Quinlivan, "Force Requirements in Stability Operations," *Parameters* (Winter 1995), at <www.army/usawc/parameters/1995/quinliv.htm>.

22. For example, see Donald H. Rumsfeld, "Transforming the Military," *Foreign Affairs*, Vol. 81, No. 3 (May/June 2002), pp. 20–32; Secretary of Defense, *Annual Report of the Secretary of Defense, 2002*, chap. 6, at <www.defenselink.mil>; Ashton B. Carter and John P. White, ed., *Keeping the Edge: Managing Defense for the Future* (Cambridge, Mass.: MIT Press, 2000); Flournoy, *QDR 2001*, chaps. 3 and 11; Report of the National Defense Panel, *Transforming Defense: National Security in the 21ˢᵗ Century*, December 1997; and Michael E. O'Hanlon, *Defense Policy Choices for the Bush Administration*, 2d ed. (Washington, D.C.: The Brookings Institution, 2002), chap. 4.

23. Quoted in John Lloyd, "Rowing Alone," *Financial Times Weekend*, August 4, 2002, p. III.

24. G. John Ikenberry, *After Hegemony: Institutions, Strategic Restraint, and the Rebuilding of Order After Major Wars* (Princeton, N.J.: Princeton University Press, 2001), pp. 246–256, and chap. 7.

25. Joseph S. Nye, Jr., *The Paradox of American Power: Why the World's Only Superpower Can't Go It Alone* (Oxford: Oxford University Press, 2002), pp. 154–163.

26. This insight is based on conversations with Harvard's Steven Miller. Also see Jason D. Ellis, *Defense by Other Means: The Politics of U.S.-NIS Threat Reduction and Nuclear Security Cooperation* (Westport, Conn.: Praeger, 2001); and Rensselaer W. Lee III, *Smuggling Armageddon: The Nuclear Black Market in the Former Soviet Union and Europe* (New York: St. Martin's Press, 1998).

27. Matthew Bunn, "A Nuclear Weapon Just Waiting To Happen," *Los Angeles Times*, August 29, 2002, at <www.latimes.com>.

28. See Douglas W. Smith, et al., *Designing a Climate-Friendly Energy Policy: Options for the Near Term* (Pew Center on Global Climate Change, July 2002), p. 8, at <www.pewclimate.org/projects/energy.cfm>.

29. The Council bases these estimates on increases in the average for automobiles to between 39 and 44 miles per gallon of gas (mpg) and for light trucks to 33 mpg. See Howard Geller, *Strategies for Reducing Oil Imports: Expanding Oil Production vs. Increasing Vehicle Efficiency*, Report No. E011 (Washington, D.C.: American Council for an Energy Efficient Economy, April 2001), at <www.aceee.org/pubs/e011/pdf>.

30. Program on International Policy Attitudes, University of Maryland, "Americans on the Global Warming Treaty," November 27, 2000, p. 27, at <www.pipa.org/OnlineReports/GlobalWarming/buenos_aires.html>.

31. This is a central argument of Henry R. Nau, *At Home Abroad: Identity and Power in American Foreign Policy* (Ithaca, N.Y.: Cornell University Press, 2002), chap. 4.

32. Quoted in Robert Rubin, "Hard Choices to Keep Growth," *International Herald Tribune*, August 1, 2002, p. 4.

33. For some suggestions on how to mitigate future international liquidity crises, see Barry Eichengreen, *Toward a New International Financial Architecture: A Practical Post-Asia Agenda* (Washington, D.C.: Institute for International Economics, 1999); and Report of an Independent Task Force, *Safeguarding Prosperity in a Global Financial System: The Future International Financial Architecture* (New York: Council on Foreign Relations, 1999).

34. The Gallup Organization, "Americans' Perceptions: World Affairs," February 2002 update, at <www.gallup.com/poll/specialReports/pollSummaries/sr020215.asp?Version=p>.

35. John E. Reilly, *American Public Opinion and U.S. Foreign Policy 1999* (Chicago: The Chicago Council on Foreign Relations, 1999), p. 12.

36. Steven Kull and I.M. Destler, *Misreading the Public: The Myth of a New Isolationism* (Washington, D.C.: The Brookings Institution Press, 1999), pp. 45–47.

37. The Pew Research Center for the People and the Press and the Council on Foreign Relations, *The View Before 9/11: America's Place in the World*, p. 1, at <www.cfr.org>. This study was completed in early September 2001.

38. Kull and Destler, *Misreading the Public*, p. 78.

39. Program on International Policy Attitudes, University of Maryland, "Americans on Defense Spending and the War on Terrorism," August 2, 2002, pp. 8–9, at <www.pipa.org/OnlineReports/DefenseSpending/overview.htm>.

40. Reilly, *American Public Opinion and U.S. Foreign Policy* 1999, p. 15; and Pew Research Center and Council on Foreign Relations, *The View Before 9/11*, p. 7.

41. Kull and Destler, *Misreading the Public*, p. 106.

42. Steven Kull and Clay Ramsay, "The Myth of the Reactive Public: American Public Attitudes on Military Fatalities in the Post-Cold War Period," in Philip Everts and Pierangelo Isernia, eds., *Public Opinion and the International Use of Force* (New York: Routledge, 2001), p. 205.

43. Eric V. Larson, *Casualties and Consensus: The Historical Role of Casualties in Domestic Support for U.S. Military Operations* (Santa Monica, Calif.: RAND, 1996), pp. xx–xxiii.

44. Bruce W. Jentleson and Rebecca L. Britton, "Still Pretty Prudent: Post-Cold War American Public Opinion on the Use of Military Force," *Journal of Conflict Resolution*, Vol. 42, No. 4 (August 1998), p. 415.

45. The gap in favor of the United States increased dramatically from 1999, when the U.S. GDP was $9.3 trillion and that of the European Union $8.6 trillion, largely due to faster economic growth in the United States and to the strengthening of the dollar. Data is available at the International Monetary Fund's world economic outlook database at <www.imf.org/>.

46. For the Swiss Confederation, see William B. Lloyd, Jr., *Waging Peace: The Swiss Experience* (Washington, D.C.: Public Affairs Press, 1958); and William E. Rappard, *Collective Security and the Swiss Experience, 1291–1948* (London: George Allen and Unwin, 1948). For the Articles of Confederation, see Frederick W. Marks III, *Independence on Trial: Foreign Affairs and the Making of the Constitution* (Baton Rouge: Louisiana State University Press, 1983); and Richard H. Kohn, *Eagle and Sword: The Federalists and the Creation of the Military Establishment in America, 1783–1802* (New York: Free Press, 1975). For the German Confederation, see Werner Conze, *The Shaping of the German Nation* (New York: St. Martin's Press, 1979); and Geoffrey Barraclough, *The Origins of Modern Germany* (Oxford: Basil Blackwell, 1949).

47. President Jacques Chirac, speaking in June 2000 before the German Bundestag, quoted in John J. Mearsheimer, *The Tragedy of Great Power Politics* (New York: W.W. Norton, 2001), p. 366.

48. For a discussion of the meaning of the phrase "comprehensive national power" as the Chinese use it, see Michael Pillsbury, *China Debates the Future Security Environment* (Washington, D.C.: National Defense University Press, 2000), chap. 5.

49. See China's Institute for Contemporary International Relations, Research Report, *Systematic Estimates of Comparative National Power*, p. 19 (mimeo). I am indebted to Robert Ross of Boston College for providing me with this study and for translating the relevant parts of it.

50. Figures are rounded to the nearest tenth of a percentage point. Angus Maddison, *The World Economy: A Millennial Perspective* (Paris: Organization for Economic Cooperation and Development, 2001), pp. 187 and 217. In order to make comparisons across countries, Maddison uses the Geary-Khammis multilateral purchasing power parity (PPP) method. PPP is a way to compare economies by determining how far the same amount of money can go in different economies. According to my calculations from International Monetary Fund (IMF) statistics, from 1970 to 2000, the United States grew at a 3.2 percent average growth rate, Japan at 3.4 percent, Germany at 2.4 percent, and mainland China at 8.1 percent. See IMF, *World Economic Outlook Database*, April 2002, at <www.imf.org/external/pubs/ft/weo/2002/01/index.htm>.

51. Since 1950, ten countries have been able to sustain average growth rates of 5 percent or greater: China, Hong Kong, Singapore, South Korea, Taiwan, Thailand, Jordan, Oman, Syria, and Botswana. These figures come from Maddison, *The World Economy*, pp. 217 and 226.

52. These points are based on conversations with Gary Jefferson, an economist at Brandeis University, who specializes in China's economy.

53. See Shuxun Chen and Charles Wolf, Jr., eds., *China, the United States, and the Global Economy* (Santa Monica, Calif.: RAND, 2001), p. 113, at <www.rand.org/publications/MR/MR1300>; and National Intelligence Council, *Global Trends 2015: A Dialogue about the Future with Nongovernment Experts*, at <www.odci.gov/cia/publications/globaltrends/2015/375954.gif>.

54. Nye, *The Paradox of American Power*, pp. 19-20.

55. For much the same conclusion, see Stephen G. Brooks and William C. Wohlforth, "American Primacy in Perspective," *Foreign Affairs*, Vol. 81, No. 4 (July/August 2002), pp. 20-34.

Index

305

Enhanced greenhouse effect, 33–34; effects of, 35–36; major contributors to, 34–35. *See also* Global warming

Environmental degradation, 31–36; forms of, 32; greatest threats of, 8; impact on U.S., 32–33; political consequences of, 32. *See also* Global warming

Environmental protection: as grand strategy goal, 7–9; state action on, 31

Ethiopia: Italian invasion of, 93, 97; war with Somalia, 159

Ethnic warfare: frequency of, 38; impact on U.S., 40–41

Eurasian great-power peace: benefits of, 9, 55–58, 150; cost of maintaining, 207, 296; encouraging, 43–44; as grand strategy goal, 7–9; as national interest, 45–47, 46*t*; in selected strategies, 204–16; threats to, 8, 79*t*, 80–81; U.S. trade and, 7, 207–9, 296–97

Eurasian great-power war: consequences of, 9, 56–57, 207–9, 212–13; history of, 192–93, 295; nuclear weapons and, 209–13; potential combatants in, 212; probability of, 57–58, 210; U.S. involvement in, 56, 192–93

Eurasian hegemon: isolationist view of, 176–77; offshore balancing view of, 176–77; potential for, 177; in selected strategies, 205

Eurasian military presence, U.S.: European security and, 214–16; impact of, 8, 55, 58, 213; importance of, 150; regional desire for, 164; in selective engagement strategy, 216–21, 231–32; U.S. economic interests and, 216–21

Eurasian security competition, 55–57

Europe: civil wars in, 250*t*; as crucial region, 123; future of, 245; interests versus U.S. interests, 169–70; military presence in, 8, 231–32; as U.S. ally, 237; U.S. direct foreign investment in, 125–30, 131*t*; U.S. military presence in, 140–41, 214–16; U.S. trade with, 124–25, 124*t*, 126–27*t*, 128*t*, 130*t*; wars in (1991–2000), 252*t*

European Common Market, 26

European security community, 214–16

European Union: as competitor state, 15, 41, 242–43; direct foreign investment in, 26; energy usage and, 59, 60*t*, 61*t*; future of, 242–43; GDP of, 242; greenhouse gas emissions and, 34; history of, 215, 299; impact on U.S., 37, 38; national sovereignty and, 243; rapid reaction force of, 243; U.S. military presence and, 215; U.S. trade with, 124, 124*t*, 126–27*t*, 128*t*

Exports, global, 20–21, 21*f*

Extended deterrence, 282

Falklands dispute, 104

Far East: civil wars in, 250*t*; wars in (1991–2000), 252*t*

Financial markets, 55–56

Financial Times, 66

First World: aid to Third World, 80; economic interdependence of, 20–27; greenhouse gas emissions and, 34–35, 42

Force use criteria, 11; public opinion on, 239–41; ranking of interests and, 261; in selective engagement strategy, 146–57, 165–68. *See also* Military power, U.S.

Foreign assets of deposit banks, 21–22, 22*t*

Foreign involvement: deciding scope of, 3; since World War II, 9

Foreign policy, U.S.: allies' undermining of, 234–35; excessive ambition in, 171, 234–35; geopolitical era in, 178; importance of, 1; objections to, 225; past successes of, 42; post-World War I, 160–62; proposed changes in, 203–4; unintended consequences of, 42

Switzerland: U.S. direct foreign investment in, 132*t*; U.S. trade with, 130*t*

Syria: attack on Israel, 211; containment and, 278; NBC weapons and, 136

Taft, Robert A., 174, 176

Taiwan: economic interdependence of, 26; NBC weapons and, 136; U.S. alliance with, 137–38; U.S. policy on, 142; U.S. trade with, 125, 129*t*, 130*t*

Taiwan Relations Act (1979), 138

Taiwan Straits crisis (1996), 142–43

Taliban, 9, 145, 146, 227, 233

Technological supremacy, U.S., 42

Technology transfer, 41

Tenet, George, 118

Terrorism: changing goals of, 51–52; deterrence and, 52; political causes of, 237–38; preemption of, 146, 230–31; public concern about, 239; state-sponsored, 18, 48, 144, 200; war on, 237–38; World Trade Center bombing (1993), 52, 255–56, 262. *See also* Conventional terrorism; Grand terrorism; September 11 terrorist attacks

Thailand, 26

Third World, 35

Threats: from grand terrorism, 19, 43, 47; to homeland security, 8, 47–55, 78*t*, 80–81; to national interests, U.S., 79–81, 79*t*, 239; from NBC weapons, 8, 43, 47–48; risks of making, 6

Tracy, Benjamin, 183

Trade, 20–27; developing nations and, 281; G-7 countries, 24–25, 25*t*; industrial countries, 25–26, 26*t*, 281; isolationist view of, 175, 195–96; threats to, 55–56, 57, 262–63. *See also* Economic interdependence; Economic openness

Trade, U.S.: Eurasian great-power peace and, 7, 207–9, 296–97; as

percent of GDP, 123; by region, 123–25, 124–30*t*; in services, 125, 130*t*, 281

Transparency: in cooperative security, 107, 110; in selective engagement, 122

Triple Entente Treaty (1907), 183

Truman administration, 105, 106, 173

Turkey: dispute with Greece (1996), 144, 284; as emerging market, 131; military power of, 133

"Two-power" standard, 15

Unilateralism: dangers of, 171, 234–35, 246; in grand strategy options, 84*t*, 86; isolationism as, 174; public opinion on, 239–41; in selective engagement, 121; U.S. leadership and, 159, 165

Union of Concerned Scientists, 228

United Arab Emirates: oil reserves of, 62; U.S. alliance with, 137; U.S. military presence and, 141

United Kingdom: alliance with U.S., 145, 275–76; as competitor state, 15; in cooperative security theory, 108; economic warfare and, 114; energy usage and, 59, 60*t*, 61*t*; European Union and, 243; Falklands dispute and, 104; greenhouse gas emissions and, 34–35; military power of, 133; nuclear arms and, 58; productivity and, 180; trade and, 24–25, 124, 124*t*, 125, 126–30*t*; transparency and, 110; U.S. direct foreign investment in, 125, 132*t*; U.S. oil imports from, 135*t*; World War II and, 160–61, 187, 191, 214. *See also* British navy

United Nations: efficacy of, 97–98, 274–75; Gulf War and, 97–98, 275–76; history of, 95–96, 173; Iraq weapons inspections, 118–19; Korean War and, 97, 275; public opinion on, 239; U.S. goals and, 224; U.S. use of, 99